Ard Chomhairle na Meáns

FIFTY FIVE YE, ...

of the

Croke Cup

All-Ireland Colleges 'A' Hurling Competition

1944 – 1948
and
1957 – 2006

by
Gerry Buckley

In association with O'Neill's Sports and Leisurewear

Leinster Leader, Naas

a

Dedication

Anybody who knows me even remotely well will know that the death of my beloved mother, Pearlie, aged only 46, in 1974, devastated me beyond belief.

That I had the stomach, as a fragile teenager, to carry on at all is down to the love and friendship of a number of people. However, two people whom I didn't even know when my mother was alive, undoubtedly contributed the most. Tom and Kitty Farrell's open house policy to me in Mullingar, in Patrick St and later when they moved to Longford Rd, kept me sane. Their eldest son, Brendan, and I became very close friends and I could never repay the Farrell family for all they did for me in those lonely times.

Unfortunately, I'm all too aware that I am a desperately thick man if I am deliberately done a bad turn. But I never, ever forget a good one. The deaths of Tom (in September 1997) and Kitty (in October 2001) were sad, sad days for me. May they rest in peace.

Gerry Buckley,
January 2007.

Editorial

The book which (hopefully!) follows is the culmination of a strange project. The year 2001 was the 50th staging of the Croke Cup and my original plan was to produce a commemorative book at that time. However, for various reasons, the plan did not come to pass but I did manage to link up with seven of the captains and profile them for the Hogan Stand magazine, along with a records section, over a two-month period.

In the interim, I brought out a book on its sister competition, the Hogan Cup, for its Golden Jubilee in 2003. Thankfully, this went off well and the captains, other team representatives and relations of the two deceased captains were treated to a memorable launch day on October 4th, 2003. This took place in the Greville Arms in my native Mullingar, courtesy of splendid organisation by the manager there, John Cochrane, himself a Hogan Cup winner in 1976 with Carmelite College, Moate. Liam Mulvihill, the GAA's excellent Director General since 1979, and the then GAA President, Sean Kelly, attended for a function superbly compered by UTV's Adrian Logan. The day went like clockwork, thank God.

Inevitably, the idea of a Croke Cup publication on similar lines would surface again and 2006 represented the 50th staging of the competition since it was brought back on to the GAA's calendar in 1957. These 50 stagings, in addition in the opening five from 1944 to 1948, constitute the 55 years documented in the pages hereafter. The format is the same - the stats on the semi-finals and finals, in addition to a profile of the captains or other team representative. 50 of the 55 men to lift the Croke Cup were interviewed, 48 face-to-face, while Jim Murray (1980) and Tim Murphy (2000) e mailed me as necessary from the USA and Australia respectively. Sadly, four captains were deceased when I started out - J. J. Bugler (1946), Michael Shalloo (1947), Ted Carroll (1957) and John Sutton (1960) - while Michael Hogan (1986) was unfortunately

unavailable. Also on a sad note, a fifth captain, Brendan O'Donoghue (1945) passed away in September 2006, but a record of our chat is included. I warmly and sincerely thank all 55 people I interviewed for their help and courtesy. For someone who never grew up when it comes to my childish love of sport, it was a great thrill to meet so many top-class hurlers from the past and present. They say you should never meet your heroes. In my case, I was certainly not disappointed.

On a personal level, this has been a trying project and I am amused, yet gratified, by Bernard Dunne's comment about my "never-ending good humour" in his Réamhrá. I felt I came across as a bag of cats at the regular meetings I had over the course of the project with Bernard, Hugh Rudden and Cora Weldon, back at our favourite haunt of the Greville Arms. The latter three people were fantastically supportive of my work at all times, as I struggled to meet self-imposed deadlines due to, inter alia, a protracted house move and a brief (thank God) but worrying illness. In the old colleges regime, they were Chairman, Secretary and Serving Officer respectively. It is my fervent wish that that we will stay in touch and I can honestly say that the GAA was very fortunate to have three such wonderful people in high office in recent years. Indeed, if I was to pick out a person whose never-ending good humour has greatly impressed me in recent years, it has been Bernard Dunne! While Portlaoise-based Michael Reynolds was less hands-on this time, he remains a man I hold in very high regard and I will certainly be dropping in to him, please God, for a bowl of soup and toasted special anytime I pass through the County Laois town.

At various stages, I sub-contracted some work to three fellow Westmeath journalists. Kieran Galvin ('Westmeath Independent') was a big help to me, as was my long-time and very genuine friend and fellow sports fanatic, Paul O'Donovan ('Westmeath Topic'). I just hope

d

he doesn't wear his 'silly cap' to the launch! I also thank Randal Scally from the 'Hogan Stand'.

My immediate boss and much valued friend in the 'Westmeath Examiner', sports editor John Fitzsimons, gave freely of his time and expertise in proof-reading my scripts. He also played a major part in ensuring that my employers were very flexible with me at crucial junctures of the book. In this context, I also warmly acknowledge the understanding attitude of former editor, Ronan O'Donoghue. He has a brilliant brain on seemingly an indefinable range of topics and his magnificent 'Offside' sports column is missed both by fellow staff and the paper's readership since his very sad departure from his role. I wish the new group editor, the affable Dave O'Connell, every success in his challenging position.

I also thank my first cousin, Ursula Kane Cafferty for her help in proof-reading. Her book from 2005, 'Suitcase Number Seven', the story of her late uncle, multi-talented sports man, Tom Cleary, is a fantastic read.

Another terrific weekly columnist with the 'Westmeath Examiner' is my great mate, Bernie Comaskey. His remarkable life story was recently chronicled in the often hilarious, often poignant, but always enjoyable autobiography, 'If Ever A Man Suffered'. Bernie divides his time roughly 50/50 between his beloved Westmeath (the biggest of our many common denominators) and his fabulous pub in Spain, Paddy's Point. The atmosphere there for sports events, especially Gaelic games, is truly unique. Bernie's son, Ian runs a property company next door to Paddy's Point and I thank them for their generous contribution to my out-of-pocket expenses in this book.

As was the case with the Hogan Cup book, O'Neill's, Ireland's leading Gaelic brand, came on board as the main sponsor of this book. Tony Towell has again shown the way and I sincerely hope that he and the powers-that-be in O'Neill's feel that they are associating their famous name with a worthwhile publication. That marvellous organisation, Genesis Fine Arts Ltd in Mullingar, have again come up trumps with superb plaques for the 55 hurlers profiled in the book, in addition to the four widows of deceased captains - Sheila Bugler, Anne Shalloo, Angela Carroll and Sheila Sutton. The company's financial controller, Donald Bell, is a pleasure to deal with in every way.

After a lot of trawling, I eventually got my hands on all the winning team photographs and I have acknowledged the source of every photograph in the book. A shining light for me in my darkest hours of despair that the book would never come to pass was former St. Kieran's, Kilkenny vice-principal, Dick McEvoy. His work for me on all matters relating to the 16-times champions was thorough and prompt. Many, many thanks, Dick. Legendary former Dublin player and manager, Kevin Heffernan - in my opinion, the man who revolutionised Gaelic football - came to my rescue in lining out the St. Joseph's, Marino side of 1945, when all else had failed. Others who don't get a mention elsewhere who helped out with the occasional query, include Westmeath's greatest-ever GAA administrator, Paddy Flanagan; last year's All-Ireland senior final referee from the Lake County, Barry Kelly; and that mine of information on the colleges scene, Alan Aherne from Wexford. A Romanian man based in Mullingar, Vali from Compu 2 Ltd, kept me calm a few times with his ability to unwind faulty cassette tapes of my interviews. I am indebted to him and his staff for their patience.

I regularly feel that the staff at the National Library in Kildare St in Dublin dread to see me coming! The nature of my work means that I often need a particular microfilm for minutes rather than hours and I run people off their feet. Two people who certainly disguise any dread at my arrival are Gerry Kavanagh and Fran Carroll. Since I started on the book writing scene in 1999, I have become quite pally with these two men. I thank them sincerely for their professionalism and good humour at all times. Indeed, they regularly send me e mails if they see or hear something which they feel is of interest to me. Incidentally, irrespective of how many hours you spend trawling though newspapers, it is virtually impossible to be 100 per cent accurate on team lineouts and substitutes who come on during the course of a game. There have been occasional conflicting data between some newspapers in these areas. I have done my utmost to be as thorough as humanly possible.

Colm McSherry, the design editor for the group of newspapers which includes the 'Westmeath Examiner', did a marvellous job on the cover for this book. I am indebted to him for his wonderful skills in his specialised field and, given that he had precious few photographs with which to work, he has played a blinder. As with my previous publications, I have utilised the very professional services of the 'Leinster Leader' in Naas. Mark Rogers is always on hand to help with relevant matters, while Philip Higgins again was outstanding in his contribution to the laying out of pages.

My once totally fluent Irish has inevitably faded with the passage of time and the few paragraphs 'as Gaeilge' which follow are the work of the Westmeath GAA County Chairman for the past 20 years, Séamus Ó Faoláin. He is a very busy man, both through his GAA commitments and his longstanding role as an Irish teacher in that fine school, St. Mary's CBS in Mullingar. His schedule is even busier since 2004 with his marriage to the lovely Sarah, an event which delighted his countless friends and admirers, including yours truly. Despite his hectic workload, Séamus is a gentleman to the fingertips and he invariably finds time to stop and talk. His genuine interest in the educational welfare of my two daughters means a lot to me.

Bhí áthas agus bród orm nuair a iarradh orm scéal Corn Uí Chrócaigh a scríobh trí

agallaimh a chur ar na captaein buacacha ó cuireadh tús leis an gcomórtas. Thuig mé ón tús go dtabharfadh mo thaighde deis dom léargas doimhin a fháil ar iomáint sna meánscoileanna ó 1944 i leith. Ní raibh díomá orm agus caithfidh mé a rá gur mhéadaigh an t-eolas uilig a bhailigh mé ó na captaein agus ó mo thaighde mo mheas agus m'ómós ar na hiománaithe agus a lucht bainistíochta sna meánscoileanna a chothaigh traidisiún na hiomána go bródúil ó thús an chomórtais sinsearaigh iomána.

Is léir dom freisin go bhfuil moladh faoi leith tuillte ag na Sagairt agus ag na Bráithre Oirmhinneacha maraon leis na múinteoirí tuaithe a thug oiliúint agus traenáil do na hiománaithe go deonach agus go toilteanach le linn na scoilbliana. Rinne siad éacht oibre, ní hamháin dá gcoláistí, ach do Chumann Lúthchleas Gael fré chéile. Is féidir a rá go cinnte dearfa gur chabhraigh na daoine agus na hiománaithe ó na meánscoileanna go mór le fás is forbairt an chluiche ársa iontaigh sa Chumann Lúthchleas Gael.

Mór an trua é, bhí ceathrar de na captaein marbh nuair a thosaigh mé ar na hagallaimh. Ach bhí ionadaithe acu uilig a thug léargas agus eolas dom ar a bhfeachtais iomána ina mblianta buacacha. Rinne mé agallamh le captaen 1945, Brendan O'Donoghue, ach cúpla mí ina dhiaidh sin, fuair Breandán uasal bás R.I.P. "Ar pháirceanna imeartha na bhFlaitheas go gcastar ar a chéile sinn arís."

Buíochas le Dia, bhí an chuid is mó acu beo agus táim an-bhuíoch do na captaein sin a thug agallaimh dom. Ghlac siad strainséir isteach ina dtithe agus bhí siad agus a muintir fial flaithiúil lena gcuid ama agus iad ag dul siar bóthar na gcuimhní iomána. Bhí siad foighneach liom freisin. Is fir faoi leith iad gach captaen acu. Guím rath Dé orthu uilig.

Gearóid Ó Buachalla,
Eanair 2007.

f

Contents

THE CROKE CUP

Réamhrá

Fearaim fíorchaoin fáilte roimh fhoilseachán an leabhair seo mar thaifead agus mar cheiliúradh ar chomórtas clúiteach iománaíochta na meánscoileanna. The publication of '55 Years of the Croke Cup' is perhaps a fitting conclusion to the All Ireland Colleges final official function. This great competition which has promoted all that is great in Hurling since its inception and has provided a unique training ground for many of the game's best known names.

May I welcome to today's launch Uachtarán Cumann Lúthchleas Gael, Nioclas Ó Braonáin, himself a Croke Cup medal holder with the famous St. Kieran's. May I also welcome Archbishop Dermot Clifford, patron of our association and Ard Stiúrthóir Liam Ó Maolmhichíl, Hogan Cup medal holder with St Mel's, Longford and all the members of Coiste na Bainistíochta. We are also honoured and privileged to have here as Fear an Tí this afternoon, the voice of the GAA, the great Michael Ó Muircheartaigh.

All Ireland Colleges recently merged with our friends and colleagues from the vocational sector and formed the new All Ireland Post Primary Committee. Ní neart go cur le chéile. Under the chairmanship of Mr Sean Fogarty, whom I also welcome here today, and extend best wishes to him in his new role. I also welcome and thank all those people here today who have served on the former All Ireland Colleges Committee.

May I welcome all the captains of the winning teams here today. I hope you have a very enjoyable day full of happy memories of your school days. Many thanks to Hugh Rudden, former secretary, for all his help on this project and to Miss Cora Weldon, our serving officer in Croke Park. Thanks also to O'Neill's Sports and Leisure for their continued support.

This project would not have been possible but for one man, Gerry Buckley. May I thank Gerry for his incredible amount of work in compiling today's book. Gerry's enthusiasm and professionalism and never-ending good humour has been an inspiration to us all.

Comhghairdeas Gearóid agus beir bua!
Bernard Ó Duinn
Cathaoirleach - Ard Chomhairle na Meánscoileanna
Bealtaine 2003 – Bealtaine 2006

Gerry Buckley

Gerry Buckley (50), is a native of Mullingar and was educated in his home town at St. Mary's CBS Primary School and St. Finian's College.

After over a quarter of a century working as an accountant, Gerry's hobby of sports writing became his new career in recent years. He is employed as a sports journalist with the 'Westmeath Examiner' in Mullingar.

This is his third book, following on from The Millennium Handbook of Westmeath Gaelic Games (2000) and Fifty Years of the Hogan Cup (2003).

Gerry has two daughters – Pearlie (23), a final year student nurse in Athlone IT, and Grace (18), a first year actuarial student in UCD.

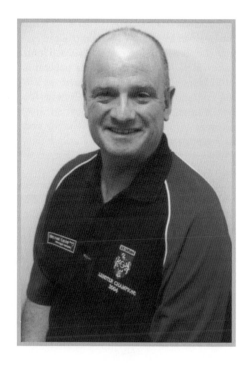

1944 – ALL-IRELAND FINAL
23 April 1944, Thurles
Referee: Phil Purcell (Tipperary)

St. Flannan's, Ennis 5-5

J. J. Bugler
(Clare)

Lou Power
(Dublin)

Tim Tuohy
(Clare)

Senan Bourke
(Clare)

Brian McMahon
(Clare)

Eddie John McGrath
(Tipperary)

Cormac McNamara
(Clare)

Jim Minogue (*capt*)
(Clare)

Michael Meagher
(Clare) (0-1)

Harry O'Meara
(Clare) (0-1)

Tommy Byrne
(Clare)

Jimmy Kennedy
(Tipperary)

Michael Shaughnessy
(Tipperary) (3-0)

John Kenny
(Tipperary) (2-3)

Brendan O'Donoghue
(Tipperary)

St. Kieran's, Kilkenny 3-3

Rick Grogan
(Laois)

John Walsh
(Kilkenny)

Colm Murphy
(Cork)

Tom O'Donnell
(Limerick)

Jimmy Dowling
(Kilkenny)

Percy Grant
(Kilkenny)

Sean Collier
(Laois)

Liam Egan
(Kilkenny)

Dick Freeman
(Laois)

Ray Cody
(Kilkenny) (2-0)

Cyril O'Loughlin
(Laois)

Paddy McGrath (*capt*)
(Kilkenny) (0-2)

Billy Gannon
(Kilkenny)

Mark Marnell
(Kilkenny) (0-1)

Michael Guerin
(Laois) (1-0)

Jim Minogue

St. Flannan's, Ennis, have more or less consistently been in the shake-up for Croke Cup honours since the competition's inauguration in 1944, but the team that made history that year by winning the Clare school's first-ever Harty Cup and Croke Cup was captained by Jim Minogue.

Jim hails from a farming background in the parish of Bodyke in East Clare. The second youngest of four boys, Jim's brother, Paddy won a Munster Cup medal with St. Flannan's in 1939 but St. Flannan's didn't win another trophy again until 1944, when Jim captained the Ennis college to Munster and All-Ireland glory. Jim recalls, "I entered St. Flannan's in 1939 and sure the hurling was great. It kept us all going. " However, St. Flannan's didn't play in the Harty Cup from 1928 to 1943, because of a dispute which arose over the extension of the GAA's ban on foreign games to colleges who participated in hurling. Jim recalls that the colleges most effected by this ban were St. Flannan's, Mungret, Rockwell, Roscrea and St. Finbarr's. Those teams all competed in their own separate competition called the Munster Cup.

Jim feels that the future winners of the Croke Cup were gelling together nicely and had captured a junior championship before losing the Munster Cup in 1943, but after that final they were told they were going back into the Harty Cup in 1943/44. "The hurling was excellent back then and we were improving with every puck of the ball, but another important turning point was the introduction of Tull Considine as team trainer. This gave the

team an added lift and new ideas were introduced as Considine was a mighty trainer. He was gifted at picking guys in certain positions. If you were weak in certain areas he would point out your strengths to overcome these weaknesses. He was a terrific man," Jim concludes. Considine would place players in the most unusual of positions but it worked and St. Flannan's improved as a result of these tactics. On his third year in the senior team, Jim was appointed captain. "I remember Monsignor Quinn was President at the time".

Although a long time ago now, Jim's memories are still quite vivid of the the games back then. "We played the Harty Cup final on Palm Sunday and we didn't really know anything about the All-Ireland. I was at home on holidays when I received a letter from the Dean of Flannan's, Fr Queally, informing us that we were going to play Kilkenny in the All-Ireland final. So the Sunday after Easter we played Kilkenny in Thurles and Mr Gardiner, chairman of Central Council, presented the cup to me that day. For a long time it was not recognised as the first All-Ireland final in colleges hurling, but later on it was. We were thrilled to beat a Kilkenny side because we had heard so much about their style and ability," Jim recalls. He feels it was unfortunate that one competition which fell by the wayside was the colleges version of the Railway Cup, which was abandoned in the mid-1950s. St. Flannan's had five players playing for Munster in that year including Jim, who is of the opinion that the competition provided a fun weekend in those spartan times. "In Kilkenny we played Leinster and we beat them. We had great craic that weekend. It was very unusual for the boarders to get out for a weekend and it was a pity that competition was dropped. "

As the Croke Cup was in its infancy, the Harty Cup remained the major target and Jim reminisces on that campaign. "We beat Limerick CBS in the first round and Thurles CBS in the semi-final. Thurles were captained by Pat Stakelum and had Paddy Kenny in the squad. We played and drew with Midleton CBS in the Harty Cup final in Buttevant, on a scoreline of Flannan's 1-10 Midleton 3-4. The replay was played in Tipperary town on April 2 and there was ferocious excitement. It was very windy and we played with the wind in the first half. Our backs were to the wall in the second half but we did manage a few more scores. One of those scores was controversial, but Fr Hamilton intervened and we were awarded the goal! We won by 4-5 to 2-2. I remember after the game receiving the Harty Cup and meeting Monsignor Quinn who was thrilled about our win.

Up to this point, the All-Ireland colleges series did not exist but due to the endeavours of Fr Hamilton, the powers-that-be introduced the championship in 1944. The first final of the Croke Cup was played on Sunday April 23 in Thurles. The 'Irish Independent' was full of praise for the participants in its brief account of that historic occasion, stating, "playing with more combination, St. Flannan's were deserving winners of a closely-fought game. There was little open play due to the keenness of the tackling on both sides. St. Kieran's, though short their provincial full back, Molloy, set the pace at the start. They then wilted under a number of sharp attacks by St. Flannan's who scored 3-2 before half time against 1-2 to St. Kieran's. In the second half, St. Kieran's put up a better fight but were unable to make up the first half leeway. " Goalscoring heroes for the winners were Michael Shaughnessy and John Kenny who raised all five green flags between them, as the Ennis college eventually won out by an eight-point margin.

Jim went on to study for the priesthood in Maynooth. Along with two of his brothers, he was part of Bodyke's only Clare SHC winning side to date in 1947, trained by Fr Purcell. However, he recalls with regret that, "Clare were often out of the Munster championship those days by the time I got home from Maynooth on my summer holidays. " After his ordination in 1951, he was posted to London where he played for Thomas McCurtain's. On moving home to the diocese of Killaloe, he spent time ministering in Kilkishen, Crusheen (being part of a great hurling revival in that small community), Newmarket-on-Fergus and Shannon. He gave much of his time to promoting underage hurling in his various parishes. For the past 16 years he has been based in Castleconnell in county Limerick, where there is "fierce good-humoured rivalry" between the neighbouring counties. Naturally, Fr Jim was absolutely thrilled with the Banner's memorable hurling breakthrough in the mid-1990s, acknowledging "the mighty work" done in this regard by Ger Loughnane.

To this day, Jim still looks out for the St. Flannan's results and his interest in colleges hurling still remains undiluted. He wonders how St. Flannan's will fare in the years ahead, relying purely on players from the local catchment area of Ennis and its surrounds. "It was different back in my time as a student. I think only Senan Bourke from Ennis was a day pupil," Jim recalls. Nowadays, Fr Jim likes the occasional game of golf to relax and is pleased to have picked up the odd prize here and there over the years, including a Thomond Cup with the Shannon club. However, Jim's great sporting love has always been hurling, but it wasn't just the game he liked. "I loved the social end of the game also. Most importantly, the contacts you met and the friends you made for life. No matter where you were, hurlers had a common bond and a common language, like my time in London when a man came up to me whom I had never met before and said, 'we heard you could play hurling', and told me they had registered me as a player."

Sadly, Jim doesn't get the opportunity to meet many of that historic Croke Cup winning side nowadays but a quick glance at the team sheet brings back mixed emotions, as some dear friends have since passed away. Jim can quickly rhyme off the occupations and current whereabouts of those still with us, some of whom went on to have distinguished hurling careers. Football always played second fiddle to hurling in St. Flannan's but Jim remembers playing football against St. Brendan's, Killarney "in the muck". Jim smiles as he reflects that, "if you lost a hurling game they would bring you across to the football pitch to try and make a footballer out of you." While there has been no formal re-union of the 1944 Croke Cup winning side, a number of them managed to meet up at some recent functions. A golf outing organised by St. Flannan's over a decade ago was the opportunity for some past players to gather together, while in 2001, the launch of Ollie Byrnes'

book, "Blue is the Colour - Hurling at St. Flannan's", was another chance to renew old acquaintances. He is also very proud of the tie-pin he received in the college when the winning Harty Cup captains over the years were honoured.

While the first-ever Croke Cup was not greeted with the pomp and ceremony attributed to it in later years, the history books will forever show that Jim Minogue was the first winning captain over 62 years ago. "It was a great team," Fr Jim concludes, "and I was thrilled to be a member of that great team, and highly honoured to be chosen as its captain." The young men of 1944 duly set the standard for countless outstanding hurlers in the famous blue and white colours of St. Flannan's over the generations.

St. Flannan's, Ennis, Croke Cup Champions, 1944.
Back row, left to right: Fr Michael Queally, Tommy Byrne, Brendan O'Donoghue, Harry O'Meara, Manus Rodgers, Mr Tull Considine, Tim Tuohy, John Kenny, Cormac McNamara, Brian McMahon, Canon Michael Quinn.
Middle row, left to right: Michael Shaughnessy, Eddie John McGrath, Jim Minogue (capt), Jimmy Kennedy, Senan Bourke.
Front row, left to right: Lou Power, Michael Meagher, Anthony O'Meara, Mick Keane, John Dooley, J. J. Bugler.
(Photograph courtesy of Ollie Byrnes, author of Blue is the Colour, Hurling at St. Flannan's)

1945 – ALL-IRELAND FINAL
29 April 1945, Croke Park
Referee: J. J. Stuart (Dublin)

St. Flannan's, Ennis 7-10

Paddy Rodgers
(Clare)

Michael Shalloo   **Mattie Neylon**   **Senan Bourke**
(Clare)   (Clare)   (Clare)

Brian McMahon   **Michael Shaughnessy**   **Jimmy Smyth**
(Clare)   (Tipperary)   (Clare)

John Ryan   **John Hanly**
(Clare) (0-2)   (Clare) (0-1)

Harry O'Meara   **Brendan O'Donoghue** (*capt*)   **Donal McNamara**
(Clare) (0-4)   (Tipperary) (2-0)   (Clare) (2-1)

Joe O'Grady   **J. J. Bugler**   **John Dooley**
(Clare) (1-0)   (Clare) (1-2)   (Tipperary) (1-0)

St. Joseph's, Marino 2-3

Jackie Copeland
(Dublin)

Liam Robbins   **Sean McLoughlin**   **Des Leahy**
(Dublin)   (Dublin) (0-1)   (Dublin)

Val McLoughlin   **Paddy Donnelly** (*capt*)   **Christy McHale**
(Dublin)   (Dublin) (0-1)   (Dublin)

Liam Donnelly   **Des Healy**
(Dublin)   (Dublin)

Paddy McHugh   **Jackie Noonan**   **Liam Healy**
(Dublin)   (Dublin)   (Dublin) (0-1)

Paddy Tully   **Pat Lawlor**   **Kevin Heffernan**
(Dublin)   (Dublin)   (Dublin) (2-0)

Brendan O'Donoghue

There was no stopping St. Flannan's in the early years of the newly-established All-Ireland colleges hurling competition. The title was retained in 1945 and, despite being domiciled in the United States for well over a half a century, that year's victorious captain, Brendan O'Donoghue, retains fond memories of his schooldays in the famous Ennis nursery.

Brendan is the youngest of a family of nine and comes from a farming background in Carrigahorig in Tipperary. At 12 years of age, he entered the famous Clare secondary school as a boarder and spent "five happy years" there, combining a sound education with the fostering of his hurling talents. He recalls the teachers who developed his academic interests and had a particular fondness for Fr Cuddy. His recollections of the president of the college, Canon Quinn, are of "a strict but fair man with a great love of horse riding".

St. Flannan's has always placed a lot of emphasis on nurturing young hurlers and the war-torn years of the 1940's were no different. "Under the inspirational leadership of the legendary Tull Considine", the college dominated the All-Ireland series. Brendan was left corner forward on the team which won the inaugural competition in 1944 in Thurles when they defeated St Kieran's, Kilkenny, thereby commencing "a healthy rivalry", which has continued all the way into the 21st century. "It was a real perk to be a hurler", Brendan recalls, with challenge games meaning that

"the hurlers saw much more of the outside world than their fellow students".

With six of the history-making side of 1944 still available, it was no surprise that St. Flannan's were again a powerful unit the following year. Brendan was "delighted to have the honour of captaining the side" in their attempt to retain the title. The Munster campaign commenced with a semi-final defeat of Thurles CBS by 6-4 to 3-5, with Brendan himself notching a memorable goal at the start of the second half. The Harty Cup final was a much tighter affair with St. Flannan's just shading North Monastery of Cork on a scoreline of 2-6 to 3-2.

The All-Ireland final meant an entire weekend away in Dublin, travelling by train to the capital on Saturday and returning on the Monday. Croke Park was the venue on Sunday April 29th, 1945, when the Ennis boys faced St. Joseph's, Marino, a team featuring a young man who was destined to become one of the GAA's most influential figures in the decades ahead, Kevin Heffernan. Despite the future Dubs player and manager notching two goals, the first to actually open the scoring, St. Flannan's won the tie comfortably by 7-10 to 2-3. An interval lead of 13 points had them well on the way to retaining their crown. Indeed, a measure of St. Flannan's dominance is such that the "Irish Independent" reporter singled out the Dublin school's goalkeeper, Jackie Copeland for making "seemingly impossible saves". The newspaper praised the victors for their "excellent all-round teamwork,

St. Flannan's, Ennis, Croke Cup Champions, 1945.
Back row, left to right: Mattie Neylon, John Ryan, John Hanly, Brendan O'Donoghue (capt),
Michael Shaughnessy, Donal McNamara, Joe O'Grady, Brian McMahon.
Front row, left to right: Harry O'Meara, Michael Shalloo, J. J. Bugler, Paddy Rodgers,
John Dooley, Senan Bourke, Jimmy Smyth.
(Photograph courtesy of Ollie Byrnes, author of Blue is the Colour, Hurling at St. Flannan's*)*

accurate shooting by the forwards and superior speed", in a game that was "too one-sided to be thrilling".

The victors also featured one of the future greats of Gaelic games in Jimmy Smyth, recognised by Brendan as "one of the finest players never to be part of a Liam McCarthy Cup winning side". Brendan clearly remembers being presented with the cup before the team and mentors enjoyed "a sumptuous meal" in Barry's Hotel, when "the announcement of the death of Mussolini took second place to our joyous celebrations"! On their return to the Banner County at 5.20 pm the following afternoon, a great welcome awaited the champions. Later in the year, Brendan was picked by Tipperary to play minor hurling but was persuaded by Tull Considine to declare for Clare, who ironically went on to lose to his native county in the Munster championship.

After leaving St Flannan's, Brendan studied in UCD, effectively giving up hurling for a few years. However, in 1949 an older brother of Brendan, a Californian-based priest, invited him to America. He stopped off in New York and has lived there since, only managing to hit the West Coast some six years ago! He hurled for both Galway and Tipperary in the late 1940s and early 1950s, in New York. He was drafted into service and served in the Korean War in 1951. Brendan later joined the Fire Department and, naturally, was extremely upset by the events of September 11th, 2001, in his adopted city. Due to the risk of losing pay in his new employment if injured on the sports field in his spare time, he gave up hurling in 1958 and contented himself in the role of spectator. He spent twenty years in the Fire Department, followed by six years in Real Estate, before easing down his work commitments after a health scare in recent years. He is a proud member of the retired Firefighters Associates of Orange County.

Brendan and his wife, Peggy (née Henry),

whose parents came from Newbridge, celebrated their Golden Wedding anniversary in 2002. They have three grown-up family, Brendan T., Raymond and Theresa, as well as four granddaughters. With a Peruvian daughter-in-law and a Swedish son-in-law, Brendan jokes that he is "part of a real United Nations"! His sons are keen soccer and American Football fans but, from their rare glimpses of hurling, they are not quite sure what to make of "the crazy game with the sticks". Brendan manages to get home to Ireland every two years or so and continues to watch out for St. Flannan's results. He feels that the game has deteriorated a little from his own playing days with less concentration on ground hurling.

Now in his late 70s, Brendan continues to play golf, having once got as low as an eight handicap. His involvement now is with a 200-strong group known as 'The Grasshoppers' and he generally plays twice a week over a variety of golf courses. He laughs when he recalls playing golf in Ireland in 1994, when a 50th anniversary re-union took place of the victorious St. Flannan's team of 1944. "Because so many of my team-mates had become priests, I could not properly air my frustrations after a mishit shot!" His other form of exercise is cycling and his distinctive mop of grey hair is often seen on the streets in Goshen as he attempts to emulate Sean Kelly from near his Irish homeland!

Not only St. Flannan's, but Ireland in general, is a totally changed place from the days when Brendan O'Donoghue and his team-mates considered it a thrill to get out of the Ennis school for trips, both to watch and play hurling. One thing that hasn't changed, however, is his alma mater's consistency in Harty and Croke Cup campaigns. This tradition still remains dear to Brendan's heart despite his many, many years' domicile in the US.

Author's Note:
Sadly, since this article was compiled, Brendan O'Donoghue passed away in New York on September 13th, 2006, aged 79. May he rest in peace.

1946 – ALL-IRELAND FINAL
5 May 1946, Croke Park
Referee: Gerry Kelly (Dublin)

St. Flannan's, Ennis 5-7

Michael Fahy
(Limerick)

Derek McNulty　　　　**Harry Sheehy**　　　　**Joe O'Grady**
(Tipperary)　　　　　　　(Tipperary)　　　　　　(Clare)

Adrian McMahon　　　　**Michael Shalloo**　　　　**Jimmy Smyth**
(Clare)　　　　　　　　　(Clare)　　　　　　　　(Clare)

Michael Shaughnessy　　　　**Paddy Gallagher**
(Tipperary)　　　　　　　　　　(Clare) (1-0)

Tommy O'Meara　　　　**John Hanly**　　　　**Larry Byrne**
(Tipperary) (0-4)　　　　(Clare) (1-0)　　　　(Clare)

Tom Lynch　　　　**J. J. Bugler (*capt*)**　　　　**Mick Keane**
(Clare) (1-0)　　　　(Clare) (2-3)　　　　　　　(Tipperary)

O'Connell Schools, Dublin 5-2

Donal Kirwan
(Dublin)

Stephen Scanlon　　　　**Jim Lavin**　　　　**Des Stanley**
(Dublin)　　　　　　　　(Dublin)　　　　　　(Dublin)

John Keating　　　　**Brendan Clancy (*capt*)**　　　　**Denis Mahony**
(Dublin)　　　　　　　(Dublin)　　　　　　　　　　(Dublin)

Sean O'Neill　　　　**Jack Finnan**
(Dublin) (0-1)　　　　(Dublin)

Brendan O'Kelly　　　　**Tom Mulligan**　　　　**Paddy Ambrose**
(Dublin)　　　　　　　　(Dublin) (0-1)　　　　(Dublin)

Terry Jennings　　　　**Eamonn Clancy**　　　　**Sean Clancy**
(Dublin) (1-0)　　　　(Dublin) (2-0)　　　　(Dublin) (2-0)

John Hanly

The early years of the Croke Cup were dominated by St. Flannan's who, after winning the inaugural All-Ireland colleges hurling championship in 1944, went on to complete a remarkable four in-a-row of successes. One of the leading lights during this golden period for the Ennis hurling nursery was Clarecastle's John Hanly, whose second of three medals came as a member of the 1946 side, captained by the late J. J. Bugler.

Growing up in the hurling stronghold of Clarecastle, John, a nephew of Mick Falvey, who played for Clare in the 1932 All-Ireland final, quickly developed a flair and love for the game. Indeed, he has vivid recollections of being told how the defeat by Kilkenny was "down to the sideline"! John played hurling every evening in the old fair green. "That's where all the youngsters in Clarecastle learned how to play," John recalls. "Timmy McMahon, the local blacksmith, encouraged us to play and was a big influence on me in those early years." To this day, John can rhyme off the list of his young hurling companions from the 1930s.

After completing his primary education in Clarecastle, John headed off to St. Flannan's. "When I first went to Flannan's, I didn't like it. It was pretty rough in those days, as all schools were." John reflects. "I had a nice life in primary school and I'm not just saying that because both my parents taught there, as they didn't make it easy for me! It was often said in those days that the college was only interested in scholarships and that it had little inter-est in games. However, the appointment of Tull Considine of Clare hurling fame as hurling coach by Canon Quinn changed all that." It was Tull who suggested to the college authorities that John and his brother, Willie be brought in for training. The brothers were reluctant to play at first, but eventually had a change of heart. "We had no intention whatsoever of playing. We usually walked to school, often in terrible weather, and staying back to play hurling after school wasn't very appealing, to go to a cold, weary and miserable dressing room, but Tull wanted us to play and we decided to give it a go. He may have seen us play underage hurling with Clarecastle. I must say that attitudes towards us changed after we joined the hurling team. After training, we were fed just like the boarders and the priests even gave us pocket money which we certainly appreciated."

The Hanly brothers' first success with St. Flannan's was in the Munster junior colleges championship when Rockwell were overcome in the final. John played at left half back and Willie lined out in the left corner forward position. There was "great excitement" in the school and throughout Ennis when St. Flannan's won their first Harty Cup in 1944, followed by the inaugural All-Ireland title. In 1945, John graduated to the senior team and Tull Considine again trained the team to Harty and All-Ireland glory, defeating St. Joseph's, Marino, in the All-Ireland decider at Croke Park. On the night before the final, St. Flannan's stayed in Barry's Hotel. The following morning, Micheal O'Hehir arrived at the hotel and each player was introduced to him, providing him with all the details he needed for his match commentary. As John gave him his details, one of the St. Flannan's mentors told the legendary commentator that his uncle, David Hanly, had broadcast the 1943 All-Ireland hurling semi-final between Cork and Galway in Ennis. John has still fond memories of arriving back in Ennis to "a hero's welcome". Indeed, in 1945, John played in a remarkable nine finals, winning seven of them. "I won junior, senior, Harty and All-Ireland medals with Flannan's, an inter-provincial colleges medal with Munster and Clare Cup and senior championship medals with Clarecastle. The two finals I lost were at minor level – the county final to Éire Óg and an awful hammering in the Munster final by Tipperary. I was burnt out afterwards".

St. Flannan's were successful again in 1946, with the late J. J. Bugler skippering them to their third All-Ireland title on the trot. They began the year by capturing the Canon O'Kennedy Shield at St. Colman's expense by 2-6 to 2-4. In the Harty final, they accounted for North Monastery on a 4-5 to 2-1 score-line at Tipperary town. John recalls "seeing stars" after being struck on the head by a North Mon forward. On a rare occasion such as this, he got "really vexed" and John would later exact retribution before the final whistle! It was back to Croke Park for the All-Ireland final when St. Flannan's completed an All-Ireland hat-trick by getting the better of O'Connell Schools by 5-7 to 5-2. The Clare school led by 1-4 to 1-1 at the interval, after what the 'Irish Independent' described as "a moderate first half", but struggled in the third quarter as their "persistent" Dublin oppo-

St. Flannan's, Ennis, Croke Cup Champions, 1946.
Back row, left to right: Joe Cummins, Paddy Rodgers, Paddy Gallagher, Adrian McMahon, Michael Shaughnessy, Joe O'Grady, Jimmy Smyth, Paddy Murray.
Middle row, left to right: Seamus Cleary, Mick Keane, Larry Byrne, Harry Sheehy, Michael Shalloo, J. J. Bugler (capt.), John Hanly, Bernard McMahon.
Front row, left to right: Leo Long, Tommy O'Meara, Derek McNulty, Michael Fahy, Tom Lynch.
(Photograph courtesy of Ollie Byrnes, author of Blue is the Colour, Hurling at St. Flannan's)

nents battled back to take the lead. However, with J. J. Bugler in fine scoring form, St. Flannan's finished strongly to retain their title.

John insists that St. Flannan's weren't at their best for the 1946 All-Ireland because a number of players had rebelled against Fr Michael Queally, who had taken over the management of the team from Tull Considine. "He wouldn't let us go to the pictures in Dublin, so we romped around the city doing things that were forbidden. Not surprisingly, we didn't play well and it took the switch of J. J. Bugler from full forward to centre forward to change the game around," he says. "If we played as well as we had been playing all year, we'd have beaten them by more". Again, there were celebrations on the homecoming to Ennis ("official, this time", John jokes), but, by now, "Flannan's were expecting to win the All-Ireland". Fr Jimmy Madden took charge of Flannan's in 1947, which was John's final year to play for the famous hurling nursery. In the Harty campaign, they beat Thurles CBS, North Mon and finally St. Colman's, Fermoy, by 4-5 to 3-6 at Thurles. John considers that his successful tussle with the highly-regarded John Thornhill in the Harty Cup final was his finest hour for his alma mater. The All-Ireland four-timer was achieved against Mount St. Joseph, Roscrea, with John becoming a member of a still-elite group to win three medals at the highest level of colleges hurling.

Looking back, John believes that the St. Flannan's players benefited greatly from playing challenge matches against senior club sides. "The training was very difficult, often times running around the field as many as ten times, then sprinting and finally hurling skills. This activity took place most evenings after school for an hour and a half. We had matches every second Sunday against club teams, principally Clarecastle, Tulla and Scariff. These games helped to toughen us up and stood us in good stead for the Harty and All-Ireland campaigns." John was also a useful footballer and in 1947 he was one of eight members of the St. Flannan's hurling team that played on the college football team. The Ennis college reached the Munster final against St. Brendan's of Killarney, but were forced to concede a walkover after their request for a postponement was turned down. Remarkably, John never wore a St. Flannan's jersey in defeat.

After leaving St. Flannan's, John trained to be a national teacher at St. Patrick's, Drumcondra. He represented Clare in senior hurling, but had no success. "We weren't that organised and were well beaten by the likes of Cork and Tipperary every year," he laments, adding that, "I lost interest, particularly as I was so far away". John's teaching career took him to both Wexford and Laois before he returned to Clare as principal of Clarecastle National School in 1960. He remained as principal until his retirement in 1993. During his time in Laois, he played for the now defunct Rovers club in the 1951 senior county final which they lost to Kyle. "They were rough days", John recalls, "often playing on pitches where the grass wasn't cut". On reflection, he considers that he may have made the groundbreaking Wexford senior team of the 1950s had he remained posted in the Model County.

John immersed himself in administration work after his playing career ended, and served as Clare County Board chairman from 1962 to 1973. He was also deeply involved in coaching at a time when it was "looked upon as a disease" by many in the GAA hierarchy, and he was one of five national coaches, the others being Ned Power (Waterford), Fr Tommy Maher (Kilkenny), Donie Nealon (Tipperary) and Des 'Snitchy' Ferguson (Dublin).

Very sadly, after just over 50 years of marriage, John's wife, Maura (née Bannon), a native of Laois and who played camogie for Galway in her time, passed away suddenly in November 2006. John has three sons, John Jnr, Tom and Andrew, and a daughter, Neasa. John and Andrew followed in their father's footsteps by successfully playing senior hurling with St. Flannan's, winning Harty and Croke Cup medals in 1976 and 1983 respectively. John also has eight grandchildren.

John Hanly has truly had a lifetime's involving in Gaelic games. After his initial reluctance, he became an integral part of the most successful college side ever in St. Flannan's. A couple of decades down the line, in Clarecastle

National School, he coached many young hurlers who were later to help in the college's Harty and All-Ireland wins of 1976, thereby ending an 18-year drought. He also coached a number of the players who famously won the All-Ireland senior hurling titles for Clare in 1995 and 1997, including team captain Anthony Daly. His on and off-the-field participation, as well as his clear recollection of stories from all aspects of his career, mark him out as a remarkable contributor to GAA in the Banner County.

J.J. BUGLER
(Born 21/10/1927, Died 30/3/2003)

John Hanly on J.J. Bugler: "J.J. and I were very close friends. He actually stayed in our house the year he was doing his Matriculation. He wasn't the biggest, but was very strong and had great courage and sense of position. He was particularly good at getting goals, and scored two in the 1946 All-Ireland final. He played in goal for the Clare seniors for a few years and had a very sharp eye. He won a county championship with Scariff in 1946 and later ran a successful business there. He continued to play hurling until his business commitments took over. I visited him a few days before his death and I was very sad at his passing."

Author's Note:
    On his death, aged 75, on 30 March 2003, J.J. Bugler was survived by his wife, Sheila and daughters, Clare, Pauline, Bernadette, Anne, Jean and Helen.

1947 – ALL-IRELAND FINAL
4 May 1947, Thurles
Referee: Phil Purcell (Tipperary)

St. Flannan's, Ennis 6-8

Michael Fahy
(Limerick)

Michael Considine
(Clare)

Paddy Rodgers
(Clare)

Peadar Keane
(Limerick)

Frank Fitzgerald
(Tipperary)

Michael Shalloo (*capt*)
(Clare)

Noel Hickey
(Tipperary)

John Hanly
(Clare)

Jimmy Smyth
(Clare) (0-5)

Larry Byrne
(Clare)

Paddy Murray
(Clare)

Derek McNulty
(Tipperary)

Sean Kenny
(Tipperary) (0-1)

Tom Feeley
(Kildare) (1-0)

Bernard McMahon
(Offaly) (5-2)

Mount St. Joseph, Roscrea 3-1

Paddy Holmes
(Limerick)

John O'Rourke
(Limerick)

Jim White
(Clare)

John Dagg
(Laois)

Paddy Carroll
(Tipperary)

Paddy Quinlan
(Tipperary)

William Power
(Tipperary)

Paddy Riordan (*capt*)
(Limerick)

John Stokes
(Limerick)

Sean Murphy
(Offaly) (2-0)

Patsy Torpey
(Tipperary)

Peter McCreery
(Kilkenny)

Tommy O'Meara
(Tipperary) (0-1)

Jim Fogarty
(Tipperary)

Vincent Cowen
(Offaly) (1-0)

Jimmy Smyth

St. Flannan's achievement in winning four consecutive All-Ireland colleges senior hurling titles, from 1944 to 1947 inclusive, has never been replicated. The fourth of these came under the captaincy of the late Michael Shalloo. The historic success also brought a third winner's medal to Jimmy Smyth, remarkably still aged only 16 at the time. Indeed, of the many outstanding hurlers who have passed through the Ennis nursery, Jimmy is still considered one of the greatest.

Jimmy's earliest hurling recollections are of his days in Kells National School where his mother, Mary Kate (née Considine) was a member of the teaching staff. "Even though I am from Ruan, I went to school in Kells where my mother taught," he remembers. "She was a sister of Paddy Considine who played junior hurling for Clare, and she took a great interest in the game herself. Every lunch break she would have us out playing hurling." Hurling was the only sport Jimmy played as a young boy. "We had a 30-acre field at the back of the house and from the age of four upwards, we played hurling there for at least four hours a day. We played with hazel sticks, a sponge ball and canisters. As a result, we were in heaven when we got to play with a hurley."

After completing his primary education, Jimmy followed in his older brother Gerard's footsteps by becoming a boarder at St. Flannan's, "as a blocky and nervous youngster, in spartan times". When he entered the Ennis college in 1943, the Second World War was at its height and hurling was beginning to take a grip in the college. "St. Flannan's was a change. Everything was a change. We were away from our natural feeding ground, but the hurling settled us down. Like it or lump it, rain or hail, we had to play", Jimmy recalls. He made the junior team in second year, while the college's seniors beat Midleton CBS after a replay to win the Harty Cup for the first time in 1944, and they subsequently defeated St. Kieran's, Kilkenny, to become the inaugural winners of the All-Ireland title. "These fellows to me were real heroes", Jimmy reflects.

The following year, Jimmy was drafted onto the senior panel by Tull Considine and made his Harty Cup debut against Thurles CBS. St. Flannan's were victorious and went on to retain their Munster and All-Ireland titles. They were successful again in 1946, winning their third All-Ireland title on the trot. Jimmy recalls his fear of being dropped for the 1946 All-Ireland after being pulled up for smoking by Fr Queally on the train to Dublin. "Smoking was one of the deadly sins in Flannan's at that time and when Fr Queally caught me having a drag, I thought I was in for it. He told me I was the kind of fellow who broke a man's heart by smoking. I knew his resolve, but he relented and I played. He was a skilful and talented footballer. He was able to kick a ball over the college and could play the better handballers with his feet. He opposed the strongest and toughest and allowed players to vent their grudges against him on the field."

Fr Jimmy Madden took charge of St. Flannan's in 1947 and in the Harty campaign, they beat Thurles CBS, North Mon and finally St. Colman's by 4-5 to 3-6 at Thurles. The Ennis school went on to capture their fourth All-Ireland title in-a-row by beating Mount St. Joseph's, Roscrea in the final on a 6-8 to 3-1 scoreline. That day in Thurles, Jimmy notched up 0-5 from play, and claims that was when he discovered his scoring touch. "I learned the secret of how to score in that All-Ireland final. I was never a scorer before that and had played all my hurling at wing back before switching to centrefield that year. Prior to this game, if I hit a shot towards goal it was, 'God direct it'. But in this game I got five points. I struck down on the ball and it went straight over the bar. Any scores I ever got afterwards I can attribute to this experience. I now had the confidence," Jimmy explains. St. Flannan's led by 4-6 to 2-1 at the interval and the 'Irish Independent' stated that, "Roscrea never got

into their stride and were in difficulties for most of the hour." The paper's reporter picked out Jimmy Smyth for special mention, applauding him for his "stickwork, ball control and fine sense of positional play". In the end, Michael Shalloo received the Croke Cup after a comfortable 6-8 to 3-1 success, with Bernard McMahon of Offaly (then a so-called 'weaker' county) showing an appetite for goals throughout.

In his first three years on the Harty team, Jimmy had known nothing but success, but that all changed in 1948 when, under his captaincy, St. Flannan's bid for a fifth consecutive Harty Cup was ended by St. Colman's in the final, after a second replay. 1949 was his final year at St. Flannan's and once again they reached the Harty final, only to lose to the holders from Fermoy by 1-3 to 4-6.

Jimmy was also a useful footballer and was part of the St. Flannan's teams which reached the 1947 and 1949 Munster senior finals. St.

St. Flannan's, Ennis, Croke Cup Champions, 1947.
Back row, left to right: Frank Garvey, Bernard McMahon, Michael Considine, Arthur Stritch,
Fr Jimmy Madden, Jimmy Smyth, Frank Fitzgerald, Barry Murphy, Paddy Haugh, Derek McNulty.
Middle row, left to right: Steve Murphy, Tom Feely, Sean Kenny, Michael Shalloo (capt),
Larry Byrne, Paddy Rodgers.
Front row, left to right: Peadar Keane, Noel Hickey.
Missing from photograph: John Hanly, Michael Fahy and Paddy Murray.
(Photograph courtesy of Ollie Byrnes, author of Blue is the Colour, Hurling at St. Flannan's)

Flannan's controversially gave a walkover to St. Brendan's, Killarney in the 1947 final and lost to Coláiste Íosagáin, Ballyvourney in the final of 1949. Jimmy recalls, "We had some very good footballers in Flannan's at that time and were unlucky not to win a Munster title. I had never seen a football before I went into Flannan's, but I played the game for three years. However, I didn't have the same 'grá' for it as I had for hurling."

He regards himself as very fortunate to have played under two great hurling coaches in Tull Considine and Fr Jimmy Madden during his years in St. Flannan's. "Tull was as far advanced as any coach is today," he claims. "Tactically, he was brilliant. He was the most articulate and knowledgeable man in hurling I have ever heard, since or before. Fr Jimmy also had a very good knowledge of the game. He brought a fresh approach to the team in '47 and his enthusiasm rubbed off on everyone." Even though times were tough in Flannan's, Jimmy has nothing only fond memories. "As someone said at the time, 'we could be thrown into the jungle and we'd survive'. It wasn't easy in those days and I suppose it was the hurling which kept a lot of lads going, myself included."

Jimmy first pulled on a Clare jersey at the age of 14 in the minor grade. It was the beginning of a long and distinguished inter-county career which spanned three decades. He was first selected on the Clare senior team in 1948 and captained the county junior side which won the Munster championship the following year, but lost the All-Ireland final to London.

His senior career really took off in the Munster championship tie with Tipperary in 1950. From 1953 to 1964, he was seldom off the Munster Railway Cup team. These years marked the high point of the competition when crowds in excess of 45,000 turned out to watch the finals in Croke Park. He won eight medals, all as a team-mate of the legendary Christy Ring (who won an astonishing 18 Railway Cup winner's medals), of whom Jimmy has "great memories".

At club level, Jimmy was a key member of the Ruan teams that won county senior cham-pionships in Clare in 1948, 1951, 1959, 1960 and 1962. "We had a very good side in Ruan and trained hard. Without the club, I wouldn't have survived on the Munster team for the length I did." While Jimmy enjoyed much suc-cess with St. Flannan's, Ruan and Munster, he failed to win anything of significance with Clare. "I played senior inter-county constantly from 1950 to '64, but we failed to win a Munster championship in that time. It was very frustrating. Needless to say, I was delight-ed when Clare finally made the breakthrough in 1995. It gave me the greatest thrill ever after all the barren years," he says.

Jimmy regards the 1953 Clare team as the best he played on. "We beat Limerick 10-8 to 1-1 in Ennis. We were later beaten by a goal by Cork who went on to win the All-Ireland in '53. Our team was just as good." In the facile win over Limerick, Smyth scored 6-4, which is a record in the Munster championship to this day. He is remarkably modest about the feat, saying "I was playing badly up to that game and yes I scored 6-4, but it's the player who is on you that suffers. Limerick had beaten us earli-er in the year, and we drew 1-7 apiece in a tournament game just weeks before." After taking a two-year break from the inter-county scene, Jimmy returned in 1967 for the latter stages of the National League. After overcom-ing Limerick and Galway in the Munster cham-pionship, Clare went under to Tipperary in the Munster final and Jimmy retired for good after that.

Having worked with Clare County Council for 15 years, Jimmy moved to Dublin in the mid 1960s where he took up the full-time position of Executive Officer with the GAA in Croke Park. He played his last game for Ruan in 1970, and ended his club career with Dublin outfit O'Connell's. "The thing I found from my time playing in Dublin is that the supporters didn't have the same passion or interest," he says. Married to Vera (née Gleeson), they have three daughters and a son, all now grown-up, as well as twelve grandchildren. Jimmy's son, Peter was also a talented hurler and won three county championships with O'Toole's.

Retired from his post with the GAA since 1987, Jimmy still maintains an interest in the

St. Flannan's hurling team, although time and geographical constraints have meant that he has very little contact with his surviving colleagues from his own secondary schooldays. His own writings on various facets of County Clare, hurling and GAA ballads in particular, are well respected. He is particularly pleased to have edited Pa Howard's tome, "Over 50 Years of Clare Hurling Teams, 1949 – 2001".

"I played in five Harty Cup finals, won three and lost two. I played in three All-Ireland finals and won all three. I owe everything to Ruan and St. Flannan's," Jimmy concludes. Many would feel, to this day, that his club, county and alma mater owe a lot to Jimmy Smyth. Such was his skill, talent and scoring ability, that he is acknowledged by many as one of the greatest forwards of all time, an opinion shared by countless GAA writers, commentators and selection committees over the years, including those charged with picking the Munster Team of the Millennium and the side containing the greatest-ever hurlers without an All-Ireland medal in the GAA's Centenary Year. He was inducted into the An Post GAA Hall of Fame in 2002 and had the unique honour of appearing on a postage stamp.

MICHAEL SHALLOO
(Born 18/1/1929, Died 11/7/2002)

Jimmy Smyth on Michael Shalloo: "Michael wasn't the most stylish hurler ever, but he was a very strong and tenacious defender who gave little away. Off the field, he was a total gentleman. He was an uncle of Sean Hehir, who was centre back on the great Clare team of the 1970s. He moved to Dublin many years ago and I was sad to hear of his death in 2002."

Author's Note:
On his death, aged 73, on 11 July 2002, Michael Shalloo was survived by his wife Anne, and their sons, Tadhg and Eoin.

1948 – ALL-IRELAND FINAL
2 May 1948, Croke Park
Referee: J. J. Stuart (Dublin)

St. Kieran's, Kilkenny 2-12

Sean Lynch
(Kilkenny)

Willie Doyle   Kieran Crotty   Nicky Murphy
(Kilkenny)   (Kilkenny)   (Kilkenny)

Tom O'Connor   Dan Galavan   Harry Ryan
(Kilkenny)   (Kilkenny)   (Kilkenny)

Lar Dunphy (*capt*)   Tom Connolly
(Laois) (0-3)   (Dublin) (0-2)

Billy Bennett   Gerry O'Malley   Mick Loughlin
(Kilkenny) (0-4)   (Laois) (1-2)   (Kilkenny)

Jim Mahony   Bill Hoban   Dick O'Neill
(Laois)   (Kilkenny) (0-1)   (Kilkenny) (1-0)

St. Colman's, Fermoy 2-2

Michael Ryan
(Waterford)

Pat O'Keeffe   Liam O'Connell   Finbarr Kelleher
(Cork)   (Cork)   (Cork)

Mick Gould   Paddy Cotter   Paddy Scully
(Cork)   (Cork)   (Cork)

Bertie Troy   Willie Joyce
(Cork) (0-1)   (Cork)

Michael Mullins   Willie Moore   Jim Twomey
(Limerick)   (Cork) (1-0)   (Cork)

Billy Abernethy (*capt*)   Jim Brew   Jim McGrath
(Cork) (1-1)   (Cork)   (Cork)

Lar Dunphy

In 1948, in the fifth staging of the new All-Ireland colleges senior hurling championship, a new name was at last inscribed on the Croke Cup, with young Laois man Lar Dunphy captaining St. Kieran's when they eventually took over from four-time champions St. Flannan's. Remarkably, the Kilkenny and Clare schools were to win no less than 30 of the first 55 finals, with one or other or both appearing in all bar 20 of the deciders between 1944 and 2006.

Lar grew up in Cullohill, not far from the Kilkenny border. "Because there was very little hurling played in the local primary school, I had to teach myself how to hurl, out in the back field," he says. Bit by bit, he taught himself the basic skills of hurling before coming to St. Kieran's on a County Council scholarship. "I furthered my skills in St. Kieran's and it was there that I learned how to win as well as lose. I started out in first year with Billy Rackard, but he got some type of bad influenza which nearly killed him and he never returned. My brother Mick (now an abbot), who was in the same class as Nicky Rackard, had gone to Kieran's before me and my eldest brother Barney played full forward for Laois. My father, also Mick, never played the game, but his brother Joe, who was in the army, played for the local club. Joe Dunphy, who was also from Cullohill and was my father's brother-in-law, was full back on the one and only Laois team to win the All-Ireland senior hurling title in 1915."

As a young first year, Lar looked up to the likes of Sean Collier. "He was part of the team that lost the 1944 All-Ireland final to St. Flannan's, who won the first of their four in-a-row that year. We couldn't believe it when they lost, as losing was something St. Kieran's were never used to," he explains. The same Sean Collier, who went on to play for Laois, was co-trainer along with Fr John Joe Reidy when St. Kieran's returned to win the All-Ireland four years later. "He came back as a head prefect and was very involved in the hurling," Lar remembers.

Lar played on the St. Kieran's senior team for three years, during which time he had many great jousts with future Dublin football legend Kevin Heffernan, who played for St. Joseph's, Marino. "I played on Heffernan a few times, even though we didn't always start out marking one another. When we beat St. Joseph's in the 1948 Leinster final, I would like to think he was moved to mark me during the game." In 1946, St. Kieran's lost the Leinster final to O'Connell Schools and they were knocked out the following year by Mount St. Joseph's, Roscrea, in the first round.

After returning from the summer holidays in September 1947, Lar was handed the captaincy. He confesses to being "the most surprised man when it was announced in the refectory by Fr John Joe Reidy". On November 20th, St. Kieran's set out on the road to Leinster and All-Ireland glory. They had home advantage against keen rivals Roscrea and, with six Kilkenny minors on board, had high hopes of coming away with victory. Lar was one of those minors, despite his Laois upbringing and residence. "I was somehow eligible to play minor for Kilkenny and we had two great games against Dublin in that year's Leinster final before losing by a point in the replay (2-4 to 3-2) in Croke Park," he recalls. The first round clash with Roscrea was one of the most stirring colleges encounters seen on Noreside for some time. Bill Hoban's goalscoring instincts and Lar Dunphy's crisp striking were key factors in Kieran's 7-7 to 5-4 win. "Roscrea were a very fit, mobile team - they were big into athletics and we always had a tough time against them," Lar says. St. Kieran's had home advantage again for the Leinster final against St. Joseph's, Marino. The Kilkenny lads settled quickly and

had established a 3-2 to 0-1 lead at the break. The Dublin representatives pulled back a goal after half-time, but they left themselves with too much to do as St. Kieran's claimed the Leinster title on a 3-6 to 1-4 scoreline.

St. Colman's, Fermoy provided the All-Ireland final opposition for St. Kieran's in Croke Park. Lar hoped that St. Flannan's, Ennis, would win out in Munster as he "wanted a crack at Jimmy Smyth, who had fabulous ability". However, having beaten St. Flannan's in a twice-replayed Harty Cup decider, the Cork side was a battle-hardened outfit who deservedly carried the favourites tag into the final. "We knew we were up against it," Lar recalls, "because Fr Reidy had brought three of us to Thurles to see one of those Harty

St. Kieran's, Kilkenny, Croke Cup Champions, 1948.
Back row, left to right: Fr John Joe Reidy, Dick O'Neill, Donie O'Brien, Harry Ryan, Kieran Crotty, Tom O'Connor, Jackie Nolan, Sean Lynch, Nicky Murphy, Tom White, Tom Vaughan, Rev Sean Collier, Mr Christy Murray.
Front row, left to right: Denis Bergin, Dan Galavan, Gerry O'Malley, Willie Doyle, Lar Dunphy (capt), Bill Hoban, Billy Bennett, Tom Connolly, Jim Mahony, Mick Loughlin.
(Photograph courtesy of Dick McEvoy, c/o St. Kieran's, Kilkenny).

Cup finals and it was one of the best games I ever saw. There wasn't a word spoken in the car that day going back to Kilkenny. We were gobsmacked by the standard of hurling. However, we stuck to our training routine while Colman's and Flannan's were knocking lumps out of one another in yet another replay. Gradually, our confidence was restored and, when the day came, we were ready. "

The early minutes of the final were anything but encouraging for St. Kieran's. Lar, uncharacteristically, missed a free from 21 yards out near the sideline and St. Colman's responded with an unanswered 1-1. However, once the threat of Cork starlet Liam Abernethy had been curbed, St. Kieran's looked a different team and a flurry of scores had them ahead by 1-6 to 1-1 at half-time. Ironically, both sides replicated their first half tally in the second moiety and St. Kieran's won their first Croke Cup by 2-12 to 2-2.

"A polished display" was how the 'Irish Independent' described their performance. "Except for a brief period in the second half when they reduced the lead to three points, Munster champions, St. Colman's were outclassed by a fitter and faster St. Kieran's", was how their match reporter summed up events in GAA headquarters that historic day. Lar was especially prominent in the final quarter, fielding high ball after high ball and making intelligent use of the possession. "We won more comfortably than we could ever have imagined," Lar reflects. "It was a very wet day and both teams were slow to get into the game. But we eventually got going and were in control until they got their second goal. We then got our second and we were able to pull away after that. We had a big advantage over Colman's in that some of us were used to playing in Croke Park. Even when it's empty, Croke Park can be an intimidating place to play in if you're not used to it and I definitely think the occasion got to Colman's." Lar fondly remembers the All-Ireland champions' return to Kilkenny. "It was a typical Kilkenny homecoming, nothing was spared. The James Stephens Band met us at the railway station and we paraded from there back to St. Kieran's. It was a wonderful occasion. "

Lar is fulsome in his praise of Fr John Joe Reidy, the man who masterminded the 1948 success, and was associated with successful St. Kieran's teams for many years. "He was a brilliant trainer and before we went out on to the pitch he would have us convinced that we couldn't lose. He was a great man to give a rousing talk before a game. He was a very passionate hurling man, so much so that he ran the length of Croke Park on All-Ireland final day without realising it. Fr Reidy was a brother of Liam Reidy, who used to play for Kilkenny. Liam used to come to our matches and would gee us up beforehand. We were fortunate in St. Kieran's to have so many good coaches. Sean Collier, then a seminarian, did great work with us, as did both of the Fr Dunphy brothers from Mooncoin. John Wilson, who played for Cavan in the 1947 All-Ireland football final in the Polo Grounds and went on to become Tánaiste, promoted football in the school and we were happy to play it because it was a change from hurling. John used to give great support to the hurling as well, and all the priests and teaching staff were very enthusiastic and supportive," Lar reflects.

After completing his education in St. Kieran's, Lar studied for the priesthood in Dalgan Park, Navan. Despite the rule then in existence that prohibited members of the clergy from playing Gaelic games, he still managed to line out for Laois and Cullohill by using a false name. "I played under Barney Dunphy, my brother's name," he reveals. "I didn't get a chance to play for Laois when they reached the All-Ireland final in 1949 but I was on the panel the following year when Wexford beat us in the Leinster semi-final. As I watched my old friend Billy Rackard lording it over all and sundry from the back line, I prayed for the opportunity to mix it with him one more time, but it wasn't to be. " In 1955, Lar was player/trainer of the Cullohill team which defeated Kyle to win their first Laois senior hurling championship. The Kyle team included future Tipperary All-Ireland winning corner back Kieran Carey, who was one of three brothers in their ranks. After spells ministering in the USA and Japan, Lar came home to guide Cullohill to their second county championship in 1964, defeating Camross in the final.

He returned to Japan before deciding to leave the priesthood in 1971. He has lived for many years in London with his partner Lynda Jefferson, herself long-since converted to the game of hurling and with an English family background in a range of sports. Lar worked in the construction business up until his retirement eight years ago. He jokes that he "dabbled" at other sports over the years, including baseball and American football while domiciled in the States. He enjoyed playing golf, which he feels is "a rhythm game" and reckons is "very different from taking 21-yard frees". Unfortunately, Lar suffered a stroke two years ago. He has made a good recovery but finds that he has to take life a little more slowly. It has not stopped him enjoying an active retirement.

Lar still continues to follow St. Kieran's fortunes closely and was delighted to travel over to a well-attended 50th anniversary of the all-conquering 1948 team, some eight years ago in the college itself. "There's something special about colleges hurling and I'm always looking out for St. Kieran's results. I kept in touch with a lot of the lads down the years, including Kieran Crotty, Jim Mahony and, up to his death, Gerry O'Malley. I have fond memories of my time in St. Kieran's," he concludes. St. Kieran's first Croke Cup win in 1948 assured Laois man Lar Dunphy and his colleagues of a special place in the college's history. "For future generations of hurling-loving students the example was set and the template was created," is how Enda McEvoy refers to the historic breakthrough in his excellent history of the great Kilkenny nursery, 'Fennessy's Field'.

1957 – ALL-IRELAND SEMI-FINAL
7 April 1957, Galway

St. Flannan's, Ennis 7-4
(B. Hennessy 2-1, P. Nealon 2-0, T. Ryan 1-0, S. Custy 1-0, F .Devlin 1-0,
O. Naughton 0-1, P. Kennedy 0-1, M. Deasy 0-1)

St. Mary's, Galway 1-6
(S. Conroy 0-4, P. Finnegan 1-0, S. Fallon 0-2)

St. Kieran's, Kilkenny, Croke Cup Champions, 1957
Back row, left to right: Kevin Mahoney, Mick Carroll, Tim Murphy, Kieran Fitzgerald, Sean Murray,
Joe O'Donnell, Dick Dowling, Martin Campion, Martin Duggan, Humphrey O'Sullivan.
Front row, left to right: Austin McMahon, Har Hickey, Martin Walsh, Miko Ryan,
Ted Carroll (capt), P. J. Mahoney, Eddie Keher, Dick Walsh, Ollie Harrington, Tom White.
Missing from photo: Dick Lynch.
(Photograph courtesy of Dick McEvoy, c/o St. Kieran's, Kilkenny)

1957 – ALL-IRELAND FINAL
28 April 1957, Thurles
Referee: Inky Flaherty (Galway)

St. Kieran's, Kilkenny 4-2

Dick Lynch
(Kilkenny)

P.J.Mahoney
(Kilkenny)

Joe O'Donnell
(Kilkenny)

Har Hickey
(Kilkenny)

Miko Ryan
(Kilkenny)

Ted Carroll (*capt*)
(Kilkenny)

Sean Murray
(Tipperary)

Kevin Mahoney
(Kilkenny)

Ollie Harrington
(Kilkenny)

Mick Carroll
(Kilkenny)

Dick Walsh
(Kilkenny) (1-0)

Eddie Keher
(Kilkenny) (1-0)

Martin Walsh
(Kilkenny) (0-2)

Dick Dowling
(Kilkenny) (1-0)

Tom White
(Kilkenny) (1-0)

Subs: Martin Campion (Tipperary) (for Harrington),
Ollie Harrington (Kilkenny) (for Campion).

St. Flannan's, Ennis 2-7

Terry Moloney
(Tipperary)

Colm Wiley
(Clare)

Joe Hoare
(Limerick)

Gerry Kennedy
(Tipperary)

Kevin Smyth
(Clare)

John Slattery (*capt*)
(Tipperary) (0-1)

Joe Keane
(Clare)

Michael Deasy
(Clare)

Brendan Hennessy
(Kerry) (0-1)

Ollie Naughton
(Tipperary)

Tom Ryan
(Tipperary) (0-1)

Paudie Kennedy
(Tipperary) (0-3)

Sean Devlin
(Galway) (1-0)

Frank Custy
(Clare) (1-0)

Patsy Nealon
(Tipperary) (0-1)

Sub: Tim Kelly (Clare) (for Custy).

Mick Carroll

A sensational finish, in which they struck three goals in the final six minutes, saw St. Kieran's snatch a dramatic victory from St. Flannan's in the 1957 All-Ireland colleges senior hurling final. Afterwards, the late Ted Carroll became the first captain to lift the Croke Cup since the competition had been removed from the GAA calendar in 1948. Ironically, Ted's twin brother, Mick also figured on the Kilkenny college side which brought the trophy to the Marble City for the second time.

The Carrolls grew up in Lisdowney where their father Paddy, whom Mick was told was "a pretty good hurler in his day", brought them to a variety of matches, together with his friend, Bill Kenny, who had played in the 1922 All-Ireland winning side when Kilkenny defeated Tipperary. Mick paints a very simple picture of practising hurling as a young boy in in the 1940s. "The Lisdowney club was revived in 1939. Ted and I were naturally close, being twins, and we would spend evening after evening watching the lads playing and training in Bill Kenny's field. They would arrive straight from a hard day's work and they often played in their clothes, as there were no tracksuits back then," Mick recalls. "We often stayed there till after dark as there was no other entertainment back then, and, as young lads, we would sit behind the goals and we would be delighted to get a puck of the ball when it would go behind. Sometimes, we would spend hours looking for the ball in the ditch as we'd only have one ball and there were no nets." Back on the family farm, two

big gates 40 yards apart were used as goals as the twins pucked the sliotar around. Although not very successful at national school level, Mick and Ted played in the school leagues in Kilkenny but they often got "hammered" in matches by schools with much bigger pupil numbers. It was not unusual to walk long distances to games at the time, and it was quite a treat to get a lift to and from games from local priests, Fr Marnell and Fr Brennan.

Mick and Ted followed the footsteps of their older brother Lar when they enrolled as boarders in St. Kieran's in September 1952 and Mick recalls that arriving in the famous nursery with new hurling boots, togs and socks was "like Christmas". The in-house hurling leagues kept the boarders suitably occupied, particularly at weekends, as there was little opportunity to visit the outside world except at Christmas and Easter, or occasional days out for National League games in Nowlan Park. As a first year, Mick looked up to the likes of senior players like Eddie Healy, Dermot Sheedy, Watty McDonald, Joe Prendergast and Paddy Walsh. However, despite St. Kieran's winning the Leinster senior title in 1953 (during the time the Croke Cup was in limbo), the mid-1950s was "a lean period" for the school. Indeed, the ensuing three years brought heavy senior championship defeats to Roscrea, Knockbeg and Ballyfin respectively, with the added ignominy of not even reaching the provincial final in any of those campaigns.

Mick was a member of the St. Kieran's

team which lost to Ballyfin in the 1955/56 semi-final in Carlow, a disappointing end to his first campaign as a senior in the black and white hoops. It had started in whirlwind fashion when he bagged 4-5 in an 11-11 to 0-0 first round win, ironically against their conquerors from the previous year, Knockbeg College from Carlow. However, a provincial junior win that season augured well for the following year, when the twin Carrolls were both on the side which defeated St. Joseph's, Fairview (Des Foley et al), by 4-9 to 1-1 in the Leinster final in Portlaoise, with Ted captaining the side to victory.

By now, Fr Tommy Maher was making a massive contribution to improving hurling in St. Kieran's. Almost a half-century later, Mick speaks in glowing terms about the famous hurling coach, whose philosophy was simple. "Even though he had no magic formula, he was still a man before his time". Mick remembers Fr Maher as "a very quiet man, who never raised his voice but gave people confidence in themselves". Many of his training sessions were innovative at the time and the hours spent perfecting hand-passing drills ultimately proved be a match-winner when the chips were down in the 1957 showdown with St. Flannan's. "There were no dieticians or sports psychologists then. Fr Maher was coach, trainer and truly a jack-of-all-trades," Mick concludes.

St. Kieran's started off their 1956/57 championship run with an easy first round victory over St. Peter's, Wexford, who had yet to become a major force in the province. This is clear as Ted Carroll's charges romped home in Carlow, winning 7-10 to 1-1, with the captain's twin brother Mick accounting for three of the goals. Mount St. Joseph's, Roscrea, were the next opponents, also at Dr Cullen Park, with St. Kieran's winning after a much tighter encounter, on a scoreline of 5-4 to 3-4. Patrician College, Ballyfin were St. Kieran's Leinster final opponents and, after the unexpected reversal in the previous season, Mick remembers the game was considered as "touch and go". As it transpired, the Kilkenny lads used the wind advantage to good effect in the first half in Athy and led comfortably at

half time by 3-3 to 0-0. In the end, St. Kieran's won by 6-3 to 3-0 and Mick recalls that "a lot of us ended up with cramps", as they held out against the wind in the second moiety.

There was great hype surrounding the Croke Cup final in St. Kieran's, now that the All-Ireland series had been restored. In a sense, the opportunity had arisen to 'retain' the trophy as Lar Dunphy had led the black and whites to success when it was last up for grabs in 1948. That side had featured Lisdowney's Nicky Murphy, thereby making the Carroll twins keen to emulate their fellow clubman's achievement. There wasn't much national media coverage about the final, but the local Kilkenny newspapers honed in on the importance of the occasion. Training was intensified and Fr Maher had the team well prepared as they got ready to face St. Flannan's. The Ennis side had convincingly defeated St. Mary's, Galway, by 7-4 to 1-6 in the first ever semi-final of the competition, three weeks before the decider in Thurles on April 28th, 1957. In particular, Fr Maher reminded the Leaving Cert lads that "it would be our last chance of All-Ireland glory with the school".

Naturally, there was a great sense of anticipation in the Carroll household in Lisdowney, although Mick vividly recalls that, while his father attended the game, "my mother went to the Cathedral in Thurles to say her prayers", adding jokingly that, "maybe that was the reason we won". Mrs Carroll clearly must have prayed very fervently, as this was certainly a game that St. Kieran's stole from under the noses of their great rivals from County Clare.

'Irish Independent' reporter, Con Kenealy reckoned that, "St. Kieran's staged what must rank as one of the most fantastic finishes of all time, when they scored three goals in the last six minutes to snatch victory by 4-2 to 2-7 over St. Flannan's, Ennis".

The Ennis side led 2-3 to 0-1 at the interval having played against the wind, and many present expected the the second half to be a mere formality. However, Mick reflects, "at the interval, Fr Maher just told us to relax, go out and play our own game and let the ball do the work and that we were capable of playing far better than we had shown in the first half". But it still looked like a certain St. Flannan's win some 15 minutes in to the second half when, despite the return to the fray of the injured Ollie Harrington to help his comrades in distress, very little had changed. Scoring only their second point of the game at the end of the third quarter, thereafter St. Kieran's played like men inspired. Sharpshooter Eddie Keher then put Dick Walsh through for the first goal. Six minutes from the final whistle, Keher was put through for another three-pointer and, moments later, Tom White raised another green flag.

As time ticked away, Fr Maher's training methods came up trumps when a Keher hand-pass found Dick Dowling, who grabbed the all-important fourth goal which left the St. Flannan's side completely numbed. Mick vividly recalls the winning goal, stating that, "as there was only one stand in Thurles at the time, a fog of dust flew up from the cinder bank on the opposite side as our followers celebrated". At the other end of the pitch, goalkeeper Dick Lynch made wonderful saves throughout the contest, while Ted Carroll played a captain's part in defence. Indeed, Mick feels that, "the longer it went on, the more we would have won by and I distinctly remember Ted going up to collect the Croke Cup. We headed back to the college where there was tremendous hype. We all got a free day the next day and the team members were allowed head home," Mick fondly remembers.

However, the year wasn't without its bad memories for Mick and he won't forget in a hurry the day the Leaving Cert results for 1957 were announced. He was in hospital awaiting an appendix operation and this caused him to miss out on a much cherished All-Ireland final appearance for the Kilkenny minor side. They were trying to avenge the previous year's defeat in the Irish Press Cup final to Tipperary (when Ted had been on a badly beaten Cats side). Alas, defeat was again Kilkenny's lot in the 1957 minor decider, albeit by a much more respectable margin of just one goal, with Ted again picking up a loser's medal.

After leaving St. Kieran's, Mick spent a year in Multyfarnham Agricultural College in County Westmeath, before moving on to study Agricultural Science in UCD. With the Dublin college, Mick won two Fitzgibbon Cup medals, with Ted going one better and winning a rare haul of three. The Carroll brothers also featured on the UCD side which won the Dublin Senior Championship in 1961, beating a strong St. Vincent's side which contained many members of the Dublin senior hurling team who lost by just a point to Tipperary in that year's All-Ireland final.

On the home front, Lisdowney had won the Kilkenny junior hurling championship in 1960, which was the only adult championship to come to the club since its formation. However, the ultimate honour of winning the Kilkenny senior title was denied them in the 1962 final by Bennettsbridge. Unlike Ted, who went on to have a long and illustrious career in the famous black and amber jersey, Mick's stint as a senior inter-county player was very brief. He played a number of National Hurling League games with Kilkenny in 1960/61, but only one championship game as Wexford beat their great rivals in the 1961 Leinster campaign.

Having finished his studies in UCD, in 1962 Mick joined the staff of the Sugar Company in Carlow town as an agricultural advisor. He enjoyed quite a degree of success on the hurling fields with the factory in inter-firms competitions. After leaving the Sugar Company in 1966, Mick spent three years in Castlerea, County Roscommon, where among his friends was the legendary Roscommon dual star, Gerry O'Malley. He also became a great pal of the former secretary of Roscommon GAA, Philly Gannon and his wife May, who helped Mick and his new bride, Rosemary (neé Stratford) settle in the area. The friendship continued long after the Carrolls left Castlerea and Mick was particularly sad when Philly died a few weeks after being guests of the Carrolls in Thurles for the Centenary All-Ireland senior hurling final in Thurles in 1984. During his time in Roscommon, Mick undertook a little coaching and also refereed Connacht minor championship games and a

Roscommon senior hurling final, joking that, "I mustn't have been too bad as I didn't get in to any rows and nobody hit me a belt".

Mick moved to Thurles as an agricultural advisor with the North Tipperary Committee of Agriculture (later Teagasc) in 1968. He and Rosemary have lived there ever since and have three grown-up children. Naturally enough, their two sons, Ciaran and Brendan are "very much Tipp men". Indeed, both played hurling at a high level and followed in their father's footsteps by winning the Fitzgibbon Cup in 1992/93, also with UCD. Brendan actually played in a Harty Cup final with Thurles CBS and went on to win a National League medal with Tipp, as well as being a member of the Thurles Sarsfields side which bridged a 31-year gap by winning the Tipperary senior hurling title in 2005. Their sibling, Deirdre is "a big Tipp follower". Ciaran, who is a former Thurles Sarsfield goalkeeper, now lives in Fermoy, and one of Mick's four grandchildren,

Ciaran's son Colm, is already shaping up as a prospective Cork hurler, which would nicely tie up Mick's connections with the recognised 'big three' in hurling!

After settling in Thurles, Mick noticed a declining interest in underage hurling in the town so, together with some friends, like former Tipp great Pat Stakeleum, as well as Brother Lombard, Connie Higgins and Michael Murphy, they formed a juvenile club called Dúrlas Óg in 1979. This club catered for youngsters up to the age of 16, at which stage they could move to any club they wanted. As the years went by, the club went from strength to strength and has now its own pitch and dressing rooms. Mick is still a trustee of the club and he enjoys his other GAA roles also. He is a member of the Development Committee of the Tipperary County Board and, using his work background, he regularly advises on pitch development and maintenance in Semple Stadium and

TED CARROLL
(Born 19/2/1939, Died 22/12/1995)

Mick Carroll on Ted Carroll: "Ted was one of the most dedicated players you could meet. His hurling career spanned an amazing 30 years, playing club hurling up to his mid-40s. This is a testament to his great commitment and loyalty to his native parish. It is also significant that the county junior championship medal, which he won in 1960, was one of his most cherished trophies. He always kept himself very fit and he had hurling in his heart at all times. While quiet and unassuming, he was a good leader and showed great example, both on and off the field. It was a terrible shock to the system when he died. A sad, sad occasion."

Author's Note:
On his death, aged 56, on 22 December 1995, Ted Carroll was survived by his wife, Angela, and their sons Pat, Donal, Ted and David, and daughter Helen.

on many other pitches throughout Tipperary. Having retired from Teagasc a few years ago, he now jokes that, "there is no day that I am bored; maybe I hadn't time for work at all over the years"! Mick enjoys a social game of golf and playing Bridge, with Pat Stakelum among his colleagues in that pastime.

There has never been a reunion of the 1957 Croke Cup winning team. Sadly, two of its members are now deceased - Miko Ryan and, of course, Ted Carroll. Mick sees 2007 as an ideal opportunity to hold a Golden Jubilee get-together. He occasionally bumps in to former team-mates such as Sean Murray, Eddie Keher and Dick Walsh at matches and other outings. Naturally, he was deeply upset when his twin brother and great friend, Ted, died suddenly in Kilkenny 11 years ago. He still recalls receiving the dreaded phone call with deep regret. Indeed, the poignancy of the event was added to by the fact that one of Ted's 1957 colleagues, Monsignor Martin Campion, was one of the first to come on the scene.

To this day, despite his Tipperary domicile, Mick Carroll looks out for his alma mater's results. "I have fond memories of the school. It was all hurling; hurling was a religion in the place," he recalls. The 1957 triumph was St. Kieran's second Croke Cup win and, to this day, it remains a particularly sweet success for all those associated with it, as the Kilkenny lads snatched victory from the jaws of defeat against arch-rivals, St. Flannan's.

1958 – ALL-IRELAND SEMI-FINAL
30 March 1958, Ennis

St. Flannan's, Ennis 6-8
(G. Jordan 4-1, F. Cleary 2-0, O. Naughton 0-4, K. Smyth 0-1, M. Deasy 0-1, N. McDonnell 0-1)

St. Joseph's, Galway 1-3
(M. Moylan 1-0, M. Deignan 0-2, J. Berry 0-1)

St. Flannan's, Ennis, Croke Cup Champions, 1958.
Back row, left to right: Paddy Brady, Kevin Smyth, Joe Williams, Gerry Jordan, Michael Deasy,
Ronnie Slevin, Paddy Vaughan, Sean Devlin, Joe Keane.
Middle row, left to right: Dick Halpin, Noel McDonnell, Terry Moloney, George Kinane,
Paudie Kennedy (capt), Ollie Naughton, Frank Cleary, Andy Hoolan, Pat Keane.
Front row, left to right: Sean Mix, John O'Mahoney, Charlie McLoughney, Seamus Maxwell.
(Photograph courtesy of Ollie Byrnes, author of Blue is the Colour, Hurling at St. Flannan's).

1958 – ALL-IRELAND FINAL
27 April 1958, Thurles
Referee: Josie Gallagher (Galway)

St. Flannan's, Ennis 3-10

Terry Moloney
(Tipperary)

Andy Hoolan   **George Kinane**   **Joe Williams**
(Tipperary)   (Tipperary)   (Tipperary)

Kevin Smyth   **Joe Keane**   **Ronnie Slevin**
(Clare)   (Clare)   (Tipperary)

Ollie Naughton   **Michael Deasy**
(Tipperary)   (Clare)

Frank Cleary   **Sean Devlin**   **Paudie Kennedy** (*capt*)
(Clare)   (Galway) (1-1)   (Tipperary) (1-9)

Paddy Vaughan   **Gerry Jordan**   **Noel McDonnell**
(Clare)   (Clare) (1-0)   (Tipperary)

Subs: Sean Mix (Clare) (for Vaughan), Paddy Vaughan (Clare) (for McDonnell).

St. Kieran's, Kilkenny 0-2

Paddy Dunphy
(Kilkenny)

Humphrey O'Sullivan   **Joe O'Donnell** (*capt*)   **Har Hickey**
(Kilkenny)   (Kilkenny)   (Kilkenny)

John Alley   **Dick Walsh**   **Sean Creagh**
(Laois)   (Kilkenny)   (Laois)

Ollie Harrington   **Martin Lanigan**
(Kilkenny) (0-1)   (Kilkenny)

Myles Kehoe   **Tom Forristal**   **Eddie Keher**
(Kilkenny) (0-1)   (Kilkenny)   (Kilkenny)

Martin Walsh   **Peter Phelan**   **William Quinlan**
(Kilkenny)   (Kilkenny)   (Kilkenny)

Sub: Pierce Freaney (Kilkenny) (for Quinlan).

Paudie Kennedy

Twelve months after a heartbreaking defeat by perennial rivals, St. Kieran's in the 1957 Croke Cup final, St. Flannan's comprehensively reversed the previous year's result, with the Ennis school being captained in their fifth All-Ireland win by Tipperary's Paudie Kennedy, who put on a particularly memorable personal display in the showdown 48 years ago.

Paudie is a native of Nenagh and he recalls that, "hurling was part of my life from the day I was able to walk. My late father, who ran a small grocery shop in the town, brought me to hurling matches when I was very young and I was steeped in the game." His first memory of receiving "proper gear" was when he played for Nenagh CBS in a primary schools game against their counterparts from Limerick. Sadly, his father died while attending a Tipperary v. Galway match in 1952, leaving behind a wife and six young children (of which Paudie was the third youngest).

Paudie confesses to have been "a Flannan's fan before I ever hurled with them at all" as his older brother, Michael (later a government minister using the full O'Kennedy family name) had attended the school before Paudie was enrolled as a boarder in September 1953. Indeed, Paudie was soon to inherit Michael's unusual nickname of 'Edjar'. Competitive matches were a rarity for colleges at juvenile level in those days, so Paudie had to be content with playing 'money matches' every day at school. Indeed, he remembers getting caught on a couple of occasions, as he attempted to slip down to the weaker games in order to win a sixpence! He feels these matches were to later give him "a competitive edge". Those early years in St. Flannan's consisted of long hours of study, combined with hurling matches in the in-houses winter leagues, where Paudie won his first medal in second year. These leagues increased in significance if the school made an early exit from the Harty Cup. As a young boy in St. Flannan's, Paudie looked up to, among others, future Tipp star, Donie Nealon, as well as Seamus and Liam Ryan ("both of whom became priests") and Paddy O'Malley. An interesting anecdote which springs to his mind concerns Billy Quinn, nowadays better known as the father of former Irish soccer star, Niall. Billy scored three goals in a National League final for Tipperary, yet tasted defeat just two months later when Thurles CBS lost to St. Flannan's in the Harty Cup.

In his Inter Cert year, Paudie was on the verge of the Harty team but a poor performance against Mick Craddock in a friendly against Thurles CBS saw him relegated to the subs with St. Flannan's succumbing to North Mon in the second round. The following year saw Paudie progress onto the senior team where he lined out at left half forward in the Croke Cup final, now back on the GAA calendar after being abandoned for eight years, but a heartbreaking defeat was the outcome against a strong St. Kieran's, Kilkenny team. "That year was a huge disappointment,"

Paudie reflects, "as I felt we lost that game because it was played during the Easter Holidays. Just picture it, the college was closed when we met for the final. We should have been on holidays and we left an empty and lonely college to play the match with no support, no buzz and no excitement. Having said that, we led by ten points and fair play to them they came back and beat us," he concludes.

Paudie was "delighted and honoured" to be selected as Harty captain in his Leaving Cert year, although not totally surprised as "I had featured on the team from third year. Generally the longest serving player was appointed captain, so long as he wasn't doing silly things like setting fire to the school!" In the 1957/58 Munster campaign Mount Sion were St. Flannan's first opponents but the Waterford school were no match for the reigning Harty champions, who were inspired by a six-goal haul from Gerry Jordan. St. Flannan's went on to beat Thurles CBS at the semi-final stage but Limerick CBS proved to be stern opposition in the Harty Cup final. "We were very lucky to win that game," Paudie recalls, "as we played against a very stiff wind in the first half and crossed the half way line only six times but fortunately we managed to get four goals from those attacks. Limerick had a terrific team and we were fortunate to come away as winners." In the end, St. Flannan's overcame a highly-rated Sexton Street side by 6-2 to 3-7 that day in Limerick.

After a comfortable All-Ireland semi-final win against St. Joseph's from Galway, on a scoreline of 6-8 to 1-3 (with goalscorer supreme Gerry Jordan on target four times on this occasion), the stage was set for a repeat of the memorable Croke Cup final of 1957. To this day, Paudie remembers the build-up and excitement to the final of 1958. "Fr Jimmy Madden was the best trainer and tactician I ever came across. He had me practising my freetaking with the aid of very high goalposts. We were treated like greyhounds and got fed on glucose, raw eggs and beef tea. We enjoyed our little perks, which also included a sugar cube as we left the dressing room for a big game, even if it left my mouth very dry. We were pampered and made feel special as we received crisp new shorts and socks. There was a huge desire in Flannan's to win that final. This was drilled home in our pep talk the night before the game."

Nobody anticipated a one-sided final but that is exactly what materialised. Paudie remembers the intense rivalry on the sideline between the respective managers". Fr Tommy Maher was in charge of St. Kieran's, while Fr Jimmy Madden ("he had an aura about him") and Fr John Shaloo ("he got you fit") looked after St. Flannan's. "They insisted that we would not concede a goal and get revenge for the previous year. I felt very confident that day and everything fell into place. I remember going over to the far sideline, which was my most difficult side, to take a free 40 yards out which normally I would dread and yet I knew on the way over that I was going to point it, because it was one of those days - I couldn't have put the ball wide that day if I tried." Indeed, Paudie remembers that there were no distinguishing numbers on the blue jerseys of St. Flannan's, but his proud young brother, Eamonn made sure that the newspapers knew who was getting the scores, as he happened to be sitting beside the reporters!

The 'Irish Independent' reported, "Producing one of their greatest ever displays, a rampant St. Flannan's ran out comfortable winners on a scoreline of 3-10 to 0-2. The match itself proved to be an utter anticlimax before a crowd of 3,000. St. Flannan's produced a match-winning move when switching Ollie Naughton to centrefield where he out hurled Ollie Harrington of whom so much was expected. St. Kieran's Har Hickey at left corner back had the game of his life but at the opposite end Terry Moloney was brilliant in the St. Flannan's goals. Kevin Smyth kept Eddie Keher subdued and Joe Keane outplayed Tom Forristal but the St. Flannan's half forward line sparkled and the outstanding member of this line was Paudie Kennedy. Tipperary has produced some first class marksmen and Kennedy more than lived up to this tradition when he brought his personal score to 1-9 shooting from almost impossible angles." St. Flannan's led by seven points six minutes before the interval and increased their lead to

13 points by the half time break (2-8 to 0-1). This time there would be no Lazarus-like recovery from St. Kieran's.

After the game, Paudie more or less repeated his victory speech from the Harty Cup final before going into the St. Kieran's dressing room to give three cheers for the losers, thereby replicating Ted Carroll's sporting gesture a year earlier. Curiously, he also has a recollection of a priest he didn't know approaching him to take his picture with the Croke Cup on cine film to send to Paudie's relative, "a nun out on the foreign missions". Paudie duly obliged but is not aware of having a relation who was a nun and he has never seen the picture since! On their return to Ennis, Paudie had to address the students in the school hall, where Fr Madden praised his captain for his own performance. "It was very unusual to get praised as an individual by Fr Madden", Paudie jokes, before adding sombrely that he was sorry that former college president, Canon Maxwell ("a fanatical hurling man") had moved on from St. Flannan's a year earlier. Another perk of the win was a day off on the Monday at home in Nenagh for "some home cooking".

An All-Ireland minor medal with Tipperary in 1957 proved to be Paudie's only inter-county success although he later garnered two Fitzgibbon Cup medals with UCD in 1963/64 and 1964/65. He also won two North Tipperary medals with Nenagh in 1957 and 1964, which he describes as "huge wins for the club". He only played once for the Tipperary senior side in an Oireachtas game but he modestly recalls it as "a bad day when my opponent was going for the ball while I was thinking of moving". Paudie is a particularly passionate club man and he rates Éire Óg

Nenagh's first county senior title in 1995 as "one of my greatest memories in hurling even though I had nothing to do with it. I thought of all the old characters who would have given their left arm to see it".

Having qualified as a veterinary surgeon, Paudie found the unsociable hours of his work a strain on his hurling career and he effectively retired from the game at the young age of 27. He still practices as a vet in Nenagh where he lives with his wife, Roscommon native, Tess McEvaddy ("who took time to adjust to a total pre-occupation with hurling in the house"). They have five grown-up children - three boys and two girls – "who are all living happily in Dublin at the present time". Outside of hurling Paudie liked a number of other sports, with badminton and squash his favourites for keeping him fit and "golf taking over in recent years", although he feels he "started it too late in life". To this day, Paudie still does a little bit of running.

Despite almost half a century having elapsed since he figured in some of St. Flannan's most memorable games of the 1950s, Paudie Kennedy retains a keen interest in his alma mater. While he occasionally meets some of his old hurling companions from St. Flannan's, he regrets that at least three of his colleagues from 1958 - Andy Hoolan, Noel McDonnell and Paddy Vaughan – are no longer with us, while there are others he has never laid eyes on since their schooldays together in Ennis. "Hurling was our life in Flannan's", he concludes. "Winning matches was our road to survival." Indeed, Paudie's description of the St. Flannan's side he captained when they trounced a star-studded St. Kieran's side as "an average team" would seem to be modest in the extreme.

1959 – ALL-IRELAND SEMI-FINAL
15 March 1959, Birr

St. Kieran's, Kilkenny 8-7
(E. Keher 2-2, M. Walsh 2-2, D. Somers 2-0, M. Lanigan 1-1, L. Kehoe 1-0, J. Alley 0-2)

St. Joseph's, Garbally 6-5
(J. Madden 2-0, O. Moran 2-0, P. Cormican 0-4, N. Kelly 1-0, J. Langan 1-0, C. Stanley 0-1)

St. Kieran's, Kilkenny, Croke Cup Champions, 1959.
Back row, left to right: Gerry Moylan, Martin Kennedy, Dan Kennedy, Sean Creagh,
Joe Delaney, Leo Kehoe, Ollie Ryan.
Middle row, left to right: Mick Drennan, Eddie Freyne, Pierce Freaney, Joe Delaney, Tom Carroll,
Tom Forristal, Patsy Foley, Paschal McCann.
Front row, left to right: Dick Somers, John Nyhan, Martin Walsh, Eddie Keher (capt),
Martin Lanigan, John Alley, Pat Duggan.
(Photograph courtesy of Dick McEvoy, c/o St. Kieran's, Kilkenny).

1959 – ALL-IRELAND FINAL
19 April 1959, Thurles
Referee: Gerry Rosengrave (Dublin)

St. Kieran's, Kilkenny 2-13

Pat Duggan
(Kilkenny)

Ollie Ryan　　　　**Sean Creagh**　　　　**Paschal McCann**
(Kilkenny)　　　　　(Laois)　　　　　　(Dublin)

Martin Kennedy　　　**John Alley**　　　　**Dan Kennedy**
(Kilkenny)　　　　　(Laois) (0-1)　　　　(Kilkenny)

Joe Delaney　　　　**Martin Lanigan**
(Kilkenny)　　　　　(Kilkenny)

Tom Forristal　　　**Eddie Keher** (*capt*)　　　**Leo Kehoe**
(Kilkenny) (1-0)　　　(Kilkenny) (0-7)　　　(Kilkenny)

Martin Walsh　　　**John Nyhan**　　　　**Dick Somers**
(Kilkenny) (0-1)　　　(Kilkenny) (1-3)　　　(Kilkenny) (0-1)

Tipperary CBS 4-2

John O'Donoghue
(Tipperary)

John Cummins　　　**Paudie Griffin**　　　**Christy O'Dwyer**
(Tipperary)　　　　(Tipperary)　　　　(Tipperary)

Seamus O'Donoghue　　**Mick Cleary**　　　**Mick McCormack**
(Tipperary)　　　　(Tipperary)　　　　(Tipperary)

Jimmy Blake　　　　**John O'Reilly**
(Limerick)　　　　　(Tipperary) (0-1)

Leo Ryan　　　　**Fonsie Condon** (*capt*)　　　**Ailbe Heuston**
(Tipperary) (1-0)　　　(Tipperary) (1-0)　　　(Limerick)

Pete O'Dwyer　　　**Bobby O'Sullivan**　　　**Michael Kirby**
(Tipperary) (1-0)　　　(Tipperary) (1-0)　　　(Tipperary) (0-1)

Eddie Keher

Perhaps the most famous captain to lift the Croke Cup was the St. Kieran's captain of 1959, the legendary Eddie Keher from Inistioge. His enormous talent as a hurler was first brought to national prominence during his years as a boarder in the famous Kilkenny nursery and, to this day, he gives due credit to his coach there, Fr Tommy Maher, for starting him on the road to a glittering inter-county career.

Remarkably, there was no hurling in Eddie's background. His late father, Stephen, was a native of County Roscommon and "played once or twice with the Roscommon footballers". Stephen spent his working life as a garda in Kilkenny, ending up as a sergeant in Ballyhale. Eddie's recently deceased mother, Noreen, was from Inistioge, a parish which Eddie describes as "always having an interest in, but not a huge tradition of hurling" and it was there that Eddie was reared. He started hurling "at a very early age", and he recalls playing "in the square outside the village" with the likes of Miko, Jim and Ollie Ryan, his next-door neighbours, whose father "was very interested in the hurling". His teacher in the local national school, Martin Walsh, was one of the main men involved in setting up the Primary School Leagues, "very important structures" which are still operational in Kilkenny.

"I got on to the Inistioge teams when I was quite young," Eddie recalls. "In one particular practice game against Thomastown, I was only eight, but I was amongst the subs on the Under-14. I remember being called in with 15 minutes to go and told to 'go out and mark that big blonde-headed guy', who turned out to be none other than future goalkeeping great, Ollie Walsh, who was playing outfield at the time!" Eddie went on to collect two Under-14 medals, but he confesses that when the time came to move on to secondary school, he "hated the thoughts of leaving home and going to a boarding school". In the end, the choice was between De La Salle in Waterford and St. Kieran's, and his parents chose the latter "at the last minute".

In his early days in St. Kieran's, Eddie looked up to senior players, Paddy Walsh, Jimmy Prendergast, Toss Molloy and Mick Connolly. There was no juvenile team at the time but, by his second year, Eddie had graduated to both the junior and senior teams. The seniors were beaten by Ballyfin, but Eddie feels that "while it was bad to be beaten, being so young, I was just delighted to be on the team". However, the following year in 1956/57, the Croke Cup was revived and Eddie and Martin Walsh were the only third year students on the side which went all the way to All-Ireland glory. "St. Flannan's were ahead of us in All-Ireland titles back then, but that All-Ireland final was extraordinary. We had only two points on the board with ten minutes to go and were behind by eight, but we came back with four late goals to steal it from them," Eddie recalls. The 'big two' met again in the 1958 Croke Cup decider, but the Ennis college gained sweet revenge to overwhelm St. Kieran's by all of 17 points. "I learned a lot from that game. In many ways, there's more to be learned from a defeat than a victory," Eddie reflects.

At the start of the 1958/59 campaign, both Martin Walsh and Eddie were in contention for the captaincy as they were the longest serving members on the team. "There was a general expectancy that I would get the captaincy but, naturally enough, I was still thrilled when Fr Maher told me I would be captain," Eddie remembers. St. Kieran's had a comfortable victory against Knockbeg College, Carlow, on a scoreline of 7-13 to 4-2 in the first round in Leinster. Patrician College, Ballyfin were their next opponents in Athy. The Laois outfit had lost some of their quality players such as Eddie's future Kilkenny team-mate, Sean Buckley, and Larry Kiely of Tipperary, who had starred in a previous victory over the black and whites. While St. Kieran's ran out 2-7 to 0-6 victors, they were certainly flattered by the seven-point winning margin. The Kilkenny college ended up being awarded the Leinster title as the other semi-final between St. Vincent's, Glasnevin, and St. Joseph's, Fairview, had ended in a draw and the teams' failure to play extra-time meant that the powers-that-be ejected both from the competition. "That was disappointing not to win it on the field of play", Eddie recalls, "but it gave us added impetus to go on and win out the All-Ireland."

"We were warned that St. Joseph's, Garbally, would be strong opponents in the semi-final. The Galway colleges hurling scene was beginning to come alive," Eddie remembers. So it proved in Birr, before St. Kieran's triumphed by 8-7 to 6-5 on March 15th. "There was the usual hype surrounding the All-Ireland final, but we tried to remove ourselves from all that as we felt it affected our performance in the final the previous year. We kept our heads down." Fr Tommy Maher had his homework done on final opponents, Tipperary CBS. "Fonsie Condon was identified as their key man, so Fr Maher switched John Alley who had been playing centre field to centre half back. I think John Alley was a tremendous player." Indeed, the Laois lad

ended up playing heroically in the final. C.F. Kenealy reported in the 'Irish Independent' the following day that "it was clear enough at an early stage that St. Kieran's were the more accomplished hurlers. As they spent more time on the attack throughout the hour, they were well worth their win." The game in Thurles was watched by about 5,000 spectators, in perfect conditions. St. Kieran's led 1-6 to 1-1 at the interval, but Tipperary drew level just eight minutes after the resumption and then took the lead for the first time a minute later.

Before the end of the quarter, Tipperary led by four points, but after this they failed to add another score and St. Kieran's went on to improve their scoreline to the extent of 1-6, to ensure themselves of victory. Eddie played a big part in the late scoring burst, notching three points in the closing stages. "He stamped himself as the best ball player of the two teams right through," according to the match report. Eddie himself recalls, "the goals kept them in it and it was always nip and tuck, but we ran out winners at the end of a see-saw game. I received the cup and was carried shoulder high across the pitch. We got a free day from school when we won. Another perk for the players was that we got a good feed and we would also get out to the pictures after every game, which was great for young fellows who were locked in for months at a time!"

Eddie is lavish in his praise of highly renowned team coach, Fr Tommy Maher. "Looking back, for St. Kieran's and everyone associated with Kilkenny hurling, Fr Maher's arrival back in St. Kieran's was a moment in history. He was way ahead of his time. All the training and coaching going on nowadays was initiated by Fr Tommy Maher. We enjoyed his analysis and pre-match talks and his coaching and his training methods. He made great hurlers out of good players. He was a tremendous influence on us." Indeed, Eddie has stayed in regular touch with his former mentor throughout the years. Another man who fostered hurling in the school whom Eddie remembers was Fr Joe Dunphy from Mooncoin, while Mick Lanigan, "a pretty successful athlete" occasionally advised Fr Maher on fitness and training regimes and subsequently joined him with the Kilkenny senior team. "As kids, when we were training we would just go out and puck the ball around, but Fr Maher put method into everything."

Eddie featured in two more All-Ireland finals in 1959, both unsuccessfully. Having won his fourth Leinster minor medal that summer, he played on the Kilkenny side which lost the decider by a point to Tipperary. Four weeks later, he came on as a sub in the Liam McCarthy Cup final replay defeat by Waterford. However, over the next 18 years, he was to become one of the most celebrated names in the history of the sport. With Kilkenny, he won six All-Ireland medals and three National League mementoes and, as a Leinster player, he won nine Railway Cup medals. Five years after winning a junior medal, he won a Kilkenny senior medal in 1968 with Rower-Inistioge, thereby qualifying him to captain the Cats to All-Ireland success the following September. He was selected on the first five All-Star teams (1971 to 1975). Indeed, had the scheme been inaugurated ten years earlier, he may well have set records which could have lasted for many, many years, as he had been a regular on the 'Gaelic Weekly' All-Stars in the 1960s. He was selected on both the GAA's all-time hurling team in Centenary Year and at the turn of the Millennium.

Eddie continued to play club hurling long after his Kilkenny career ended, actually garnering a county junior medal aged 47! He was never much into indoor sports, due to ongoing foot problems on hard surfaces. Indeed, he remained indebted over the years to a cobbler from Thomastown whom he recalls simply as "Mr Reilly" for solving a painful problem with the old-fashioned boots, then the norm, during hot summers when the pitches were rock hard. He enjoys playing golf, despite being a late starter to the game due to hurling commitments, both playing to an advanced age and many stints as a coach and selector at club and inter-county level. He now plays off a handicap of ten, joking that when he once got as low as nine, he won a bet off his former

Kilkenny colleague, Fr Tom Murphy, who reckoned Eddie would never make single figures! Many of his meetings with St. Kieran's colleagues from the team of 1959 now take place on the golf course and he can rhyme off the whereabouts of most of the team at his ease. There was never a formal reunion of the side.

After school, he worked with Killeen Paper Mills for a period of six months, before then passing his exams for the Provincial Bank (later part of AIB Bank). He worked in St. Stephen's Green and Capel Street in Dublin, before being transferred to Kilkenny city, Carlow and finally, Callan. Since his retirement from the bank in 1997, Eddie has been engaged in quite an amount of promotional and journalistic work and has since written a book, 'Hurling Heroes'. Nowadays, he enjoys his involvement with the No-Name Club, an organisation that provides young people with the opportunity to socialise without alcohol/drugs, and which he helped to found in 1978.

Eddie and his wife Kay (née Phelan), originally from Gowran, live in Inistioge and they have five grown-up children - two sons and three daughters, as well as seven grandchildren. His son, Eamon (who is an accountant and now lives in Australia), played in a Croke Cup final with St. Kieran's, while his other son, Colm, is principal of Stella Maris Secondary School in Tramore. Two of Eddie's daughters, Deirdre and Clodagh, enjoyed playing hockey in Loreto Convent in Kilkenny and St. Leo's in Carlow. His other daughter, Catherine, played camogie in St. Brigid's Convent, Callan.

Eddie Keher reflects that "school was tough and you'd wonder how guys survived if they weren't interested in hurling. The hurling always gave you something to look forward to." He has always retained an interest in St. Kieran's and was prominent in the Past Pupils Union for a number of years. "The priests there were wonderful," concludes the man who went on to be a truly great ambassador for college and county, and the game of hurling in general, with the awarding of an Honorary Doctorate of Science by the University of Limerick to him in December 2006 being a fitting tribute.

1960 – ALL-IRELAND SEMI-FINAL
27 March 1960, Croke Park

St. Peter's Wexford 4-4
(E. Doyle 1-2, P. Murphy 1-0, B. O'Neill 1-0, M. Jordan 1-0, W. Redmond 0-1, M. Rossiter 0-1)

St. Mary's, Galway 3-7
(P. Fahy 1-5, M. Caulfield 1-0, M. Niland 1-0, J. Whiriskey 0-2)

1960 – ALL-IRELAND SEMI-FINAL (REPLAY)
10 April 1960, Croke Park

St. Peter's, Wexford 2-5
(W. Redmond 1-0, M. Rossiter 1-0, P. Murphy 0-2, T. Byrne
0-1, B. O'Neill 0-1, E. Doyle 0-1)

St. Mary's, Galway 1-4
(J. Setright 1-0, M. Connolly 0-2, M. Niland 0-1, P. Fahy 0-1)

North Monastery, Cork, Croke Cup Champions, 1960.
Back row, left to right: Tony Brady, Micheal Murphy, Jim Burke, Con Mulcahy, Michael Prior,
Paddy Duggan, Jim McGowan, Denis Daly, Jerry Gibbons
Middle row, left to right: Fachtna O'Sullivan, John Hickey, Paddy Marshall, Dave Moore,
John Sutton (capt), Brian Twomey, Eugene O'Connor, Paddy McMahon, Pat Curley.
Front row, left to right: Billy Fitton, Dave Joyce.
(Photograph courtesy of Pat Curley).

1960 – ALL-IRELAND FINAL
8 May 1960, Thurles
Referee: Josie Gallagher (Galway)

North Monastery, Cork 1-9

Fachtna O'Sullivan
(Cork)

Jim Burke	**John Hickey**	**Paddy McMahon**
(Cork)	(Cork)	(Cork)

Paddy Marshall
(Cork)

John Sutton (*capt*)
(Cork)

Brian Twomey
(Cork)

Dave Moore
(Cork) (0-1)

Eugene O'Connor
(Cork) (0-1)

Micheal Murphy
(Cork)

Pat Curley
(Cork) (1-4)

Paddy Duggan
(Cork)

Dave Joyce
(Cork) (0-1)

Con Mulcahy
(Cork) (0-2)

Billy Fitton
(Cork)

Subs: Jerry Gibbons (Cork) (for Duggan), Michael Prior (Cork) (for Fitton).

St. Peter's, Wexford 1-4

Jim O'Neill
(Wexford)

Raymie Aylward
(Wexford)

John Doyle
(Wexford)

Jimmy Roche
(Wexford)

Tommy Byrne
(Wexford)

John Murphy
(Wexford)

Michael Jordan
(Wexford)

Paddy Merrigan
(Wicklow)

Eamonn Doyle
(Wexford) (0-1)

Michael Rossiter
(Wexford)

Peadar Murphy (*capt*)
(Wexford) (0-1)

Brian O'Neill
(Wexford)

Willie Redmond
(Wexford) (0-1)

Johnny Mullane
(Wexford)

Jim Byrne
(Waterford) (1-1)

Sub: Pat Gallahue (Wexford) (for Mullane).

Pat Curley

At the ninth time of asking, the early Croke Cup monopoly of St. Flannan's and St. Kieran's was eventually broken in 1960, when Cork school, North Monastery brought the trophy back to the banks of the Lee. The history-making side was captained by the late John Sutton and it featured the following year's skipper, Pat Curley, at centre half forward.

Pat Curley was born in Cork in 1942, and he attended national school in Mayfield, although he quickly points out that he has never met the area's most famous son - Roy Keane! From primary school in Mayfield, Pat progressed to the North Mon where he spent six happy years gaining a valuable education. He is not aware of any great sporting tradition in the family. Pat's involvement in hurling blossomed when he attended North Mon and then joined the emerging Brian Dillon's club. Pat shows his allegiance to Mayfield when he recalls his hurling heroes from his early years. "There was a McCarthy guy playing for North Mon in 1955 when they won the Harty Cup and he was one of my heroes as I attended the final that day. I also remember Tom O'Donoghue as a particular favourite of mine, and he eventually won an All-Ireland senior medal with Cork in 1966. Tom was also from Mayfield but didn't attend the Mon, but you must remember that the Christy Ring era was coming to an end and Cork weren't winning too many All-Irelands back then."

When Pat entered North Mon he claims, "the talent wasn't there to succeed." The Mon had won the Harty Cup in 1955 but the only success in the late 1950s came in the Dean Ryan Cup, with Pat part of winning junior sides in 1958 and 1959. He was selected for the Mon senior side for four years, but it wasn't until his third year on the team that the talent in the school gelled. In the 1959/60 campaign, the Mon defeated St. Colman's, Fermoy, before dethroning reigning champions, Tipperary CBS in the semi-final in Buttevant by 3-11 to 0-7. Pat recalls the Harty Cup final on March 27th 1960. "We were playing Limerick CBS, who were going for a Munster double, and they were a real concern and a threat, but we managed to beat them in Thurles. Brother Vaughan, our trainer, gave me a specific job to do. I normally played centre forward but that day he put me in right half back and asked me to try and stop one of their main players. I also recall Limerick possessing one great player by the name of Paddy Murphy that day." In the end, the Mon regained the Harty Cup on a scoreline of 0-10 to 1-4.

In the Croke Cup final North Mon faced St. Peter's of Wexford, who had just won their first Leinster senior title and had fought off the stiff challenge of St. Mary's from Galway after a replay, to reach their first Croke Cup final. "We never worried or got too excited about the Croke Cup because the Harty Cup is huge in Munster and after winning that we thought we were the best team in the world. It was almost an anti-climax." He was pleased with his own display in the final, played in

Thurles, as he scored 1-4 on the day. The goal arrived near the end of the contest and sealed the victory for the Cork side. "We had a terrific team and tremendous players all around us," Pat recalls proudly. "Eugene O'Connor, Dave Moore, Con Mulcahy, David Joyce and Micheal Murphy were all great players, while the late John Sutton was a tremendous back. The 'Irish Independent' reported from that momentous occasion, "North Monastery's superior hurling artistry enabled them to withstand the challenge of St. Peter's. The Cork boys proved worthy custodians of the trophy. Crisp, attacking teamwork and courage were dominant factors and decisive against a Wexford team which although less skilful, displayed an ample measure of strength, stamina and spirit. The Slaney boys called the tune, bulldozing their way to a two point lead but the Mon were not found wanting. Centre forward, Pat Curley successfully adopted the role of a deep lying third midfielder. It was a desperately close match, fought throughout with tremendous pace and vigour, but in the red hot heat of exchanges, skill was too often secondary to strength and ruthlessness. "

John Sutton became the last young man to lift the old Croke Cup and, to this day, Pat remembers the post-match euphoria. "We were an excited bunch of players and we felt very privileged when a double-decker bus met us at the station and carried us through Cork city up to the North Mon to begin the celebrations in earnest. As All-Ireland winners we were like gods in the school and were given many little privileges which included being fattened up on soup and bread for our tea breaks, while some 'baddies' not associated with the hurling team, chose to go smoking around the back of the school!" Recalling the training and preparation for matches back in those days, Pat holds Brother Vaughan in high esteem. "I think he only arrived around 1960 and took over the team with Brother Kavanagh and Brother Minogue as his assistants. Brother Vaughan was a tough taskmaster and he took no prisoners. He soldiered on with us in a big way. He used to train us two or three evenings a week. The North Mon training ground was at the very top of Fair Hill, so we had to drag our bikes up the hill and then endure a very tough training session, but at least we were able to free-wheel down the hill and that was very enjoyable. The training was very tough especially in winter. We were kept fit and then on match days the brothers would always be aware of the dangerous players on the opposing side. "

North Mon almost achieved a Munster double in 1960 but the footballers were beaten in the Munster semi-final. Pat remembers that, "we had some excellent footballers back then, including Terry Moore, who later played international rugby with Ireland and Eugene O'Connor, but hurling was the main sport in those years. " Indeed, later that year, Pat was on the Cork minor football team but unfortunately they suffered defeat to Galway in the All-Ireland final. In Pat's Leaving Cert year of 1960/61 he was appointed team captain and the Munster crown was retained. "We beat Ennis CBS and then Thurles CBS in the Harty Cup final in Buttevant (1-11 to 1-9) but we were too cocky against St. Kieran's in the All-Ireland final. In a game that was never a contest they taught us a lesson in hurling, but they were a tremendous side," Pat sportingly acknowledges.

After leaving North Mon in 1961, Pat started working with CIE and was transferred to Ballyhaunis in County Mayo. However, an opportunity to join the army soon arose and Pat ended up in the Curragh. "There was no sporting ban in the military, even though there was outside of it, so I was able to play in all the army competitions in hurling, football, rugby and soccer," Pat recalls. Being domiciled in County Kildare, Pat won an All-Ireland junior hurling medal with the Lilywhites in 1962, defeating London 4-7 to 2-4 in the final. Among his team-mates was Larry Kiely, a future senior hurling medallist with Tipperary and international show jumper. The following year, Pat was commissioned in the army and in 1964 he qualified as a pilot and he ended up in Gormanston in County Meath, where he taught at the Flying School there. Although continuing to play hurling and football with the Air Corps it was around this time his connections with Cork began to fade and injuries began to slow him down. Pat then "became an alickadoo" in the army and his responsibilities included the administration of a range of sports, with Gaelic football being the principal activity promoted. He organised the Defence Forces GAA tour of the United States in 1986 and Australia in 1990, having "blackmailed all our friends and business acquaintances to fund the trips".

While he finished his football and hurling career when still in his mid-20s, Pat has no regrets as his Air Corps career put an end to his dream of returning to his native Cork to play hurling with Glen Rovers and possibly the Rebel County. His brother, Peter kept the Curley name going on the hurling fields when he won an Under-21 All-Ireland medal in 1966, after a memorable three-game saga against Wexford. Pat married Anne Berry from Killeigh (near Tullamore) in 1966, allowing him "to wish Offaly well once they are not playing Cork", and they have lived in Santry for over 39 years. Pat retired from the Air Corps in 2000 but has worked on a temporary basis from time to time with the Central Statistics Office since then. They have five grown-up children - four sons and one daughter. Joanne and Peter both live in the US, while Robert, Barry and John Paul live in Dublin. None of

Pat's sons got heavily involved in the GAA but they had strong leanings towards soccer and athletics, with Robert obtaining a scholarship to Louisiana in the States, where he spent six years before returning home.

While Pat was present for a 25-year reunion of his school year in the mid-1980s, it was not specifically for the winning Croke Cup team. "It was great to meet Brother Vaughan again, but unfortunately Fachtna O'Sullivan, our goalkeeper on that team, died a few years after the All-Ireland final win, and Dave Moore also died suddenly as, of course, did John Sutton. I haven't met many from our Croke Cup winning side since, although I did meet Eugene O'Connor when I visited Perth in Australia a number of years ago", Pat reflects.

Some 45 years after leaving North Monastery, Pat Curley thinks back on his youth and he laments the huge decline in the influence of the Christian Brothers in education and sport. He is of the opinion that, "North Mon is changed nowadays and it's not the North Mon of old from a sporting viewpoint. " For his part, his tenure in the famous Cork nursery was "very, very happy", with the Croke Cup win of 1960 undoubtedly one of the real highlights of his schooldays.

JOHN SUTTON

(Born 26/4/1942, Died 3/9/1993)

Pat Curley on John Sutton: "I would not like to have played against John Sutton. John was a quiet, strong man and solidly built. He was a blocky guy, but he never got upset. Once he was on the pitch you knew you could depend on him. John shored up the rearguard to great effect. I was very sad at his passing because he was such a quietly pleasant guy. "

Author's Note:
On his death, aged 51, on 3 September 1993, John Sutton was survived by his wife, Sheila and their sons, Paul and Mark.

1961 – ALL-IRELAND SEMI-FINAL
26 March 1961, Thurles

North Monastery, Cork 1-8
(P. Curley 1-1, C. Mulcahy 0-3, N. Crowley 0-2, B. Fitton 0-1, S. O'Mahony 0-1)

St. Molaise's, Portumna 1-1
(P. Mannion 1-0, M. Derrivan 0-1)

St. Kieran's, Kilkenny, Croke Cup Champions, 1961.
Back row, left to right: Martin Walsh, Jim Walsh, Tom Holden, Peter Duggan, Rory O'Moore,
Pat O'Connor, John Delaney.
Middle row, left to right: Jim Langton, Matt Walsh, Jim Gannon, Michael Tennyson,
Jimmy O'Brien, Pat Drennan, Nicholas Forristal.
Front row, left to right: Maurice Aylward, John Loughnane, Ollie Ryan, Pierce Freaney (capt),
Noel Rohan, Tom Forristal, Patsy Foley.
(Photograph courtesy of Dick McEvoy, c/o St. Kieran's, Kilkenny)

1961 – ALL-IRELAND FINAL
23 April 1961, Thurles
Referee: Matt Spain (Offaly)

St. Kieran's, Kilkenny 8-8

Patsy Foley
(Kilkenny)

Peter Duggan　　　**Nicholas Forristal**　　　**Noel Rohan**
(Laois)　　　　　　　(Kilkenny)　　　　　　　(Kilkenny)

Pat Drennan　　　**Ollie Ryan**　　　**Michael Tennyson**
(Kilkenny)　　　　　(Kilkenny)　　　　　(Kilkenny)

Jim Gannon　　　**John Loughnane**
(Kilkenny)　　　　　(Tipperary)

Tom Forristal　　　**Pierce Freaney** (*capt*)　　　**John Delaney**
(Kilkenny) (3-1)　　　(Kilkenny) (1-4)　　　(Kilkenny) (0-1)

Martin Walsh　　　**Rory O'Moore**　　　**Maurice Aylward**
(Kilkenny) (0-1)　　　(Laois) (2-0)　　　(Kilkenny) (2-1)

North Monastery, Cork 1-4

John Buckley
(Cork)

Vincie Murphy　　　**Denis Daly**　　　**Ken Owens**
(Cork)　　　　　　　(Cork)　　　　　　(Cork)

Tony Brady　　　**Pat Curley** (*capt*)　　　**Noel Crowley**
(Cork)　　　　　　(Cork)　　　　　　(Cork)

Micheal Murphy　　　**Paddy Duggan**
(Cork)　　　　　　　(Cork)

Billy Fitton　　　**Con Mulcahy**　　　**Gerry Gibbons**
(Cork) (0-1)　　　(Cork) (0-3)　　　(Cork)

Tadhg O'Sullivan　　　**Jim McGowan**　　　**Bob O'Connell**
(Cork)　　　　　　　(Cork)　　　　　　(Cork) (1-0)

Sub: Michael Lehane (Cork) (for O'Sullivan).

Pierce Freaney

Although he left Semple Stadium without a trophy on April 23rd 1961, Pierce Freaney led St. Kieran's College, Kilkenny to their third Croke Cup success in five years that afternoon, after they cruised to victory over reigning champions, North Monastery from Cork in the final.

While his father played some football, Pierce, an only son, had no direct hurling background, although his uncle displayed some hurling skills to him as a youngster. A native of Clodiagh, Pierce wittily describes his place of birth as the hyphen in the name the Rower-Inistioge. "I wasn't from the Rower and I wasn't from Inistioge. I was from in between, so I suppose I was from the hyphen," he jokes. Pierce won a scholarship to St. Kieran's and his early heroes as a young boy in the college included Eddie Keher, Ollie Harrington ("a classy hurler"), Ted and Mick Carroll and Martin Walsh ("a sneaky corner forward"). While competing in the first year leagues, Pierce lost two front teeth, but this didn't put him off the game despite his mother being less than impressed. "Anyway, hurling for your college was the only legitimate way of getting out of school in those days. It was a very strict regime back then. It was similar to a prison, except the food was worse," he jokes.

Pierce's early experiences on the senior team were of a mixed variety. Having been a substitute in 1958 when St. Kieran's lost heavily to St. Flannan's in the Croke Cup final, a year later he was still a sub as St. Kieran's overcame Tipperary CBS to regain the trophy.

However, in 1960 St. Kieran's didn't make it out of Leinster, as they lost to their fierce rivals, St. Peter's of Wexford. "1958 was a significant experience for me," he recalls, "as I was only 15 years old and coming on in an All-Ireland final and, although it wasn't for very long, it made me feel special. " Just 12 months later, he modestly confesses to have been outhurled by his Garbally opponent in the All-Ireland semi-final. "I was dropped for the final. I was very disappointed, but it was the right decision. However, I've never been let forget the 1960 Leinster final against St. Peter's. It was played in New Ross and the wind was blowing across the pitch. I was on a solo run in the last minute with my head down. Everyone (even people who weren't at the game!) saw John Alley, the team captain, screaming at me for a pass, as he was in acres of space, but I never heard him and my shot which was heading over the crossbar was caught by the wind and dropped short. We lost by a point (3-6 to 2-10) and I was never let live that down as Peter's won their first Leinster senior hurling title", he concedes, despite scoring 2-3 on the day.

One man above all others who was the mainstay of hurling in St. Kieran's in those years was Fr Tommy Maher and Pierce sings his praises. " Fr Maher had a knack of cajoling guys to do things they didn't realise they could do, or didn't want to do. He had a presence about him. He never needed to wave a big stick; he was the nicest man in the world, but always in control. Fr Maher was light years ahead of his time as he was into sports psychology before it was ever invented! He would do his homework and always go and see the opposition and tell you everything about your opponent the day before a game. He had Humphrey O'Sullivan, a tough and experienced corner back up against me in training when I was 15 and shouldering me in an effort to toughen me up and I needed that." Pierce remembers, in one instance that he needed to see the doctor after one of the challenges.

Pierce won three Leinster junior hurling college medals with St. Kieran's and having captained the team to a provincial title at that level, "the natural progression" was to be handed the senior captaincy in his Leaving Cert year. A facile victory over Knockbeg College from Carlow by 5-12 to 0-3 in the Leinster quarter-final was the first championship game of the 1960/61 campaign. It was obvious that the Kilkenny side was strong, but Pierce recalls that "everyone knew that semi-final opponents, St. Peter's had a good team too". Interestingly, if Fr. Maher was unavailable for training it was the captain's job to take the session, so Pierce had to go and collect the balls and other equipment from Fr Maher's room. Noticing a jotter on Fr Maher's desk, curiosity got the better of Pierce and a quick glance enabled him to spot "a ring around a particular St. Peter's player and this was to signify that he was the weakest player on their team and sure enough Tom Forristal was put on this player come match day". Pierce goes on, "I clearly remember the instructions being dished out in the hall the evening prior to the game against St. Peter's, based on Fr Maher's knowledge of St. Peter's strengths and weaknesses. Tom Forristal ran riot and poor Dan Quigley, the St. Peter's full back, didn't know whether to come out or stay in, and before they knew where they were, Forristal had got two or three goals. We were well ahead at half time and in the end we only won by a few points (4-6 to 2-7), but being honest Fr. Maher won that game for us with his tactics. That was the big game because after we beat St. Peter's we knew we could beat anyone," Pierce concludes. So it

proved, as St. Kieran's easily defeated Patrician College, Ballyfin in the Leinster decider by 8-14 to 2-2, with Pierce helping himself to 1-6 in that final.

Despite this, Pierce feels that "North Mon were red hot favourites to retain the Croke Cup and we were warned by our teachers that we would be lucky to come within 20 points of these Cork guys. So we went out to show these guys we were no underdogs and we would put up a good fight. In the end we ran through them and blew them out of it. I felt comfortable in my role as captain and freetaker. Centre half forward was not my favourite position as I would have preferred the wing, but all we had to do was make sure Tom Forristal got possession. In the end, we won very easily with a fantastic team. " Indeed, the 'Irish Independent' described the match as an "effortless win for St. Kieran's. " Reporter, Donal Carroll felt the game was, "a final without thrills or atmosphere", while describing St. Kieran's as, "a side of great skill and purpose, a wonderfully fit and dedicated team which played with supreme confidence all through". Despite playing against the wind and the sun in the first half, the Kilkenny boys were ominously ahead by 3-6 to 1-4 at the interval. The Harty champions were unable to add to their total on the change of ends, while their Leinster counterparts, with Jim Gannon and John Loughnane completely dominating the midfield exchanges, tacked on a further 5-2 to emerge as very comfortable winners.

Referring to the absence of a trophy at the end of the game, Pierce recalls that, "we knew before the final that there would be no cup presentation so it wasn't a surprise, but I just remember a few friends running onto the pitch and lifting me shoulder high off the pitch. One memory from the final is the referee handing me the sliotar at the final whistle and it remains a treasure of mine to this day. A free day from school followed and we were all allowed home. I remember sneaking back in to the college very late, trying to avoid the headlights from the priests' cars!" A couple of weeks later, Bishop Patrick Collier arrived in St. Kieran's and presented the newly-designed Croke Cup to Pierce and the team. "The next morning, we paraded into the dining hall with the new cup and received a standing ovation," Pierce recalls. However, it wasn't all fun and games, with Pierce reflecting that, "in those days we hurled through hail, rain and snow and it was difficult then to turn around and give your full attention to your Leaving Cert. One minute it was hurling and winning matches and the perks that went with it, and the next minute we were in shock studying, but in the end I got on ok in the Leaving. "

Pierce won two All-Ireland MHC medals with Kilkenny in 1960 and 1961 and when he left St. Kieran's, he went to work in Carlow for the Sugar Company and there he hurled with a club called Pearses, which Pierce is quick to point out "was named after the patriot and not me"! He jokes that he was "a professional hurler," as he feels he was kept on at the factory for his hurling skills by the company accountant, Jimmy Phelan from Kilkenny. Pierce went on to play with the promising Carlow side of the 1960s but still managed to play Leinster SHC for Kilkenny in 1968, despite being hampered by illness. He passed out as a garda in 1965 and married Kilkenny native, Emir Bourke a year later, and he was stationed in Cork where he joined the famous St. Finbarr's club, winning a Cork SHC medal in 1968. Three years later, he was transferred to County Kildare, and to this day he still lives in Newbridge. Lining out with his home club, the Rower-Inistioge, was proving difficult due to travelling, so Pierce curtailed this by playing for Kildare side, Suncroft, with whom he reached a county senior final where "Ardclough hammered us". He played briefly for the Lilywhites in the 1970s but he concedes that "the interest was not great in the county team". Pierce was coaxed out of retirement in the GAA's Centenary Year to help Suncroft win the junior championship and he ended up as a goalie playing senior hurling before he finally retired with Sarsfields from Newbridge.

Since then, Pierce has been involved in underage coaching with Sarsfields in Newbridge, in addition to holding a number of administrative positions with the club. Nowadays, he is the Recruitment and Training Officer for Leinster referees, having taken up refereeing after retiring from the playing fields. Unfortunately, he lost 90 per cent vision in one of his eyes, an injury which was sustained, ironically, while refereeing a colleges hurling game. Having retired ten years ago from the Gardaí, he is now employed as the manager in Newbridge Shopping Centre. Naturally, Pierce takes a keen interest in his son, Enda's football playing career, which has seen him play for Kildare at a number of levels. His daughters, Maeve and Aideen live in Boston and Foxrock respectively, while Pierce and Emir have five grandchildren. Pierce enjoys a regular game of golf, playing off a 12 handicap, while squash was another sport he played "at a reasonably high level" over the years.

Pierce Freaney reflects that, "a lot of people hate school, but as a result of hurling I loved every minute of it." While the 1961 team never had a formal get-together, he has met many of his former team-mates over the years, at class reunions and elsewhere. Many shrewd pundits rate the St. Kieran's team from 45 years ago as the best ever to represent the college and the brief wait to collect the new Croke Cup was surely worth it, with the black and white squad of '61 proudly inscribed as the inaugural winners of the trophy, still played for to this day.

1962 – ALL-IRELAND SEMI-FINAL
1 April 1962, Kilkenny

St. Peter's, Wexford 4-8
(J. Kennedy 2-0, P. Quigley 1-3, M. Rossiter 1-1, E. Doyle 0-3, D. O'Neill 0-1)

St. Molaise's, Portumna 1-2
(N. Lane 1-0, P. Mannion 0-1, T. O'Hara 0-1)

St. Peter's, Wexford, Croke Cup Champions, 1962.
Back row, left to right: Pat Quigley, Conor O'Rafferty, Walter Shortle, Mick Kinsella,
Paddy O'Brien, Tom Kavanagh, Martin Tobin, Dan Quigley, Kevin Kielthy, Brian Doyle.
Front row, left to right: Richard Weafer, Donal Doyle, Vincent Staples, John Kennedy,
Michael Rossiter (capt), Dermot O'Neill, Nicky Scallan, Billy Foley, Eamonn Doyle.
Missing from photograph: Pat Cullen.
(Photograph courtesy of Power and Glory, The Story of Gaelic Games in St. Peter's College, Wexford)

1962 – ALL-IRELAND FINAL
15 April 1962, Thurles
Referee: Matt Spain (Offaly)

St. Peter's, Wexford 0-10

Donal Doyle
(Wexford)

Paddy O'Brien　　　**Dan Quigley**　　　**Tom Kavanagh**
(Wexford)　　　　　　(Wexford)　　　　　(Wexford)

Walter Shortle　　　**Mick Kinsella**　　　**Vincent Staples**
(Wexford)　　　　　　(Wexford)　　　　　(Wexford)

Eamonn Doyle　　　　**Martin Tobin**
(Wexford) (0-6)　　　　(Wexford)

Michael Rossiter (*capt*)　　**Conor O'Rafferty**　　**Pat Quigley**
(Wexford)　　　　　　　(Wexford) (0-2)　　　(Wexford) (0-2)

John Kennedy　　　**Nicky Scallan**　　　**Dermot O'Neill**
(Wexford)　　　　　(Wicklow)　　　　　(Wexford)

Sub: Pat Cullen (Wexford) (for Tobin).

Ennis CBS 2-4

Mick Hayes
(Clare)

Paddy Flynn (*capt*)　　**Tony Vaughan**　　　**Paddy Corbett**
(Clare)　　　　　　　(Clare)　　　　　　(Clare)

Sean O'Leary　　　**Vincent Hogan**　　　**Gus Considine**
(Clare)　　　　　　(Clare)　　　　　　(Clare)

Michael Meagher　　　　**Garry Stack**
(Clare) (0-1)　　　　　(Clare) (0-1)

Vincent Loftus　　　**Sean Coffey**　　　**Michael Hanrahan**
(Clare) (1-1)　　　　(Clare)　　　　　(Clare) (0-1)

Des Guerin　　　**Sean McMahon**　　　**Pat Coffey**
(Clare)　　　　　(Clare) (1-0)　　　　(Clare)

1962 – ALL-IRELAND FINAL (REPLAY)
6 May 1962, Croke Park
Referee: Gerry Fitzgerald (Limerick)

St. Peter's, Wexford 4-11

Donal Doyle
(Wexford)

Paddy O'Brien   **Dan Quigley**   **Tom Kavanagh**
(Wexford)   (Wexford)   (Wexford)

Walter Shortle   **Mick Kinsella**   **Vincent Staples**
(Wexford)   (Wexford) (0-1)   (Wexford)

Eamonn Doyle   **Martin Tobin**
(Wexford)   (Wexford)

John Kennedy   **Conor O'Rafferty** **Pat Quigley**
(Wexford)   (Wexford) (1-5)   (Wexford) (0-5)

Billy Foley   **Michael Rossiter** (*capt*) **Pat Cullen**
(Wexford) (1-0)   (Wexford)   (Wexford) (1-0)

Subs: Dermot O'Neill (Wexford) (1-0) (for P. Quigley), Nicky Scallan (Wicklow) (for Cullen).

Ennis CBS 2-4

Mick Hayes
(Clare)

Paddy Flynn (*capt*)   **Tony Vaughan**   **Paddy Corbett**
(Clare)   (Clare)   (Clare)

Sean O'Leary   **Vincent Hogan**   **Gus Considine**
(Clare)   (Clare) (0-2)   (Clare)

Michael Meagher   **Garry Stack**
(Clare)   (Clare)

Vincent Loftus   **Sean Coffey**   **Michael Hanrahan**
(Clare) (0-1)   (Clare)   (Clare) (0-1)

Des Guerin   **Sean McMahon**   **Pat Coffey**
(Clare)(2-0)   (Clare)   (Clare)

Sub: Jim Quinn (Clare) (for Considine).

Michael Rossiter

Two years after their first ever appearance in the All-Ireland final ended in defeat to North Monastery, St. Peter's of Wexford made amends in 1962 when they brought the Croke Cup back to Slaneyside for the first time, under the captaincy of dual colleges player, Michael Rossiter.

Of farming stock, Michael was the eldest in the family and he grew up in the South Wexford village of Kilmore. His earliest hurling memories are of pucking a ball around in a field behind the family home. It was during his time in Kilturk National School, however, that he began to take a serious interest in both hurling and football. "The curate in Kilmore, Fr McDonald, was very keen on hurling and football and he was a big influence on me. The Rackard Cup leagues started in 1956 and we were very successful in those. We won both the hurling and football leagues in '56 and '57," he explains.

While there had been no family history of going to St. Peter's, Michael entered the famous Wexford college as a boarder in September 1957 and fondly recalls the "buzz" that had been created by Wexford's hurling achievements of the mid-1950s. Wexford won back-to-back All-Ireland senior hurling titles in 1955 and 1956, and interest in the game was at an all-time high. After learning the ropes at junior level, Michael graduated to the senior team in 1959/60 and was part of the history-making side which won the Leinster 'A' title for the first time on March 20th, 1960, in New Ross. Perennial favourites and reigning provin-

cial and All-Ireland champions, St. Kieran's were dethroned by a point that day, by 2-10 to 3-6. Michael was full of admiration for older teammates such as team captain, Peadar Murphy ("a beautiful hurler"), John Doyle, Raymie Aylward and Paddy Merrigan. The Wexford lads were forced to give second best to North Monastery in the All-Ireland final, but they had broken the mould in Leinster. It also heralded the arrival of St. Peter's as one of the most feared and respected hurling nurseries in the country.

St. Kieran's exacted revenge the following year at the penultimate stage in the province, but under Michael's captaincy, which he feels was awarded to him for "longevity of service", St. Peter's were a determined bunch when they reassembled for the 1961/62 academic year. "We learned from the mistakes that were made in 1960 and '61, and our attitude in '62 was that we could beat anyone. To win the All-Ireland was our Holy Grail. We were very fit and focused, and thankfully everything went according to plan."

Fielding a team entirely made up of boarders, St. Peter's opened their campaign with an emphatic 11-10 to 1-3 victory over Franciscan College, Gormanston in the Leinster semi-final at Croke Park. Midfielder Eamonn Doyle was superb for the winners who dominated from start to finish, with Pat Quigley bagging 4-2 further forward. There was a huge shock in the Kilkenny derby in the other side of the draw, so St. Peter's faced Kilkenny CBS in the Leinster final at New Ross on March 18th. The

Wexford lads were far from impressive as they were held to a 1-6 each draw, with substitute, Dermot O'Neill scoring their goal.

St. Peter's improved immeasurably for the replay which took place at Dr Cullen Park in Carlow a week later. Their forwards were far sharper, taking practically every chance that came their way, while Eamonn Doyle had another outstanding game at midfield. The Slaneysiders led by 1-3 to 0-0 at the interval with Dermot O'Neill again getting a crucial goal. Three minutes after the restart, John Kennedy added another and this effectively ended the game as a contest. Further goals from Pat Quigley and Nicky Scallan saw St. Peter's run out 4-3 to 1-4 winners and the Leinster crown was on its way to Summerhill for the second time. St. Peter's then played their third major match in as many weeks when they squared up to St. Molaise's of Portumna in the All-Ireland semi-final at Nowlan Park. This proved to be a very one-sided contest with the Leinster champions claiming a 4-8 to 1-3 victory and qualifying for their second All-Ireland final in three years.

Michael recalls the campaign as "a hard slog". There was a great emphasis on staying fit but Michael feels that, "we always felt we were fit and could beat any opponents". Having said that, they knew nothing about first-time Croke Cup finalists, Ennis CBS. As it transpired, poor finishing, a problem which had first surfaced in the drawn Leinster final, returned to haunt St. Peter's in the All-Ireland final against Ennis CBS at Thurles on April 15th. They registered nine first half wides and, despite having wind advantage, could only manage five points before the break, but they showed a lot of character in the second half to earn a second bite of the cherry. The 'Irish Independent' highlighted the Wexford side's wastefulness when reporting, "Opportunity knocked not twice, but three times for St. Peter's at sunny but chilly Thurles. But by fluffing three golden first half chances, they failed to open the door, and it was only with a point from a free five minutes from time that they avoided defeat by Ennis CBS in the final of the All-Ireland Colleges SH championship."

The replay was staged before the National Hurling League final between Kilkenny and Cork in front of a large crowd at Croke Park. Having had little or no experience of playing at GAA headquarters, the occasion seemed to affect many of the Ennis players and St. Peter's took full advantage by powering to a 4-11 to 2-4 victory. Indeed, the 'Irish Independent' described the victory as "effortless" for a side playing "with tremendous confidence". The Wexford side got off to a flying start and posted 1-2 in the opening eight minutes with Billy Foley scoring the goal. A second major by Eamonn Doyle had them perched on a 2-5 to 0-3 interval lead. They continued to take the game to the Harty Cup winners after the restart and ten minutes in, substitute Dermot O'Neill bagged their third goal. Conor O'Rafferty added a fourth shortly afterwards to put the result beyond doubt. A belated Ennis rally, saw corner forward Des Guerin score two goals in the closing minutes, but they were mere consolation scores. So much in control were St. Peter's that Michael remembers the acceptance speech as being the most difficult duty he had to perform. "From about the tenth minute onwards, my biggest worry was about having to make the speech," he jokes. "We were playing so well that I knew we weren't going to be beaten. There were great celebrations afterwards, but the hype died down when we got back to Wexford. We might have had a free day – that was about it – and everything got back to normal in a short space of time."

1962 is still remembered in St. Peter's College as the year of the draws. Not only did the hurling team draw twice en route to winning the All-Ireland, the senior footballers and junior hurlers bowed out of their respective championships in replays. Michael also captained the St. Peter's football team in 1962 from the centre half back position, when they were beaten by eventual All-Ireland champions, St. Mel's of Longford after a replay in the Leinster semi-final. The Wexford lads were unlucky not to win the first day when a number of questionable refereeing decisions went against them. "We thought the referee was their 16th man. It was a lovely game and you felt you were walking on air. We had a very good football team, and it was probably more highly regarded than the hurling side. If we had beaten St. Mel's, we could have pulled off an All-Ireland double," he says. Michael laughs when recalling the 'perks' of being a college footballer and hurler in those days. "We got oranges and we had our aching legs rubbed with oils. They were generally just rubbed in mud," he jokes.

Michael is fulsome in his praise of St. Peter's hurling manager, Ned Power and his football counterpart, Fr Paddy Curtis. "Ned and Fr Curtis were great managers. Ned was in charge of the hurling team and Fr Curtis looked after the footballers. There was a great understanding between them. They worked as a team. Fr Jackie McCabe also did a lot of work behind-the-scenes. The amount of time and effort they put into it was tremendous, every day and often at weekends," he says.

Michael represented Wexford at minor level in both codes, losing out in the 1962 Leinster hurling decider to Kilkenny. He also played senior football with the county for a short time, and recalls marking Kerry great, Mick O'Connell in a National Football League match in 1963. Reflecting back on that day, Michael regrets that he wasn't as fit as he would have liked. "I would really have enjoyed it had I been fully fit."

After studying medicine in UCD, Michael went to England where he practised as a doctor in the Derby area from 1968 to 2002, at which point he returned to Ireland to reside in Kilmore. His medical studies and, later his time constraints as a doctor, meant that his GAA career ended prematurely. He did "a little bit of rowing", but concedes that, "when I went to Dublin to study, that was it as far as Gaelic games were concerned". Indeed, he can only recall playing "one soccer match" during his lengthy English sojourn.

Michael is married to Belfast native, Colette (nee Napier) and they have six grown-up children, three boys and three girls ("now scattered round the world"). He smiles when recalling bringing up his family in England. "I seemed to spend my life going to swimming pools, wind surfing and water skiing!" He laughs when recalling being asked at a medical job interview did he play golf. He feels his negative reply got him the position as it ensured he would spend his days in the surgery rather than on the golf course!

Walter Shortle is the only real contact that Michael Rossiter has with his hurling teammates in the intervening 34 years since their All-Ireland triumph. "I was very happy in school. I enjoyed the days out with the teams, singing stupid songs all the way to Carlow. There were no McDonald's or Burger King then. St. Peter's was a wonderful place to be." And the steps of the Hogan Stand was a wonderful place to be also, on May 6th, 1962, Croke Cup in hand.

1963 – ALL-IRELAND SEMI-FINAL
7 April 1963, Limerick

St. Finbarr's, Farranferris 7-9
(J. Dineen 3-1, S. Barry 2-1, D. Harrington 1-0, J. Hennessy 1-0, T. McEvoy 0-2, C. O'Leary 0-2,
M. Donegan 0-1, L. McAuliffe 0-1, P. Crowley 0-1)

St. Mary's, Galway 2-6
(P. O'Toole 2-1, F. Coffey 0-3, T. Canavan 0-2)

St. Finbarr's, Farranferris, Croke Cup Champions, 1963.
Back row, left to right: Fr Denis Forde, Mr Christy Ring, Paddy Crowley, Johnny Collins,
Vincent Hodnett, Jerry Hennessy, Liam McAuliffe, Sean Barry, John Dineen,
Dr Carthach McCarthy.
Front row, left to right: Tom McEvoy, Donal McCarthy, Frank Crowley, John Hennessy,
Connie O'Leary (capt), Mick Donegan, Kevin Collins, Denis Harrington.
(Photograph courtesy of Farna's Hurling Story, by Tim Horgan)

1963 – ALL-IRELAND FINAL
5 May 1963, Croke Park
Referee: Stephen Gleeson (Limerick)

St. Finbarr's, Farranferris 4-8

Kevin Collins
(Cork)

Frank Crowley
(Cork)

Vincent Hodnet
(Cork)

Donal McCarthy
(Cork)

Johnny Collins
(Cork)

Connie O'Leary (*capt*)
(Cork) (0-1)

Jerry Hennessy
(Cork)

Mick Donegan
(Cork) (1-1)

Paddy Crowley
(Cork)

Sean Barry
(Cork) (2-4)

Liam McAuliffe
(Cork)

Tom McEvoy
(Cork) (0-1)

John Hennessy
(Cork)

John Dineen
(Cork) (1-0)

Denis Harrington
(Cork) (0-1)

Patrician College, Ballyfin 3-4

Mick Davitt
(Dublin)

David Delaney
(Laois)

John O'Shaughnessy
(Laois)

Paddy Enright
(Limerick)

Liam Purcell
(Laois)

Seamus Behan
(Laois)

Thomas McGee
(Laois)

William Cronin
(Cork)

Pat Bradley (*capt*)
(Westmeath) (0-3)

Ray Niland
(Westmeath) (1-0)

Sean Gaffney
(Tipperary) (0-1)

Eamonn Egan
(Westmeath)

Declan Hayes
(Kilkenny) (1-0)

James Mullane
(Limerick)

Martin Mahoney
(Laois) (1-0)

Connie O'Leary

When St. Finbarr's, Farranferris, won their first Harty Cup in 1963, they went all the way to All-Ireland glory. Their outstanding centre half back and captain, Connie O'Leary, still holds treasured memories of those ground-breaking successes, despite being domiciled in London for almost 40 years.

A stalwart of the Blackrock club through all underage levels, Connie received his primary school education at Scoil Chríost Rí in Turner's Cross. He comes from a family of six girls and three boys and, while his two younger brothers were never heavily involved in sport, he concedes that his sister, Margaret, proved to be "the most successful of the family in sport", as a very talented camogie player with Cork.

Connie's late father, Denis, who played junior hurling with Cork, had ambitions that his eldest son would become a priest, an undoubted factor in Connie being sent as a boarder to St. Finbarr's back in the late 1950s. For his part, Connie jokes that he "didn't fancy the Sunday work" involved in such a career move! As a young teenager in Farna, he looked up to the likes of Gerard O'Herlihy, Mick Ryan and Derry Scully. Connie had a degree of success in his early years, winning all Cork Colleges competitions, but the Dean Ryan and Harty Cups eluded him. He graduated to the senior team as a very young goalie, but the following year in 1960/61, Farranferris suffered the heartbreak of 'defeating' Ennis CBS in the Harty quarter-final in Buttevant by a point, but losing a subsequent re-fixture. The powers-that-be deemed that Farna's winning goal had come during excessive injury time allotted by referee, Stephen Gleeson, whose watch had allegedly been affected by the heavy rain. "That was very unfortunate as we had a brilliant team that year," Connie laments.

Connie clearly recalls the day when he was asked to take on the role of team captain of St. Finbarr's for the 1962/63 campaign. Dr Carthach McCarthy asked him if he fancied the job and he replied, "I would be really chuffed and I will take on the responsibilities and do my best." Connie and his team-mates had no bother defeating Sullivan's Quay in the first round of the championship that year. "We beat them very heavily, but in the next round we were very lucky to get through against St. Flannan's who had thrashed us in the Dean Ryan Cup the previous year. We went into that game very nonchalantly. We went in with the attitude that we'd have a good game, as we were not going to win, but we stole through and we never looked back," Connie recalls. In the end, Farna won by 5-7 to 4-6, with Seanie Barry (who had captained the side and scored just a single point when drubbed by St. Flannan's a year earlier in the Dean Ryan Cup) accounting for no less than 3-5 of their total.

The same player added a further 1-6 to his scoring tally in the semi-final defeat of Thurles CBS, leaving reigning champions, Ennis CBS as St. Finbarr's opponents in the Harty Cup final to be played on St. Patrick's Day, 1963. History was made in Thurles on March 17th when

Farna triumphed by 4-9 to 4-3, despite a late Ennis CBS rally. "We were lucky there wasn't another ten minutes left, but we were always on top in that game," Connie reflects. St. Finbarr's wore numberless jerseys and it took the Ennis mentors quite a while to pinpoint the threat of Seanie Barry, who again wreaked havoc with a huge total of 3-5. The driving rain failed to dampen the enthusiasm of players, mentors and supporters as Connie was presented with the prestigious Harty Cup. Indeed, Connie recalls that many dignitaries called to the school in the ensuing days, including Jack Lynch and the Lord Mayor of Cork. "I ended up appearing on television and we didn't even have a telly in our house," Connie laughs.

In the All-Ireland semi-final in Limerick, St. Finbarr's had a very comfortable win over St. Mary's, Galway, on a scoreline of 7-9 to 2-6. However, it wasn't one of the major powers in Leinster who awaited in the final. Surprisingly, it was Patrician College, Ballyfin from Laois who had beaten St. Kieran's, Kilkenny, in the provincial decider. "We had played St. Kieran's earlier in the year in a challenge game when there was heavy snow on the ground. We went to see St. Kieran's play in the Leinster final and we knew that when Ballyfin beat them, they must be good." Connie remembers an "unbelievable build-up" to the Croke Cup final, which was postponed by a week due to the death of the Ballyfin parish priest. "The porridge wasn't half as thick as it was supposed to be. I think we were on diets and Sister Peter used to give us some kind of vitamins. It wasn't cocaine, but it was great stuff," Connie jokes.

"Many of the lads hadn't been to Dublin before and it was every lad's ambition to go to see Nelson's Pillar. I remember we travelled up on a train and the Cork Hibs soccer team were on the same train, as they were playing Shelbourne in the FAI Cup final the next day. They were beaten and we really wound them up on the way back to Cork when we had our cup," Connie says with a smile. The team stayed in the Hollybrook Hotel and were treated to an evening at the cinema. Indeed, those who wanted to further partake of fun and frolics that night back at the hotel were well monitored by the watching duo of Dr McCarthy and Christy Ring!

Connie sportingly acknowledges that, "we stole that final. We were only a couple of points up having played with a gale force wind in the first half. However, Dr Mac made some switches and we ripped them off. It was the most workmanlike team ever, but only for Seanie Barry's scores I don't think I would have been lifting any silverware." Donal Carroll agreed with this assessment in his match report in the 'Irish Independent'. "Farranferris take Croke Cup but by a flattering margin," was how he judged the final. The report continued, "it was the ability of their mentors to plug gaps which staved off the fiery challenge of Patrician College, Ballyfin. At the finish, the seven-point margin was highly flattering when the game is viewed over the entire hour."

When Ballyfin scored 1-2 in their first three attacks they gained sufficient confidence to play a strong attacking game. With the wind advantage on the change over, Ballyfin, leading 3-4 to 1-6 after 40 minutes seemed set to take their first Croke Cup. However, as the report stated, "Farna's ace score-getter, Sean Barry, thundered into the game from the centre forward spot in the second half. Displaying craft and cuteness far beyond his years he notched 2-4 of his side's total but left an even bigger imprint on the final tally." After the euphoria of winning, Connie recalls, "the speech was nerve-racking as there must have been 50,000 people present for the Waterford against Tipperary National League final which was on after our final." He laughs when recalling that he asked for three cheers for Farranferris before he remembered the gallant losers from Ballyfin! The reception for the team back in Cork was another memorable occasion, as Connie recalls being chaired up the streets of Cork, with the crowds out in force and car horns blowing.

The president of the college, Dr McCarthy, who combined that role with that of team trainer, gets great praise from Connie for his part in the victory. "He was very good at encouraging lads. You must remember a lot of young lads arrived in Farranferris from foot-balling areas and saw hurleys for the first time in the college. He spent hours and hours training us and he could give a great team-talk." The legendary Cork maestro, Christy Ring also was a huge influence on Connie and his colleagues. "Christy would show us how to take a sideline cut with the sliotar buried in the mud and still put it over the crossbar from the sideline." While in Farranferris, Connie "ate, slept and drank hurling" and he thought nothing of getting up at 6am before Mass and training "in the freezing cold" before break-fast. Other teachers whom he recalls for fos-tering the game include Fr Denis Forde, Fr Eddie Keown and Fr Brian Kelly. Connie "never went near football", although he feels that the school could easily have produced a quality team in the big ball game. However, "Dr Mac encouraged hurling, hurling, hurling".

Connie played minor hurling for Cork in 1962 and lined out for the seniors while still a teenager, playing Oireachtas Tournament and National League games. He played for Blackrock in the 1963 Cork senior final, where they were beaten by a UCC side which included some Blackrock players who chose to actually play for the university side. Emigration to England in 1967 meant that he would never win a coveted Cork SHC medal. In London, he played with Brian Boru's. He had a fair degree of success, both with his adopted club and with London. Indeed, in the 1975/76 club championship, Brian Boru's ran Galway champions, Ardrahan to two points in the All-Ireland quarter-final. A few years later, they come up against Blackrock, of all teams, at the same stage. 1973 was a particularly noteworthy year as London defeated Galway in Ballinasloe in the All-Ireland quarter-final, before putting up a decent showing against

champions-elect, Limerick in the penultimate round. Connie also lined out at corner back on the London side which reached the All-Ireland intermediate final that year. Unfortunately, they were "trounced by Kilkenny".

Having worked for Dunlop in Cork after school, Connie was out of a job when the fac-tory closed down. His brother-in-law offered him a job in his business in London and he has been there ever since, employed in security work over the years. He is married to Eileen (née Rowe), a London lady whose mother was from Roscommon and they live in Hammersmith. They have four grown-up chil-dren - daughters, Kerrie, Sinéad and Katherine - while their son, Bryan, who now lives in Dublin, was once on the books of Chelsea F.C. as a youth. Connie and Eileen have one grandson, Jack.

Connie travels home to Ireland at least once a year and he loves meeting up with his old Farna colleagues. Three (who had no problem with working on Sundays!) became priests - Fr Johnny Collins, Fr Vincent Hodnet and Fr Sean Barry. In July 2006, Connie was very upset to hear of the death of his "very good friend", Mick Donegan, whose company he enjoyed on trips home. He still remains in touch with 1963 team-mate, Denis Harrington, as well as the next Farna man to raise aloft the Croke Cup (in 1969), Donal Collins.

"While we might have hated some aspects of school when we were there, looking back they were brilliant days", Connie O'Leary concludes. "There was great camaraderie," he reflects. No doubt, this camaraderie con-tributed enormously to the never-to-be-for-gotten Harty and Croke Cup wins over 43 years ago.

1964 – ALL-IRELAND SEMI-FINAL
12 April 1964, Birr

Limerick CBS 4-5
(T. Clohessy 3-0, N. Carroll 1-1, E. Cregan 0-3, E. Grimes 0-1)

St. Mary's, Galway 4-2
(T. Connolly 2-0, N. Keogh 2-0, J. McLoughlin 0-2)

1964 – ALL-IRELAND SEMI-FINAL
19 April 1964, Croke Park

St. Peter's, Wexford 8-7
(N. Rochford 2-0, T. Royce 2-0, P. Bernie 2-0, F. O'Neill 1-1, J. Furlong 1-1, E. Ryan 0-4, E. Furlong 0-1)

St. MacNissi's, Garrontower 2-5
(E. Black 1-4, C. Donnelly 1-0, E. Donnelly 0-1)

Limerick CBS, Croke Cup Champions, 1964.
Back row, left to right: John Leonard, Eddie Power, Tom Crowe, Donal Manning, Philip Aherne, Michael O'Brien, Roddy Hayes.
Middle row, left to right: Pat Nash, John Finucane, Gerard Boland, Walter Maloney, Noel O'Gorman, J.J. Fitzpatrick, Seamus Shinnors, Pat Doherty.
Front row, left to right: John Kennedy, Brian Cobbe, Tom O'Brien, Eamon Cregan (capt), Niall Carroll, Eamon Grimes, Donal Russell, Tommy Clohessy.
(Photograph courtesy of Noel Earlie, c/o Limerick CBS)

1964 – ALL-IRELAND FINAL
26 April 1964, Croke Park
Referee: Aubrey Higgins (Galway)

Limerick CBS 6-7

Seamus Shinnors
(Tipperary)

Tom O'Brien
(Limerick)

Noel O'Gorman
(Tipperary)

J. J. Fitzpatrick
(Limerick)

Donal Russell
(Limerick)

Donal Manning
(Limerick)

Eddie Power
(Limerick)

Pat Doherty
(Limerick)

Eamon Cregan (*capt*)
(Limerick) (0-2)

Pat Nash
(Limerick) (2-2)

Brian Cobbe
(Limerick) (1-1)

Eamon Grimes
(Limerick) (2-0)

Michael O'Brien
(Tipperary)

Niall Carroll
(Limerick)

John Kennedy
(Limerick) (1-2)

Sub: Roddy Hayes (Clare) (for M. O'Brien).

St. Peter's, Wexford 4-5

Phil Berry
(Wexford)

Michael Merrigan
(Wexford)

Enda Murphy
(Wexford)

Jim Kinsella
(Wexford)

Jimmy Furlong
(Wexford)

Michael Fitzpatrick
(Wexford)

Matty Doyle
(Wexford)

Eamonn Furlong (*capt*)
(Wexford) (0-1)

Eugene Ryan
(Wexford)

Paddy Bernie
(Wexford)

Tom Royce
(Wexford) (1-4)

Finbarr O'Neill
(Wexford)

Noel Rochford
(Wexford)

John Furlong
(Wexford) (2-0)

John Quigley
(Wexford)

Sub: Dave Bernie (Wexford)(1-0) (for O'Neill).

Eamon Cregan

"My two highlights in hurling were winning the Harty Cup in '64 and the All-Ireland with Limerick in '73. They're the ones that stand out in my mind." So says Limerick hurling legend, Eamon Cregan, and it shows just how much the groundbreaking successes of his alma mater Limerick CBS in winning the Munster and All-Ireland Colleges titles meant back in 1964, when he was the team captain and midfielder supreme.

Eamon and his older brother, Michael, who captained Limerick CBS in the 1962 Harty Cup campaign, were both reared on a diet of hurling. Their father, Ned played for Limerick during the Mick Mackey era and he won an All-Ireland medal in 1934 when the Shannonsiders beat Dublin after a replay. "He used to bring us to the Gaelic Grounds when we were small." Eamon explains. In the mid-1950s, the Cregan brothers began their hurling careers with Claughaun. Eamon was just 11-years-old when he helped the city club to victory over South Liberties in an Under-16 championship final. "When I first went up to Claughaun, I was only ten and because I was so small, they decided to put me in goal. The following year, which was 1957, we won a county Under-16 championship. There was no Under-14 grade back then, so the Under-16 team was the only team I could play for. I've been involved with Claughaun now for over 50 years."

Eamon received his primary education in Model National School on O'Connell Avenue which, in hurling terms, was "a type of springboard" for the Claughaun club. He also attended St. Patrick's National School for a year and a half, with some success on the hurl-

ing fields. In 1958, he entered Limerick CBS, or Sexton Street as it was known at the time. The young Eamon had been fully aware of the prestige and glamour that was attached to the Harty Cup before he enrolled in the CBS. "I was always interested in the Harty Cup. It was the number one schools competition at that time. Limerick CBS had a fantastic side in '58, with players like Pat Murphy and Paddy Cobbe. They played St. Flannan's in the Harty final in front of a crowd of 15 to 20,000. It was a very bad day; it was pouring rain. Flannan's scored three early goals and I think Limerick ended up losing by a few points. But most of those lads had the bonus of winning All-Ireland minor medals with Limerick later that same year. It was a tremendous time, going to the likes of Buttevant on the train."

Eamon played Harty Cup for four years, making his debut as a goalkeeper in 1961 when Limerick CBS lost to St. Flannan's. "I remember it being a miserable day and I couldn't get my puck-outs any further than 40 yards because the wind was so strong, and none of the full backs would take the pucks," he jokes. Ennis CBS beat "one of the best Limerick CBS teams" in 1962, en route to Harty success, and further disappointment followed in 1963. There was one hugely significant development in 1963, though, which saw Br Michael Burke and Br Jim Hennessy take charge of team affairs. "That was the turning point," Eamon says. "Br Burke and Br Hennessy turned our fortunes around. They were brilliant tacticians and only for them, I don't think we would have won as much as we did. The 1964 team wasn't perhaps the most skilful, but it had lots of heart and that's what made the difference. Br Burke and Br Hennessy worked very well together. Br Hennessy coached the backs and Br Burke looked after the forwards. Their game plan was to move the ball as quickly as possible. We played a Limerick style of hurling. We didn't do a lot of physical work in training - we concentrated on hurling, hurling, hurling, and the physical work we did was overseen by Stevie Keogh, who was in the army."

As the most experienced player on the 1964 team, Eamon was an obvious choice for the captaincy. "I remember Br Burke pulling me aside one day and telling me I was being made captain. I had gone back to repeat Maths and I was probably chosen on the basis that I had captained the Limerick minor team in the All-Ireland final the previous year. I was only delighted to be handed the role." The road to Croke Park began for Limerick CBS when they defeated North Monastery in their opening game of the Harty Cup in Kilmallock by 6-9 to 1-11. Eamon suffered concussion during the first half, but returned to the fray for the second half. "If a player got concussed now, he would be told to stop playing for a fortnight, but it was different in those days. I wasn't right, the lights were out, but they decided to reintroduce me after half-time at full forward. My head eventually cleared and I moved back to midfield." Newmarket-on-Fergus was the venue for a second round win over a fancied Ennis CBS team, when Limerick CBS overcame a three-goal interval deficit to win by 3-10 to 4-2. In the Harty semi-final, Limerick enjoyed a very comfortable victory over Coláiste Chríost Rí in Thurles, romping home by 10-9 to 0-2. A talking point which Eamon recalls was the involvement of the Doherty brothers in opposite camps. Pat lined out alongside Eamon in the Limerick midfield, while his brother, John was full back on the Chríost Rí team.

A huge crowd watched Limerick CBS finally get the better of old rivals St. Flannan's in the final at the Gaelic Grounds. Centre forward, Brian Cobbe scored a hat-trick of goals as the Harty Cup returned to Sexton Street for the first time since 1932, winning out by 6-10 to 4-7. "We were under a lot of pressure

going into the final," Eamon remembers. "We went into the game as favourites, even though we hadn't won the Harty Cup in 32 years. But to their great credit, the management got us mentally right and all the Bovril we were fed stood to us", he jokes. "The funny thing about that team was that each match we played, one player or other would score at least a couple of goals. You weren't depending on the same players all the time. The celebrations were something else after the final. When Br White came to Limerick CBS in 1958, his objective was not to build buildings but to win the Harty Cup! I've no doubt that the '64 success gave Limerick CBS the confidence to go on and win again in '65, '66 and '67."

However, in the All-Ireland semi-final at Birr, the Sexton Street boys received a major fright before prevailing against St. Mary's, Galway, on a 4-5 to 4-2 scoreline. "We got one hell of a scare," Eamon recalls. "Things didn't go well for us in the first half and they were ahead at half-time. But Tommy Clohessy came into his own in the second half by scoring three goals to send us through to the final. Going into matches as out-and-out favourites is not a great thing," he concludes.

Limerick's All-Ireland final opponents were St. Peter's of Wexford. Capturing the sense of occasion, the 'Irish Independent' reported, "Limerick CBS, resplendent in their trim maroon and white outfits, made a grand first entrance at Croke Park. They had their own pipe band to rouse the crowd with tuneful airs and crisp figure-marching. They made an even more spectacular exit for, after defeating gallant St. Peter's, Wexford by 6-7 to 4-5, they left to a rising crescendo of cheers and applause and with team captain, Eamon Cregan proudly bearing aloft the Croke Cup." Indeed, Donal Carroll in his report referred to Eamon as "a truly delightful striker and hurling artist".

The Munster side got off to a disastrous start, conceding a goal after just ten seconds. It took Limerick three minutes to get back onto level terms, but they pulled away to lead 3-2 to 1-3 at the interval, despite having played into the wind. Early in the second half, St. Peter's scored a goal to get themselves back into contention. The last quarter was a ding-dong affair with scores coming in quick succession. Only four points separated the teams with ten minutes remaining, but it was Limerick who pulled away again in the closing stages, scoring 1-1 without reply. Limerick's six goals were shared between wing forwards, Pat Nash and Eamon Grimes (who scored two each), centre forward, Brian Cobbe and John Kennedy, who lined out at top of the left. "It was a tremendous feeling to win that game. We didn't know much about St. Peter's - we just stuck to our own game plan. The legs had just gone from under me in the '63 All-Ireland minor final which we lost to Wexford. I think the prospect of playing in Croke Park had got to me somewhat. But this time there was no talk and we just had to go out and play. After the game, Br Burke just whispered a few thoughts to me in Irish for the speech. It was an unbelievable time for all of us and for all our supporters from Clare, Tipp and Limerick."

After the All-Ireland Colleges victory, Eamon quickly graduated to the Limerick senior team, making his debut as a substitute against Dublin in a National League game in November 1964. He made his first championship start against Waterford the following year, lining out at midfield. Also in 1965, he played in the Munster football final against Kerry. "We led Kerry by seven points at half-time, but they came back to beat us. That Limerick football team was backboned by lads who had been in Limerick CBS," he says.

Eamon played senior hurling for Limerick from 1964 to 1983, both as a defender and a forward. He was a key member of the team that beat Kilkenny in the 1973 All-Ireland final, and also played in the 1980 final loss to Galway. He was honoured with All-Star awards in 1971, 1972 and 1980. "It's scandalous that we haven't won the All-Ireland since 1973," he laments. With Claughaun, Eamon won eight county senior football championship medals and three senior hurling. Indeed, there were doubles in 1971 and 1986. He also garnered Under-16, minor hurling and football championship honours with the club. "There was never a dull moment," he reflects.

Sandwiched between two spells as Limerick senior hurling manager, Eamon managed the Offaly hurlers between 1993 and 1996, during which time they won two Leinster championships and the Liam McCarthy Cup in 1994. Not surprisingly, he had mixed emotions after the latter success. "As someone who all my life wanted to see Limerick win an All-Ireland, it was a strange feeling to be in charge of a team that deprived them of one. Limerick had 12 wides in the first half and they lost their focus. It just goes to show that a game isn't over until you're back inside in the dressing room with the trophy."

Eamon is married to Ann (née Crowley) and they have five children - Gary, Ciara, Niamh, Caoimhe and Brian. He is full of praise for his very supportive wife during his time-consuming involvement in hurling in various capacities. Eamon is employed as secretary/manager of Newcastlewest Golf Club. The former RTÉ Sunday Game analyst still keeps in touch with many of his old Limerick CBS team-mates, whose whereabouts he can freely rhyme off. Most of these attended last year's memorable reunion of the four Harty Cup winning teams (1964-1967) in the Castletroy Park Hotel in the city. "We trawled the world to get lads together for the night. The '63/'64 panel were always close and everybody who played with Sexton Street have this bond that we will never lose," Eamon states. Players were presented with commemorative ties on a night where glorious memories were shared by all and sundry, including joint-trainer, Jim Hennessy. He continues to keep an eye out for the CBS' results but concedes that the big choice of secondary schools on Shannonside makes it very difficult for Limerick CBS (now St. Michael's) to build a strong team.

"There was something special about Sexton Street," Eamon Cregan reflects. "Our team of '64 had leaders everywhere on the pitch." However, Eamon's team-mates would undoubtedly concur that their captain led by example and his special talent was hugely instrumental in their historic successes over 32 years ago.

1965 – ALL-IRELAND SEMI-FINAL
2 May 1965, Croke Park

St. Kieran's, Kilkenny 5-8
(M. Delaney 2-0, T. Holohan 1-3, F. Power 1-3, D. Prendergast 1-2)

St. Mary's, Galway 5-7
(A. Rabbitte 2-0, P. Fahy 2-0, J. Gibbons 1-0, A. Henry 0-3, J. McLoughlin 0-3, M. O'Connell 0-1)

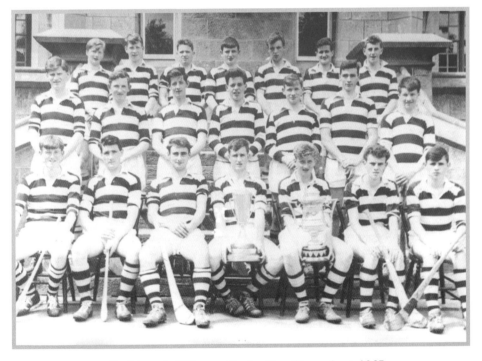

St. Kieran's, Kilkenny, Croke Cup Champions, 1965.
Back row, left to right: Mick Delaney, Michael Moore, John Lacey, John Maher, Billy Tobin,
Martin O'Neill, Ber Butler.
Middle row, left to right: Richie Teehan, Vincent McNamee, Michael Cody, Paddy Dunne,
Brendan Morrissey, Dick Prendergast, Eddie Bolger.
Front row, left to right: Eamon Tobin, Seamus Purcell, Davie Freyne, Tom Nolan (capt),
Tom Holohan, Frank Power, Pat Alley.
(Photograph courtesy of Dick McEvoy, c/o St. Kieran's, Kilkenny)

1965 – ALL-IRELAND FINAL
16 May 1965, Clonmel
Referee: Aubrey Higgins (Galway)

St. Kieran's, Kilkenny 6-9

Michael Moore
(Kilkenny)

John Maher   Vincent McNamee   Eamon Tobin
(Tipperary)   (Kilkenny)   (Kilkenny)

Pat Alley   Michael Cody   Richie Teehan
(Laois)   (Kilkenny)   (Kilkenny)

Ber Butler   Tom Nolan (*capt*)
(Kilkenny) (1-1)   (Kilkenny) (2-0)

Tom Holohan   Dick Prendergast   Frank Power
(Kilkenny)   (Kilkenny) (1-4)   (Kilkenny) (2-1)

Seamus Purcell   Davie Freyne   Mick Delaney
(Kilkenny)   (Kilkenny) (0-1)   (Laois) (0-2)

Sub: Brendan Morrissey (Kilkenny) (for Butler).

Limerick CBS 6-1

Tony Brennan
(Limerick)

John Leonard   Donal Manning   Tony Cronin
(Limerick)   (Limerick)   (Limerick)

Michael Keogh   Wally Moloney   Donal Russell (*capt*)
(Limerick)   (Limerick)   (Limerick)

John Finucane   Pat Doherty
(Limerick)   (Limerick)

Pat McCarthy   Michael O'Brien   Tommy Clohessy
(Limerick)   (Tipperary)   (Limerick) (1-1)

Matt Grace   Liam Ryan   Eamon Grimes
(Limerick) (1-0)   (Limerick) (1-0)   (Limerick) (3-0)

Subs: Aidan Murphy (Limerick) (for Finucane), Michael Hennessy (Limerick) (for McCarthy).

Tom Nolan

Despite a Leinster and All-Ireland campaign which featured three Houdini-like escapes, St. Kieran's, Kilkenny ultimately won the Croke Cup for the fifth time in 1965 with a well-balanced side captained from midfield by Tom Nolan.

A native of Conahy, Tom reckons that, "I must have acquired some hurling skills from my mother, a Kilkenny woman, who was apparently a very good camogie player", before adding in a humorous way that, "my father was a Kilkenny man and he claimed to be a great hurler but, to be honest, I don't think he ever played hurling!" When he reflects on his early hurling memories, the name Joe Phelan immediately springs to his mind. Joe, an elderly man, "who always seemed to be on a bike", took an interest in coaching the young lads around the area. "Come to think of it we were all on bikes back then as there were no cars in those days," Tom recalls. He also remembers Fr Kearns from Castlecomer, after whom the GAA pitch in the locality is now named, taking a particular interest in his hurling development. Other names who spring to his mind are Dermot Healy's father, Paddy 'Ger', "one of the few people at the time who had a car", and local milkman, Lar Carroll, whose lorry was often used to transport the budding young local hurlers to various venues around Kilkenny.

When second level education beckoned, Tom followed the lead of his two brothers and his cousins (including the 1957 Croke Cup winning captain, Ted Carroll) by enrolling in St.

Kieran's. For Tom, as was the case for many young students at that time, entering boarding school was "frightening". However, hurling was a great distraction when homesickness threatened to take over and "watching Pierce Freaney lift the Croke Cup in 1961, in just my second year in the college, was a great inspiration". The in-house leagues for first year students provided Tom with his first taste of competitive hurling. "Teams for those leagues were chosen on a graded basis of best down to worst, starting with the captain and I was at the bottom of the list, so you could say, I started at the very bottom of the ladder," Tom modestly reflects. However, he soon climbed the ladder and he matured into the captain of the St. Kieran's junior side which won the 1963 Leinster championship.

There was no All-Ireland championship at that level but Tom progressed to the senior side for the 1963/64 campaign, but the Kilkenny lads were unable to deny St. Peter's, Wexford, who won by 3-5 to 3-4 in New Ross in the Leinster semi-final. Tom was appointed as team captain in his Leaving Cert year of 1964/65 by the legendary Fr Tommy Maher, whom he feels was "the best coach in the country at that time and an excellent tactician". Before St. Kieran's first game of the championship against Cistercian College, Roscrea, Fr Maher warned his team "about a big fellow playing at full forward". It turned out to be a future Kilkenny senior hurler and Irish rugby international, Ned Byrne. "When I saw him, I immediately felt pity for our full back," Tom jokes. However, despite the presence of the towering number 14, St. Kieran's won very handily by 8-11 to 4-1 in Mountrath. Ironically, a future Kilkenny hurling legend was to prove even more of a scourge in the provincial semi-final. Dublin school, Belcamp OMI, who went on to win the Leinster football crown that season, featured Frank Cummins. "Of course, we didn't know at the time who Frank Cummins was," Tom recalls, "but Fr. Maher warned us not to concede any 21-yard frees. So what did we do early in the game? Yes, we conceded a 21-yard free and Cummins buried it in the back of the net." In the end, St. Kieran's were fortunate to draw that game in Athy (their 2-4 cancelling out Belcamp's 3-1), with Tom scoring a late equalising point, urged on by Tommy Murphy, who was then a seminarian. "We were very close to defeat as the final whistle was blown just after the puck out," Tom concludes. St. Kieran's went on to win the replay by 7-5 to 5-4, also in Athy, withstanding a spirited Belcamp comeback in the process.

The Kilkenny college faced their fierce rivals, St. Peter's, Wexford, in Carlow in the Leinster Final. Torrential rain poured in the first half and Tom feels the game "turned out to be tight and a little dirty". A tangle with John Quigley resulted in Tom and the future Wexford star both being sent off. "Fortunately the team raised their game and the lads played very well and won it by a couple of points," says Tom. Indeed, it took a late goal by Frank Power to edge St. Kieran's over the line by 4-5 to 4-3. The All-Ireland semi-final against St. Mary's, Galway, "was supposed to be an easy one", Tom recalls, but this proved to be anything but the case. The game was a curtain-raiser to the National Hurling League semi-final between Kilkenny and Wexford, but the early arrivals in Croke Park from Noreside got a serious fright. With Frank Power again proving to be the team's scoring saviour, St. Kieran's eked out a one-point win over the Connacht champions. "That game proved that there were no stars in our team, but we showed great character and determination. It really spurred us on," Tom remembers. "There

was great hype surrounding the build up to the Croke Cup final against Limerick CBS," Tom recalls. "Fr Tommy Maher arranged a challenge game against the Kilkenny senior side and I distinctly remember running into the great Pat Henderson, but sure he nearly broke every bone in my body," Tom reflects. "There was also a game arranged against the seminary side and we managed to beat them and they weren't a bit happy about that. St. Kieran's hadn't won the Croke Cup in four years and that year, above all years, we weren't expected to win, as we had just scrapped through all our games. This time Fr Maher had us forewarned about Pat Doherty playing at centrefield and a little blonde guy playing corner forward by the name of Eamon Grimes."

However, having made the Croke Cup final by the skin of their teeth, the Kilkenny lads came good on the big day. Indeed, the 'Irish Independent' reporter was very impressed with St. Kieran's performance in the All-Ireland final, expressing his opinion that they displayed "a brand of fitness, fire and fury hardly hinted at in their earlier engagements". Tom Nolan was described as "a brilliant captain" and his side was ahead by 5-5 to 4-1 at half time. However, the reigning All-Ireland champions from Shannonside rallied in the third quarter, "moving with great power and considerable fluency", according to Donal Carroll's newspaper account, and the margin was only three points (5-7 to 6-1) with 15 minutes to go. The crowd of approximately 6,000 was enthralled, but an unanswered 1-2 from the black and whites swung the tie firmly in their favour in the time remaining. That day Tom nabbed what he modestly describes as "two lucky goals", as St. Kieran's captured the Croke Cup for the fifth time. Afterwards, the triumphant side retired to Clonmel where they "enjoyed a meal in the hotel but the hype was nothing like it would be nowadays," Tom says. "We also enjoyed the extra meals we got and little perks which the team were allowed during the year, and our day off school the day following the All-Ireland, but it was straight down to study duties immediately after our return," according to Tom.

Tom played for Kilkenny minor hurlers in

both 1964 and 1965, but failed to win a provincial title either year, with unheralded Laois and Dublin winning out in Leinster in those two years, respectively. After his Leaving Cert, Tom decided to go to London. Ironically, on the flight over, he met his old friend Fr Kearns. His mentor as a young boy advised Tom to take the bus into the city to meet his brother. "In London, you'll have to work the buses," was Fr Kearns' advice. So, despite "not having a clue" where he was heading, Tom resisted the temptation to get a taxi and "ended up cursing Fr Kearns" until he saw his brother coming! Playing hurling in London was a culture shock for Tom after the highly-organised regime in St. Kieran's. Tom hurled with Geraldines, "but the interest wasn't the same and the players weren't as good, so you'd end up picking up more injuries". He lived in London from 1966 until 1972, during which time he married Patricia, a Sligo woman, "who's into football". Moving back to Ireland to work with PMPA, Tom played in the Business Houses League and PMPA's renowned boss, Joe Moore was "thrilled" when Tom and his team-mates won the league title.

In later years, Tom played with St. Brigid's of Blanchardstown before finishing his hurling career with Blackhall Gaels in County Meath, when he moved to live in Dunboyne. He has fronted his own insurance business in Kells since 1985, practising as Tom Nolan Insurance Brokers Ltd. Tom and Patricia have two sons and four daughters, as well as five grandchildren. Over the years, Tom played "a bit of racquet ball", using some of the skills garnered from his handball exploits in St. Kieran's, but nowadays his favourite pastime is golf, playing off a 12 handicap. He retains an interest in his alma mater, despite the geographical restraints of living in Dunboyne since 1988. The winning team of 1965 met up for 25 and 40-year reunions. To the best of Tom's knowledge, only Frank Power from the Croke Cup winning squad is deceased, while Michael Cody is the only panellist he manages to meet occasionally in recent times.

"We had no Eddie Keher or Henry Shefflin or D.J. Carey on our team," Tom Nolan recalls candidly. However, despite getting out of jail on a few occasions, the St. Kieran's team he captained in 1965 had a bond which drove them over the line that year and their place is assured in the illustrious history of the Kilkenny nursery.

1966 – ALL-IRELAND SEMI-FINAL
3 April 1966, Cavan

St. Mary's, Galway 4-5
(J. Hughes 2-0, T. Rabbitte 1-1, L. Hannify 1-0, P. Fahy 0-2, R. Glynn, 0-1, M. O'Connell 0-1)

St. Mary's, Belfast 1-5
(S. Rice 1-0, G. Mallon 0-2, P. Curran 0-1, C. Carson 0-1, A. Hamill 0-1)

1966 – ALL-IRELAND SEMI-FINAL
24 April 1966, Nenagh

Limerick CBS 8-9
(S. Burke 5-1, E. Grimes 1-2, M. Grace 1-1, P. Doherty 0-4, L. Ryan 1-0, G. O'Donoghue 0-1)

St. Kieran's, Kilkenny 3-9
(P. Dunne 0-6, B. Morrissey 1-0, S. Walsh 1-0, M. Delaney 1-0, D. Prendergast 0-2, J. J. Ryan 0-1)

Limerick CBS, Croke Cup Champions, 1966.
Back row, left to right: Ignatius Cantillon, Sean O'Donovan, Walter Shanahan, Willie Cusack, Pat Hartigan, Pat Doherty, Aidan Murphy, Donal Manning, Paddy Phelan, Gerry McKeon.
Middle row, left to right: Ger Fitzgibbon, Tony Cronin, Gerry O'Donoghue, Pat McCarthy, Eamon Grimes (capt), Liam Ryan, Matt Grace, Sean Burke, Richie Grace.
Front row, left to right: Conor Cregan, Dave Tuohy, Tony Brennan, Sean Foley.
(Photograph courtesy of Noel Earlie, c/o Limerick CBS)

1966 – ALL-IRELAND FINAL .
1 May 1966, Birr
Referee: John Dowling (Offaly)

Limerick CBS 8-9

Walter Shanahan
(Limerick)

Pat Hartigan	**Donal Manning**	**Aidan Murphy**
(Limerick)	(Limerick)	(Limerick)

Gerry McKeon	**Sean Foley**	**Tony Cronin**
(Limerick)	(Limerick)	(Limerick)

Pat Doherty   **Paddy Phelan**
(Limerick) (0-1)   (Limerick)

Eamon Grimes (*capt*)	**Gerry O' Donoghue**	**Pat McCarthy**
(Limerick) (1-3)	(Limerick) (1-2)	(Limerick) (1-2)

Matt Grace	**Liam Ryan**	**Sean Burke**
(Limerick)	(Limerick) (2-0)	(Limerick) (2-0)

Sub: Richie Grace (Limerick)(1-1) (for McCarthy).

St. Mary's, Galway 2-2

Michael Hurney (*capt*)
(Galway)

Michael Murphy	**Paddy Moore**	**Stan Whiriskey**
(Galway)	(Galway)	(Galway)

Paddy Fahy	**Willie Cummins**	**Mattie Cooney**
(Galway)	(Galway)	(Galway)

John Rabbitte   **Mick O'Connell**
(Galway)   (Galway)

Sean Nealon	**Padraig Fahy**	**Ray Glynn**
(Galway)	(Galway) (1-2)	(Galway) (1-0)

Tony Rabbitte	**Jimmy Hughes**	**Liam Hanniffy**
(Galway)	(Galway)	(Galway)

Subs: John O'Malley (Galway) (for Hughes), Francis Donoghue (Galway) (for J. Rabbitte).

Eamon Grimes

After ending a 32-year famine for Harty Cup honours in 1964, Limerick CBS won two All-Ireland titles and a remarkable four-in-a-row of provincial crowns. Two years after playing a starring role in Limerick CBS's first All-Ireland Colleges triumph, Eamon Grimes captained the Sexton Street hurling nursery in 1966 to their second Croke Cup success and their third Harty Cup victory on the trot.

Hurling didn't feature in Eamon's life until about the age of ten when he changed primary schools. "There was no hurling played at all in Roxboro National School, which was the first school I attended," he said.

"But when I was in fourth class, I left to go to John the Baptist in Limerick, which had close links with the CBS. There my interest in the game developed. We played in various schools competitions, winning the Leader Cup when I was in fifth and sixth class. My father, Edward, didn't play the game. Indeed, his schools background was in rugby and he won a Munster Junior Cup medal with Presentation in 1927. He became a great hurling supporter and, sadly, he actually died from a massive heart attack when watching a game between Limerick and Waterford at the Gaelic Grounds in 1975."

Eamon entered Limerick CBS in the early 1960s when the likes of Mick Tynan, Bernie Hartigan, Eugene O'Brien and the Kelleher brothers were the marquee names. "I remember the school getting to a Harty Cup semi-final one year with a great team. They were fine hurlers and I wanted to be as good as them," he recalls. Eamon played Harty Cup hurling for three years, making his first appearance at wing forward in the All-Ireland winning year of 1964. There were joyous scenes after Limerick CBS defeated old rivals, St. Flannan's in front of an estimated 14,000 spectators at the Gaelic Grounds to end their long wait for Harty Cup success. In the All-Ireland semi-final at Birr, the Sexton Street boys overcame St. Mary's of Galway after a tough battle. All roads led to Croke Park for the All-Ireland final, and Limerick CBS gave their legion of supporters plenty to cheer about as they powered to a 6-7 to 4-5 victory over St. Peter's, Wexford. Limerick CBS successfully retained the Harty Cup in 1965, but their bid for back-to-back All-Ireland titles ended in disappointment when they lost the final to St. Kieran's in Clonmel. "It just didn't gel for us that day," Eamon laments.

Eamon was voted in as captain for the 1965/66 campaign following a meeting of players in the school canteen. "I was the longest on the team by then, so that was probably why I was given the captaincy," he modestly says. Limerick CBS's first objective was to complete a hat-trick of Harty Cup wins. A first round victory over Ennis CBS was followed by a semi-final win against North Monastery. They then faced Thurles CBS at Buttevant. The Tipperary school enjoyed the upper hand in the opening half, but calling on all their experience, Limerick fought back to claim a 6-5 to

5-3 victory. "We had a terrible bad start and were well down at the break. We got an awful dressing down from Br Burke during half-time and it obviously had the desired affect as we played much better in the second half. Sean Burke scored a goal just after half-time and we took it from there. I had started the game at corner forward but ended up moving out to midfield for the second half. It was a huge honour to collect the Harty Cup on behalf of the team - the All-Ireland nearly comes second to it."

Buoyed by their second half comeback against Thurles, Sexton Street went on to exact sweet revenge on St. Kieran's in the All-Ireland semi-final at Nenagh. Producing an exhibition of hurling, they ran out 8-9 to 3-9 winners, with corner forward Sean Burke scoring a whopping 5-1. Following their demolition of the Leinster champions, Limerick CBS were installed as hot favourites for the final against St. Mary's. The Galway side had given Limerick an almighty scare in the 1964 All-Ireland semi-final, but on this occasion the Harty winners justified their favourites' tag with a 25-point victory in Birr on May 1st, 1966.

"After what had happened two years before, there was no way we were going to take St. Mary's for granted. It was drilled into us. Everything clicked for us and it turned out to be quite a one-sided affair. We knew we had it kind of won after the first ten minutes and probably the hardest part for me was making the speech afterwards!" According to the 'Irish Independent', Limerick's victory would have been even more comprehensive but for an outstanding performance by the Galway goalkeeper. The report stated, "St. Mary's first appearance in an All-Ireland Colleges hurling final was hardly an auspicious occasion as Limerick CBS romped to their second Croke Cup title in three years by the overwhelming margin." Limerick scored 8-9 (remarkably, exactly what they had done in the All-Ireland semi-final) and their opponents could only muster 2-2. Yet, St. Mary's goalkeeper, Michael Hurney was the star of a very one-sided, unexciting final and even the most ardent admirers of the winners could not deny the

courage and skill of this fine performer. According to the 'Irish Independent', "Hurney was under constant pressure. His backs failed to give him the required protection but he still managed to bring off a serious of really brilliant saves. Galway could never compare in speed, skill or team-work with their superbly fit and more experienced opponents who revelled in lightning attacks which generally began at midfield, but also quite frequently from the half back line. In Eamon Grimes, Gerry Donoghue and Paddy McCarthy, they had a swift and clever half forward line whose work was invariably carried on by opportunists Liam Ryan and Sean Burke, who notched two goals apiece."

An early goal from Burke set Limerick on their way and they scored 2-2 without reply in the opening quarter. The Munster kingpins led by 3-4 to 0-1 at the interval and, after a slow start to the second half, they added 5-3 in the final 18 minutes to leave their Galway opponents well and truly demoralised. One of Eamon's abiding memories of the Harty and Croke Cups was the huge crowds that attended the games. "You could have had anything up to 20,000 people at a Harty Cup final. We had massive support and a lot of that was down to the hunger for success in Limerick at the time. With the exception of the 1955 Munster championship win, the county had had nothing to cheer about since 1940. I was part of teams which reached the 1963 and 1965 All-Ireland minor finals, but we lost both to Wexford and Dublin respectively. So every effort was made to ensure that we were successful and we got great support from all Limerick people."

Eamon had the height of respect for Br Jim Hennessy and Br Michael Burke, who masterminded the All-Ireland victories of 1964 and 1966.

"We were fortunate to have had two contrasting but great people over us in Br Hennessy and Br Burke. Br Hennessy was very outgoing, while Br Burke was astute and a great reader of the game. They were years, years, years ahead of their time from a tactical point of view. Br Burke went on to be a Limerick senior selector a few years later. We also had very good people working behind the scenes in army man, Stevie Keogh, who was the physical trainer, and Con McGrath, who was a man from Kilkenny with an almighty interest in hurling. Others I recall being a great help were Mr Noonan and Mr Frawley." While he also played football for the school, Eamon modestly states that, "I couldn't kick a ball 20 yards and was just on because I had a bit of speed".

While still a student in Limerick CBS, Eamon made his senior inter-county debut in a National League game against Wexford in New Ross in the early part of 1966. He made his Munster championship debut later that year against Tipperary in Cork. "I'll never forget it," he reflects. "I was marking Len Gaynor, who was the toughest opponent I ever played against, without a shadow of a doubt. The following day, I was back in Limerick CBS sitting my Leaving Cert."

Eamon went on to enjoy a long and distinguished career in the green and white of Limerick. The obvious highlight was captaining the Shannonsiders to All-Ireland glory in 1973 against Kilkenny. The Cats reversed this result the following year. He also made an appearance as a substitute in the 1980 All-Ireland final loss to Galway and he won All-Star awards in both 1973 and 1975. With South Liberties, he won four senior county championships in 1972, 1974, 1976 and 1978 and he also won ten East Limerick senior hurling championship medals. "We were very unlucky not to win an 11th," he remembers.

After leaving school, Eamon trained as a psychiatric nurse but, on the day of his final exam, he was offered a job with Halpin's Tea and duly accepted it. He subsequently worked for Beamish and Crawford for 30 years, retiring in 2004. He jokes that he is now "busier than ever" catching up on painting and decorating chores at home! Eamon is married to Limerick lady, Helen and they have two grown-up children, Eamon Jnr (28), who won a Munster 'B' hurling medal with St. Clement's, and Karen (20). He regularly meets up with his old friends from Limerick CBS, mainly on the golf course, and he enjoys giving a weekly hurling coaching session in Donoughmore National School. His connections with wealthy businessman, J. P. McManus commenced when Eamon was his 'runner' as a bookie. "He is one of the best friends any man could have", Eamon says of the man who famously named a horse Grimes in his honour and pulled off the very prestigious Galway Plate with the horse. "For good measure, I backed him at 10/1 that day," Eamon laughs.

Undoubtedly, the achievements of the Sexton Street boys during this glorious period for the school in the mid-1960s laid the foundations for Limerick's All-Ireland senior triumph of 1973, the county's first in 33 years. Eamon Grimes looks back on his schooldays with affection. "Even down to the privileges for the hurlers of getting soup and Bovril and Mrs Murphy's home-made jam in the canteen, the Limerick CBS days were the best of my life," he concludes.

1967 – ALL-IRELAND SEMI-FINAL
9 April 1967, Croke Park

St. Peter's, Wexford 7-12
(P. Murphy 3-1, J. Murphy 3-0, T. Royce 1-4, M. Casey 0-3, P. Bernie 0-2, M. Quigley 0-2)

St. Mary's, Belfast 1-3
(S. Rice 1-0, A. Hamill 0-2, K. Carson 0-1)

1967 – ALL-IRELAND SEMI-FINAL
9 April 1967, Nenagh

Limerick CBS 5-9
(M. Grace 2-1, R. Grace 1-4, S. Burke 1-1, W. O'Connor 1-1, G. McKeown 0-2)

St. Mary's, Galway 2-4
(J. Hannify 2-0, M. O'Connell 0-2, J. Rabbitte 0-1, C. O'Malley 0-1)

St. Peter's, Wexford, Croke Cup Champions, 1967.
Back row, left to right: Mogue Doyle, John Quigley, Larry Harney, Laurence Kehoe, Tom Royce, Liam O'Loughlin, Michael Nolan, Jim Quigley.
Front row, left to right: Watty Ffrench, Martin Casey, John Murphy, Martin Quigley, Larry Byrne, Paddy Breen, Paddy Bernie (capt), Peter Murphy.
(Photograph courtesy of Alan Aherne and Kevin Kehoe, authors of
Power and Glory, The story of Gaelic Games in St. Peter's College, Wexford)

1967 – ALL-IRELAND FINAL
23 April 1967, Portlaoise
Referee: John Moloney (Tipperary)

St. Peter's, Wexford 5-13

Laurence Kehoe
(Wexford)

Jim Quigley
(Wexford)

Mogue Doyle
(Wexford)

Paddy Breen
(Wexford)

Larry Harney
(Wexford)

John Quigley
(Wexford) (0-1)

Larry Byrne
(Wexford)

Michael Nolan
(Kildare)

Liam O'Loughlin
(Wicklow) (1-1)

Peter Murphy
(Wexford) (0-4)

Tom Royce
(Wexford) (2-1)

Paddy Bernie (*capt*)
(Wexford) (1-4)

John Murphy
(Wexford)

Martin Casey
(Kerry/Wexford) (0-1)

Martin Quigley
(Wexford) (1-1)

Limerick CBS 5-13

Tony Fitzgerald
(Limerick)

Alo Flannery
(Limerick)

Pat Hartigan
(Limerick)

Davy Tuohy
(Limerick)

Gerry McKeown
(Limerick)

Sean Foley
(Limerick)

Christy Campbell
(Limerick)

Pat McCarthy (*capt*)
(Limerick) (0-1)

Michael Hanley
(Limerick) (0-1)

Sean Condon
(Limerick) (0-1)

Mattie Grace
(Limerick)(1-1)

Richie Grace
(Limerick) (2-6)

Conor Cregan
(Limerick) (0-1)

Willie O'Connor
(Limerick) (1-2)

Sean Burke
(Limerick) (1-0)

Sub: Gerard Quinn (Limerick) (for Campbell).

1967 – ALL-IRELAND FINAL (REPLAY)
7 May 1967, Croke Park
Referee: John Moloney (Tipperary)

St. Peter's, Wexford 5-11

Laurence Kehoe
(Wexford)

Jim Quigley
(Wexford)

Mogue Doyle
(Wexford)

Paddy Breen
(Wexford)

Larry Byrne
(Wexford)

John Quigley
(Wexford)

Larry Harney
(Wexford)

Michael Nolan
(Kildare)

Tom Royce
(Wexford) (1-4)

Peter Murphy
(Wexford) (1-1)

Martin Quigley
(Wexford) (1-0)

Paddy Bernie (*capt*)
(Wexford) (0-4)

John Murphy
(Wexford) (1-1)

Liam O'Loughlin
(Wicklow) (1-0)

Martin Casey
(Kerry/Wexford) (0-1)

Limerick CBS 3-6

Tony Fitzgerald
(Limerick)

Alo Flannery
(Limerick)

Pat Hartigan
(Limerick)

Davy Tuohy
(Limerick)

Gerry McKeown
(Limerick)

Sean Foley
(Limerick)

Christy Campbell
(Limerick)

Pat McCarthy (*capt*)
(Limerick) (0-1)

Michael Hanley
(Limerick)

Sean Condon
(Limerick) (1-0)

Mattie Grace
(Limerick) (1-0)

Richie Grace
(Limerick) (1-4)

Conor Cregan
(Limerick)

Willie O'Connor
(Limerick) (0-1)

Sean Burke
(Limerick)

Sub: Liam Minihan (Limerick) (for Cregan)

Paddy Bernie

Despite the fact that the school only won its first Leinster senior hurling 'A' title in 1960, the rest of the 'swinging sixties' proved to be a very successful period for St. Peter's, Wexford, with the Croke Cup making its way to Summerhill for the second time in 1967. The winning captain, a mere eight months after he lifted the Irish Press Cup, was Paddy Bernie.

Paddy Bernie was brought up in the parish of Ferns which he describes as "a GAA stronghold", where "lots of hurling and football" was played. Paddy's late father, Mick, played for Wexford and Paddy describes him as "a Gaelic games fanatic". Paddy recalls that a photograph of his father playing a football match against Westmeath was regularly shown (only to Westmeath people!) in the house where he and his brothers grew up. As Paddy was from Ferns, going to secondary school in St. Peter's College, Wexford was not a natural progression. "At the time, there was no secondary school where I lived. Lads used to have to ride on the bikes to Enniscorthy and mostly that's what lads my age were doing. I suppose my father had a few pounds and could afford to send us as boarders to St. Peters, and that's why we ended up down in Wexford," he explains.

When Paddy entered St. Peter's in September 1962, Vinny Staples and Conor O'Rafferty were just two of the star hurlers in the school. Paddy also recalls the reputations of players like Dan Quigley and Mick Kinsella, who were part of the first St. Peter's team to win the Croke Cup in 1962.

Paddy was part of a "very good juvenile team" which won the Leinster title in 1963, before going on to win a Leinster junior title in 1965. These teams formed the backbone of the side that won the senior All-Ireland crown in 1967. "The juvenile team was so good at the time that most of them made the senior team in their second year (1964) and got to the All-Ireland final against Limerick. I think we didn't do too badly against a strong Limerick team," says Paddy, who has vivid memories of the captain of that Limerick CBS team. "I don't think I had seen a hurler like Eamon Cregan at the time. He could do anything, left or right. He was a massive player." The fact that a young and inexperienced St. Peter's team reached the All-Ireland final in 1964 (with Paddy featuring at right half forward), and performed creditably in the decider, rose expectations of further success in the school. However, age-old rivals, St. Kieran's proved to be the spoilsports in the Leinster finals in the two ensuing seasons, winning by two and five points in 1965 and 1966 respectively.

Paddy was among those who made the speedy graduation from the juvenile to the senior team, but he was slightly surprised to be chosen as senior captain for the 1966/67 campaign. "John Quigley was a brilliant player and he would probably have been expected to be the captain of the hurling team, but he was appointed captain of the football team. I suppose it was a great honour for me because

Quigley was a great player. I had captained the Wexford minor hurling team to win the All-Ireland in September 1966 and I think on the strength of that I was offered the job."

St. Peter's only had to win two matches to win the Leinster title in 1967. They began their campaign on February 12th in Wexford, easily defeating town rivals, Wexford CBS 6-12 to 2-2. Paddy scored 1-3 in that game, a scoring feat he matched in a memorable victory (3-10 to 4-5) over St. Kieran's, Kilkenny in the final in Carlow on March 19th. "Any games we ever had with Kieran's were always close, tough matches that time. They were always the toughest to play. I don't know what way they were coached, but Kilkenny teams are similar today. They have their homework done," Paddy feels.

Having secured their fourth Leinster senior title, the Wexford school's thoughts turned to launching an assault on All-Ireland honours but Paddy remembers there were some doubts about the team's capacity to make the necessary step-up. "Even though there were plenty of good players on the team, there were a few weak spots, we thought." Paddy believes the contribution of two of the non-Wexford players, Martin Casey from Kerry and Liam O'Loughlin from Wicklow, helped to overcome any perceived weaknesses. Liam was regarded as "more of a footballer", but Paddy felt the Wicklow native played a vital role in the team's ultimate success. The All-Ireland semi-final against St Mary's, Belfast was a very one-sided affair as St. Peter's cruised to a 7-12 to 1-3 win. "To be honest, we could have beaten them by as much again," says Paddy. "There were lads taken off and other lads given a chance when the game was won."

The build-up to the All-Ireland final against old rivals, Limerick CBS understandably generated plenty of "buzz and excitement". "The players got special treatment. It was a good time to be playing on the senior team. They did look after us," Paddy reflects. Portlaoise was the venue for the All-Ireland final. The game had all the hallmarks of a classic, with the sides finishing level on a scoreline of 5-13 each. "It was a great game and I remember

there were some great displays by both sides," Paddy says.

However, his abiding memory is "thinking that the game was finished", until Martin Quigley came to the Wexford side's rescue with an equalising goal in the dying moments of the game. Indeed, the 'Irish Independent' report refers to Quigley's last-ditch goal as giving St. Peter's "the extra chance they richly deserved". Paddy felt that the desire of the St. Peter's players to maintain the "winning feeling" they had cultivated was vital in the team's spirited comeback.

The teams had the honour of playing in Croke Park in the replay, which was staged on May 7th as a curtain-raiser to the Wexford-Limerick National Hurling League semi-final. The replay was, in Paddy's words, "a different match totally", with Peter's emerging convincing winners on a scoreline of 5-11 to 3-6. "From almost the start of the game, we were in control. We were sort of easing down at the end, that's the way I felt. Limerick weren't the same outfit at all." The 'Irish Independent' report praised St. Peter's for "displaying energy in abundance, coupled with the ability to pick off scores from long range". They led by 3-4 to 0-4 at the interval and a further goal, within 90 seconds of the resumption, effectively ended the game as a contest.

The 'Irish Independent' staff reporter felt that most of the damage came from an in-form half forward line of Peter Murphy, Martin Quigley and Paddy himself, who chipped in with four points as well as playing a part in many other scores. Paddy's own particular highlights of the replay were the "excellent performances" of Larry Byrne at wing back, Michael Nolan at midfield and Tom Royce in attack. As for the dreaded acceptance speech on receiving the Croke Cup, Paddy quips, "I still know it off by heart like the 'Our Father'! Wexford played on the same day and there was a big crowd in Croke Park and that would have added to the occasion. I can remember people congratulating us and shaking hands with us afterwards. We had to show off the cup to the lads on the 'far side' (the student priests in the seminary in St. Peter's), whom we weren't allowed to talk to at the time.

They were equally enthusiastic and they enjoyed the occasion," Paddy recalls.

Over the years, St. Peter's have had a very impressive record in replays and Paddy feels that this was largely down to their coach, Ned Power. "We didn't lose too many replays that he was involved in because he was able to read the game and learn the weaknesses of the opposing team." Ned Power was a great influence. I think one of his greatest attributes was the fact that he could get 15 minds thinking and working along the same lines. He tried to get that message across to any team he was ever involved in. Some people took it on board and some didn't. Whenever it was taken on board, it was very successful." Paddy also fondly remembers the contribution of Fr Paddy Curtis, who gave encouragement to the players that was "second to none" and the "infectious enthusiasm" (for hurling particularly) of Tony O'Connor from Galway (later Fr Tony, and a brother of Bernie, of Galway fame) and Sligo man Vincent Forde (mainly for the big ball game). In St. Peter's at that time, the two coaches (Ned Power and Fr Paddy Curtis), the team captain, vice-captain (Tom Royce in 1967) and the two prefects all had a say in picking the team.

Within a few weeks of winning the Croke Cup, the small matter of sitting the Leaving Cert had to be faced and Paddy recalls that knuckling down to the books represented an "anti-climax" following the high of All-Ireland success at Croke Park. Paddy then became more acquainted with the 'far side' as he went on to study in the seminary. "I was very much aware of the All-Ireland the following year (when Wexford won the Liam McCarthy Cup) and I was at the match, one of the first times we were allowed to go to anything like that. The following year, our club, Ferns St. Aidan's, got to the county final for the first time ever and I would have played on the team in the summer time. Then when I went back to the seminary, I wasn't allowed out for any of those matches." After his days in St. Peter's were over, Paddy played hurling for the Wexford Under-21 team and he represented the county in senior football. The Ferns man was called on to the senior hurling panel in 1977 and he

claims to have been "the last Wexford man to receive a Leinster medal until 1996. The only reason for that was I was a sub on the team in 1977. When the presentation was made they forgot I was on the panel, but I chased up a medal!" Paddy explains.

Although he moved to Gorey in 1974 (a town in which he still resides), the only club he played hurling with was Ferns St. Aidan's. He won a couple of intermediate championship medals but a senior county title eluded him. Paddy recalls getting "a smack of a hurl across the side of the face" in a first round club championship match in 1978. That incident hastened the end of Paddy's hurling career which, he admits, was drawing to a close in any case. As hurling commitments became less demanding, Paddy found the time to play tennis, squash and golf, while he played rugby for both Enniscorthy and Gorey as a full back.

Sadly, Paddy's father died at the age of 52 in 1970, just three years after Paddy captained St. Peter's to the All-Ireland title. "I suppose it had an influence on my playing career because when he died I took over the family business, even though I was in St. Peter's in the seminary at the time." Paddy's grandfather started P Bernie & Son in 1888 and the building and decorating business is still going strong under Paddy's direction to this day. He is married to Ann (née Kelly) from Borris, Co. Carlow and the couple have three children. Catherine is the eldest and she works as an accountant with IIB Bank in Dublin. Michael works for Heineken, while the youngest, Ann Marie, is a pharmacist.

Paddy still retains an interest in the sporting fortunes of St. Peter's although he has found it difficult to attend many of their games. He has kept in touch with many members of the 1967 team on "a casual basis", although a formal reunion of the team has never taken place. After winning the All-Ireland title in 1968 (Paddy's brother, Dave, was a member of that team), Wexford hurling endured some lean times and Paddy feels the "lack of continuation of the way Ned Power was thinking" was the county's "biggest downfall of all". Although Power was involved with

Wexford in the 1970s, Paddy says "his influence would have been lessened" by the strength of the clubs in the county. "All Wexford teams, without him, had to be twice as good as Kilkenny to beat them because of the type of system they played to," he comments. Tony Doran quite rightly has a special place in the hearts of Wexford hurling followers and Paddy acknowledges that he was a "great player".

However, Paddy feels Doran's exceptional prowess under the high ball caused a fixation in Wexford with route-one hurling, when a more subtle approach may have borne more fruit. "Tony Doran would get the ball regardless of what way it came in. Once Tony Doran was gone, these high balls were the backs' delight," Paddy concludes.

While Paddy Bernie never became an established senior inter-county hurler, his interest in Wexford's fortunes never waned and he continues to be a deep thinker about the game he loves. This love of the ancient game was undoubtedly nurtured in his years in St. Peter's during their golden era of the 1960s.

1968 – ALL-IRELAND SEMI-FINAL
7 April 1968, Croke Park

St. Peter's, Wexford 4-14
(W. French 1-5, J. Kavanagh 1-2, P. Lawless 1-2, M. Byrne 1-0,
M. Casey 0-2, A. Kavanagh 0-1, M. Quigley 0-1, P. Kennedy 0-1)

St. Joseph's, Garbally 2-5
(T. Frehill 1-3, N. Kilroy 1-0, S. Silke 0-1, J. Lyons 0-1)

St. Peter's, Wexford, Croke Cup Champions, 1968.
Back row, left to right: Larry Harney, Declan O'Brien, Anthony Shiggins, Anthony Harte,
David Power, Michael Murphy, Seamus Kane, Aidan Kerrigan, Andy Kavanagh,
Denis Kinsella, Willie Doyle.
Front row, left to right: Watty Ffrench, Martin Byrne, Phil Kennedy, Martin Quigley, Martin Casey,
Larry Byrne, Paddy Breen (capt), Joe Kavanagh, Peter Lawless, Jim Quigley.
*(Photograph courtesy of Alan Aherne and Kevin Kehoe, authors of
Power and Glory, The story of Gaelic Games in St. Peter's College, Wexford)*

1968 – ALL-IRELAND FINAL
12 May 1968, Clonmel
Referee: John Moloney (Tipperary)

St. Peter's, Wexford 4-3

Denis Kinsella
(Wexford)

Paddy Breen (*capt*)   **Jim Quigley**   **Michael Murphy**
(Wexford)   (Wexford)   (Wexford)

Larry Harney   **Larry Byrne**   **Aidan Kerrigan**
(Wexford)   (Wexford)   (Wexford)

Martin Casey   **Phil Kennedy**
(Wexford) (1-2)   (Wexford)

Joe Kavanagh   **Martin Quigley**   **Watty Ffrench**
(Wexford) (1-0)   (Wexford) (0-1)   (Wexford)

Declan O'Brien   **Peter Lawless**   **Martin Byrne**
(Wexford) (1-0)   (Wexford)   (Wexford) (1-0)

Sub: Anthony Harte (Wexford) (for Lawless).

Coláiste Chríost Rí, Cork 3-6

Jim Cremin
(Cork)

Fergus Cronin   **Mick Bohane**   **Sean McCarthy**
(Cork)   (Cork)   (Cork)

Ned Callanan   **Brendan Cummins (*capt*)**   **Martin Doherty**
(Cork) (1-0)   (Cork)   (Cork)

Der Cogan   **Dan Callanan**
(Cork)   (Cork) (2-4)

Billy Cogan   **Seamus Looney**   **Brian O'Loughlin**
(Cork)   (Cork)   (Cork)

Eamon Fitzpatrick   **Pat Mackey**   **Kevin Doherty**
(Cork)   (Cork) (0-2)   (Cork)

Sub: Mick McCarthy (Cork) (for K. Doherty).

1968 – ALL-IRELAND FINAL (REPLAY)
19 May 1968, Croke Park
Referee: John Moloney (Tipperary)

St. Peter's, Wexford 5-10

Denis Kinsella
(Wexford)

Paddy Breen (*capt*)   **Jim Quigley**   **Michael Murphy**
(Wexford)   (Wexford)   (Wexford)

Larry Harney   **Larry Byrne**   **Aidan Kerrigan**
(Wexford)   (Wexford)   (Wexford)

Martin Casey   **Phil Kennedy**
(Wexford) (1-2)   (Wexford)

Martin Byrne   **Martin Quigley**   **Watty Ffrench**
(Wexford) (1-1)   (Wexford) (1-5)   (Wexford) (0-1)

Joe Kavanagh   **Seamus Kane**   **Declan O'Brien**
(Wexford) (0-1)   (Wexford)   (Wexford) (2-0)

Coláiste Chríost Rí, Cork 4-5

Jim Cremin
(Cork)

Fergus Cronin   **Mick Bohane**   **Sean McCarthy**
(Cork)   (Cork)   (Cork)

Brian Murphy   **Brendan Cummins (*capt*)**   **Martin Doherty**
(Cork)   (Cork)   (Cork)

Der Cogan   **Dan Callanan**
(Cork)   (Cork) (0-4)

Billy Cogan   **Seamus Looney**   **Brian O'Loughlin**
(Cork)   (Cork) (1-0)   (Cork)

Eamon Fitzpatrick   **Ned Callanan**   **Pat Mackey**
(Cork) (2-0)   (Cork) (1-0)   (Cork) (0-1)

Paddy Breen

The year of 1968 was probably the greatest ever in the history of Wexford GAA and it was also a year to cherish for Paddy Breen.

He was one of five members of the 1967 All-Ireland winning St. Peter's team who also lined out on the starting team for the 1968 final, when he had the honour of captaining the Wexford college when it won two Croke Cups in-a-row, only the second school to do so.

Paddy was one of a family of seven (two sisters and four brothers) who grew up in the parish of Horeswood which, he says, "wasn't very renowned for hurling or football". As Paddy puts it, "we always had a team here but we never seemed to get anywhere." However, Paddy's father, Jimmy won a county championship medal with the local club. It wasn't for football or hurling reasons that Paddy and his brothers went to school in St. Peter's. Paddy recalls it had more to do with the advice of the local parish priest. He remembers playing hurling in primary school, but he states that "it wasn't organised hurling". "We were farmers so local lads would meet in our field and play 7-a-side or 5-a-side games. When we went to St. Peter's, we started playing with the local parish," says Paddy, adding that parish leagues in the area "used to be hot and heavy".

When Paddy entered St. Peter's there was still a warm afterglow from the school's first All-Ireland success in 1962 but, in Paddy's recollection, this "buzz" soon wore off. Having won a Leinster junior title in his third year in the school, Paddy graduated to the senior team the following year and was a valuable member of the side which regained the Croke Cup after a five-year wait in 1967. In terms of promoting hurling in St. Peter's, Ned Power and Fr Paddy Curtis are the two figures who stand out in Paddy's mind, and he describes Power as his "mentor". A lay teacher in the school and a native of Kilkenny, Ned's passion for hurling had a major influence on innumerable young players who entered the Wexford college. "He was married to the hurling," Paddy jokes. Two student priests from the seminary in St. Peter's would also be involved in training the senior team and, in Paddy's view, they played a crucial role. "They were the men that pushed us and then Ned took over," he says. Ned placed considerable emphasis on training and the gym. He was "big into that end of things", Paddy recalls.

Paddy doesn't remember exactly when he was awarded the honour of captaincy for the 1967/68 campaign but, interestingly, he recalls the decision caused resentment, which continued to linger many years later. "I don't know when I was appointed to that position. To this day, I think some people resent the fact that I was captain." St. Peter's had a custom whereby the captain of the senior team would help out with the training of the juniors. This was one of the rules set down by legendary coach, Ned Power, but it was not a task for the faint-hearted. "You had to get all the junior teams out training as well. That was part of the role; we had to get them out. It was a tough old job," recalls Paddy. He remembers previous senior captains "going through the locker rooms with the hurl in the hand", and it was not unusual to witness "a few smacks of the hurl" being applied. Young players were, occasionally, quite literally frightened out on to the training field. "There was an element of that in it, I suppose, forcing fellas to go out. We weren't, of course, as ruthless as the fellas before us," Paddy laughs.

St. Peter's began their attempt to regain the Leinster crown with a facile 8-9 to 1-3 win over Kilkenny CBS in New Ross on February 11th. Belcamp OMI provided the opposition in the Leinster semi-final in Carlow, in a match that was played on St. Patrick's Day. St. Peter's led 5-4 to 0-1 at half-time but, remarkably, the Dublin side managed to score six goals in the second half. However, St. Peter's survived the onslaught to claim a 6-10 to 6-2 victory. The fact that St. Peter's defeated their great rivals from Kilkenny, St. Kieran's, in the Leinster final made victory all the sweeter a week later. It was a hard-earned win in Croke Park, with a second-half goal by Martin Casey proving crucial in the Wexford side's one-point victory (2-4 to 0-9). The All-Ireland semi-final took place in Portlaoise on April 7th, when St. Peter's faced St. Joseph's, Garbally. The Leinster champions convincingly dismissed the Ballinasloe side's challenge on a 4-14 to 2-5 scoreline.

Paddy himself was not conscious of the fact that St. Peter's All-Ireland final opponents, Coláiste Chríost Rí from Cork, were going for a unique double of All-Ireland colleges football and hurling titles. "I was never aware of it, but then again I wasn't deeply into the GAA as such," he says. "There were things going on in the college that I didn't know about. We were on the field most of the time, outside hurling and then smoking. We were the first senior class to get smoking privileges." As for meals, Paddy doesn't recall much by way of special treatment, although "raw eggs and oranges" were doled out in the hope of enhancing players' performances. Having been part of the All-Ireland success in 1967, Paddy already had considerable experience under his belt. However, even in 1968, he feels that the

importance of the All-Ireland final occasion was somewhat lost on him. "For some reason or other, it didn't seem to register that we were in an All-Ireland, the importance of it. I never had any speech made for the day or anything," he recalls. In common with the previous year, a replay would be required before St. Peter's were crowned All-Ireland champions in 1968. Martin Casey was the Wexford boys' saviour in the drawn game, his late goal forcing a 4-3 to 3-6 draw in Clonmel. While acknowledging that the game ended in "a welter of excitement", the 'Irish Independent' report was less than complimentary about the overall game. Tom O'Riordan wrote, "while there was an abundance of enthusiasm and stout-hearted effort from both sides, as a spectacle the final fell well below expectations."

Croke Park was the venue for the replay and St. Peter's triumphed (5-10 to 4-5) in a thrilling encounter. This time, the 'Irish Independent' applauded the contestants for their "copybook display". In his match report this time, Tom O'Riordan hailed the performances of Martin Casey, Phil Kennedy, Aidan Kerrigan and Martin Quigley, while the display of centre-back Larry Byrne was deemed so impressive that he was predicted to command a place on the Wexford senior county team "in the very near future". Despite trailing by 1-2 to 4-0 at the end of the first quarter, St. Peter's led at the break by a point (3-5 to 4-1), before pulling away in the second half. Paddy vividly remembers the presentation of the Croke Cup and it appears that it was far more nerve-wracking than the match itself. "The match was over and, all of a sudden, we had won an All-Ireland and I was supposed to be captain. All these officials came along and tried to get me off the field. I looked around and wondered 'how am I going to make a speech?' I could see our Irish teacher, Jim Golden, in the distance but I couldn't get near him. I was being hustled off the field and up to the stand. I didn't know what to do, I didn't know where to go and I felt like going through the ground. I made a speech and I thanked everyone, did the usual thing, three cheers or whatever. What way I said it, I don't know, but back at the college a few days afterwards, the Irish teacher hardly spoke to me!"

The county of Wexford itself completed a famous double in September 1968, when the Slaneysiders won All-Ireland senior and minor hurling titles. Indeed, Wexford's senior camogie team got in on the act by also winning the All-Ireland title that year. Four former St. Peter's pupils were part of the Wexford senior team in 1968 while, on the same day, Paddy Breen won an All-Ireland minor medal. However, strangely enough for such a prominent underage player, Paddy's hurling career was over by the time he was 19. After finishing school in St. Peter's, Paddy worked on the family farm for about eight months. He then began to look for a job in the local ESB power station. "I was hanging around for that, then I went into the building game with a local builder, Matty Wallace, while waiting on my job in the power station and I'm still waiting on it," he jokes. Paddy worked with Matty Wallace for nine years but eventually went out on his own. Nowadays, he is one of three partners who run GMB Construction, a company involved in civil engineering and property development projects. While Paddy didn't take up any other sports after quitting hurling, he likes to engage in "physical work" at the weekends and he enjoys gardening.

Paddy is married to Philomena (née Cummins), whose brother used to be heavily involved in Horeswood GAA and they live in Campile. The couple have three children, two girls and one boy. Elizabeth graduated from UCD with a science degree last year and is now pursuing further studies. The second eldest, James (19), is a mechanical engineering student in Cork IT and is very interested in music. The youngest, Bríd, is a second year student in Holy Faith Convent in New Ross.

Paddy admits that he has not kept in touch with many of his team-mates from 1968, and that there are some players he has actually not even seen since their days in St. Peter's, as there has never been a reunion of the boys of '68. While Paddy has kept an eye out for St. Peter's results over the years, finding the time to attend games has often proved difficult. Ironically, he now has close ties with one of St. Peter's arch-rivals on the sporting field, Good Counsel, New Ross. He has been on the Board of Management of Good Counsel for the past seven years, having been first elected as a parent representative.

In 1961, a school uniform was introduced for students of St. Peter's College and a school crest was designed. Fr Thomas Rossiter, the then president of St. Peter's, decided upon the Latin motto 'Disce prodesse', which is translated as, 'Learn to be useful'. During his time playing hurling for St. Peter's, that was certainly a maxim that Paddy Breen and his hurling colleagues lived up to in the school's glorious era in the late 1960s.

1969 – ALL-IRELAND SEMI-FINAL
20 April 1969, Thurles

St. Finbarr's, Farranferris 9-10
(F. O'Brien 3-2, K. O'Driscoll 3-0, P. Lucey 1-2, T. Crowley 1-1, D. J. Collins 0-3, J. Hegarty 1-0, N.Crowley 0-2))

Our Lady's, Gort 3-1
(B. Brennan 2-0, M. Donoghue 1-0, M. O'Connor 0-1)

St. Finbarr's, Farranferris, Croke Cup Champions, 1969.
Back row, left to right: Gerry Hennessy, Teddy O'Donovan, Kieran O'Driscoll, Pat Lucey,
Donal G. Collins.
Middle row, left to right: Jerry O'Sullivan, Jimmy Hegarty, Ger O'Keeffe, Tim Crowley,
Noel Crowley, Denis Ryan.
Front row, left to right: Fr Michael O'Brien, Dominic Holly, Frank O'Brien,
Donal J. Collins (capt), Bishop Cornelius Lucey, Tony Whooley, Kevin Murray,
Dr Carthach McCarthy.
(Photograph courtesy of Tim Horgan, author of Farna's Hurling Story)

1969 – ALL-IRELAND FINAL
27 April 1969, Thurles
Referee: John Moloney (Tipperary)

St. Finbarr's, Farranferris 5-15

Gerry Hennessy
(Cork)

Dominic Holly   **Teddy O'Donovan**   **Jerry O'Sullivan**
(Cork)   (Cork)   (Cork)

Ger O'Keeffe   **Tony Whooley**   **Kevin Murray**
(Cork)   (Cork)   (Cork)

Noel Crowley   **Donal G. Collins**
(Cork)   (Cork)

Kieran O'Driscoll   **Tim Crowley**   **Donal J. Collins** (*capt*)
(Cork)   (Cork) (0-6)   (Cork) (0-5)

Jimmy Hegarty   **Frank O'Brien**   **Pat Lucey**
(Cork) (1-0)   (Cork) (4-2)   (Cork) (0-2)

St. Kieran's, Kilkenny 2-1

Brendan Kennedy
(Tipperary)

John Brophy   **Timmy Cleary**   **Joe Brennan**
(Kilkenny)   (Tipperary)   (Kilkenny)

Gerry McCarthy (*capt*)   **Dick O'Shea**   **John Prendergast**
(Kilkenny)   (Kilkenny)   (Kilkenny) (1-1)

John Mahon   **Mick O'Shea**
(Laois) (1-0)   (Kilkenny)

Paddy Bollard   **Gerry Gleeson**   **Tom Barry**
(Kilkenny)   (Laois)   (Kilkenny)

Pat Kearney   **Mick Gannon**   **Michael Dillon**
(Kilkenny)   (Kilkenny)   (Kilkenny)

Sub: Joe Brennan (Kilkenny) (for Cleary),

Donal Collins

In Tim Horgan's excellent book *Farna's Hurling Story*, 1969 is referred to as the 'Year of Glory', which is hardly surprising considering that St. Finbarr's, Farranferris won all before them that year. However, the highlights were the Harty and Croke Cup victories under the captaincy of Donal Collins.

Donal is the eldest of eight children (seven boys and one girl) born to Daniel and Margaret Collins. He was reared on the family farm in Aghilles and, from the outset, his late father, who excelled as a pole vaulter and was a clever footballer, instilled a love of sport in him. He recalls "gobbling up stories about Christy Ring" from his father. Five of the Collins boys – Dinty, Bernard, Christy, Anthony and Vincent went to Skibbereen Technical School, while the other two, Donal and Francis, attended Farranferris where they enjoyed great success with the Harty teams and later became Cork hurlers. Donal admits that he had played little or no hurling before he came to Farna. "There was a bit of junior hurling played in Skibbereen, but football was the only game played in Castlehaven. We went to Ballyhillow school in Leap where our teacher, Peter Williams, encouraged us to play football and indeed, hurling. In Castlehaven school, Malachy O'Sullivan did the same and the combined Leap and 'Haven teams won a couple of schools competitions against Timoleague. It wasn't until I went to Farna that I got involved in hurling in a big way, just like Francis did afterwards and our first

cousin, Michael Dineen from Ballydehob. The three of us went on to play with Farna, Blackrock and Cork."

Donal came to Farna as a boarder from Castlehaven in September 1964, just over a year after the school had won its first Croke Cup. He confesses that few of his classmates in Farna had ever heard of Castlehaven, and even fewer were aware that a GAA club actually existed in the West Cork outpost. He jokes that he was sent to St. Finbarr's as "it was a question of getting rid of some of us". Looking back, over 40 years later, he wonders "if it wasn't for the hurling, would I have stuck it at all", referring to the often lonely and harsh regime prevalent in boarding schools in those days.

"Fr Donal Linehan was the man who taught us to play hurling as soon as we entered Farranferris, and those of us who made the grade later came under the guidance of Fr Michael O'Brien. Both men did a lot for the game." Donal, who looked up to the likes of Tim Joe Coakley, John Hennessy, Donal McCarthy, Paddy Crowley and Noel Dunne ("he once didn't give Eamon Grimes a puck in a Harty game"), Brian Tobin, Dan O'Brien and Frank Long, quickly picked up the skills of the game. So quickly, in fact, that he received the Hurler of the Year award in his first year at Farna. In second year, he won a White Cup medal and that team would form the nucleus of the great 1969 side. He made the Harty team in 1967, but despite receiving some useful advice from the legendary Christy Ring ("he was a God to us"), the year ended in disappointment for Farna when they lost the final to Limerick CBS by 1-5 to 4-9. "It was a step too far for what was a young Farna team and we were overawed by the occasion," Donal reflects. There was some consolation gained from winning the Callaghan Cup, though, with Donal grabbing 2-3 in the final against North Mon.

Two years later, a stronger and more mature Farna team returned to the big stage. Donal was honoured to be appointed captain, having "got wind of it" during the summer holidays. "I would give the odd word here or there, but I wasn't one for great motivational speeches. I would leave that to others," he recalls modestly. By then, Fr Michael O'Brien had become the great driving force behind the team and revenge was sweet when they beat Limerick CBS well in the opening round of the Harty Cup. To this day, Donal can rhyme off the date of that game - October 20th 1968. Indeed, he was in the wars that day and needed "three or four stitches" to treat a head wound. In their next outing at Buttevant, Farranferris had a very comfortable win over Thurles CBS. They then beat St. Colman's, Fermoy by four points ("we were complacent and relieved to get out of it that day") and qualified to meet holders Coláiste Chríost Rí in the first ever all-Cork Harty Cup final.

Not surprisingly, the game created enormous interest in the city, but heavy rain saw it postponed by a week. When it eventually took place at the old Athletic Grounds, it proved to be one of the great Harty Cup deciders. "Because it was the first time two Cork teams met in the final, there was unbelievable hype and I couldn't study for a fortnight beforehand," Donal remembers. "An unplayable pitch meant that it couldn't be played the first day, so the game was put on as part of a double-header with the football final between St. Brendan's and Coláiste Iosagáin the following Sunday. There must have been in excess of 20,000 supporters at the final and we knew that we would need to improve on our semi-final performance." As it happened, Farna beat Chríost Rí by 6-6 to 3-7, but it was only in the closing ten minutes that they managed to put

daylight between themselves and the holders, whose fans had been chanting, 'we are the champions'. The sides were level at 1-4 apiece at the interval and, according to Donal who feels he played badly in the opening half an hour, a few reassuring words from Christy Ring in the dressing room at half-time did the trick for Farranferris.

"There was fierce tension during the first half and you could see how tense both Fr O'Brien and Dr McCarthy were when we went in at half-time. But 'Ringie' was very calm about the whole thing. He told us we were playing well and said we would win because we were playing into the Blackrock goal in the second half. He said we'd get a rake of goals and he was right. I scored a goal from a '21' and Tim Crowley scored another to put us out of sight. It was a huge thing to win the Harty - it has such a great tradition - and anything we won after that would have been looked upon as a bonus." Indeed, Donal can recall almost every puck of the ball in the Harty final some 37 years later.

Following their successful Harty Cup campaign, Farna enjoyed two easy victories in the All-Ireland series. "We physically overpowered Gort in the All-Ireland semi-final and had a surprisingly comfortable win over St. Kieran's in the final. We had beaten them in a challenge match earlier in the year, but not by the same margin we beat them by in the All-Ireland," Donal recalls.

Farranferris overcame St. Kieran's by a margin of 23 points in a woefully one-sided Croke Cup decider at Thurles. Dominant in every facet of the play, Farna steamrolled their Kilkenny opponents and their diminutive full forward Frank O'Brien had a day to remember when helping himself to 4-2. "That was the last chance for a lot of us and we were determined to finish our time in Farna as All-Ireland champions. The majority of us were around the 18 mark and we were physically bigger than most of the teams we played." The 'Irish Independent' reckoned that Farna gave "a fluent display of controlled hurling", adding that, "seldom has a college team possessed so many long and clean strikers of the ball". Leading by 2-6 to 1-1 at the interval, wind-assisted Farna pulled away at their ease on the change of ends.

Donal remembers Fr O'Brien as being a "great motivator and disciplinarian, who was ahead of his time. He instilled tremendous belief in us. He told us we were tougher than the other teams because we were basically a bunch of lads from the country, and we believed him. I think he modelled our style of hurling on Limerick CBS. He was a great believer in wing to wing play and didn't advocate the more traditional direct style of hurling." Donal actually enjoyed the Croke Cup final, claiming that, "my nerves were gone after the Harty final". His most vivid post-match memory is of emulating his fellow Corkonian, Noel Cantwell, after Manchester United's FA Cup final win six years earlier, by throwing the lid of the Croke Cup in the air, much to the horror of the watching staff from Farna!

After leaving Farranferris, Donal won two All-Ireland Under-21 medals with Cork as well as National League and Munster championship honours with the county seniors in 1972, coming on as a sub in the All-Ireland defeat by Kilkenny. With his adopted Blackrock, he won five county championships and three All-Ireland club souvenirs in 1972, 1974 and 1979. Donal often regrets not having had a longer inter-county career with Cork. "I probably didn't have the self-belief and didn't look after myself enough. That's a big regret of mine," he concedes.

Donal's job with Hibernian Insurance took him to Kilkenny in 1980 where he won a county championship with James Stephens in 1981 and a then record fourth All-Ireland club medal the following year, coming on as a sub when Mount Sion were defeated in the decider. After overcoming an eye injury, sustained while playing for 'The Village', he retired in 1984 at the age of 34. Donal spent 12 years on Noreside, during which time Kilkenny beat Cork in three All-Ireland senior finals and he jokingly remembers having to endure "some dreadful slagging." After returning to Cork, Donal got involved with Blackrock again and served as a selector under Fr O'Brien for a period in the mid-1990s. He became a Cork selector in 2003 when the Rebels were beaten once again by Kilkenny in the All-Ireland final. "I have a very bad record against Kilkenny," he concedes, while adding that he "had great friends there and met lovely people." He speaks very highly of Donal O'Grady as a coach. In late 2006, he was re-appointed as a Cork senior selector by Gerald McCarthy.

When Donal led Farranferris to All-Ireland glory in 1969, Castlehaven were a junior 2 club in the South-West division. But in the years that followed, they made remarkable progress and in 1989, their fairytale rise through the ranks was complete when they were crowned Cork senior football champions. The Castlehaven team was captained by former Kildare player Larry Tompkins, who incidentally was 'recruited' for Castlehaven and Cork by Donal's younger brothers Anthony and Vincent in New York.

Donal's younger brother, Francis, himself a Croke Cup winner in 1974, was a member of the winning 'Haven team and how fitting it was, given the huge role the Collins family had played in transforming the tiny club into a household name. Dan Collins encouraged all his sons to play football and had the pleasure of seeing them feature in many of Castlehaven's groundbreaking successes. Castlehaven won a junior 2 title in 1969, the South-West junior championship in 1973 and the county junior title three years later when five of the Collins boys were involved. Then came the county intermediate championship and the 'Haven's promotion to the senior ranks. With six Collins' brothers playing and one a sub, they reached the county final only to lose to St. Finbarr's. But the 'Haven atoned for that disappointment with their historic success in '89 and have been a force to be reckoned with in senior football ever since. Donal particularly enjoyed playing in 7-a-side competitions with his brothers where they had an unbeaten record over the years, although he modestly confesses that, "I was never much good at football" - this despite having won a Munster SFC 'B' medal in 1969 with Farna.

A keen golfer - he was secretary of Kilkenny Golf Club when domiciled there -

Donal has remained in the insurance business and now works with O'Leary Insurances Ltd in Cork. Very sadly, his wife Evelyn died suddenly last March after 32 years of marriage, much to the distress of Donal and his grown-up children, David (an accountancy student) and Yvonne (a psychologist). David plays for Blackrock, but has had his share of shoulder injury problems.

Donal Collins still keeps in touch with many of his former team-mates and attended a number of school reunions over the years. He regrets the recent closure of his alma mater which gave him so many pleasant sporting memories in the 1960s, culminating in marvellous Harty and Croke Cup triumphs in 1969, many of which games Donal can recall in minute detail.

1970 – ALL-IRELAND SEMI-FINAL
22 March 1970, Birr

Kilkenny CBS 3-7
(J. Giles 1-2, R. Dunne 1-0, W. Young 1-0, T. Neary 0-3, G. Burke 0-1, B. O'Brien 0-1)

Presentation College, Athenry 1-9
(M. Donoghue 1-3, G. Gorley 0-2, F. Burke 0-2, P. Flannery 0-1, G. Holland 0-1)

North Monastery, Cork, Croke Cup Champions, 1970.
Back row, left to right: Oliver Jordan, Harry Kennedy, Derry Sexton, Mick Corbett,
Ger Hanley, Sean Long.
Middle row, left to right: Kieran O'Connor, Frank Coughlan, Dave O'Brien, Donal Buckley,
Tony Radley, Mick O'Mahony, Richie Fitzgerald.
Front row, left to right: Donal O'Grady, Seamie O'Connell, Vivian O'Brien,
Des O'Grady (capt), Tadhg Harris, Joe O'Donovan, Stevie Greene.
(Photograph courtesy of Gerry Kelly and Liam O'Brien, c/o North Monastery, Cork)

1970 – ALL-IRELAND FINAL
26 April 1970, Dungarvan
Referee: John Moloney (Tipperary)

North Monastery, Cork 2-13

Dave O'Brien
(Cork)

Mick O'Mahony
(Cork)

Donal Buckley
(Cork)

Vivian O'Brien
(Cork)

Kieran O'Connor
(Cork)

Tadhg Harris
(Cork)

Des O'Grady (*capt*)
(Cork)

Mick Corbett
(Cork) (0-3)

Stevie Greene
(Cork) (0-3)

Derry Sexton
(Cork) (0-3)

Ger Hanley
(Cork) (2-2)

Frank Coughlan
(Cork) (0-1)

Seamie O'Connell
(Cork) (0-1)

Kilkenny CBS 2-8

Joe Bourke
(Kilkenny)

Pat Grace
(Kilkenny)

Seamus Brophy
(Kilkenny)

Paddy Phelan
(Kilkenny)

Ger Bourke (*capt*)
(Kilkenny)

Tom Gaffney
(Kilkenny) (1-0)

Richard Dunne
(Kilkenny)

Sean McGarry
(Kilkenny) (0-1)

Bill Young
(Kilkenny) (1-1)

Barry O'Brien
(Kilkenny)

Tom Neary
(Kilkenny) (0-2)

Jimmy O'Brien
(Kilkenny) (0-3)

Jimmy Giles
(Kilkenny) (0-1)

Subs: Pat Mulcahy (Kilkenny) (for B.O'Brien), Christy Murray (Kilkenny) (for Young).

Des O'Grady

Des O'Grady felt part of a worthy tradition during his time in North Monastery and captaining the famed Cork hurling nursery to Croke Cup glory in 1970 was one of the proudest moments of his sporting career.

Des grew up on the northside of Cork city in Sarsfield's Terrace, off Blackpool. Even though Des' late father, Jim, lived on the northside, he played with St. Finbarr's on the southside, which was "very unusual at the time." Des, who had three siblings, has early memories of playing hurling with his only brother, Donal and other friends in Bell's Field, at the top of Patrick's Hill. He went to primary school in North Presentation Convent and moved on to North Monastery after making his First Holy Communion. "When we went to the Mon, all the talk was about hurling and more hurling. The Brothers were totally immersed in the game and many of them imposed their own native county style of play," Des recalls. In his youth, Des looked up to close neighbour Michael Ellard, who later became a reporter with the Cork (Irish) Examiner. "We felt it was an honour to play with him as he was a very good hurler. Unfortunately when he left school, he didn't play on for too long because of the job commitments," says Des.

Success with North Mon eluded Des at juvenile and junior level. Other Cork schools like St. Colman's, Fermoy and St. Finbarr's, Farranferris provided tough opposition. In addition, Sullivan's Quay "were coming on the scene" and Coláiste Chríost Rí were "mush-rooming in both hurling and football". The competition in Cork and in Munster as a whole was "very good at the time", Des points out. He was on the Mon's Harty Cup team for three years, but medals didn't come his way until the third of these. He was surprised when chosen as captain of the 1969/70 team. "Brother Barry, who was in charge of hurling in the school at the time, told me before the first match that I was going to be captain. It was a surprise to me certainly and it was probably a surprise to the rest of the lads as well! I was lucky to be picked. It was a great honour, certainly, and I took it very seriously," he says. Having suffered early exits in the previous two years, the Mon's expectations were low when they met Ennis CBS at Charleville in the first round. "It was close enough but we got there, which was a big relief to us because I thought I'd never see the second round of a Harty!" The Mon's next Harty Cup match was a local derby against Sullivan's Quay. "There was a lot of talk about the match beforehand because the Quay had people back repeating the Leaving. They had a very good team," says Des. There was a humorous incident during the game when a Mon supporter bore the brunt of Br Barry's frustration with how things were going. "Br Barry, who was standing on the sideline with a bunch of hurleys, was asked by one of our more enthusiastic supporters, when we were about seven points down, 'will we win Brother?' and he got the hurleys thrown at him!" However, the Mon eventually triumphed after a "tremendous comeback". Having got out of jail, the Mon realised the Harty Cup was now an achievable target. "I think that's where the spark was lit really. That made us as a team." St. Flannan's, Ennis, were North Monastery's opponents in the Harty Cup semi-final in Charleville on March 1st. Joe McKenna, the future Limerick star, was undoubtedly the St. Flannan's dangerman. "We were very much afraid of him," says Des, "and special plans were made to deal with the threat he posed, but our defence was outstanding that day". Des feels the team's high level of fitness was a significant factor in that 0-8 to 1-2 win over St. Flannan's. "We did a lot of physical training. We had trained hard, even over the Christmas holidays. Our fitness definitely told that day. We played a kind of a running game."

Charleville was again the venue for the Harty Cup final against Limerick CBS, surprise winners over St. Colman's in the other semi-final. "There was no stone left unturned when it came to preparation," Des remembers. "Even Christy Ring was brought in to the dressing room at half-time to say a few words to us. That might have made a little difference and given us a bit of an edge. I never felt we were going to lose that match." The Mon won that Munster final 6-8 to 4-7, with a second-half goal from Stevie Greene proving the "turning point". 1969/70 was the first year the All-Ireland colleges hurling championship was played on a 13-a-side basis. Des believes this format suited the Mon. "Playing on a full-sized pitch with 13 left space and we utilised the space. We thought about the kind of team we were going to put out. It actually suited us big time because we didn't have an outstanding full-back and we didn't have an outstanding centre-forward." The Mon tended to move centre-forward Derry Sexton ("a big strong man") to the full-forward position. "That kind of pushed their centre-back back on top of the square which opened it up for our very speedy forwards," Des remarks.

Victory in the Munster final saw the Mon qualify for the All-Ireland decider in Dungarvan against Kilkenny CBS. The Noresiders had narrowly beaten Presentation, Athenry, in the semi-final. "We had beaten them in a challenge earlier in the year and they were a typical Kilkenny team. If you didn't hit the ball fast, you weren't going to get a second chance, as you'd be hooked or blocked," says Des. "Maybe it fell our way that St. Kieran's weren't there, with all their tradition, but certainly Kilkenny CBS still put it up to us that day. I remember it was a dour, hard struggle. It was a kind of dull day. Ger Hanley was our top scorer, he got the two goals and they were vital. Our backs did reasonably well and I remember Kilkenny pushed us all the way, but all through the second half I didn't think we were going to be beaten." Des was conscious of the burden of captaincy in the All-Ireland final and he feels his personal performance suffered as a result. "A lot of the game seemed to bypass me." The 'Irish Independent' described the final as "a disappointing game". The Mon led by a point (1-4 to 0-6) at the interval and while there was very little between the sides in the third quarter, the Cork lads gradually pulled away and they were well in control when Tom Gaffney nabbed a late consolation second goal for the Kilkenny boys.

Des hadn't given any thought to delivering his acceptance speech before the match, but saying the 'cúpla focail' proved no trouble. Recalling the homecoming, he says, "Traditionally in the Mon, we always paraded the cup up and down Patrick Street to show the other schools in Cork who were the top dogs! It was no different that day." The North Mon team had a sizeable contingent of "country boys" in 1970. "The Mon was the school in Cork for so long that pupils came from all over and a lot of them came for the hurling," remarks Des. When the victorious team arrived at the gates of the school, a bonfire greeted them. The entire student body assembled in the schoolyard the following day and everyone was given a couple of days off. It was "all part of building the tradition". As for the Leaving Cert, Des believes the school's hurling exploits did not have a detrimental effect on results. "Strangely enough, I think the set of results that year were very good. I don't think our results or books suffered at all."

Unsurprisingly, the Mon also had a fine football team in Des' Leaving Cert year. The school entered the Corn Uí Mhuirí, "basically as extra training for hurling, but we actually drew with Coláiste Íosagáin, who had Mickey Ned O'Sullivan in their ranks", Des recalls.

Des is loud in his praise of the team mentors. "I must pay compliment to the people who were in charge of the team. There was Br Barry and Murt Murphy, who was a lay teacher in the school and he was only in his first or second year and wasn't much older than the students. He became a very good trainer of Cork teams later on. Br Miniter was a hard man and he didn't baulk at the physical stuff. If you didn't come off the training field with your knuckles cut, he'd be asking questions. Br Barry was the main man. His main strength I suppose was that he'd scare the living hell out of us! He was a very practical kind of man and he did a lot of the organising and looked after us well with soup and sandwiches. Murt Murphy did more of the coaching on the hurling side. I'm not sure that Br Barry knew or pretended to know a whole deal about hurling, but he knew about organising and how to get the best out of fellas. Murt Murphy put the gloss on it with his coaching and the way he studied the opposition, which was a new thing to me. The switches they made always seemed to work."

Des studied in UCC for whom he played in both the Fitzgibbon Cup and the Sigerson Cup, winning a Fitzgibbon Cup medal as a sub in his first year. "I didn't play much hurling afterwards. I suffered a broken wrist and I found it hard to play after that. I also went to England for a couple of years and when I came back I found it hard to break in to the club side, the 'Barr's. I played a few senior matches but I don't have a senior county hurling medal." However, success on the football field provided ample consolation. "We always looked on both games as being equal, as we are a dual club and I was lucky enough to make it on the senior football team." Des won county football medals with St. Finbarr's in 1976, 1979 and 1980, and he is the holder of two All-Ireland Club medals, won in 1980 and 1981. Des never played hurling for Cork at underage or senior level, but he did wear the famous red and white jersey for the senior footballers and played in the Munster final in 1977 against the legendary Kerry team of the time. It was "the year of the famous three stripes on the Cork jersey" and Des recalls the events of almost 30 years ago as, "shocking carry-on altogether". He humorously goes on, "unfortunately, Billy Morgan was the only GPA we had! It was horrendous stuff. You couldn't build a team on it. I think it shot Cork football in the foot for a long time after that."

When Des returned from England, he did the H.Dip and started teaching in 1976. He taught in Thurles CBS for two years and trained the school's Harty Cup team. Des then took up a teaching post in Macegan College, Macroom, before moving to Coachford Community School in 1985, where he has been a Maths and Irish teacher ever since. He is in charge of Gaelic games in the 600 pupil co-educational school. Des is married to a Cork lady, Maura (née McCarthy) and they live in Ovens. They have four children, two boys (neither of whom attended the Mon) and two girls, ranging in ages from 24 to 17.

Des retains a keen interest in the sporting fortunes of North Mon and he's still in touch with members of the 1970 team, particularly Tadhg Harris, who is actually his brother-in-law. Others are well scattered with the passing of time, but he meets some of his former team-mates occasionally. An unusual reunion of the team did take place ("it ended up being very informal", he jokes), when they were invited to play a challenge match against the school Harty Cup team in the mid-1970s.

As a brother of former Cork hurling manager Donal O'Grady, who led the Rebel County to the All-Ireland title in 2004, Des is keenly aware of the huge sacrifices inter-county players have to make nowadays. Pointing to players like Donal Óg Cusack, Seán Óg Ó hAilpín and Diarmuid O'Sullivan, Des says, "these fellas are totally committed and surely they deserve some reward." Although not an advocate of 'pay for play', Des firmly believes that players should be "looked after properly and it's a pity that they don't have a scheme where they're given tax allowances and tax relief. I think that would be a great help as it's actually costing some lads money to play".

Des O'Grady looks back fondly on his schooldays, praising the Brothers, who are now more or less phased out nationwide, but who certainly weren't rewarded financially for their long hours of devotion to Gaelic games in the likes of North Monastery. Des recalls his days in the Mon as "the happiest of my life", with the Harty and Croke Cup wins of 1970 very much the icing on the cake.

1971 – ALL-IRELAND SEMI-FINAL
28 March 1971, Limerick

St. Finbarr's, Farranferris 4-8
(G. Hennessy 1-4, J. O'Donoghue 1-3, F. O'Regan 1-0, B. Murphy 1-0, M. Crowley 0-1)

Presentation College, Athenry 2-6
(S. Hynes 0-6, J. J. Kane 1-0, G. Cullinane 1-0)

St. Kieran's, Kilkenny, Croke Cup Champions, 1971.
Back row, left to right: Terry Brennan, Martin Gibbons, Joe Ryan, Brian O'Shea, John Power,
Tony Teehan, John Dunne, Jimmy Walsh, Billy Fitzpatrick, Martin Healy.
Middle row, left to right: Des Kennedy, Richard Beck, Jimmy Moore, Brian Cody, Louis Campion,
Ger Woodcock, Pat White, Nicky Brennan, Noel Minogue.
Front row, left to right: Pat Kearney (capt), Joe Reidy.
(Photograph courtesy of Dick McEvoy, c/o St. Kieran's, Kilkenny)

1971 – ALL-IRELAND FINAL
9 May 1971, Thurles
Referee: John Moloney (Tipperary)

St. Kieran's, Kilkenny 8-6

John Dunne
(Kilkenny)

Jimmy Walsh   **Louis Campion**
(Kilkenny)   (Offaly)

John Power   **Brian Cody**   **Tony Teehan**
(Kilkenny)   (Kilkenny)   (Kilkenny)

Ger Woodcock   **Nicky Brennan**
(Kilkenny)   (Kilkenny) (0-2)

Pat Kearney (*capt*)   **Noel Minogue**   **Pat White**
(Kilkenny) (1-0)   (Kilkenny) (1-1)   (Kildare) (2-3)

Billy Fitzpatrick   **Joe Ryan**
(Kilkenny) (4-0)   (Limerick)

St. Finbarr's, Farranferris 5-8

Tadhg O'Sullivan
(Cork)

John Lysaght   **Declan Meade**
(Cork)   (Cork)

John Collins   **Joe O'Connor**   **Denis O'Keeffe**
(Cork)   (Cork)   (Cork)

Barry Murphy (*capt*)   **Dan O'Dwyer**
(Cork)   (Cork)

Tom Fogarty   **John O'Donovan**   **Gerry Hennessy**
(Cork) (1-5)   (Cork) (1-0)   (Cork) (1-2)

Michael Crowley   **Fintan O'Regan**
(Cork) (1-0)   (Cork) (1-1)

Subs: Brendan Gallagher (Cork) (for Lysaght), Brendan Manley (Cork) (for Meade), John O'Regan (Cork) (for O'Connor).

Pat Kearney

Remarkably, long before the world's best golfers even heard of the place, a young boy named Pat Kearney began hurling on what is now the first fairway of Mount Juliet Golf Course, where children from Oldtown and neighbouring townslands spent hours playing with a sliotar. From those early days, Pat's hurling career took off, with the highlight being captaining St. Kieran's, Kilkenny, when they won their first Croke Cup in six years, back in 1971.

"Mount Juliet, where my late father Jimmy worked, was a great place to grow up. There was, of course, no golf course there at the time but there was great freedom in those fields," Pat recalls. In those particular fields, Pat attempted to copy his heroes from that era like 'Cha' Whelan and Ollie and Tom Walsh, before he progressed to playing underage hurling in all the grades for his local Thomastown, "a club that had a great tradition". Ironically, the Kearney family's introduction to Leinster colleges hurling had begun a few years earlier, as Pat's older brother, Seamus, turned out for local rivals, Kilkenny CBS. "I have great memories of hurling in St. Kieran's. It was the only sport in the college back then, but you could just see the odd game of soccer creeping in. You couldn't really call it soccer, so it ended up being a cross between Gaelic and soccer," says Pat, as he reflects on the loosening of 'the Ban', back in the early 1970s.

"One of the great aspects of St. Kieran's winning in 1971 was that it was their first All-Ireland after a gap of six years. There was a lull

there in the senior team when I entered the college but the internal leagues were organised every year and they remained the catalyst for producing so many great hurlers over the years." There was never a shortage of people to referee these games which involved many teams, as there were seventy or eighty students in each year with few activities other than hurling. According to Pat, "six years without an All-Ireland title was like an eternity to a coach like Fr Tommy Maher".

He vividly recounts a nice story about the importance of hurling to Fr Maher, even in the midst of the primary function of the college, the education of its students. "We were let out of the college to go to Nowlan Park in Kilkenny to see the matches and, one particular Sunday, Kilkenny had beaten Tipperary in the National Hurling League, so on Monday morning we thought it would be a good idea to talk hurling rather than do Maths. So the hurling chat was going great until someone suggested that perhaps hurling was a little over the top in Kilkenny and almost like a religion. "Well it wouldn't be such a bad one. Now open your books for Pythagoras' Theorem", was Fr Maher's immediate response.

At the start of the 1970/71 senior campaign, Pat was fairly confident of doing well as the team had won juvenile and junior championship, over the preceding years. "Victory was all the sweeter in 1971 as we had lost out in Leinster in 1970 and I had actually played in the Croke Cup final in 1969 where we all played poorly and got heavily beaten by St. Finbarr's".

Recalling his shock at being named as captain of the side, Pat modestly says, "I was very, very surprised as there were a lot better hurlers on the team and I hadn't been a captain on any of the previous teams. When you look at players of the calibre of Brian Cody, Billy Fitzpatrick, Nicky Brennan and Tony Teehan, they were all great players, so it was an honour to be given the captaincy but it wasn't a difficult job when you were playing with these quality players. You just had to look after your own position on the team."

All these years later, one game still sticks out in Pat's mind. "Our first round game against Callan CBS in Piltown remains vivid as we were extremely lucky to come out of it. Even though we entered the game with confidence, the first round of a championship can always be tricky." While acknowledging that Callan CBS had a good side, Pat feels that a lot of the St. Kieran's players, including himself, didn't perform on the day. "We were lucky to win but it proved to be a watershed," Pat reflects. He remembers Tony Teehan getting split across his head through his helmet, but Ger Woodcock and Nicky Brennan dominated at midfield and goals from Billy Fitzpatrick and Noel Minogue, plus a brace from Pat White, helped St. Kieran's to triumph by 5-9 to 5-1. In the Leinster final, played in New Ross, St. Peter's, Wexford proved no match for the Kilkenny side. Two goals from Joe Ryan saw the future champions open up a lead of 2-6 before St. Peter's opened their account in the 20th minute, with St. Kieran's running out comfortable winners on a scoreline of 2-15 to 1-7.

Pat has clear memories of the build-up to the final against St. Finbarr's, Farranferris. "Despite the failure to win the Croke Cup in the previous six years, there was no added pressure preceding the final," Pat recalls. "Dermot Healy was our trainer and he was excellent - his achievements with Offaly in later years would bear that out - but he'd never mention anything like the six-year gap. We didn't do any great physical training as regards running but we did do an unmerciful amount of skills work. It didn't matter whether it was hail, rain or snow. I remember all our hand-passing drills and the sliotar getting stuck in the mud, but we kept at it and it was worth it in the end. We were naturally fit as we trained every day and played many challenge matches against local minor club sides like James Stephens and Shamrocks and the St. Kieran's seminary side".

As the colleges championships were played on a 13-a side basis in the early 1970s, Pat clearly remembers "relentless" scoring. "You would get down the field for a score and then the ball would go straight up the other end of the field for another score". Indeed, such was the case in the Croke Cup final played on Sunday May 9th in Semple Stadium, Thurles. The 'Irish Independent' reported that "a stronger, fractionally faster, St. Kieran's College showed many instinctive natural touches of skilful hurling in a dazzling climax to the season". Two late first half goals by the winners meant that St. Finbarr's lead of 2-4 to 2-3 was overturned and St. Kieran's led by 4-3 to 2-4 at the interval. A second half goal feast ensued with future Kilkenny senior star Billy Fitzpatrick on fire, as evidenced by his four-goal tally. Although Farna had entered the game as favourites, Fr Maher's charges had responded in dynamic fashion. "There was a great buzz lifting the Croke Cup and later on back in the school", Pat recalls, "but I was soon reminded that you didn't get any extra marks for this achievement in the Leaving Cert which was lurking just around the corner!"

Three and a half decades later, Pat acknowledges the great contributions of St. Kieran's hurling mentors. "We were indebted to Fr Tommy Maher and Dermot Healy for our success. They did trojan work. Other seminarians would also help out like Liam Cassin and Johnny Ryan who gave up their time to referee games", Pat reflects. His father also encouraged him to hurl through his college years even if they didn't always agree on hurling matters. "My dad loved hurling and was always willing to give his views on the game and he loved reading one of the leading GAA journalists of that era, John D. Hickey".

Pat played minor hurling for Kilkenny but they lost out by a goal to Cork in the All-Ireland final in 1971. However, he went one better at Under-21 level where the Cats beat Waterford by a point (3-8 to 3-7) in the final. When he finished in St. Kieran's, Pat furthered his education in St. Patrick's, Drumcondra, where he hurled with fine players he admired such as Ger Loughnane and Sean Hehir (Clare), Brian O'Keeffe (Westmeath) and Brian Cody (Kilkenny). He played local soccer until he was nearly 40 and also continued to hurl for Thomastown until his late 30s, but he has always remained a fan of the underage grades. "It doesn't matter if you don't make it to the senior grade of your sport. I remember there was great camaraderie all the way up at Under-12, Under-14, Under-16 and minor and these are great levels of hurling in their own right. They are still vitally important to the game of hurling once they are enjoyed," according to Pat.

A national teacher by profession, Pat taught in Kildare town, Portlaoise, Inistioge and finally Paulstown, where he was principal for 21 years, after which he took early retirement and nowadays he claims to be "a small-time sheep farmer!" Married to an Inistioge woman Nellie (née Malone), Pat's love of hurling has never dwindled and he applauds the recent restructuring of the hurling championships by the GAA to incorporate the Christy Ring and Nicky Rackard Cups. "This gives the so-called 'weaker' counties an opportunity to play in Croke Park", as he recalls the great contribution made by Kildare's Pat White to St. Kieran's 1971 triumph. To this day, Pat still continues to look out for St. Kieran's results.

Nowadays, Pat Kearney loves to play a round of golf. The man who first learned his hurling skills in the fields which are now part of one of Europe's best known golf courses jokes, "I would be better off with a hurl to get around the course some days". However, these endless hours practising as a young boy with hurley and ball in hand, later enabled Pat to go on to be a winner in his own right and lift the Croke Cup for St. Kieran's in 1971.

1972 – ALL-IRELAND SEMI-FINAL
26 March 1972, Birr

St. Kieran's, Kilkenny 7-5
(G. Freyne 2-1, J. Reidy 2-0, J. Quane 2-0, B. Fitzpatrick 1-1, J. Dunne 0-1, B. Cody 0-1,
N. Minogue 0-1)

Our Lady's, Gort 3-1
(V. Mullins 1-1, G. Curtin 1-0, A. Connolly 1-0)

St. Finbarr's, Farranferris, Croke Cup Champions, 1972.
Back row, left to right: Eddie Forde, Richie Cotter, Michael Coughlan,
Tadhg Murphy, Ger Duggan.
Middle row, left to right: Sean O'Shea, John Delaney, Brendan Manley, Joe Hyde,
Pat Kelleher, John O'Regan.
Front row, left to right: Fr Michael O'Brien, Billy Mackesy, Tadhg O'Sullivan, Tom Fogarty (capt),
Bishop Cornelius Lucey, Declan Meade, Dan O'Dwyer, Brendan Gallagher, Fr Michael Murphy.
(Photograph courtesy of Tim Horgan, author of Farna's Hurling Story)

1972 – ALL-IRELAND FINAL
30 April 1972, Thurles
Referee: Mick Spain (Offaly)

St. Finbarr's, Farranferris 3-7

Ger Duggan
(Cork)

John O'Regan   **Brendan Gallagher**
(Cork)   (Cork)

Brendan Manley   **Sean O'Shea**   **Declan Meade**
(Cork)   (Cork)   (Cork)

Dan O'Dwyer   **Richie Cotter**
(Cork) (0-2)   (Cork)

Tom Fogarty (*capt*)   **Pat Kelleher**   **Billy Mackesy**
(Cork) (0-3)   (Cork)   (Cork)

Tadhg O'Sullivan   **Michael Coughlan**
(Cork) (2-1)   (Cork)

Subs: Tadhg Murphy (Cork)(1-1) (for Kelleher), Joe Hyde (Cork) (for Coughlan),
Eddie Forde (Cork) (for Cotter).

St. Kieran's, Kilkenny 2-5

Pat Dunphy
(Kilkenny)

Johnny O'Shea   **Louis Campion**
(Kilkenny)   (Offaly)

Maurice Power   **Brian Cody**   **Martin Gibbons**
(Kilkenny)   (Kilkenny) (0-1) (Kilkenny)

Ger Woodcock   **John Dunne**
(Kilkenny) (0-2)   (Kilkenny) (0-1)

Billy Fitzpatrick (*capt*)   **Noel Minogue**   **Joe Reidy**
(Kilkenny) (1-1)   (Kilkenny)   (Kilkenny) (1-0)

John Quane   **Ger Freyne**
(Limerick)   (Kilkenny)

Tom Fogarty

When St. Finbarr's, Farranferris avenged their 1971 All-Ireland final defeat by St. Kieran's College 12 months later, they were captained by Kinsale man, Tom Fogarty, ironically dethroning his father's alma mater in a closely-fought Croke Cup final in Semple Stadium.

Being the son of a Kilkennyman, it was inevitable that Tom would develop an interest in hurling. His late father, Joe, attended St. Kieran's College and helped them to win a Leinster senior colleges hurling title in 1931, before he moved to Cork as an adult, to work in the Department of Agriculture. Tom's interest in the game was further heightened by a renewed interest in hurling which took place in Kinsale during his youth. "There was a revival in hurling in Kinsale when I was growing up and I was lucky enough to win Under-14, Under-16, minor and Under-21 championship medals with the club. The likes of John Kirby, who was a Midleton man and Jack Barrett, who was Cork County Board Chairman, did fantastic work with the underage in Kinsale at that time. But for various reasons, we failed to reproduce those successes at adult level in the years that followed", Tom laments. On completing his primary education, Tom's mother "hoped I would become a priest", so next stop was almost inevitably Farranferris, but young Tom was more than happy with this move. "Fellas like Brian Tobin from Kinsale had gone to Farna a few years before me and I wanted to go as well. All I wanted to do was play hurling and Farna was the place to do that. In any case, there was no secondary school for boys in Kinsale at the time, although a small number of boys had just begun to attend the local convent girls' school".

Tom attended St. Finbarr's from 1967 to 1973, returning to repeat his Leaving Cert in the latter year. His early heroes in the school included Tim Crowley and Donal Collins. When he reflects back on his time in Farna, Fr Michael O'Brien, who is regarded as one of the great hurling coaches of the time, dominates his thoughts. "Fr O'Brien was the man who made it all happen. He was a fantastic coach, a hard taskmaster, but you took it. He was way ahead of his time when it came to coaching. We were playing an advanced style of hurling back then as Newtownshandrum and Cork were to play in later years. We played a running style of hurling which probably suited the 13-a-side game that was in operation at the time. We all knew what our jobs were. You made the runs because you knew the ball was coming to you. We chased everything and it was a very effective style of hurling. I suppose the only drawback for a lot of fellas was that they found it difficult to revert back to the more traditional style of direct hurling when they went back to their clubs. Fr O'Brien trained us hard and you could feel yourself improving with each session. Our achievements were incredible when you consider that there were only about 280 pupils in the school and, not alone that, but most of them were from West Cork where hurling plays second fiddle to football," Tom reflects.

Tom had played under 14-and-a-half and had won a Dean Ryan Cup medal under Fr O'Brien's tutelage before he claimed a place on the Harty Cup panel while still a second year in 1969. That year was arguably the most successful in the sporting annals of Farranferris. Practically every trophy worth winning came to the college - the Harty and All-Ireland, the Dean Ryan Cup for the first time, the Cohalan Cup and even the Munster 'B' football trophy. The only piece of silverware to elude them was the Callaghan Cup. The year's highlight was, of course, the winning of the Croke Cup, following a facile 5-15 to 2-1 victory over St. Kieran's. "Because I was only a non-playing sub in '69, I didn't get a medal and I was basically told that there would be further opportunities to win one". Tom made the senior team in 1970, but had to wait until the following year to win his first Harty Cup medal on the field of play. Farna defeated St. Flannan's in the provincial decider, despite the Ennis side having the likes of future Clare stars, Ger Loughnane, Johnny Callinan, Tim Crowe and Colm Honan in their ranks, as well as Tipperary's, Liam Heffernan. The Cork college went on to contest the All-Ireland final which they lost to St. Kieran's.

There was no lack of motivation in the Farranferris camp when they embarked on a new campaign in 1971/72, with the by now vastly experienced Tom Fogarty in the role of team captain. This honour was bestowed on him at a team meeting, where he was proposed and seconded. "The captaincy was irrelevant but I still felt I had to lead by example. Even though we only had a handful of survivors from the '71 team, most notably Tadhg O'Sullivan, Declan Meade and Dan O'Dwyer, who was a fantastic player for us in both years, we had our sights set on making up for the previous year's disappointment. I have no doubt that we would have won it in '71 had

we not been told to concentrate on our studies after we beat Flannan's in the Harty Cup final. We weren't as focused as we should have been. Another motivating factor for us in '72 was what we felt was a derogatory comment about us attributed to Fr Maher from St. Kieran's after the '71 final which we found drove us on," Tom remembers.

En route to retaining the Harty Cup, Farna's first win was over Coláiste Chríost Rí in the old Athletic Grounds, "after which we knew we were good enough". A victory over North Monastery in "a very tight game" provided Farna with their stiffest test in the semi-final. North Mon featured the likes of Tom Cashman, John Norberg, Liam Shanahan, Donal O'Grady and Seanie Farrell (who was Down manager in 2005). Tom recalls that "we only pulled away in the last quarter when our inner-belief drove us on". In the Harty decider, St. Finbarr's recorded an impressive win over St. Flannan's by 6-11 to 2-7, with Tom himself bagging 1-4 and youthful sub, Tadhg Murphy helping himself to a vital 1-1 haul. "The final was played on a terrible day in Charleville and I can remember hitting four or five early wides. But we eventually adapted to the wet and windy conditions and played very well to run out comfortable enough winners in the end."

"Once you won the Harty, the All-Ireland was a bonus. Having said that, we wanted another crack at Kieran's and there was a great buzz in the build-up to the game", Tom says. Unlike in 1971 when Farna had to overcome Presentation College, Athenry, to reach the All-Ireland final, they qualified automatically for the national decider in 1972. The final proved to be a tremendous contest, with the 'Irish Independent' report particularly praising "a second half of brilliant hurling as both teams blossomed in the overcast conditions". Despite having wind advantage in the opening half, the Farna boys only led by 2-1 to 1-2 at the interval, with both goals coming from Tadhg O'Sullivan. St. Kieran's dominated the third quarter to move four points clear, but then came the Farna fightback. Young Tadhg

Murphy again came on as an impact sub and Tom Fogarty moved to a more central position where his point from a free sparked a great resurgence. Further points from Fogarty, Murphy and O'Sullivan levelled matters before Dan O'Dwyer ("pound for pound, as good as there was") slotted over two points, and the icing on the cake was provided when Murphy slammed home a third goal with time almost up, after a great move involving Tom Fogarty, Billy Mackesy and Dan O'Dwyer. "We won that game because our backs were unbelievable and we carried the ball against the wind in the second half," Tom explains.

"St. Kieran's played a similar style of hurling to us but we kept plugging away and our determination to make amends for the '71 final really came to the fore in the closing stages when the game was up for grabs."

Tom speaks of the tremendous pride Farna players had when they donned the famed saffron jersey. "You were playing for the school and the team, and not for yourself. There was always fierce pride in the jersey. We always got great support from the school president, Fr Murphy, Fr Buckley, Seanie O'Riordan (who would later succeed Fr O'Brien as senior team coach), Fr Keohane and the rest of the teaching staff. When I received the Croke Cup from Archbishop Morris, I was receiving it for everyone. My role was irrelevant after that." Amazingly, Tom left Farna without an actual All-Ireland medal in his possession. "I missed out as a sub in '69, but when we won the All-Ireland again in '72, I didn't get one either. There weren't enough medals for the subs, I think, but I'm certainly not bitter about it," he says.

Tom came back to repeat his Leaving Cert in St. Finbarr's in 1973. In his repeat year, he was overage for the Harty team, but was delighted to be afforded the opportunity to work alongside Fr O'Brien in a coaching capacity. "I learned a lot about coaching that year and it stood to me years later when I trained Kinsale to beat Carrigaline - who were coached by the Canon (Fr O'Brien) - in a junior championship match. After the game,

he proclaimed, 'the pupil has finally outshone the master', and that was the greatest compliment I ever got." Tom also enjoyed his successful exploits in Munster 'B' football with Farna. "We would have been good enough to give the 'A' championship a rattle, as we had a lot of West Cork guys on the team and both Sean O'Shea and Seanie Murphy went on to achieve great things in football," he says.

Tom garnered an All-Ireland minor hurling medal with Cork in 1971 and represented the county at Under-21 level for two years, lining out at full forward on the team which beat Wexford in the 1973 All-Ireland final. To this day, he remains in awe of Seanie O'Leary's semi-final performance against Galway that year. Because of what he describes as "unbelievable competition for places - you had the likes of Seanie and Jimmy Barry (Murphy) coming through" - Tom failed to break into the Cork senior team, being confined to playing a few challenge games. Sadly, he was forced to retire with a cruciate ligament injury at the age of just 23. "I was playing a game of soccer during a minor football training session that I was taking and it just happened. I knew straight away that I was in trouble," he explains. Tom trained Kinsale for a period after that in "an unbelievably competitive South-East division" and his hopes of guiding them to glory were hit by emigration during the 1980s. "The club hasn't recovered since," he laments.

Tom qualified as a primary teacher in St. Patrick's, Drumcondra, but soon decided that teaching wasn't the career for him, and nowadays he works for a shipping inspection company, Control Union. "Even though I live close to Páirc Uí Rinn in Cork city, I don't get to see a lot of matches because my job involves a lot of travelling. But when I'm around, I try to see as many games as possible."

Married to Margaret (Mandy), Tom has three children, Catherine, Claire ("the greatest Cork hurling supporter of all time") and Luke. All three have inherited his love for the GAA and Catherine and Luke have represented Bishopstown and Blackrock in camogie and underage hurling respectively. Over the years, Tom continued to follow the hurling fortunes of his alma mater and attended the class reunion which included the all-conquering 1972 team in 2001. "Somebody couldn't count," Tom jokes, "as it took place after 29 years, but it was a very enjoyable occasion and it was like you had never left the place."

The doors of St. Finbarr's, Farranferris, are now locked forever as a secondary school, much to the dismay of Tom Fogarty. He reflects that "it was great to have played with and against so many star players". Many of those star players were team-mates and opponents in the memorable Harty and Croke Cup campaigns of 1972, when Tom had the honour of lifting the two best best-known trophies in colleges hurling.

1973 – ALL-IRELAND SEMI-FINAL
25 March 1973, Limerick

Our Lady's, Gort 4-6
(P. O'Connor 3-6, N. Lane 1-0)

St. Finbarr's, Farranferris 2-6
(J. Crowley 2-2, J. O'Flynn 0-2, T. Murphy 0-1, J. Higgins 0-1)

St. Peter's, Wexford, Croke Cup Champions, 1973.
Back row, left to right: Oliver Murray, Jim White, Michael Murphy, Nicky Fanning,
John Moynihan, Jerome Lordan, Brian Furlong, John Greene, Larry Rowe, John Whitty,
Michael Doyle, Tom Kavanagh, John Conran, Ben Bernie.
Front row, left to right: Nicky Cardiff, Declan Rowesome, Paddy Kinsella, Billy Rowesome,
Mr Ned Power, Andy Doyle (capt), Fr Paddy Curtis, Pat Hanrick, Noel Barry,
Denny O'Connor, Paud O'Brien.
(Photograph courtesy of Alan Aherne and Kevin Kehoe, authors of
Power and Glory, The story of Gaelic Games in St. Peter's College, Wexford)

1973 – ALL-IRELAND FINAL
8 April 1973, Thurles
Referee: Jimmy Rankins (Laois)

St. Peter's, Wexford 2-6

John Greene
(Wexford)

Andy Doyle (*capt*)   **Brian Furlong**
(Wexford)   (Wexford)

Tom Kavanagh   **Billy Rowesome**   **Paud O'Brien**
(Wexford)   (Wexford)   (Wexford)

Declan Rowesome   **John Moynihan**
(Wexford)   (Wexford) (0-2)

Paddy Kinsella   **Pat Hanrick**   **Denny O'Connor**
(Wexford)   (Wexford) (0-2)   (Wexford) (0-2)

Michael Doyle   **Nicky Fanning**
(Wicklow) (2-0)   (Wexford)

Our Lady's, Gort 2-6

Kevin Fahy
(Galway)

Ger Murphy   **Ger Curtin**
(Galway)   (Galway)

Pat Broughan   **Declan Brogan**   **Pascal Quinn**
(Galway)   (Galway)   (Galway)

Martin Glynn (*capt*)   **Gerry Curtin**
(Clare)   (Galway) (1-0)

Pat O'Connor   **Anthony Brennan**   **Anthony Connolly**
(Clare) (0-4)   (Galway) (1-0)   (Galway)

Bernard Forde   **Noel Lane**
(Galway)   (Galway) (0-2)

1973 – ALL-IRELAND FINAL (REPLAY)
15 April 1973, Portlaoise
Referee: Jimmy Rankins (Laois)

St. Peter's, Wexford 4-15

John Greene
(Wexford)

Andy Doyle (*capt*)   **Brian Furlong**
(Wexford)   (Wexford)

Tom Kavanagh   **Billy Rowesome**   **Paud O'Brien**
(Wexford)   (Wexford)   (Wexford)

Declan Rowesome   **John Moynihan**
(Wexford) (0-2)   (Wexford) (0-1)

Paddy Kinsella   **Pat Hanrick**   **Denny O'Connor**
(Wexford) (0-1)   (Wexford) (0-5)   (Wexford) (1-5)

Michael Doyle   **Nicky Fanning**
(Wicklow) (2-1)   (Wexford) (1-0)

Our Lady's, Gort 1-5

Kevin Fahy
(Galway)

Ger Murphy   **Ger Curtin**
(Galway)   (Galway)

Pat Broughan   **Declan Brogan**   **Pascal Quinn**
(Galway)   (Galway)   (Galway)

Martin Glynn (*capt*)   **Gerry Curtin**
(Clare)   (Galway) (0-1)

Anthony Connolly   **Anthony Brennan**   **Pat O'Connor**
(Galway) (0-1)   (Galway) (1-0)   (Clare) (0-3)

Bernard Forde   **Noel Lane**
(Galway)   (Galway)

Andy Doyle

The fourth and, to date, last young man to captain St. Peter's to an All-Ireland senior hurling title was Andy Doyle and, remarkably, it took a final replay to decide the destination of the Croke Cup in 1973, as had also been the case in the Wexford college's previous wins in 1962, 1967 and 1968.

Andy's family background was not steeped in hurling tradition. His late father was a farmer and the duties of the land left little time for anything else. Andy attended Ramsgrange National School and occasionally matches were played against neighbouring schools like Gusserane and Horeswood. Indeed, Andy recalls getting "hammered" frequently in such games. At that stage, there was "no activity" in the local GAA club, St. James' "at underage level". "My first recollection of any kind of serious hurling or football was when I went to St. Peter's College," says Andy. From the day he entered St. Peter's as a boarder, he "just liked the place, full stop". He concedes that he "basically went there to hurl and to play football." When Andy started in Peter's, he "knew nothing" about the finer points of either hurling or football, but he did possess "a great will to learn".

When Andy enrolled in St. Peter's in 1968, Wexford hurling was on a major high after the All-Ireland senior and minor double. It was also a glorious period for St. Peter's, who had won back-to-back All-Ireland titles in 1967 and 1968. For an impressionable youngster, there was no shortage of heroes in the school. "You looked up to them all and

respected them equally because, if not, you could find yourself in serious trouble!" Andy jokes. "These lads were 'handy'; they were handy with their hurls and they were tough. But when I look back, I always remember one name, one man that I always highly respected. He was, and is, a nice guy and that's Martin Quigley. He was a great mentor and a great role model for any young lads coming into the place." During Andy's time in St. Peter's, there were sports prefects and it was their job to mobilise the student body to play hurling and football. This was effectively the entire P.E. activity in the school, along with some handball. "I remember some years ago one very famous Wexford hurler by the name of George O'Connor cornering me at a funeral to say that, only for I pulled him out to play hurling when it was my turn to be a sports prefect, he might never have gone on to be a hurler," Andy recalls fondly.

As for the coaches and team mentors in St. Peter's, Andy says Ned Power was the "major force". He goes on, "Ned was at the heart of St. Peter's through a lot of its successes. I remember him bringing us into a classroom one evening and telling us that being successful as a hurler opened doors in your career." Kerry native Martin Casey, later of Buffer's Alley and Wexford fame, was a seminarian in St. Peter's and was Ned's chief assistant, while Andy also remembers the contribution of the late Fr Paddy Curtis, who managed many college football teams. Internal mini-leagues in the school played a crucial role in Andy's development as a hurler, but he was "shocked" when told he was to captain the senior team for the 1972/73 campaign, while still eligible for the junior grade. "I was not, and would not be, a star hurler. I was a man to do a job. That is the only reason that I can think of that might qualify me for the honour that was bestowed upon me. I viewed it as an honour from the word go because we were very serious about out intentions for that year," recalls Andy modestly.

His favourite venue was Dr Cullen Park in Carlow but neither of St. Peter's provincial games took place there that year. St. Peter's defeated Kilkenny opposition in both games in their Leinster campaign. They overcame Kilkenny CBS in the provincial semi-final on March 4th in New Ross on a scoreline of 4-7 to 1-2. It's not an encounter Andy likes to dwell on, as unsavoury incidents after the final whistle marred the match. "Numerous scuffles broke out between rival players as the tension of the occasion caused an ill-disciplined reaction from the Kilkenny team", states Power and Glory - The Story of Gaelic Games in St. Peter's College, Wexford (published to mark the official opening of Ned Power Park in 1991). Sadly, St. Peter's lost midfielder Noel Barry for the remainder of the championship due to a shoulder injury sustained in that match against Kilkenny CBS. The Leinster final took place in Croke Park on March 18th and Andy describes the 3-12 to 1-7 win over St. Kieran's of Kilkenny, with Pat Hanrick nabbing a very impressive 2-7, as "a very sweet victory because we had suffered many humiliating defeats from St. Kieran's over the years. The years when we had good teams they nearly always succeeded in avoiding us by being beaten by somebody else first. It's probably fair to say that we were on a mission in that final."

In 1973, teams in the colleges hurling and football championships were 13-a-side, with no full-back or full-forward. Andy, who had won a Leinster colleges JFC medal in 1971/72, was one of two corner-backs on the St. Peter's team and his "basic philosophy" was that opposing forwards had to earn their "right of passage" to get near the goal he was

defending. One incident at a training session in the build-up to a big game stands out in Andy's mind. On that occasion, team-mate John Moynihan bore the brunt of Andy's no-non-sense approach. "John would have come out the worse for wear and Ned Power came down and threatened to expel me from the team!" At that time, St. Peter's teams trained predominantly in Coolcotts (a pitch away from the campus) and the boarders were training virtually seven days a week. The skills of the game were practised repeatedly until they were mastered. Andy also believes that two tough practice matches played during the year (against De La Salle of Waterford and St. Finbarr's, Farranferris) proved very significant in the march to ultimate glory. St. Peter's did not have to play a semi-final and went straight through to the All-Ireland decider. In that final, they would face unexpected opponents in Our Lady's, Gort, who sensationally beat reigning Croke Cup champions, St. Finbarr's, Farranferris in the All-Ireland semi-final. "We had no sense of complacency. We knew they would have a different style of hurling because we were always hearing that Connacht hurling was different from Leinster hurling".

"We didn't have any idea what the team from Gort had that enabled them to beat the Munster team and that was a great reason to be fearful," says Andy. In the first instalment of the final, Andy was marking Noel Lane, who went on to become a prominent inter-county senior hurler for Galway. The first game was played on a "hot day in Thurles" and it was a "blow for blow" affair, with neither side able to establish a clear advantage. It ended level (2-6 each), with Michael Doyle scoring both goals for the Wexford boys. "I suppose we were exceptionally nervous because of the pressure we felt under. Simple basic mistakes probably cost us that game at the end when we missed a free," says Andy. St. Peter's led by 1-5 to 1-3 at half time, but overall the 'Irish Independent' felt that "a draw was undoubtedly the most equitable result". Andy feels that St. Peter's players "probably felt relieved that they had got out of jail".

"We would have felt that we didn't play up to our potential on the first day. But we went back to the replay with one absolutely enormous confidence-booster, as every other All-Ireland we'd won to date in St. Peter's had come after a replay. We were pretty much raring to go because we nearly let it slip the week before." The replay was played in O'Moore Park, Portlaoise and this time there was no doubting the Wexford side's superiority, with St. Peter's romping to a 4-15 to 1-5 win. "Virtually everybody was spectacular that day", Andy remembers proudly. One aspect of the replay that clearly stands out in his mind was the "phenomenal support" St. Peter's had. "The hair was standing on the back of our heads when we went out onto the field. There were far more parents there and it was the biggest support that we probably ever had at a match for St. Peter's."

Damien McElroy of the 'Irish Independent' reported, "the Wexford lads outhurled and outclassed the opposition throughout the field, and even though Gort never relented in their efforts to seriously challenge for supremacy, their rewards were slight due to the robust, but always fair, tackling of the St. Peter's defence." Ahead by 1-9 to 0-2 at the interval, St. Peter's coasted to victory on the change of ends. The prospect of collecting the cup was daunting for Andy, in particular saying the few words 'as Gaeilge', but thankfully "everything worked out". Andy has vivid memories of the homecoming as the Croke Cup was brought back to Summerhill for the fourth time. "We arrived home that night to a terrific welcome in the college. We had bonfires and all kinds of things. It was 25 years later at a class reunion before I learned of a lot of the shenanigans that went on that night!" When the celebrations died down, the Leaving Cert beckoned, but it wasn't something that fazed Andy who had no great worries about the Leaving Cert because, "as far as I was concerned, I was only there for the hurling"! At that point, Andy planned to work on the family farm. However, he went on to study at Kildalton Agricultural College in County Kilkenny, with whom he won an All-Ireland medal in their inter-colleges tournament. He then applied for a scholarship to University College, Dublin, and, from there, he says his

career started "by default". He won two Fitzgibbon Cup medals with UCD in 1978 and 1979, and a Leinster senior hurling medal as a Wexford panellist in 1976 although, in hindsight, he feels he "may have been brought too early on to the panel". Andy graduated from UCD with an Agricultural Science degree and then pursued postgraduate studies. He worked and taught in UCD for a number of years. In 1989, he left UCD to join the 'Farmer's Journal', where he has worked as a journalist ever since. After receiving a presentation from St. James', Ramsgrange, in recognition of captaining St. Peter's to the All-Ireland title, Andy vowed never to play for any other club. He played junior hurling and intermediate football for St. James'. However, the pressures of work made it increasingly difficult for him to maintain the fitness levels required and he quit hurling in the mid to late-1980s. Whilst Andy says there were "some terrific hurlers" on the 1973 St. Peter's team, he adds that some players - and he modestly includes himself in this category - were there to do a job to enable the more skilful performers to work their magic. "It's probably ironic that none of that St. Peter's team went on to play senior hurling with Wexford," Andy says, with "John Conran, a substitute in 1973, about the only one that stayed with it."

Andy is married to Margaret, who hails from Ballon, County Carlow, and they have two sons, Andrew (18) and Eoin (15). In 1983, the newly married couple moved to Naas, where Andy has been actively involved in the local GAA club ever since and he is currently chairman of the Grounds Committee. He had a ten-year stint with the camogie club, before getting involved in underage hurling and football. Both Andrew (whose interest in Gaelic games only mushroomed in his teens, but now actually dabbles in hurley manufacturing) and Eoin ("who has huge heart and skill") are promising GAA players. The Gaelic Athletic Association remains a huge part of Andy's life, but he has "grave concerns" about the possibility of professionalism creeping into the GAA, while accepting that inter-county players "should be well looked after". His opinion is that "the real unsung heroes in the GAA are the people who continue to play for the enjoyment of it, having never won anything."

Andy Doyle concludes by saying, "we have a huge sense of pride in the county jersey but, when you're in school, the school jersey actually becomes more important. That's the way we felt and that's what brought us an All-Ireland. We had absolutely enormous pride in the jersey that we wore for St. Peter's and it helped us to put in a lot of effort. We also had great respect for the college itself and I remember Fr John O'Brien emphasising to us to 'be a sportsman'. We had a great sense of camaraderie with the younger lads in the college who viewed us, to a degree, as heroes. We weren't heroes. We were only ordinary guys who wanted to win for ourselves and for the college." Nowadays, Andy has very little contact with his former team-mates, mainly due to geographic constraints but is very conscious of their individual whereabouts. The Ramsgrange native lifted the Croke Cup in 1973, but the pride he felt at wearing the school's famous green and white jersey is still very evident 33 years later.

1974 – ALL-IRELAND SEMI-FINAL
7 April 1974, Nenagh

St. Kieran's, Kilkenny 5-12
(B. Fennelly 2-5, J. Prendergast 1-2, K. Brennan 1-2, T. Doheny 1-1, D. Reid 0-1, S. Brennan 0-1)

Our Lady's, Gort 1-4
(G. P. Fahy 1-1, P. Gill 0-2, P. O'Connor 0-1)

St. Finbarr's, Farranferris, Croke Cup Champions, 1974.
Back row, left to right: Teddy Murphy, Jim O'Sullivan, Kieran O'Driscoll, Denis Forde, Martin O'Sullivan, Paudie O'Regan.
Middle row, left to right: John Whooley, Martin Moir, Tim Cashman, Michael Murphy, Tim Hourihan, Pat Hayes, J. J. Murphy, Ger McEvoy, Finbarr Crowley, Frank Tobin, Denis Cronin, John O'Reilly, Gerry Crowley.
Front row, left to right: Fr Michael O'Brien, John Higgins, Tadhg Murphy (capt), Bishop Cornelius Murphy, Francis Collins, Johnny Crowley, Fr Michael Murphy.
(Photograph courtesy of Tim Horgan, author of Farna's Hurling Story)

1974 – ALL-IRELAND FINAL
28 April 1974, Dungarvan
Referee: Noel Dalton (Waterford)

St. Finbarr's, Farranferris 2-11

Finbarr Crowley
(Cork)

Denis Forde   **Jim O'Sullivan**
(Cork)   (Cork)

Johnny Crowley   **Michael Murphy**   **Francis Collins**
(Cork) (0-1)   (Cork)   (Cork) (0-1)

Kieran O'Driscoll   **Tim Hourihane**
(Cork)   (Cork) (0-1)

John Higgins   **Tadhg Murphy** (*capt*)   **Ger McEvoy**
(Cork) (1-4)   (Cork) (1-2)   (Cork) (0-1)

Frank Tobin   **J.J.Murphy**
(Cork) (0-1)   (Cork)

Sub: Paudie O'Regan (Cork) (for J. J. Murphy).

St. Kieran's, Kilkenny 1-12

Pat Bolger
(Laois)

Paddy Prendergast   **Joe Doran**
(Kilkenny)   (Laois)

Pat Power (*capt*)   **Jimmy Walsh**   **Richie Reid**
(Kilkenny)   (Kilkenny)   (Kilkenny)

Jimmy Lennon   **Frank Holohan**
(Kilkenny)   (Kilkenny)

Brendan Fennelly   **Kieran Brennan**   **Seamus Brennan**
(Kilkenny) (0-10)   (Kilkenny) (0-1)   (Kilkenny) (1-1)

Tom Doheny   **Jimmy Prendergast**
(Kilkenny)   (Kilkenny)

Sub: Harry Ryan (Kilkenny) (for S. Brennan).

Tadhg Murphy

Nine years before he secured his place in GAA folklore by scoring the goal which ended Kerry's incredible eight-year reign as Munster senior football champions, dual star Tadhg Murphy was an inspirational captain of the St. Finbarr's, Farranferris, team that won the Munster and All-Ireland senior hurling titles, thereby bringing the Harty and Croke Cups to the banks of the Lee.

Tadhgie, as he was known to all in Farna, is a native of Blossom-grove, Glanmire, and is the youngest of two boys and four girls. He confesses to have been "bred, born and reared into the game of hurling". His father Bertie, a prominent Sarsfields and Cork hurler in the 1930s, was a selector when Cork won the Liam McCarthy Cup in 1952 and fulfilled a similar role with successful Cork junior and minor hurling teams. Tadhg's uncles, Tom and Jamesie also represented their county at senior level. Tadhg attended Knockraha National School but it was with Sarsfields juvenile team that his hurling skills first came to notice. He was just 11 when he played in goal on the Sars' Under-14 team that won the East Cork championship in 1967. The following year, Sars won both the county hurling and football championships and they were successful again in the 1969 and 1970 under 14 hurling championships, with Tadhg captaining the team in '69. He has particularly fond memories of Michael Barry from those formative years, whom he describes as "a wonderful worker and a father figure".

Although his older brother and future Cork hurling manager, Bertie Óg, had opted to attend Coláiste Chríost Rí two years earlier, Tadhg's hurling instincts brought him to Farranferris in 1969. He recalls how his decision was influenced by Farna's All-Ireland success the previous school year. "I wanted to go to Farna because they were Harty Cup and All-Ireland champions at the time. I told my parents and they had no objection. I lived close to the college and went in as a day pupil. Most of the lads were boarders, but I fitted in alright," he says. "As a first year, I looked up to the likes of Tom Fogarty, Barry Murphy and Tadhg O'Sullivan. They were the guys you aspired to be as good as when your time came. We played hurling all the time and football was only secondary to it, despite Tim Horgan's best efforts to promote the game. Fr John Buckley (later Bishop Buckley) was in charge of the first successful Farna team I played on, the 1971 under 14-and-a-half side. Seanie O'Riordan was trainer of the under 15-and-a-half team the following year and he made me captain. We went all the way to the Munster final where were lost to De La Salle in Lismore after being three goals up with 20 minutes to go."

Tadhg's great skills saw him graduate to the Farna senior team at the age of 15 ("a dream come true"), and he won the first of three Harty Cup medals in the All-Ireland winning year of 1972. Fr Michael O'Brien used him regularly as a substitute during that successful campaign, and young Tadhg repaid the legendary Farna coach's faith in him by scoring 1-

I in both the Harty Cup and Croke Cup deciders. "As was the case in '74, the '72 team was very close-knit. I think that was something that stood to us. Even though we had small numbers, we always felt we would be there or thereabouts in the Harty Cup because we were such a united group." Tadhg won his second Harty medal in 1973, but a surprise loss to Gort in the All-Ireland semi-final ended Farna's hopes of putting All-Ireland titles back-to-back. "I wouldn't put the defeat down to complacency. We didn't play particularly well and Gort played out of their skins and were the better team on the day," Tadhg sportingly acknowledges.

From being the baby of the team in 1972, Tadhg was the experienced head on the 1974 side and it came as no surprise when Fr O'Brien made him captain. "I was in line for the captaincy in '74 because it was my third year playing Harty Cup and I was delighted when Fr O'Brien announced it to me. I thought because I was a day pupil that it might count against me, but I got the nod and got great support from everyone." Farna set out with the intention of completing a four-in-a-row of Harty Cup successes and this was achieved courtesy of a series of facile victories in their Munster campaign. In their two pre-Christmas games, St. Finbarr's annihilated North Mon by 5-13 to 0-3 in the Athletic Grounds, followed by a 7-8 to 4-3 win over St. Colman's, Fermoy, in Midleton, with Tadhg nabbing 2-5 and 2-6 respectively in those games. The Harty semi-final in Charleville was also very much one-way traffic, with Tadhg's 0-7 contributing to Farna's 5-19 to 2-3 victory. Remarkably, Limerick CBS, who had achieved their own famous four-in-a-row at Farna's expense in 1967, were even more comprehensively defeated by Tadhg and his colleagues in the Munster showdown in Charleville. Farranferris won the Harty final by 10-11 to 2-2, having scored 4-9 without reply in the opening half. A rampant Farna attack had posted 8-9 before Kieran Canty finally opened Limerick's scoring account in the 40th minute. A quietly-fancied Limerick outfit was left bamboozled by the sheer brilliance of the Farranferris team on the day, with Tadhg's fine

personal haul of 2-2 being even superseded by Ger McEvoy's whopping 4-3 and J.J. Murphy's hat-trick of goals.

Farranferris' opponents in the All-Ireland final at Dungarvan were old rivals, St. Kieran's, who had certainly learned from Farna's experience a year earlier and had outclassed Our Lady's, Gort in the semi-final. "St. Kieran's was by far our toughest game that year," Tadhg remembers. "We were never in danger in our earlier games and we absolutely annihilated Limerick CBS in the Harty final. It was hardly an ideal way to go into an All-Ireland final, but we showed enough resolve to win. It was a total contrast to the previous games we played. There was no quarter given or taken in the final and we had to dig deep. Scores were very difficult to come by. St. Kieran's were really up for it, and it was only in the closing stages that we managed to pull away," Tadhg remembers.

Backed by the breeze, the Cork men got off to a flyer when John Higgins goaled after just 45 seconds - " a very soft goal", according to the 'Irish Independent' match report - but St. Kieran's quickly settled and were five points up before some telling changes brought Farna back into contention. A goal from team captain, Tadhg helped Farna to a 2-4 to 1-5 interval lead. At this juncture, Tom O'Riordan reported that, "the exchanges reached their expected high standards as the second half reached its exciting climax." Fr O'Brien's charges were four points clear with eight minutes remaining before Brendan Fennelly fired over four frees to restore parity for St. Kieran's. A replay looked to be on the cards until late points from the bespectacled Ger McEvoy and Tadhg Murphy gave Farna the title. For many observers, it was entirely fitting that Tadhg should score the last point in what was his final game for Farna. "There was a big crowd in Dungarvan and because the All-Ireland club hurling final between Rathnure and Blackrock was on afterwards, we were able to do a lap of honour, after my attempt at the usual cúpla focail. Bringing the cup back to Farna was a special occasion - there was huge excitement," Tadhg fondly recalls.

According to Tadhg, Farna's performance in

the All-Ireland final was all the more praise-worthy as the players had been mistakenly treated to a full meal about an hour-and-a-half before the throw-in. "We went into Lawlor's Hotel for tea and sandwiches before the game and, while we were settling in, Fr O'Brien went out to see someone. Whatever happened, we were served a full lunch by mistake - steaks and spuds and vegetables and, naturally, we didn't refuse them. When Fr O'Brien returned, he was horrified to see what was going on, as our much-loved mentor John 'Kid' Cronin and ourselves were tucking in to the big feeds. But luckily, it didn't cost us the match!"

Tadhg claims that Fr O'Brien was years ahead of his time as a hurling coach. "He introduced drills, tactics, cross-field passing and intelligent use of the hand pass to our game. He was big in to the discipline side of things and he wouldn't tolerate dirty play. You played by his rules and the rules of the game. Seanie O'Riordan and Fr Buckley were also top-class hurling coaches at Farna. There was different thinking needed for 13-a-side hurling, as it gave more open space to the forwards." To round off a memorable 1974, Tadhg went on to win All-Ireland minor hurling and football medals with Cork later that year. He was joined on the minor hurling team by Farna colleagues Kieran O'Driscoll, Ger McEvoy and future Cork senior stars Johnny Crowley, Tom Cashman and Dermot McCurtain. Two years after captaining Farranferris to the highest honours in colleges hurling, Tadhg skippered the Cork Under-21 hurlers to All-Ireland success. He also represented the Under-21s in 1975 and 1977 when they were beaten in both years by Kilkenny in the All-Ireland finals. Tadhg was called up to the Cork senior hurling panel in 1977 and was introduced as a sub in the thrilling All-Ireland final victory over Wexford.

Ironically, in the years that followed, Tadhg became much better known as a football star. In 1986, he was an integral member of the Glanmire team which won the county intermediate football championship. He also won two senior football championship medals with divisional side, Imokilly in 1984 and 1986, and claimed an All-Ireland junior medal with Cork in 1987. Yet all his achievements - and there were many - pale into insignificance when the magical moment from the 1983 Munster football final is mentioned. The late, late goal which beat the Kingdom has cemented his place in GAA history. His longevity in the small ball game is remarkable, as Tadhg played senior hurling for Sarsfields for 25 years, from 1975 to 1999 inclusive. Even more astonishingly, he never missed a championship game during that time. "I was lucky with injuries, thanks be to God," he says, while acknowledging his disappointment in not actually winning a Cork SHC medal. He accepts that "the dual player is not feasible in the modern game".

In recent years, he trained Waterford club, Ardmore to win county junior and intermediate championships. He also managed the Sarsfields Under-14 team, which included his son, Tadhg Óg, which won the All-Ireland Féile title for the first time in 2000 in Belfast. His training commitments have restricted his participation in other pastimes such as golf.

Tadhg is married to Catherine (née Kenneally) - no mean sports star herself, having represented Munster in hockey and tennis and having won a Munster Minor Camogie medal with Cork in 1974 - and in addition to Tadhg Óg (already a member of the Sarsfields senior hurling team), they have a daughter, Katie.

For many years, Tadhg Murphy has worked in the insurance business and he is currently a director of Jardine Lloyd Thompson in Cork. He continued to follow the fortunes of Farranferris over the years and describes the school's recent closure as "tragic", having often helped out his alma mater in fundraising campaigns, as required. He still comes in contact with former team-mates such as Johnny Crowley, Francie Collins, John McEvoy, Finbarr Crowley and Mike Murphy on a regular basis, all of whom, like Tadhg, were members of the hugely-impressive Harty and Croke Cup champions in 1974.

1975 – ALL-IRELAND SEMI-FINAL
23 March 1975, Limerick

Coláiste Iognáid Rís, Cork 8-10
(J. Murphy 3-0, T. Beckett 2-2, T. Cullinane 2-0, P. Crowley 0-6, J. Barry 1-1, T. Howard 0-1)

Our Lady's, Gort 5-2
(G. Linane 2-0, B. Forde 2-0, V. Deely 1-0, J. Curtin 0-2)

St. Kieran's, Kilkenny, Croke Cup Champions, 1975.
Back row, left to right: Mick Meagher, Pat Gannon, Paudie Brennan, Dick Dalton, Gordon Ryan, Jim Lennon, Brendan Broderick.
Middle row, left to right: Michael Cuddihy, Jimmy Prendergast, Kevin O'Shea, Declan Fitzpatrick, Paddy Prendergast, Toddy Farrell, Richard Marnell.
Front row, left to right: Fr Diarmuid Healy, Seamus Brennan, John Ryan, Kieran Brennan (capt), Martin Joyce, Harry Ryan, Lester Ryan.
(Photograph courtesy of Dick McEvoy, c/o St. Kieran's, Kilkenny)

1975 – ALL-IRELAND FINAL
20 April 1975, Thurles
Referee: John Moloney (Tipperary)

St. Kieran's, Kilkenny 6-9

Richard Marnell
(Kilkenny)

John Ryan
(Tipperary)

Jim Lennon
(Kilkenny)

Harry Ryan
(Kilkenny)

Paddy Prendergast
(Kilkenny) (0-1)

Michael Cuddihy
(Kilkenny)

Jimmy Prendergast
(Kilkenny) (1-1)

Declan Fitzpatrick
(Waterford) (0-1)

Gordon Ryan
(Kilkenny) (0-1)

Kieran Brennan (*capt*)
(Kilkenny) (2-3)

Seamus Brennan
(Kilkenny) (0-1)

Kevin O'Shea
(Kilkenny) (1-1)

Paudie Brennan
(Kilkenny) (2-0)

Coláiste Iognáid Rís, Cork 2-3

Bernard Dooley
(Cork)

Tom Falvey
(Cork)

Frank Walsh
(Cork)

Damien Philpott
(Cork)

Dermot McCurtin
(Cork)

Liam O'Sullivan
(Cork)

Billy Collins
(Cork)

Paul Crowley
(Cork) (0-1)

Jim Barry
(Cork) (1-1)

Terry Howard (*capt*)
(Cork)

Tom Beckett
(Cork)

Theo Cullinane
(Cork)

Jim Murphy
(Cork) (1-1)

Sub: Joe Quinlan (Cork) (for Falvey).

Kieran Brennan

"The only real mystery was how the side compared to the best of those who have previously won the Croke Cup down through the years." So wrote Tom O'Riordan in the 'Irish Independent' on April 21st, 1975, the day after a St. Kieran's side, captained by Kieran Brennan, brought the All-Ireland Colleges senior hurling crown to the Kilkenny school for the seventh time.

Kieran Brennan is a native of Conahy and he comes from a famous family to wear the black and amber. Remarkably, however, he maintains that the hurling came from his mother's side, rather than his late father ("a very fair man, who always praised you for doing your best"). Indeed, Kieran's maternal uncles had been part of the St. Lachtain's-Freshford side which won the Kilkenny SHC in both 1961 and 1963.

Kieran recalls entering St. Kieran's in 1970 as a first year boarder, when his brother, Nicky was preparing to sit the Leaving Certificate. The following May, Nicky scored two points in the defeat of St. Finbarr's, Farranferris, with the Noresiders regaining the Croke Cup after a six-year absence. That victorious side also featured future Kilkenny star defender and manager, Brian Cody, and another player destined to become a major household name at inter-county level, Billy Fitzpatrick. Kieran looked up to these players, as well as to team captain Pat Kearney, Tony Teehan and Noel Minogue. "For young fellows like us to even talk to them was amazing", he reflects. Coming as he did from "an unsuccessful rural

club where you'd be lucky to get a game every year", young Kieran was thrilled to be in a situation where hurling was an integral part of the school ethos. He started with two years on the juvenile side, contesting Leinster finals in both years, one successfully.

A further two year cycle ensued on the junior team during which time Kieran graduated to the senior squad and was selected at centre half forward, a rare honour for a 15-year-old. However, St. Peter's of Wexford spoiled the party in the 1973 Leinster final, winning by 3-12 to 1-7 in Croke Park in a game shown live on television, en route to their fourth, and to date last, All-Ireland success. The following season St. Kieran's triumphed in Leinster, reversing the result against St. Peter's in some style (5-11 to 2-3), but were defeated in the Croke Cup final by two points in a thriller in Dungarvan by their old adversaries from Farranferris. Kieran chipped in with a point in the decider, but his abiding memory of the 1973/74 school year was a bad chest infection he sustained around Christmas. This hampered his training and playing for some time.

When Kieran returned to St. Kieran's the following September, training recommenced as always and he was thrilled when he was told he would be the senior captain for his final year. "We did serious training and, as the bulk of the team were boarders, there was no question of guys missing training", Kieran recalls. A championship game against St. Peter's was almost an annual occurrence, but there was no doubting the superiority of St. Kieran's this year, as evidenced by the 8-15 to 3-3 scoreline. Their Leinster final opponents on March 23rd in Carlow were Presentation College, Birr. Indeed, this on-field rivalry led to a lifelong friendship with Offaly's Aidan Fogarty, who went on to live in Kilkenny. St. Kieran's won the final comfortably (6-12 to 4-3), despite Kieran carrying a knee injury, and progressed to the All-Ireland final against Coláiste Iognáid Rís.

The Cork school suffered that year from the demands of the wonderful achievement of winning the Munster finals in both codes, with effectively the same bunch of players. This dual pressure certainly contributed to a somewhat one-sided final in which Kieran notched a personal tally of 2-3 against the Harty Cup champions. Kieran "absolutely loved the 13-a-side" experiment which took place in colleges GAA in the 1970s, to which he modestly attributes many of his scores with no full back to face! The open game often led to a glut of scores, but the 'Irish Independent' attributed the victory specifically to St. Kieran's "ability to beat an opponent on the pull to the ground ball, allied to great speed in all sectors of the field, their physique, strength and fitness".

The glory of the occasion was "spoiled a little" for Kieran when the newly-crowned champions were not allowed parade the trophy on a lap of honour in Thurles. Indeed, Kieran and his brother, Paudie, together with another team member, Michael Cuddihy, were "quickly brought down to earth" when they had to line out for Conahy Shamrocks against Muckalee that evening, with the Croke Cup left in the boot of a car! Kieran smiles when he remembers that "the only perk for the hurlers those days was the magnificent smell of food at the top table" compared to the more mundane offerings which went to other students on match days!

Kieran is one of five brothers who attended St. Kieran's. Nicky, Kieran and Paudie all won Croke Cup medals. However, Gearóid, in Kieran's view, was "the most unfortunate hurler of all of us" in that his time in the famed nursery coincided with a period in the latter part of the 1970s when "the whole thing went into a slide". On the other hand, Canice's schooldays saw St. Kieran's become very much the dominant force in the land and he annexed three winner's medals in 1988 (as a sub), 1989 and 1990.

Diarmuid Healy receives great praise from Kieran for his role in producing great college sides. Later to be the man most associated with the emergence of Offaly as a major hurling power, Diarmuid was well known to Kieran through his club connections with Conahy. "At the time, Fr Tommy Maher's influence was all over the place", Kieran reflects. "He was a famous guy and when you needed a hurley you went up to his room. You were very wary in his presence, as a young fellow coming from a rural area", Kieran reflects.

Later in 1975, Kieran won a minor All-Ireland with Kilkenny. He went on to don the black and amber at all levels in a glittering career, which saw him win an All-Ireland Under-21 medal in 1977, two All-Ireland senior medals in 1982 and 1983, two National League mementoes (1982 and 1986) and an All-Star award in 1984. He had the honour of captaining Kilkenny in 1985. Incredibly, he played his last game for Conahy Shamrocks at the age of 43 in 2000, after making an enormous contribution to the cause of his club from the Under-10 grade upwards. He has put much of his expertise back into the game as a trainer to Portlaoise, Graigue Ballycallan, James Stephens and, of course, his beloved Conahy Shamrocks.

Kieran joined the Defence Forces as a cadet after finishing secondary school in St. Kieran's. He was commissioned in 1977 and was stationed in Limerick. He did a B Comm at UCG and, up to 1989, he was based at the Curragh Camp. From 1989 to 1997 he was near home in Kilkenny city and since then has been in the air base in Baldonnell, followed by Clonmel and he is now back in the Curragh. He undertook three overseas tours of duty, two to Lebanon in 1982/83 and 1997/98 and, a third, to Kosovo in 2004. "Army life and commuting to training were difficult but the sacrifices were well worth it," Kieran reflects.

The Brennan connection with St. Kieran's continued on into the next generation. Kieran is married to Maria and they live in Kilkenny city, where their two sons, Kieran and Shane, "have togged out with pride" in the distinctive black and white jersey. Indeed, Kieran Jnr has successfully followed his father's career path in the Defence Forces.

With his brother Nicky now well established as the GAA President, Kieran Brennan's great love of hurling continues to this day. Comparing teams of the past is a hazardous occupation and Tom O'Riordan's query over 31 years ago about the merits of Kieran and his team-mates can never be scientifically answered. However, a scoring return of 20-36, as against 9-9 conceded in three games, says an awful lot about the All-Ireland champions of 1975, in a campaign Kieran will always treasure and one which, amazingly, was to be followed by a whopping 13-year Croke Cup famine.

1976 – ALL-IRELAND SEMI-FINAL
4 April 1976, Nenagh

Presentation College, Athenry 2-11
(P. Hurney 1-2, M. Duffy 1-2, G. Dempsey 0-4, J. Connolly 0-2, L. Kennedy 0-1)

Kilkenny CBS 2-7
(M. Nolan 1-2, M. Langton 0-4, A. Bergin 1-0, A. Malone 0-1)

St. Flannan's, Ennis, Croke Cup Champions, 1976.
Back row, left to right: John Moran, Martin Meehan, John Mullins, Barry Smythe, Cyril Lyons,
P. J. Deasy, John Hanly, John Tierney, Conor O'Dwyer, Jarlath Colleran, Michael Gleeson.
Front row, left to right: John Power, Ger Lyons, Eddie Sutton, Brian Donnellan, Brian Coffey,
Leo Quinlan (capt), John Murphy, Bernard Lynch, Seanie McMahon, Paddy O'Malley,
Michael Walsh.
(Photograph courtesy of Ollie Byrnes, author of Blue is the Colour, Hurling at St. Flannan's)

1976 – ALL-IRELAND FINAL
2 May 1976, Nenagh
Referee: Jimmy Rankins (Laois)

St. Flannan's, Ennis 3-7

John Tierney
(Tipperary)

Paddy O'Malley   **Michael Gleeson**
(Limerick)   (Tipperary)

John Hanly   **Barry Smythe**   **Jarlath Colleran**
(Clare)   (Clare)   (Clare)

Martin Meehan   **John Power**
(Clare) (0-1)   (Clare)

John Moran   **Brian Donnellan**   **Cyril Lyons**
(Clare)   (Clare)   (Clare) (1-1)

Leo Quinlan (*capt*)   **John Murphy**
(Clare) (1-4)   (Clare) (1-1)

Sub: P. J. Deasy (Clare) (for Power).

Presentation College, Athenry 4-4

Christy Kilkelly
(Galway)

Philip Powell   **Gerry Hardiman**
(Galway) (0-1)   (Galway)

Gerry Naughton   **Richie Walsh**   **Pat Lally**
(Galway)   (Galway)   (Galway)

Pascal Ryan   **John Ryan**
(Galway) (1-0)   (Galway) (1-0)

Joe Connolly   **Gerry Dempsey (*capt*)**   **Pat Hurney**
(Galway) (1-0)   (Galway) (0-1)   (Galway) (1-1)

Martin Duffy   **Louis Kennedy**
(Galway) (0-1)   (Galway)

Sub: Kieran Jordan (Galway) (for Kennedy).

1976 – ALL-IRELAND FINAL (REPLAY)
16 May 1976, Nenagh
Referee: John Moloney (Tipperary)

St. Flannan's, Ennis 3-9

Brian Coffey
(Clare)

Michael Gleeson　　　　**Paddy O'Malley**
(Tipperary)　　　　　　　　(Limerick)

John Hanly　　　　**Barry Smythe**　　　　**Jarlath Colleran**
(Clare)　　　　　　　(Clare)　　　　　　　(Clare)

Martin Meehan　　　　**John Moran**
(Clare) (0-2)　　　　　　(Clare) (2-0)

Brian Donnellan　　　**P. J. Deasy**　　　**Leo Quinlan** (*capt*)
(Clare)　　　　　　　　(Clare) (0-3)　　　　(Clare) (0-1)

Cyril Lyons　　　　**John Murphy**
(Clare) (0-2)　　　　　(Clare) (1-1)

Presentation College, Athenry 1-7

Christy Kilkelly
(Galway)

Philip Powell　　　　**Gerry Hardiman**
(Galway) (0-1)　　　　　(Galway)

Gerry Naughton　　　**Richie Walsh**　　　**Michael Delaney**
(Galway)　　　　　　　(Galway)　　　　　　(Galway)

Pascal Ryan　　　　**John Ryan**
(Galway) (0-1)　　　　(Galway) (0-1)

Joe Connolly　　　**Gerry Dempsey** (*capt*)　　**Pat Hurney**
(Galway)　　　　　　(Galway) (0-2)　　　　　(Galway) (1-0)

Martin Duffy　　　　**Pat Lally**
(Galway) (0-2)　　　　(Galway)

Leo Quinlan

By the standards set over the years in St. Flannan's, Ennis, 18 years without a Harty Cup title is an eternity and the young man privileged to end that famine as Croke and Harty Cup winning captain in 1976 was Leo Quinlan, who led the college to a succession of titles in his schooldays.

Leo, a native of Sixmilebridge, hails from a very strong hurling background. "There was always hurling spoken in the daily family life," says Leo, which is not surprising as his three uncles on his mother's side played for Tipperary in their great three-in-a-row era of 1949 to 1951, with Mick, Jack and Dinny all winning All-Ireland senior hurling medals. Leo's mother, a Ryan from Roscrea, and his father who was from Killavilla in County Offaly, arrived in the hurling-mad village of Sixmilebridge as a result of the advent of Shannon Airport. "My late father had the best of both worlds as he cheered for Tipperary when they had successful years and then for Offaly when they had their golden years, so he really couldn't lose," Leo jokes. While in national school there was little emphasis on hurling, but "once Danny O'Dea joined the teaching staff there was nothing but hurling, as he organised a school team and everything just took off from there".

While his older brother, Michael went to Árd Scoil Rís in Limerick, Leo admits he went to St. Flannan's in 1971, mainly for the hurling but he quickly points out that, "you will perform better academically if you are happy with the rest of your life and I was happy hurling."

Later on, his younger brother, Enda ended up winning Harty and Croke Cup medals in 1979 with St. Flannan's. Entering St. Flannan's in 1971, Leo quickly toughened up and learned his hurling in the "very well structured and organised" first year leagues which eventually shaped the backbone of the 1976 championship winning side. Ger Loughnane, Colm Honan, Sean Stack and Johnny Callinan were just some of the older students whom Leo admired. "They were brilliant hurlers," says Leo, recalling a number of future Clare senior heroes in the mid-1970s. 'Basher' Hickey ("also a great handballer"), 'Pudsy' Ryan and Robert Gill are other hurlers whose names come flooding back to Leo from that era. He fondly remembers "looking forward to going to the Harty Cup games in those days, although there were years when we might only see one or two championship games. For example, I remember a particular game in Charleville against Farranferris when they railroaded through Flannan's."

Success came quickly for Leo in the blue and white jersey. "In 1974, we entered the White Cup which is for Munster teams at Under-15½ age level and we won it. I was captain and the nucleus of that side went on to win the Croke Cup in 1976. The training sessions were tough but enjoyable", Leo recalls. "Father Seamus Gardiner and Father Willie Walsh were superb trainers and they always kept us going, showing us the skills of the game. Training was after school and it was never a problem for them to bring us home afterwards to places like Sixmilebridge, Kilkishen, Quin, Clarecastle and Newmarket. Looking back, it was remarkable that Mike Walsh from Kiltimagh in County Mayo was one of the boarders on the team in that year." Leo vividly remembers his first game for St. Flannan's senior side when he was just 16 and still in fourth year. "It was in 1975 against De La Salle, Waterford, and the game ended in a draw. Between the draw and the replay, which we lost, that was the first time I really paid attention to any team talk, as Fr Seamus Gardiner drilled home to us how serious these matches were and just why we were doing all this training. It consisted mainly of ball work and the sessions would often be stopped and we would be told what was expected of us in each position. There was very little emphasis on physical fitness."

Some 30 years later, Leo has kept a detailed record of his games for St. Flannan's. The first game on the road to the Croke Cup saw the Ennis college play a Harty Cup opener on October 15th 1975 in Emly against Coláiste Iognáid Rís from Cork, who had won a Munster football and hurling double in 1975. The Rebel side were favourites, but "a young, determined and fit St. Flannan's side" won comprehensively by 1-16 to 0-5 and laid down a marker for the rest of the Munster teams. "We were fortunate to see one of the best Harty Cup games ever the week before, when we witnessed North Mon beat Limerick CBS in their first round game and Fr Walsh was so impressed by the Mon that he said after the game, 'we'll pull away quietly'. At half time in the semi-final against North Mon on March 7th 1976, also in Emly, we were only leading 0-3 to 0-1 but Fr Gardiner really got on to us that day. He switched the team and I ended up playing wing back and I remember Fr Walsh, a shrewd, quiet man who always concentrated on the defensive side of the game, reminding us to keep it tight. Fr Gardiner was able to read the opposition and was a very organised person who always got to know who was refereeing before every game took place. We beat North Mon 2-6 to 0-6 and ended up playing De La Salle, Waterford, in the Harty

Cup final on April 4th. Colleges hurling games in those days were big occasions and everyone went to matches. There was a great buzz as all the students sang songs, wore school colours and looked forward to the announcement of the school team. This time we were favourites but we won in style and it was a fierce enjoyable win. In particular, I remember the performance of Barry Smythe ("a great athlete") at centre half back, especially when things got tough. We won by 2-9 to 3-4 in Bansha and Cyril Lyons got a vital goal that day. It was a huge win and a great relief for everyone in St. Flannan's after an 18-year wait. The importance and significance of that Harty Cup win only sank in afterwards as past pupils, former players and captains all attended a civic reception in Ennis for the team".

Just a few days after Leo picked up another medal as Dean Ryan Cup winning captain against Limerick CBS, St. Flannan's headed to Nenagh to face surprise finalists Presentation College, Athenry, in the Croke Cup final and they were fairly confident of winning, despite changing from a traditional 15-a-side format to 13-a-side. He reflects, "Athenry had some good players like the Ryan twins, John and Paschal and in the end we were lucky to draw. We really didn't play well and the game passed us by. They had a guy called Joe Connolly whom we nicknamed 'The Indian' because of his long black flowing hair. The Galway side got a grip on the game but we just managed to stay in it. One incident stands out and that was when Michael Gleeson dived on a ball in the dying minutes of the game to block a shot from an Athenry forward, to save the match and we escaped with a draw." The 'Irish Independent' report from the drawn game states that, "after looking down and out when trailing by 3-5 to 1-0 late in the opening half, Presentation Athenry staged a magnificent recovery to gain a draw". Indeed the report confirms that "St. Flannan's hardly got out of their own half after the interval, and had it not been for their extraordinary amount of wides, 17 in all, then the Connacht side would have become All-Ireland champions". At the end of what the paper described as "a marvellous afternoon's entertainment" the sides were level, with Leo finishing the drawn match with a personal tally of 1-4.

However, Leo points out that, "we showed a different attitude for the replay, which was also played in Nenagh a fortnight later. We were over-confident entering the drawn game as we had just won the Harty Cup. This time, we didn't let complacency set in and we had a fierce never-say-die attitude, the seeds of which were sown in our early college years, which probably was the difference. Our strength and determination in the second half of the replay won the cup for us." The 'Irish Independent' points out that it was "the ability to raise their game when such an occasion demanded which proved to be St. Flannan's advantage at the crucial three quarter stage of this replay. It was not the classic expected, as the near gale force wind saw to that but there was no shortage of honest effort on the part of both sides." The sides were level 1-4 each after ten minutes, with John Moran netting for St. Flannan's with a fortuitous effort and it wasn't until late in the second half that another Moran goal and a third green flag from John Murphy that victory was sealed. He still remembers the post-match euphoria, saying that, "fortunately Fr Gardiner helped me with my speech and gave me a few lines to say as I accepted the Croke Cup. As we headed back to St. Flannan's for a reception and meal after the game, there was a tremendous buzz and excitement within the school. We were made feel like heroes."

"Returning to our studies was very difficult after all the craic and excitement," Leo reflects, adding that, "Fr Gardiner taught a few of us French and he used to take us for extra lessons after school. Only he realised we were so far behind in our studies because of our efforts in winning the Croke Cup and now the Leaving Cert was just around the corner. Some of us who were just 17 repeated the Leaving Cert in 1977, but on the hurling field St. Colman's, Fermoy, beat us in the Harty Cup final by 0-7 to 0-3. We really regretted playing that game. It took place in dreadful conditions, and we shouldn't have played that day as the weather was so poor." While there has been no official re-union of the team since, there

have been school reunions after ten and 25 years where thankfully most of the players turned up. Unfortunately, Paddy O'Malley and Jarlath Colleran from the St. Flannan's side of 1976 have since passed away. Leo goes on, "years later, I remember meeting a guy in UCG and he shook hands with me. I had no idea who he was and then he told me he was Gerry Dempsey and that 'we shook hands before' (for the Croke Cup finals of 1976) and ever since we have been great friends".

On the club scene, Sixmilebridge reached the senior county final in 1976 where Leo played in goals. Unfortunately, he was unable to prevent Newmarket-on-Fergus from triumphing that day. However, the good times were set to roll for Sixmilebridge and the following year the county championship was won. It was Sixmilebridge's first ever championship victory and since then they have gone from strength to strength. Leo is proud of the five county medals on his mantelpiece. However, a particular disappointment for him was the defeat by St. Finbarr's of Cork in the Munster club final replay on January 22nd 1978. "In the drawn game (on December 18th 1977), we were losing by 2-3 to 0-0 in Tulla and we came back and went ahead and we were in control with ten minutes remaining, but thick fog descended and the match was abandoned and would you believe we lost the replay (0-6 to 2-8)".

While Leo played minor and Under-21 for Clare he felt there was not the same preparation, organisation or effort put in as had been the case in St. Flannan's and, as a result, the teams were not successful. "I guess we didn't have quite the same respect for the Clare trainers as we did for Fr Gardiner and Fr Walsh. Training wasn't the same and we just went through the motions and Tipperary or Cork would just come along and hammer us in the first round", he recalls ruefully. Leo was slightly more fortunate playing with the Clare senior team of the late 1970s and early 1980s, but once again championship silverware eluded him. He forced his way onto the Clare panel which won the 1978 National League final and lost the Munster final to Cork on a scoreline of 0-11 to 0-13. The Sixmilebridge native also played in the championship sides of 1980 and 1981 where in the latter year, Limerick defeated the Banner County in the Munster final. However, at third level, Leo continued to be successful with UCG when he was part of a number of strong college sides. "We had a very strong team back then with such notable quality players like Joe McDonagh, Joe Connolly, Pat Fleury and the late Niall McInerney." Leo won a Fitzgibbon Cup medal in 1980, with Gerry Dempsey as a team-mate on a side trained by Brian Cody's brother, Eamon, when UCG defeated UCC by 0-10 to 1-5 in the final in Galway. Having completed a BComm and HDip, Leo took up a teaching job in St. Mary's College in Galway and joined Liam Mellowes, the Galway city club side in 1983, with whom he made a quarter-final appearance in the county championship. He returned to Sixmilebridge later in the decade and won two more Clare county medals with the club. He retired from the game of hurling in 1993, three years before his beloved Sixmilebridge won the All-Ireland club championship.

For 11 years now, Leo has been a teacher of Business and Maths in Coláiste Mhuire in Ennis and he was particularly pleased to have coached the school camogie team to win the All-Ireland junior 'B' title in 1999. He lives just outside Sixmilebridge and has two sons, Shane (14) and Tim (12) who at present are attending Ennis CBS. Up to now, they have shown more interest in spectating than actually playing the game of hurling but they are particularly interested in swimming and shooting respectively. However, Leo still keeps an eye out for St. Flannan's results. In recent years, he has trained the Sixmilebridge senior team with quite a degree of success. The 'Bridge contested four successive Clare SHC finals under Leo, winning out in 2000 and 2002, as well as garnering a Munster club title in 2001, before losing an All-Ireland semi-final (after a replay) to Kilkenny kingpins, Graigue-Ballycallan.

To this day, Leo acknowledges that there is still "a great bond" among the survivors of the 1976 St. Flannan's team. The ending of the 18-year Harty and Croke Cup famine brought unconfined joy to the school and the town of Ennis. The mighty St. Flannan's of Ennis have never looked back since.

1977 – ALL-IRELAND SEMI-FINAL
3 April 1977, Nenagh

St. Colman's, Fermoy 2-10
(J. Mangan 1-2, J. Monaghan 1-0, G. O'Regan 0-2, W. Cashman 0-2, J. Hartnett 0-2,
M. Mellerick 0-2)

Presentation College, Athenry 2-3
(J. Ryan 1-1, G. Burke 1-0, P. Ryan 0-1, L. Kennedy 0-1)

St. Colman's, Fermoy, Croke Cup Champions, 1977.
Fourth row, left to right: Michael Healy, Sean O'Brien, Tom Abernethy, Martin Hinchion,
John Boylan, John Hartnett, Willie Cashman.
Third row, left to right: Mr John Whyte, Fr Sean Cotter, Joe Aherne, John Mangan,
Jimmy Monaghan, Pat Fitzgerald, John Redmond, Michael Lyons, Fergus Tighe, Fr Donal Coakley.
Second row, left to right: Michael Mellerick, Gerard O'Regan, Jimmy Walsh, John Lenihan (capt),
Con Spillane, Tadhg Coakley, John Kenneally, Tom Murphy.
Front row, left to right: Tim Taylor, Batty Joyce, Ned Brosnan, Kieran Keohane.
(Photograph courtesy of John Lenihan)

1977 – ALL-IRELAND FINAL
1 May 1977, Thurles
Referee: Jimmy Rankins (Laois)

St. Colman's, Fermoy 2-13

Martin Hinchion
(Cork)

Pat Fitzgerald
(Cork)

Jimmy Walsh
(Cork)

Con Spillane
(Cork)

Willie Cashman
(Cork) (0-1)

Sean O'Brien
(Cork) (0-1)

Tadhg Coakley
(Cork)

John Hartnett
(Cork) (0-2)

Tom Murphy
(Cork) (0-1)

Gerard O'Regan
(Cork) (0-5)

John Lenihan (*capt*)
(Cork)

Michael Mellerick
(Cork) (1-0)

Jimmy Monaghan
(Cork) (0-1)

John Mangan
(Cork) (1-0)

John Boylan
(Cork) (0-2)

St. Kieran's, Kilkenny 1-9

Joe Phelan
(Laois)

Tom White
(Laois)

John Joe Dowling
(Kilkenny)

Michael Manning
(Kilkenny)

Martin Prendergast
(Kilkenny)

Mick Meagher
(Kilkenny)

Liam Leahy
(Kilkenny)

Pat Gannon (*capt*)
(Kilkenny) (0-3)

Gordon Ryan
(Kilkenny) (0-3)

Martin Morrissey
(Kilkenny) (0-2)

Michael Broderick
(Laois)

Dick Moffitt
(Kilkenny)

Michael McGrath
(Kilkenny) (0-1)

Ned Kelly
(Kilkenny) (1-0)

Matt Reid
(Kilkenny)

John Lenihan

Remarkably, in 1977, there were new champions in the All-Ireland Colleges senior 'A' competitions in both codes. Even more remarkable was that both schools were under the patronage of St. Colman! Newtownshandrum's John Lenihan, captained St. Colman's, Fermoy, to Croke Cup glory that year from an unaccustomed centre half forward berth, thereby setting the trend for future champions from the County Cork college.

John loved hurling long before he entered secondary school and he has fond memories of reaching a North Cork Under-12 final as Newtown captain, before succumbing to Mallow. He recalls that, "Colman's was the place to go", both as a promising hurler and with parental notions that he might consider later life as a priest! Ironically, John's late father, Michael, played football for two counties, because his work as a creamery manager saw him change allegiance from Wexford to Limerick, but he always encouraged his son to pursue his love of the small ball game.

John first entered the hallowed gates of St. Colman's in September 1972. Initially he made the Under-14 side and, so impressive was the young team, that John recalls one of the teachers saying, "this team is going to win the Harty". Having been starved of Munster senior success since 1949, there was a deep desire within the school to return to former glory.

The frustration in St. Colman's in failing to capture the elusive trophy was compounded in John's first year. In 1972/73, a very promising side whom John feels "would probably have won the Harty", was ejected from the competition along with defeated opponents North Monastery, after a series of objections and counter-objections. John feels that this further fuelled the desire in his classmates to win out when their chance would come. John looked up to a fellow Newtown student, Pat Coughlan, from that unlucky team. On the inter-county scene at that time, John was a big fan of Seanie O'Leary, a past pupil of St. Colman's, as well as John Buckley, also of Newtownshandrum, a holder of a rare hat-trick of minor All-Ireland medals.

John made the senior team in 1975/76 and they reached the Munster semi-final, losing in a replay to De La Salle, Waterford. He recalls that "a very shrewd individual", John Whyte, became involved in the training of the team. This was quite unusual for a lay teacher at the time. John attributes his since-deceased coach with "bringing a different outlook to the game" and instilling into the squad "a confidence which made all the difference". John had been the team captain at juvenile and Under-16 level and retained the honour for the 1976/77 Harty campaign, having edged out Jimmy Walsh by the narrowest of margins in a vote among the players after the first training session of the year. "It wasn't that I was the best hurler on the team", John says modestly, "but I just did my job as best I could". Other advocates of hurling at the time in the school were Fr Sean Cotter, "who was involved for years" and Fr Donal Coakley, whom John recalls as "a fitness fanatic".

The great promise shown in their formative years shone through in early round defeats of three famed nurseries North Monastery, Limerick CBS and Coláiste Iognáid Rís. Looking back, John reflects, "all members of the team were playing well and it looked very good for us". Arch-rivals St. Flannan's, Ennis, awaited St. Colman's in the Harty Cup decider. The reigning All-Ireland champions were defeated by 0-7 to 0-3 in "very wet conditions in Emly" on March 13th, 1977. "Great celebrations" ensued that evening and for the next few days at the school. John has fond memories of "the support given to the team by the people of Fermoy and the whole of the wider area of North Cork/East Cork".

St. Colman's had lost their only previous All-Ireland final in 1948 and were denied the opportunity to go one step further in the following year as the All-Ireland series was disbanded from 1949 to 1956 inclusive, for reasons never fully clarified to this day. Naturally, there was a great determination to win the elusive Croke Cup and emulate the feats of two other Cork schools - North Monastery and St. Finbarr's, Farranferris. In order to reach the decider, the Fermoy lads had to overcome the Connacht champions, Presentation College from Athenry, in the semi-final. They accomplished this task with seven points to spare in Nenagh on April 3rd. However, John feels that the performance was not particularly inspiring. "It brought us back to reality and we knuckled down after the semi-final".

Regular centre forward, Michael Lyons, had been badly injured after the Harty campaign and John found himself in unfamiliar territory for the two games in the All-Ireland series with Tadhg Coakley ("a very good young hurler") stepping into wing back in John's place. John did not particularly fancy his new position but felt that as captain he owed it to the mentors and fellow players to give it his best shot. He didn't consider himself to be a natural scoring forward but was determined to reduce the effectiveness of opposing centre half backs.

Seven points was again the winning margin in Semple Stadium on May 1st when the mighty St. Kieran's, Kilkenny, were overcome in the Croke Cup final. John reckons that the margin was flattering with two late goals needed to seal the issue. In his absence, the half back line performed heroically with Willie Cashman and Sean O'Brien both scoring inspirational points. The 'Irish Independent' reporter's opinion was, as follows, "that incalculable capacity to lift their performance at a stage when the opposition seemed poised to take control was the ingredient which made it a day of glory for St. Colman's". The winners led by 0-8 to 1-2 at the interval and had a narrow escape when the Kilkenny side had a 'goal' controversially disallowed soon after the resumption. It wasn't until the closing stages that St. Colman's put some daylight between themselves and the seven-times champions from the Marble City, with John Mangan's last-minute goal being very much the icing on the cake. "The celebrations went on for many a long day," John recalls, "maybe too much so!"

John openly admits that some players suffered academically because of their hurling exploits and he decided to repeat four subjects in his Leaving Certificate the following year at Charleville CBS. He went on to play at centrefield on the school side, together with four Newtownshandrum colleagues, which regained the Munster 'B' colleges hurling title after a long absence. He jokes that his father's attitude was, "not this all over again"! However, John went on to gain All-Ireland 'B' honours and complete a truly remarkable double. His status as a day pupil in Charleville contrasted with being a boarder in Fermoy but he retains links with both his alma maters. He was very impressed with the huge turnout for a reunion of the Charleville CBS squad earlier this decade, while he also keeps in regular contact with five of the St. Colman's panel. With boarding being phased out nationwide, John feels that sides such as Charleville CBS will be among the teams to watch out for in the near future.

John joined AIB Bank in 1978 and his love of hurling and all sports continued in his new career, with his employers always supportive of staff who participate in sport. He enjoyed a number of overseas trips representing the bank in the company of such high-profile colleagues as Nicky English (Tipperary), Ger Fitzpatrick (Waterford) and Noel Crowley (Cork). John won a Cork IHC medal in 1981 with Newtownshandrum and he captained the senior side which reached the quarter-final three years later. He rejoiced at his club's breakthrough in 2000 when they won the Cork senior hurling crown for the first time ever with "a young and talented team led by Ben and Jerry O'Connor", and which also included John's nephew, James Bowles. The nucleus of this team went on to win the AIB All-Ireland club title in 2004. John himself only retired from hurling as a player in his mid-40s a few short years ago.

His banking career has brought John to Clonmel, Newmarket, Kilfinane, Killarney, Macroom and back to Killarney again, a town in which he now resides with his wife, Mernie (a native of Cahirciveen) and their four young children, Jack (10), Emma (8), Michael (5) and Lisa (2). His current role with AIB Bank is as Financial Planning Manager covering all of Kerry and advising on wealth management. He plays golf off a 14 handicap and hopes to reduce this when his hurling commitments are less time-consuming in the future. He also enjoys tennis and dabbled at both soccer and rugby in Charleville. One of his sisters, Ann, is

a nun and is a proficient 13-handicap golfer, while his niece, Niamh Bowles, outscores her uncle with a remarkable ten All-Ireland camogie medals!

John's undoubted love of hurling has seen him give huge commitment to his beloved Newtownshandrum for over 25 years, during which time he served as treasurer for over six years and was involved in the purchase of their new grounds in the GAA's Centenary Year in 1984. He was honoured by the club with the Clubman of the Year award in 1986. The following year, he led Macroom to the Mid Cork junior 'B' title after a long absence. Since his return to Killarney, he has been heavily involved with the Dr Crokes club and is currently manager/coach to the club's intermediate hurlers. Indeed, he also coaches the Under-10s where his son Jack is "showing great promise". John will always encourage all his children to participate in hurling and football. While he realises that hurling takes very much a back seat in football-mad Kerry, John is there "for the long haul" when it comes to promoting the small ball game. "If Kerry can do it in football, there is no reason why they can't in hurling," he enthuses.

John Lenihan's enthusiasm for Gaelic games remains undiminished by the passage of time. This enthusiasm first came to the fore almost 30 years ago when he led St. Colman's to their first Croke Cup.

1978 – ALL-IRELAND SEMI-FINAL
16 April 1978, Carlow

St. Peter's, Wexford 1-9
(T. Wright 1-0, J. O'Dwyer 0-2, S. McDonald 0-2, J. White 0-2, B. Foley 0-1,
J. Kavanagh 0-1, B. Curtis 0-1)

Our Lady's, Gort 0-4
(P. Piggott 0-1, P. Conroy 0-1, G. Broderick 0-1, A. Moylan 0-1)

Templemore CBS, Croke Cup Champions, 1978.
Back row, left to right: Br Joe Perkins, Pat Treacy, Jim Kennedy, Pat McGrath, Brendan Russell, Timmy Stapleton, Peter Brennan, Br Pat Seaver, Jim Maher, Richard Stapleton, Eamon Cody, Pat Cormack, Mick Ryan (Clonmore), Mr. John Costigan.
Front row, left to right: Joe Bourke, Liam Farrelly, Mick Ryan (Borrisoleigh), Joe Sweeney, Pat Hassett, Noel Farrelly, Martin Bourke (capt), John Hanley, Frankie McGrath, Bobby Ryan, Noel Fogarty.
(Photograph courtesy of Martin Bourke)

1978 – ALL-IRELAND FINAL
7 May 1978, Kilkenny
Referee: Noel Dalton (Waterford)

Templemore CBS 2-11

Pat Hassett
(Laois)

Martin Bourke (*capt*)
(Tipperary)

Peter Brennan
(Tipperary)

Richard Stapleton
(Tipperary)

Pat Cormack
(Tipperary)

Mick Ryan
(Tipperary)

Jim Maher
(Tipperary)

Pat McGrath
(Tipperary) (0-4)

Mick Ryan
(Tipperary)

Brendan Russell
(Tipperary) (0-1)

Pat Treacy
(Tipperary) (0-1)

Noel Fogarty
(Tipperary) (0-2)

Joe Bourke
(Tipperary)

Eamon Cody
(Tipperary) (2-1)

Bobby Ryan
(Tipperary) (0-2)

Sub: Joe Sweeney (Tipperary) (for J. Bourke).

St. Peter's, Wexford 1-4

Pat Cleary
(Wexford)

Joe Sinnott
(Wexford)

Nicky Casey
(Wexford)

Padge Dunphy
(Wexford)

Brian Foley
(Wexford)

John McDonald
(Wexford) (0-1)

Edmond O'Neill
(Wexford)

John O'Dwyer
(Kilkenny) (0-1)

Tony Wright
(Wexford)

John Kavanagh
(Wexford)

Larry Kavanagh
(Wexford)

Pat Creane
(Wexford) (0-1)

Mick Farrell
(Wexford) (0-1)

Jim White (*capt*)
(Wexford)

Pat Doyle
(Wexford) (1-0)

Sub: Brendan Curtis (Wexford) (for J. Kavanagh).

Martin Bourke

Well over a quarter of a century after leading Templemore CBS to their unique Harty and Croke Cup successes, multi-talented team captain, Martin Bourke has clear memories of the historic campaign which brought the two prestigious trophies to the Premier County for the only time ever.

Martin is the second youngest of seven boys (he has no sisters) and, as a nine-year-old, he suffered the trauma of the death of his father. Despite this, he has fond childhood memories and the love of Gaelic games which he developed back in the late 1960s and early 1970s remains with him to this day. He can still nonchalantly reel off details of underage games from that period - from his days in the street leagues, playing as an Under-15, though six years under the age limit, right through to his adult involvement. Indeed, he was a valued squad member of the Clonmore team which won the Mid-Tipperary No 1 junior hurling crown in 1975 at the tender age of 15. Over the years, Martin's commitment to the local cause was total. He laughs while recalling the stalwarts who gave freely of their time and energy to foster juvenile talent. "Mick Russell," he recalls, "thought nothing of squeezing ten or more lads into his car to transport them to and from matches."

This local camaraderie was a great plus in Templemore CBS, a day school of approximately 270 pupils back in the 1970s. Martin spent six happy years there commencing in 1972. He represented the school in the Rice Cup, Pearse Cup and Kinnane Cup grades and had the satisfaction of winning a Corn Phadraig (effectively the Harty 'B' competition) medal in 1975. He was a member of the school senior team in 1976 and 1977 and was "thrilled" to be named as captain later that year prior to the commencement of his Leaving Cert year in 1977/78.

A comprehensive 3-15 to 0-3 first round defeat of Coláiste Iognáid Rís in Emly was too one-sided to evaluate the real merit of the Templemore side. However, hurling fans sat up to take notice when the famed St Finbarr's of Farranferris were overcome in Cashel on November 16th, 1977. He remembers "a brilliant pass from Brendan Russell, who was a son of Mick, to Noel Fogarty in the dying moments" bringing the goal which ensured a 1-9 to 1-8 victory. The Harty Cup semi-final was not scheduled until well into 1978, but training continued right through the winter, including the Christmas holidays. Indeed, Martin remembers Brother Perkins ("a fanatic for the game") organising get-togethers over the festive period. "He arrived in a green van from which you could see and smell the smoke, long before he arrived!"

Undaunted by interruptions to training in January caused by severe snowfalls, preparations continued in February and all this hard graft paid dividends on March 5th in Kilmallock with a 3-8 to 1-8 win over another famous nursery, North Monastery of Cork. The build-up to their debut in the Harty Cup final sparked off "astonishing community support and enthusiasm". Around 6,500 people thronged the grounds at Emly, "with the maroon flags of Templemore undoubtedly outnumbering the blue of St Flannan's of Ennis". The Clare-based college were very experienced at this level and looked like potential runaway victors for much of the game, at one time holding a daunting nine-point lead. However "judicious switches from the mentors, as well as superb spirit from the lads" saw the Tipperary representatives stage a remarkable comeback for a two-point victory on a scoreline of 3-5 to 2-6. "Emotional scenes" greeted the final whistle and celebrations continued long after Archbishop Morris presented Martin with the prestigious Harty Cup. "A tremendous welcome" awaited the new Munster kingpins on their arrival home in Templemore and a couple of free days ensured the entire school population could treasure the memories.

While the annexing of the Munster trophy was a massive achievement in itself, a steely determination existed in the school to go one better than Tipperary CBS in 1959 and become the first side from the county to capture the Croke Cup. Nowlan Park was the venue on May 7th 1978 when four-time champions St Peter's, Wexford, provided the opposition in the All-Ireland final. A memorable display by the lads from Templemore resulted in a ten-point victory on a wet day in Kilkenny. The margin was flattering in that the game was closely contested until the final ten minutes, but much of the blame for this was down to the winners' huge total of 14 first half wides. Templemore led by 0-7 to 1-1 at the interval, with the 'Irish Independent' reporting that, "the Tipperary boys made so many openings from their outfield dominance that really at times it did not resemble a real contest".

Jim Maher gave a fine display on the half back line, where he was joined in the second half by Bobby Ryan, the man who would hold up the Liam McCarthy Cup in Croke Park over 11 years later, thus ending Tipperary's 18-year famine at the highest level. In the end, it took two late goals from Eamon Cody (the second from a free), to seal the issue before Martin was presented with the Croke Cup amid delirious scenes. "Our team manager, John Costigan, was so excited that he broke red lights in Kilkenny en route home to yet another round of celebrations in Templemore," Martin recalls. On a serious note, though, Martin is loud in his praise of "the enormous contribution made to hurling in the school for a period of over 30 years" by John Costigan, himself a corner back in Tipperary's dramatic All-Ireland senior final defeat by Wexford in 1968. Now retired from teaching, John is serving as chairman of the Tipperary County Board.

Martin left Templemore CBS in the summer of 1978 and he feels that the euphoria of the inaugural successes in that year perhaps lessened the resolve to repeat the triumphs the following year. He is adamant that the team of the 1978/79 academic year was very strong and lost out somewhat tamely in the Harty semi-final to St Flannan's, who proceeded to annihilate all subsequent opposition en route to another Croke Cup success. His alma mater is now known as Our Lady's Secondary School, Templemore, and they have never managed to repeat the feats of 1978, despite a number of promising Harty campaigns.

Martin played on two Tipperary teams in All-Ireland junior hurling finals, unfortunately losing both, to Wexford in 1985 and Kilkenny three years later (the second as captain). He managed to stay fit over the years and he won three Masters All-Ireland medals with Tipp in the early part of this decade. His club is J. K. Bracken's (named after one of the seven G.A.A. founder members, Templemore's Joseph Kevin Bracken) an amalgamation of Templemore, Clonmore and Killea. Martin experienced many ups and downs in his long club career but played senior championship hurling in the early and late 1980's. He also had a fair degree of success on the football fields in a county where the big ball game invariably takes second place.

He remains loyal to his roots and nowhere is the love of his homeland more evident than in Martin's superb 528-page book 'The GAA History of Clonmore, Killea and Templemore'. This magnificent tome was published in

December 1988 and is astonishing in its detail. His own assiduous style saw Martin produce another invaluable publication just five years later - 'A History of Camogie in Co. Tipperary, 1904-2003', in conjunction with Seamus King. At the time of writing, he is working on two further books - a history of GAA in Mid-Tipperary and a book of photographs covering all aspects of the GAA, for the same region.

In 1988 also, he won the Tipperary Ciba Geigy Clubman of the Year award. He is heavily involved in nurturing local underage talent and takes particular pride in the progress of camogie in the locality, having been one of the driving forces in setting up the Templemore club back in 1989. Numerous successes in Féile and other competitions have greatly pleased him. He was a Tipperary senior camogie selector in 2005 and 2006, with his county reaching the All-Ireland final on both occasions. He helped to set up the Tipperary Camogie Supporters Club in 2002 and is cur-

rently PRO and secretary of that noteworthy fundraising group.

After completing his Leaving Certificate in 1978, Martin studied Engineering in UCD. When he graduated in 1982, he went to work for Bord na Móna and had a number of bases round the Midlands. He is currently employed as a utilities engineer with Taro Pharmaceutical in Roscrea. Martin is a single man.

The history-making Croke Cup squad held an emotional reunion for the tenth anniversary of their win in 1988. While originally a 25th celebration was in the pipeline in 2003, the sudden death of panel member, Liam Farrelly dampened enthusiasm in the lead-up to the proposed event and it never took place. Yet, a strong bond still exists in the Templemore vicinity among Martin Bourke and his colleagues, whose exploits in 1978 will always be recalled with great fondness by players, mentors and supporters alike.

1979 – ALL-IRELAND SEMI-FINAL
31 March 1979, Nenagh

St. Flannan's, Ennis 4-15
(T. Howard 1-4, R. Colleran 1-3, P. Colleran 1-2, J. Morey 1-2,
G. Corry 0-2, M. O'Grady 0-1, G. McInerney 0-1)

St. Mary's, Galway 1-1
(P. Burke 1-0, G. Kilcommons 0-1)

St. Flannan's, Ennis, Croke Cup Champions, 1979.
Back row, left to right: Martin Corry, Pat Collins, Anton Conroy, Peter Barry, Tom Howard,
Michael Deasy, Damien Kennedy, Julian Crimmins, Brendan McNamara, Enda Quinlan.
Front row, left to right: Flan McInerney, Tommy Neville, Ian Conroy, Philip Colleran,
Gerry Corry, Gerry McInerney (capt), Jimmy Morey, John Moroney, Ray Colleran,
Seanie McMahon.
(Photograph courtesy of Ollie Byrnes, author of Blue is the Colour, Hurling at St. Flannan's)

1979 – ALL-IRELAND FINAL
29 April 1979, Thurles
Referee: Seamus Brennan (Galway)

St. Flannan's, Ennis 3-15

Pat Collins
(Clare)

Tommy Neville　　**Enda Quinlan**　　**John Moroney**
(Clare)　　　　　　(Clare)　　　　　　(Clare)

Flan McInerney　　**Seanie McMahon**　　**Michael Deasy**
(Clare)　　　　　　(Clare) (0-1)　　　　(Clare)

Ray Colleran　　　**Peter Barry**
(Clare) (0-2)　　　　(Clare)

Brendan McNamara　　**Philip Colleran**　　**Gerry McInerney** (*capt*)
(Clare)　　　　　　(Clare) (0-2)　　　　(Clare) (0-7)

Gerry Corry　　　**Tom Howard**　　　**Jimmy Morey**
(Clare) (0-1)　　　(Clare) (2-1)　　　(Clare) (0-1)

Sub: Martin O'Grady (Clare) (1-0) (for McNamara).

Presentation College, Birr 2-3

Val Smith
(Offaly)

Sean Guinan　　　**Ken Hogan**　　　**Colman Murphy**
(Offaly)　　　　　(Tipperary)　　　(Offaly)

Pat Cotter　　　**Brendan Colclough**　　**Liam Grogan**
(Offaly)　　　　　(Offaly)　　　　　(Offaly)

Jimmy Carroll　　　**Paddy Corrigan**
(Offaly)　　　　　　(Offaly) (0-2)

Noel Teehan　　　**Joe Verney** (*capt*)　　**Aidan Rosney**
(Offaly)　　　　　(Offaly) (1-0)　　　(Offaly) (1-0)

Kevin Kinsella　　**John McLoughlin**　　**Seamus Coughlan**
(Offaly)　　　　　(Offaly) (0-1)　　　(Offaly)

Sub: John Murphy (Offaly) (for Teehan).

Gerry McInerney

When former Clare and Munster sharp-shooter Gerry McInerney looks back on his long hurling career, the years which stand out are 1979 and 1996. This is hardly surprising considering he savoured All-Ireland glory in both years, with his first major success coming when he captained the famed St. Flannan's, Ennis, to Harty and Croke Cup success, remarkably with an all-Clare team.

Growing up in the hurling stronghold of Sixmilebridge, it was inevitable that Gerry would take up the camán. His late father, Jack, was deeply involved with the club, as well as his uncles, Dermot and Michael 'Guiney'. Along with Eugene O'Connell, Sean Meehan and another St. Flannan's hero of the mid-1970s, Leo Quinlan, these men were involved in the training of the first Sixmilebridge team to represent Clare at the All-Ireland Féile na nGael finals in 1975. Gerry was part of the 'Bridge team that travelled to Youghal to take part in the Under-14 hurling festival. "My father took a great interest in the club, and was very active at underage level," Gerry explains. "He instilled a love for hurling in me and in my brothers, Flan and Declan who all played the game as well. In fact, Flan played alongside me on the Flannan's team that won the All-Ireland in '79 and Declan also helped Flannan's to win a Croke Cup in 1983".

Gerry entered St. Flannan's as a day pupil in 1973 and his earliest memories are of sitting beside the aforementioned Leo Quinlan on the school bus in and out from Sixmilebridge. "Leo was someone I used to look up to when I first went to Flannan's. He captained them to win their first Munster and All-Ireland titles in 18 years in 1976 and he was one my the heroes, along with the likes of John Hanly, Barry Smythe and P.J. Deasy. Hurling was the main topic of conversation whenever I sat beside Leo." Gerry chose to attend the Ennis nursery because "if you wanted to go places in hurling, you pencilled in Flannan's". He played on the Under-15 team (trained by fellow Sixmilebridge man, Fr Hugh O'Dowd, who had played in the club's first county final, a defeat by Scariff in 1952) and the Dean Ryan, without any success, before graduating to the senior team.

Success eluded Gerry during his first two years on the St. Flannan's senior team. They lost the Harty Cup finals of 1977 and 1978 to St. Colman's, Fermoy ("in an absolute deluge in Emly"), and Templemore CBS ("one that we left behind us") by four points and two points respectively. It then looked as though he would leave the Ennis hurling nursery without any silverware to his name. However, he put that right in 1979 when he came back as a Leaving Cert repeat to skipper the blue and whites to Harty and All-Ireland honours. "My chance of winning anything with Flannan's looked to have disappeared when we lost the 1978 Harty final to a Bobby Ryan-inspired Templemore. They went into the final as underdogs and everything appeared to be going according to plan when we held a big lead at half-time. But they staged a great comeback in the last ten minutes to beat us and, like Colman's the previous year, Templemore went on to win the All-Ireland." Gerry, as well as Mike Deasy (O'Callaghan's Mills) and 1978 captain, Seanie McMahon (Newmarket-on-Fergus), who is now a well-known inter-county referee, decided to repeat the Leaving Cert in 1979 in a final attempt to win the Harty Cup. "After the disappointment of the previous two years, we felt we had something to prove. Seanie was one of the most outstanding colleges players of my time and we said we'd give it one last crack. It was our last chance to pick up a coveted Harty medal. Schooling became secondary," Gerry says, frankly.

Gerry remembers being asked by Fr Willie Walsh (nowadays the Bishop of Killaloe), who was joint-manager of the St. Flannan's team along with Fr Seamus Gardiner, if he was serious about repeating the Leaving. When he said 'yes', the captaincy was bestowed upon him. The failures of 1977 and 1978 had left deep scars in many of the St. Flannan's players and there was clearly a fierce determination to make amends in 1979. The road to success began in Emly, which was to become St. Flannan's home-from-home during the Harty campaign. In the opening round, St. Flannan's easily accounted for Coláiste Iognáid Rís from Cork on a 7-14 to 3-2 scoreline. Future Cork goalkeeper, Ger Cunningham, lined out at centre forward for Iognáid Rís but, despite his immense physical presence, he couldn't make any headway against outstanding centre half back, Seanie McMahon. The semi-final was a repeat of the 1978 final and provided St. Flannan's with an opportunity to avenge that loss. Templemore put their Harty and All-Ireland titles on the line, but proved no match for a driven Ennis side who powered to a 2-8 to 0-9 victory in "a dogfight of a game".

St. Flannan's opponents in the final were old rivals North Monastery. Again, the Ennis lads were by far the better team and the result was never in doubt after full forward, Tommy Howard found the net just after half-time. North Mon had defender Paul

O'Connor dismissed as the game was slipping from their grasp and they eventually succumbed to a 1-3 to 2-11 defeat. Tony O'Sullivan, who would make his name with Cork in the years that followed, "wasn't given a puck by John Moroney". Indeed, Tomás Mulcahy, who captained Cork to win the Liam McCarthy Cup in 1990 and is now a hurling analyst with RTÉ, failed to make the North Mon starting side. In the All-Ireland semi-final at Nenagh, St. Flannan's had an even bigger win over St. Mary's, Galway, and the Harty champions cruised to a facile 4-15 to 1-1 win.

The 1979 St. Flannan's team was highly unusual in that it contained 15 Clare men. For the All-Ireland final against Presentation College, Birr, at Thurles on April 29th, the team showed one change from that which won the Harty Cup with Sixmilebridge's Jimmy Morey replacing Martin O'Grady of Scariff at left corner forward. There were five players from Gerry's beloved Sixmilebridge on the starting team and another two among the substitutes. On the day, St. Flannan's powered to a 3-15 to 2-3 victory over the Offaly men. However, they struggled with their shooting in the early stages and found themselves 0-2 to 1-1 in arrears after Joe Verney goaled for the underdogs. At this stage, the 'Irish Independent' reported that, "the fare was very exciting with both sides throwing everything into getting some early dominance".

However, a series of positional changes had the desired effect as St. Flannan's stormed back to take a 1-10 to 1-1 lead into the interval, with Tommy Howard scoring their goal in the 24th minute. Howard's second goal just after half-time broke Birr's resistance and 'Irish Independent' correspondent Tom O'Riordan reckoned that, "the remainder of the match was pretty much one-sided". Gerry himself scored 0-7 and was joint-top scorer with Howard, who bagged 2-1. "We didn't really know what to expect against Birr. We expected to be facing St. Peter's or St. Kieran's, but Birr came out of nowhere to win the Leinster title. We hardly knew anything about them, except that they had a very good trainer in Brother Denis and we had the height of respect for him and his team." Gerry recalls, "however, on the day, future Tipperary goalie, Ken Hogan, who played full back for Birr, found Tommy Howard a real handful."

Gerry still has vivid recollections of the joy which followed St. Flannan's All-Ireland victory. "There were great celebrations. I can still remember the huge crowds that used to go to the games and the buzz in the school before every match in the Harty Cup. The school used to run five or six buses to every match, which meant that everybody was involved. The banter and the atmosphere, the colour and the chanting; they were terrific and the whole school was involved. Sadly, I don't think that's the case anymore." Gerry remembers Fr Willie Walsh and Fr Seamus Gardiner as being meticulous in their preparation of the team. "The two lads were great organisers. They paid great attention to detail and left nothing to chance. We got anti-flu injections at Christmastime and the boarders who hurled often got an extra spud or two! Everyone knew what they had to do before going out on the pitch. All the training was done with the ball. We did very little physical training, because the attitude of the management was that fellas were naturally fit at that age. In training, Fr Willie would take the backs, Fr Seamus would work with the lads further up the field and Fr Hugh would be brought in on match days to assist them with the tactical side of things. In general, the priests in the school were great."

Gerry was a Clare minor for three years and a county Under-21 player for four years, but had no success in either grade. He made his senior debut for Sixmilebridge in 1978 and, a year later, as well as captaining St. Flannan's to All-Ireland glory, he won minor, Under-21 and senior championship honours with the club. Gerry singles out Kevin 'Trixie' Twomey for his input into these successes. Gerry joined the Clare senior panel in 1980 and was given his first competitive start against Westmeath in a National League game at Castletown-Geoghegan. Conditions were far removed from the days when everything was laid on in St. Flannan's, with "showers consisting of an outdoor tap with cold water". However, Gerry remained loyal to the cause

of the Banner but, in his 11 years with the Clare seniors, he unfortunately lost two Munster finals and two National League finals. St. Flannan's old boy, Joe McKenna scored 3-3 to sink the Banner County in the 1981 Munster final, and Cork beat them by three points in the provincial decider of 1986 in Killarney. By contrast, Gerry enjoyed a hugely successful club career. In all, he won seven senior county championship medals and two Munster club championships with the 'Bridge. "The pinnacle" of his career came when he was left corner forward and vice-captain of the Sixmilebridge team which comfortably defeated Dunloy from Antrim to win the All-Ireland club title on St. Patrick's Day in 1996. Gerry actually led out the team for the final in Croke Park but regular captain, Ian Mulready, who was unable to play due to injury, actually received the cup. "It brought an identity and a sense of belonging to the whole community", Gerry fondly recalls.

Gerry has worked as a journalist with the 'Clare Champion' newspaper since he left St. Flannan's. Since retiring from playing hurling in 1998, he has concentrated mainly on sports reporting (ironically, more football than hurling orientated in the colleges scene) but, as this involves a great deal of weekend work, he hasn't been able to coach any teams. "Because I'm working every weekend, I can't give the commitment to coaching. In fairness to my employers, they cut me a lot of slack when I was playing so I can't really complain," Gerry concedes. He plays golf as a member in Dromoland, but again work commitments mean that he doesn't get to play as often as he would like. Gerry is married to Ann (neé Corry), a native of Tulla, whose brothers Denis and Matthew also played for Clare. Gerry and Ann live in Sixmilebridge and they have three young children, Niamh (8), Cian (7) and Fiachra (4). He feels that "it's a bit early to think about whether the lads will attend Flannan's".

Gerry McInerney, who was selected on the Harty Cup Team of the Millennium, has kept in touch with many of his old St. Flannan's teammates and, in 1999, he attended the 20th anniversary of the all-conquering team which he had skippered. He can easily rhyme off the whereabouts of his colleagues from 27 years ago. He confesses to have been very saddened by the death some years back in a traffic accident of corner back, John Moroney and, at the time of writing, Gerry is glad to be recuperating well from a health scare of his own. "I had a lot of disappointments in hurling, especially with Clare," Gerry concludes, "but I feel lucky to have experienced what it is like to win an All-Ireland with club and college. I cherish the Harty and All-Ireland colleges medals and I have absolutely fond memories of St.Flannan's",

1980 – ALL-IRELAND SEMI-FINAL
30 March 1980, Roscrea

Birr Community School 0-7
(A. Rosney 0-4, J. Carroll 0-2, J. Dooley 0-1)

St. Joseph's, Garbally 1-4
(J. Campbell 1-0, S. Ruane 0-2, M. Neville 0-1, N. Kelly 0-1)

1980 – ALL-IRELAND SEMI-FINAL (REPLAY)
6 April 1980, Thurles

Birr Community School 2-15
(J. Dooley 1-4, K. Kinsella 1-2, A. Rosney 0-4, P. Corrigan 0-4, J. Guinan 0-1)

St. Joseph's, Garbally 3-4
(J. Campbell 2-0, H. Bleahein 1-0, O. Kilkenny 0-1, S. Ruane 0-1. N. Kelly 0-1, L. Jennings 0-1)

North Monastery, Cork, Croke Cup Champions, 1980.
Back row, left to right: Mr Donal O'Grady, Martin Lee, Frank Higgins, Dave Geaney,
Tony O'Donovan, Eddie O'Callaghan, Mick O'Donoghue, Liam Coffey, John Rea, Neil Kenneally,
Dermot O'Callaghan, Cathal Twomey, Mr Murt Murphy.
Middle row, left to right: Mick Higgins, Brendan Burns, Thomas O'Neill, Robert Allen,
Jim Murray (capt), Tony O'Sullivan, Paul O'Connor, Tomás Mulcahy, Martin Lyons, Packie Murphy.
Front row, left to right: Paddy Connery, John Horgan, Terry O'Mahony, Ricky Walsh,
John Drinan, Kevin Doran.
(Photograph courtesy of Gerry Kelly and Liam O'Brien, c/o North Monastery, Cork)

1980 – ALL-IRELAND FINAL
27 April 1980, Thurles
Referee: John Moloney (Tipperary)

North Monastery, Cork 5-11

Mick Higgins
(Cork)

Paddy Connery　　　　**Tony O'Donovan**　　　　**Jim Murray (*capt*)**
(Cork)　　　　　　　　　　(Cork)　　　　　　　　　　(Cork)

John Rea　　　　　　　**Paul O'Connor**　　　　　**Thomas O'Neill**
(Cork)　　　　　　　　　　(Cork)　　　　　　　　　　(Cork)

Martin Lee　　　　　　**Kevin Doran**
(Cork)　　　　　　　　　　(Cork)

Liam Coffey　　　　　　**Martin Lyons**　　　　　**John Drinan**
(Cork) (0-1)　　　　　　　(Cork) (1-0)　　　　　　　(Cork) (0-1)

Robert Allen　　　　　　**Tony O'Sullivan**　　　　**Tomás Mulcahy**
(Cork) (0-1)　　　　　　　(Cork) (2-8)　　　　　　　(Cork) (2-0)

Birr Community School 3-7

Brendan Kehoe
(Offaly)

Paul Ryan　　　　　　　**Ken Hogan**　　　　　　**Colman Murphy**
(Offaly)　　　　　　　　　(Tipperary)　　　　　　　(Offaly)

John Murphy　　　　　　**Eugene Conroy**　　　　**Aidan Gleeson**
(Offaly)　　　　　　　　　(Tipperary)　　　　　　　(Offaly)

Philip Joyce　　　　　**Paddy Corrigan (*capt*)**
(Offaly)　　　　　　　　　(Offaly) (1-2)

Aidan Rosney　　　　　**Jimmy Carroll**　　　　　**Kevin Kinsella**
(Offaly) (1-4)　　　　　　(Offaly)　　　　　　　　　(Offaly) (1-1)

Pat O'Connor　　　　　**John Guinan**　　　　　　**Joe Dooley**
(Offaly)　　　　　　　　　(Tipperary)　　　　　　　(Offaly)

Sub: Val Smith (Offaly) (for O'Connor).

Jim Murray

In 1980, the famous Cork nursery, North Monastery, won the Croke Cup for the third time, remarkably continuing a sequence of winning in the first year of the decade for the third time in-a-row. The team was skippered by Jim Murray and, despite being domiciled in Boston for most of the intervening 26 years, he retains fond memories of hurling from his schooldays

Jim grew up in the Blackpool/Farranree area of Cork city. "Blackpool was Glen Rovers territory", Jim says, recalling that his grandfather, Denis Daly Snr, with whom Jim's family lived, had played with Glen Rovers in the 1920s and 1930s. Indeed, he was the first Glen man to be picked to play for the Cork seniors. Jim's next-door neighbour, Dinny Stanton, a St. Finbarr's man, was a sub on the 1931 Cork team which played against Kilkenny three times before winning that year. He had a replica of the Liam McCarthy Cup in his house which had been presented to the players. Jim remembers playing hurling outside the house on Spangle Hill with his grandfather. "He could still cut a ball over a house, even in his 70s," Jim recalls with pride.

"Hurling was big in the area, as well as soccer", Jim reflects. One of his uncles played in an FAI Cup final with Cork United. Jim continues, "I ended up playing hurling with Na Piarsaigh because my favourite uncle, Denis Daly, played senior with them. He won a Harty Cup with the Mon, while his uncle - my granduncle, Willie Byrne - also played Harty

with the Mon in the late 1920s before emigrating to America. He was a decorated US Marine during World War II but his son told me that his proudest possession was a colleges hurling medal he won with the Mon! He gave me a team photograph from 1928 (which includes Jack Lynch's brother) and features the Dr Callaghan Cup which I was presented with in 1980."

Given his background, it was no surprise when Jim was enrolled in North Monastery. From the outset, he considered it "an honour" to be involved in Gaelic games in the school. "It was always a very professional set-up from Under-12 right up to the Harty Cup. The brothers and teachers were committed to winning and it was reflected in every aspect of their approach, from training to equipment, to pitches. I remember Br Burke (a Galway man) and Br. O'Neill (a Kilkenny man), who were hurling fanatics, giving us their opinions on different styles of hurling when we were very young. Later, Br Kinsella from Wexford talked about mixing different styles to speed up the game even more."

Jim won Cork Colleges hurling and football medals in a variety of age groups. However, he concedes that "the feeling was that if you didn't win a Harty and All-Ireland those successes weren't worth much". He recalls that when Donal O'Grady and Murt Murphy started training the Harty teams, "expectations were very high". By Jim's Leaving Cert year of 1979/80, the Mon had not won the Harty Cup or Croke Cup for ten years. In his first two years on the senior team, Jim played when North Monastery lost to Templemore CBS in the 1978 Harty semi-final and to St. Flannan's in the 1979 final, with both their conquerors going on to All-Ireland glory.

Looking back over a quarter of a century later, Jim has vivid recollections of his Harty days. "We were very disappointed at our performance in 1979. It didn't help that our full back and captain, Bill Kenneally - who is now also in Boston - got carried off injured after ten minutes and that Paul O'Connor was sent off by referee, John Moloney before half-time! When I got back to the dressing room and saw Murt Murphy's face and his disappointment, it was then I realised how important it was to win a Harty and All-Ireland. The man was devastated. The players who were left for the following year like myself, Tony O'Sullivan and Paul O'Connor were determined that we wouldn't let that happen in our last year. Donal and Murt were ruthless in their approach to preparing us both physically and mentally in 1980."

As it transpired, Jim's year as captain of the Mon had its ups and downs. He accepted the trophy for the Cork Colleges final, after the defeat of St. Colman's, in a lot of discomfort after picking up a nasty finger injury, requiring the insertion of steel pins. Indeed, the surgeon at Cork Regional Hospital told Jim that he was "gone from hurling for the year". Having defeated Limerick CBS in the Harty first round, the Mon got over Templemore CBS in the semi-final on a scoreline of 3-12 to 2-4 in Bansha. "It was frustrating to be on the sideline that day," Jim reflects, "but the team did a good job winning it".

Dr Con Murphy made a special glove to protect Jim's fingers, but he wasn't named to start the Harty Cup final against St. Colman's, Fermoy. "That was Donal's psychological game, I think." Jim recalls the drawn final in Buttevant on March 23rd as "a cracker". He played at centre half back and he admits that he was "limited by the injury". He remembers St. Colman's being "up for the game", with Mick Boylan, Pat Hartnett and Joe Noonan playing well for the Fermoy school. "The clash

between Paul O'Connor and Joe Noonan at midfield was one of the best I've ever seen. Both of them were superb hurlers with different styles. Tony O'Sullivan and Tomás Mulcahy would be the names that jump out in our forward line. I played with Tony from the time I was seven with Na Piarsaigh right up to senior and with some Cork teams also, and he was worth two goals before a match even started. Mick Boylan (someone I became good friends with later in college and played with on Fitzgibbon Cup teams), marked him and Tony brought him all over the field!" The game ended in a draw - North Monastery 3-6 St. Colman's 2-9 - before a big crowd. Jim feels that "the second game, a week later, was even more frenetic". The Mon, despite being reduced to 14 men, finally came out on top by 2-10 to 2-5, but "it was a battle from start to finish". He remembers being presented with the cup with about eight people around him. "The rest of the team and the crowd had spilled out onto the streets of Buttevant celebrating!"

There was a four week gap between winning the Harty replay and the Croke Cup final, as the Mon got a bye into the final. Jim didn't know much about their final opponents from Birr Community School except that Fr Bertie Troy, a well-known Cork hurling figure, was training them, "so we weren't taking anything for granted". However, shortly after the Harty Cup win, Jim was rushed to the hospital with a massive infection due to his finger and he was hospitalised for three weeks. He studied for his Leaving Certificate exams in hospital in Cork. He got frequent visits from Donal O'Grady, Murt Murphy, as well as Br Ó Mathúna and Br Tallon, the principals of the Mon. "By the time I got out I was hungry for hurling and still had plenty of time to prepare for the final. I remember the doctors letting me off my intravenous drip to go home to have a photo with the Harty Cup taken with my grandfather", Jim recalls with a smile.

The day of the final was "dry and sunny". Jim reckons that he and his team-mates had prepared well for it and the benefit of having played two finals in the Harty Cup stood to them. "I remember Semple Stadium as being a perfect pitch for hurling. I think overall we were too strong for Birr. I went back to my natural corner back position and Paul O'Connor played centre back where he had an outstanding game." The 'Irish Independent' reported that the Mon put on "a superb display", particularly praising their "lethal forward division". Future Cork senior star, Tony O'Sullivan, singled out as "a particular menace", nabbed 2-8 on the day. Although the game was still up for grabs at half time, with the winners ahead by 2-4 to 1-3, an unanswered scoring burst of 3-3 early in the second moiety ended the game as a contest. Indeed, the 'Irish Independent' concluded that, "a stout-hearted effort from Birr in the final quarter" merely took "the lop-sided look off the scoreboard".

Jim's view is that, "the Croke Cup was the icing on the Harty Cup cake for us". The Mon were a young team - 13 of the 15 would have been eligible to play the following year. "We had great coaches and the whole school and the north side of Cork city got behind us. It was an unbelievable year, which in hindsight I don't think I appreciated or enjoyed as much as I should have." Indeed, his father told him before he passed away that it was the most enjoyment he got from watching his son playing hurling. "It was a great experience getting the whole school behind us including some pupils and teachers who didn't have a great interest in hurling."

Bringing the cups around to all the different schools and businesses was also "a nice experience". Jim realised for the first time how important winning the Harty and All-Ireland was to people in clubs, families and the area in general, "which was going through a tough time employment-wise". The week after winning the All-Ireland, the Mon beat St. Flannan's in the Dean Ryan Cup with the same team less two. Jim also featured when they won the Munster Colleges football Under-17 Frewen Cup with a lot of the same players. It was, as Jim reflects, "quite a haul".

Jim is loud in his praise of the mentors behind the Mon's victories in 1980. "Donal O'Grady was very cerebral and he dissected every player's performance. A wasted clearance or pass drove him nuts and I was on the receiving end of his tongue-lashing a few times, usually in Irish, as he taught me Irish and History! Murt Murphy brought a passion to the game that I've rarely seen. He understood more than anyone what a Harty Cup and All-Ireland meant as he was involved in previous victories."

With Na Piarsaigh, Jim won an array of underage county championships in both hurling and football. He was on the Cork minor football panel which won All-Ireland in 1981, defeating Derry in the final. He also played minor hurling for Cork for two years and Under-21 for a couple of years. "Fr O'Brien would have been the dominant figure coaching in Cork at the time and I was one of the many men influenced by his professional approach to hurling at whatever level he coached." He won two Fitzgibbon Cup medals with UCC in 1982 and 1983 and also played on the Combined Universities team. "I had a lot of happy memories playing with Mick Boylan, Nicky English, Paul O'Connor, Danny Buckley, John Grainger, Mick Allen ... the list goes on". Jim later had "a few runs" with Cork senior hurling team.

Jim emigrated to the US in 1987. There, he played with the Cork Hurling Club in Boston, winning five New England county championships and one All-American championship. He was delighted to have played in Gaelic Park in New York for a few years with the Cork team. He feels that "the standard of hurling in Boston and New York in the late 1980s and early 1990s was great".

After his secondary schooldays ended, Jim went on to do a degree in Law in UCC, eventually becoming a solicitor. He got another Doctor of Law degree from a law school in Boston and he has his own law practice there for the last ten years. He and his wife, Kate have four sons - Liam (7), Finn (6), Drew (4) and Teddy (2). His children "love the game of hurling" and he is thrilled that there is "a great youth programme for Gaelic football and hurling in Boston". Indeed, he intends to devote some of his free time to coaching in the years ahead.

Clearly, geographic constraints have not

dimmed Jim Murray's love of Gaelic games. While some of his colleagues in the Mon team went on to become household names, Jim's emphasis was on teamwork. "We had a solid core of good hurlers who all got along well together but, more importantly, were each prepared to do what it took to win the game." And win they did in style, producing memorable displays of hurling in a great season in 1979/80.

Three Croke Cup winning captains were selected on the Harty Cup Team of the Millennium in 2000: Eamon Grimes, Limerick CBS (1966), extreme right front row, Gerry McInerney, St. Flannan's (1979), second from right back row, Brian Hurley, North Monastery (1994), fifth from right back row. *(Photograph courtesy of Ollie Byrnes, author of Blue is the Colour)*

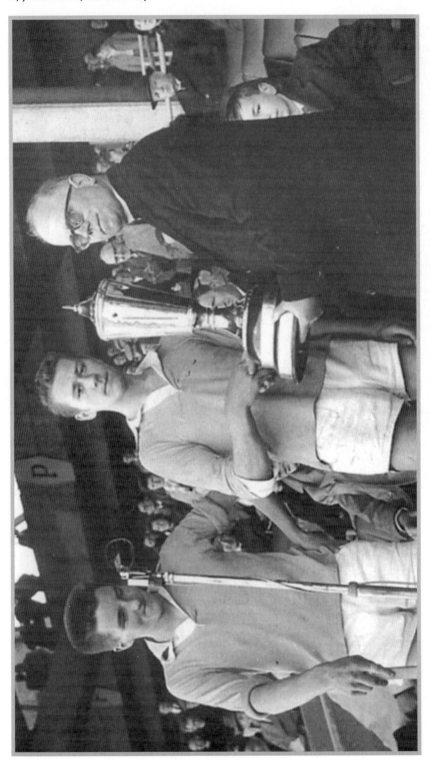

Connie O'Leary, St. Finbarr's, with the Croke Cup in 1963.
(Photograph courtesy of Tim Horgan, author of Farna's Hurling Story)

Eamon Cregan, Limerick CBS, with the Croke Cup in 1964.
(Photograph courtesy of Noel Earlie, c/o Limerick CBS)

Paddy Breen, St. Peter's, with the Croke Cup in 1968.
(Photograph courtesy of Paddy Breen)

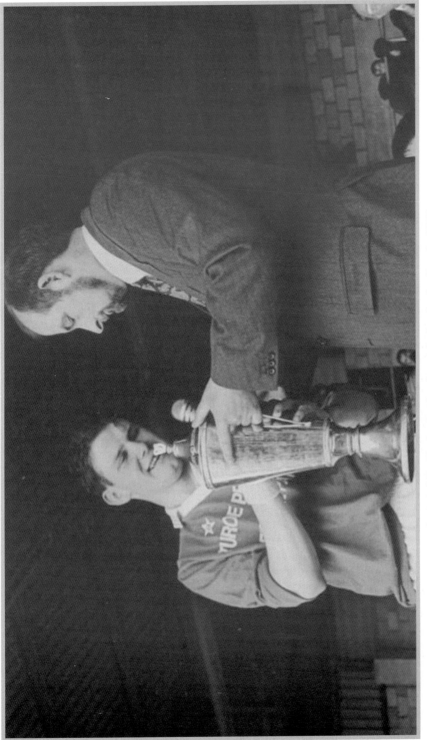

Cathal O'Reilly, St. Raphael's, with the Croke Cup in 1995.
(Photograph courtesy of Cathal O'Reilly)

Maurice O'Brien, St. Colman's, with the Croke Cup in 2002.
(Photograph courtesy of Maurice O'Brien)

Conor Connolly, Dublin Colleges, with the Croke Cup in 2006.
(Photograph courtesy of Tony Stack)

Templemore CBS, Croke Cup champions, 1978, ten year reunion in 1988

Back row, left to right: Kieran McDonnell, Joe Bourke, Br Perkins, Jim Maher, Liam Farrelly, Pat McGrath, Brendan Russell, Noel Farrelly, Pat Cormack, Eamon Cody, Peter Brennan, Pat Hassett, Br Seaver.

Front row, left to right: Frankie McGrath, Bobby Ryan, John Hanley, Br Norris, Martin Bourke (capt), Mr John Costigan, Richard Stapleton, Mick Ryan (Borrisoleigh), Joe Sweeney, Mick Ryan (Clonmore).

Missing: Pat Treacy, Jim Kennedy, Timmy Stapleton and Noel Fogarty.

(Photograph courtesy of Martin Bourke)

1981 – ALL-IRELAND SEMI-FINAL
12 April 1981, Thurles

North Monastery, Cork 1-9
(J. Chisholm 1-1, D. McCarthy 0-3, J. Drinan 0-2, D. Geaney 0-1, T. O'Mahony 0-1,
T. McCarthy 0-1)

Our Lady's, Gort 0-4
(A. Cunningham 0-3, J. Byrne 0-1)

Kilkenny CBS, Croke Cup Champions, 1981.
Back row, left to right: Stephen Whearty, Paddy Blanchfield, Brian Young, Andy Ryan,
Tommy Bawle, Tony Henderson, Paul Burke, Michael Lawlor, Dave Foley, Michael Maher.
Middle row, left to right: Michael Walsh, Paul Bateman, Paul Fennelly, Paul Cleere (capt),
Billy Walsh, Seamie O'Leary, Eddie O'Leary, Eddie Kennedy, Br A.C. Minniter.
Front row, left to right: Eamon Nolan, Michael Dermody, Jim Nugent, Joe Kennedy,
Denis Dermody, Michael Geoghegan.
(Photograph courtesy of Kilkenny CBS, Edmund Rice 150 souvenir booklet)

1981 – ALL-IRELAND FINAL
10 May 1981, Waterford
Referee: John Moloney (Tipperary)

Kilkenny CBS 3-5

Billy Walsh
(Kilkenny)

Michael Maher
(Kilkenny)

Eddie Kennedy
(Kilkenny)

Michael Walsh
(Kilkenny)

Dave Foley
(Kilkenny)

Tony Henderson
(Kilkenny)

Joe Kennedy
(Kilkenny)

Tommy Bawle
(Kilkenny) (1-1)

Paul Cleere (*capt*)
(Kilkenny)

Paul Burke
(Kilkenny)

Michael Geoghegan
(Kilkenny)

Michael Lawlor
(Kilkenny) (2-0)

Brian Young
(Kilkenny)

Seamie O'Leary
(Kilkenny) (0-4)

Eamon Nolan
(Kilkenny)

Sub: Eddie O'Leary (Kilkenny) (for Nolan).

North Monastery, Cork 1-8

Donnacha O'Leary
(Cork)

Christy O'Donovan
(Cork)

Brendan Byrnes
(Cork)

Paddy Connery
(Cork) (0-1)

Liam Coffey
(Cork)

Frank Higgins
(Cork)

Ricky Walsh
(Cork)

Kevin Doran
(Cork)

Paul Murphy
(Cork)

Terry O'Mahony
(Cork) (1-1)

Dave McCarthy
(Cork)

Teddy McCarthy
(Cork) (0-1)

Robert Allen
(Cork) (0-2)

John Drinan (*capt*)
(Cork) (0-2)

John Chisholm
(Cork) (0-1)

Paul Cleere

On May 10th, 1981, Kilkenny CBS finally emerged from the daunting shadow of their neighbours and great rivals, St. Kieran's, to claim colleges hurling's greatest honour. The historic team was captained by Paul Cleere, who, to this day, retains fond memories of his schooldays and that ground-breaking success in particular.

Paul is one of five sons born to Joe and Eileen Cleere, both natives of County Kilkenny. While Joe was a psychiatric nurse, it was his role as caretaker at Nowlan Park that brought Paul first into contact with Gaelic games. He fondly recalls that both his parents were "fanatical hurling supporters" from his earliest memories.

Young Paul displayed talent with the sliotar from a very tender age. However, when it came to deciding on his secondary education, there was no talk of enrolling in the famous nursery of St. Kieran's and Paul followed the lead of his older brothers into the Christian Brothers school. His eldest brother, Mick, enjoyed no senior success in the CBS but eventually wore the treasured black and amber county jersey and, indeed, was a sub on the side which narrowly lost the Liam McCarthy Cup showdown to Tipperary in 1991.

Paul represented the CBS at juvenile and junior level, before graduating as a 14-year-old goalkeeper to the senior team. He played in the 1979 Leinster senior final when the CBS were defeated (2-4 to 2-13) in "a stormy encounter" by Presentation College, Birr, in Athy. The following year Paul won a Leinster junior medal. This grade does not go any further than provincial level and Paul feels that "there certainly was no great expectation in the school that the 1980/81 academic year would bring the ultimate honours at senior level".

Team trainer, Brother Minniter (later Father Minniter) appointed "a delighted" Paul as captain of the senior team early in the campaign. It was to provide four very tight games against some of the biggest hurling nurseries in the country. St. Peter's of Wexford were beaten in a semi-final replay by a single point, a noteworthy accomplishment in its own right when one recalls that all four All-Ireland triumphs by the Slaneysiders had been achieved in replays. Paramount to the one point victory was Brian Young's personal contribution of 2-4. Old rivals and reigning Leinster champions, Birr (now under the guise of Birr Community School), came through the other side of the draw. In a dramatic Leinster final on April 5th, again in Athy, "a hobbling Michael Lawlor scored a wonderful goal" which secured a 1-8 to 1-7 victory, despite a late onslaught from the Offaly school inspired by Ken Hogan, later the Tipperary netminder and manager.

Reigning All-Ireland champions, North Monastery had easily disposed of the challenge of Our Lady's, Gort, in the only semi-final and were raging hot favourites to retain their crown. From the CBS' perspective, there was a five-week delay until the Croke Cup final, but "the hype in the school and throughout Kilkenny city was great," Paul reflects. However, "very few pundits" gave the CBS a chance of dethroning the famed Cork side. Ironically the school's only previous appearance in a Croke Cup final had been against the same opposition in 1970. Brother Minniter, himself "a great tactician", had by now brought in Ollie Walsh to assist with training and Paul remembers "the buzz" which the involvement of the legendary goalkeeper gave in the build-up to the final in Waterford.

Come All-Ireland final day, Paul recalls, Tony Henderson produced "a classic display" at centre half back ("I always felt he would have been a Kilkenny senior had he not emigrated to Australia"), and the CBS shocked their Leeside rivals and held out for an historic three-point win. The 'Irish Independent' sub-heading read, "North Mon sunk by freak goal" (referring to Tommy Bawle's 90-yard free seven minutes from the end of what it described as "a fine game"). However, Paul's own abiding memory was of making a save and instant clearance from a 21-yard free as stand-in goalie in the dying moments, despite having shipped "a very severe challenge" some 15 minutes earlier in his midfield role. There was never a lot between the teams, with the winners ahead by 1-3 to 0-5 at half-time. Indeed, Tom O'Riordan's report felt that the lessening of the rain on the change of ends helped the teams to produce "a second half of outstanding fare".

Paul remembers "wild celebrations in Walsh Park", with the joyous mood continuing all the way back to Kilkenny where the St. Patrick's Band led the newly crowned Croke Cup champions to a reception from Mayor Kieran Crotty at the courthouse. The success was remarkable for a day school who had for so long attempted to emulate the feats of St. Kieran's, whose ranks had very often included stars from neighbouring counties along with a majority from County Kilkenny. One of the county's all-time greats, Jim Langton, himself a CBS past pupil, visited the school soon after the victory and "a tremendous sense of pride filled pupils and staff alike".

In addition to Brother Miniter, Paul praises a number of other teachers who played their parts in the fostering of hurling in the school. Sean Breathnach, a past pupil who had been on the teaching staff for many years, "had an enormous input, particularly in juvenile hurling". Paul also speaks highly of the involvement in his time in the CBS of Mick O'Flynn and former Laois player, Johnny Mahon. "The dedication of these men was all the more admirable in a day school with fewer recreational facilities than its boarding counterparts." 1981 continued to be memorable for Paul as he won an All-Ireland minor hurling medal in September as a playing sub on the side which defeated Galway in the Irish Press Cup decider. That team was captained by full back, Eddie Kennedy, who had been "a colossus" on the CBS fifteen in the same position earlier in the year. The year was rounded off nicely when Paul was appointed to the staff of AIB Bank. His banking career has taken him to Dungarvan, Cork and finally back to his native Kilkenny, where nowadays he is employed as the branch manager in High Street. Being based locally means that he regularly meets a number of his old CBS comrades, with the recent Silver Jubilee of the Croke Cup triumph (which has never been replicated) undoubtedly prompting more and more trips down memory lane.

Paul never lost his love of hurling and he achieved a lifelong ambition in October 2001 when his beloved O'Loughlin Gaels won their first Kilkenny senior hurling title. Despite having had ongoing trouble with both knees, he continued to guard the Gaels' net through the pain barrier and was overjoyed at this historic breakthrough. The following year, he retired from hurling to concentrate on being a selector, allowing younger brother, Kevin to man the goals! He was thrilled to be part of the backroom team when the Gaels defeated Birr in the Leinster club final in November 2003. Three months later, another emerging club, Cork's Newtownshandrum, heartbreakingly stopped the Kilkenny lads in their tracks in a replayed All-Ireland semi-final, en route to All-Ireland glory. Over the past couple of years, Paul has become more involved at underage level with O'Loughlin Gaels, as a selector with both the Under-14s and Under-21s.

Paul's old hurling injuries regularly came back to haunt him, but he is thrilled with the success of a new metal hip replacement. He jokingly adds that this has improved his golf game! A keen golfer (he plays off a handicap of eight), Paul juggles his sporting and family interests, due in no small part to his "understanding wife", Eileen, a native of Lisdowney. Given their parents' love of hurling, it is no surprise that they have two daughters who are keen and successful camogie players, Karen at Under-16 level and Bronagh as an Under-10, both of course with O'Loughlin Gaels.

A Leinster triumph in 2006 for Kilkenny CBS didn't materialise into All-Ireland success, but there will be no past pupil prouder than Paul Cleere should his alma mater again have its name inscribed on the prestigious Croke Cup in the years ahead.

1982 – ALL-IRELAND SEMI-FINAL
25 April 1982, Thurles

St. Peter's, Wexford 1-18
(T. Dempsey 0-11, F. O'Leary 0-4, S. Kelly 1-0, L. Turner 0-1, G. Lyons 0-1, J. Harding 0-1)

Our Lady's, Gort 1-9
(P. Taaffe 1-7, S. Keane 0-1, A. Cunningham 0-1)

St. Flannan's, Ennis, Croke Cup Champions, 1982.
Back row, left to right: Ray Sampson, Michael Kelly, John Purcell, Tom Quinlivan,
Jim McInerney, John Corbett, Tom O'Halloran, Conor Fanning, John Murphy, Louis Mulqueen,
Michael Moynihan, Declan Nealon.
Front row, left to right: Brendan Flynn, Gearóid Mannion, Dick Quirke, John Russell,
Eoin McMahon, Peter Leyden (capt), Niall Romer, Enda O'Flaherty, Sean McCarthy,
Tim Murnane.
(Photograph courtesy of Ollie Byrnes, author of Blue is the Colour, Hurling at St. Flannan's)

1982 – ALL-IRELAND FINAL
9 May 1982, Thurles
Referee: John Moloney (Tipperary)

St. Flannan's, Ennis 1-4

Eoin McMahon
(Clare)

Ray Sampson
(Limerick) (0-2)

Conor Fanning
(Clare)

John Russell
(Clare)

Jim McInerney
(Clare)

John Murphy
(Clare)

Tom O'Halloran
(Clare)

Louis Mulqueen
(Clare)

Michael Kelly
(Tipperary) (1-1)

Niall Romer
(Clare)

Peter Leyden (*capt*)
(Clare)

Tom Quinlivan
(Clare)

Dick Quirke
(Tipperary)

John Corbett
(Clare)

Gearóid Mannion
(Clare) (0-1)

Subs: Timmy Murnane (Limerick) (for Romer), Enda O'Flaherty (Clare) (for Corbett), Sean McCarthy (Clare) (for Mulqueen).

St. Peter's, Wexford 1-4

Matty Foley
(Wexford)

Pat O'Callaghan
(Wexford)

Austin Finn
(Wexford)

Tom Byrne
(Wicklow)

Dermot Prendergast
(Wexford)

Liam Turner
(Wexford)

Paddy Donoghue
(Wexford)

Tom Dempsey (*capt*)
(Wexford) (0-3)

Gay Lyons
(Wexford)

Fintan O'Leary
(Wexford)

Michael Byrne
(Wexford)

John Harding
(Wexford)

Sean Kelly
(Wexford) (1-0)

Justin Roche
(Wexford) (0-1)

Eamonn Sinnott
(Wexford)

1982 – ALL-IRELAND FINAL (REPLAY)
16 May 1982, Thurles
Referee: John Moloney (Tipperary)

St. Flannan's, Ennis 2-9

Eoin McMahon
(Clare)

Sean McCarthy　　　**Conor Fanning**　　　**John Russell**
(Clare)　　　　　　　(Clare)　　　　　　　(Clare)

Tom O'Halloran　　　**John Murphy**　　　**Niall Romer**
(Clare)　　　　　　(Clare) (0-2)　　　　　(Clare)

Michael Kelly　　　　**Peter Leyden** (*capt*)
(Tipperary) (0-1)　　　　　(Clare)

Jim McInerney　　　**Tom Quinlivan**　　　**Ray Sampson**
(Clare) (0-1)　　　　　(Clare)　　　　　　(Limerick)

Dick Quirke　　　**Gearóid Mannion**　　　**Enda O'Flaherty**
(Tipperary) (1-2)　　　(Clare) (1-2)　　　　(Clare) (0-1)

Sub: Louis Mulqueen (Clare) (for O'Halloran).

St. Peter's, Wexford 0-10

Matty Foley
(Wexford)

Pat O'Callaghan　　　**Austin Finn**　　　**Tom Byrne**
(Wexford)　　　　　　(Wexford)　　　　　(Wicklow)

Dermot Prendergast　　　**Liam Turner**　　　**Paddy Donoghue**
(Wexford)　　　　　　　(Wexford)　　　　　(Wexford)

Tom Dempsey (*capt*)　　　**Gay Lyons**
(Wexford) (0-4)　　　　　(Wexford) (0-2)

Fintan O'Leary　　　**Justin Roche**　　　**John Harding**
(Wexford) (0-1)　　　(Wexford) (0-1)　　　(Wexford) (0-2)

Eamonn Sinnott　　　**Michael Byrne**　　　**David O'Connor**
(Wexford)　　　　　　(Wexford)　　　　　(Wexford)

Sub: Richard Lambert (Wexford) (for O'Connor).

Peter Leyden

In 1982, St. Flannan's College celebrated its centenary in the best possible fashion by winning the Croke Cup for a then record eighth time.

The famed Ennis nursery were captained that year by Peter Leyden when they defeated St. Peter's, Wexford after a replay to become All-Ireland champions once again.

Peter hails from a well-known hurling family in Clarecastle. His brothers, Christy, Paddy and Timmy all played for the local club and Peter himself claims that "pulling on the black and white jersey of Clarecastle was one of my biggest joys". Peter's father, Michael, died when he was only nine-years-old, leaving his mother, Johanna to rear the family. "She was my most important influence, while my brother, Christy provided my first hurley and boots and got me hooked," he says. Another "massive influence" on him was John Hanly, the principal of Clarecastle National School. John had been a key member of the St. Flannan's teams which dominated the Harty Cup and Croke Cup competitions during the mid-to-late 1940s. "I can't speak highly enough of John and you couldn't have had a better man teaching you the skills of the game."

After completing his primary education, Peter entered St. Flannan's. By coincidence, the diocesan college were landlords of the Leyden family home and surrounding farmlands in Clarecastle. "I felt that Flannan's was ours and ours was Flannan's," he jokes. In his early days in the college, Peter looked up to the likes of Gerry McInerney, Brendan McNamara, the Deasys, John Moroney, Seanie McMahon, Tommy Neville, Gerry Corry and Tommy Howard. "They were the stars of college hurling, while at senior level for Clare I admired Johnny Callinan, who went on to be a good friend of mine," he reflects. Indeed, Peter's memories of the All-Ireland winning year of 1978/79 and other campaigns around that time are vivid. "I can remember supporting the Harty team in places such as Cloughjordan, Oola, Emly and Bruff. It was a big thing when you were in first or second year to get off school to go to those games."

Peter played for St. Flannan's in the White and Dean Ryan Cups before graduating to the senior team, as a repeat Leaving Cert. So it came as a big surprise to him when he was called aside and told he would captain the team in the 1982 Harty and All-Ireland campaigns. "I was astounded when Fr Willie and Fr Hugh told me I had been chosen as captain. It was my first year on the Harty team and I mightn't have known the rest of the lads as well as some captains would. It was a fantastic honour and I was probably chosen because I had captained various Clarecastle underage teams. I wasn't the world's greatest stylist in hurling, but I had confidence I could do a job."

St. Flannan's beat three Cork sides - Coláiste Chríost Rí, St. Finbarr's, Farranferris, and North Monastery - en route to winning the Harty Cup. In the first round, they overcame a Chríost Rí side whose top player was future Manchester United and Republic of Ireland soccer star, Denis Irwin. A great comeback was needed in the penultimate round at Emly before the Farna boys were ousted by 3-7 to 1-9 in "a hard-fought encounter". In the final at Bruff on March 28th, the Ennis boys were boosted by a brace of goals by Dick Quirke en route to a 2-7 to 1-7 victory, thus ending North Mon's bid for a third title in-a-row. "North Mon, who were spearheaded by Teddy McCarthy, had been fancied to beat us. Whereas we were a team of average hurlers, they were the team of stylists. We played as a united team and it was a fantastic day. The win meant a lot to Clare people in general as the county team was starved of success at the time," he recalls.

"We all felt there was an onus on us to perform, given that it was the college's centenary," he says. "We pulled out all the stops in training to achieve a certain standard. Our trainers, Fr Willie Walsh and Fr Hugh O'Dowd realised from an early stage that our team was limited from the point of view of superstars, with perhaps the exception of Ray Sampson and John Russell. But we were prepared to listen and do what we were instructed to do, and we also had the ability to graft. We had a fantastic backline and it wasn't unusual for some of the lesser lights to stand out in training and in games."

With the Harty Cup safely tucked away, the boys in blue set their sights on All-Ireland success. However, they were fortunate to get a second bite of the cherry against St. Peter's, Wexford at the end of a poor quality drawn All-Ireland final at Thurles which produced just ten scores. "Seldom does a hurling match appear slow when it follows a football game but certainly this was the case during the first half of the All-Ireland Colleges final in Thurles. A change in formation played a major role in St. Flannan's, Ennis, salvaging the two points which forced a draw with St. Peter's, Wexford before a crowd just in excess of 5,000," the 'Irish Independent' reported. St. Peter's shot six wides before Michael Kelly opened the scoring for St. Flannan's in the 12th minute. Tom Dempsey eventually got St. Peter's off the mark, but St. Flannan's went on to lead by 1-1

to 0-2 at the break thanks to a Kelly goal from a 20-metre free. The standard of play improved considerably after the break, and the Leinster champions put themselves in a strong position when Sean Kelly found the net nine minutes after the restart. Gearóid Mannion replied with a point for Flannan's, but the momentum stayed with the Wexford lads and it took a great intervention from goalkeeper, Eoin McMahon to deny them. When Justin Roche's sideline cut split the posts to make it a two-point game with 14 minutes remaining, St. Flannan's reacted by moving star defender, Ray Sampson to left half forward and Peter Leyden in the opposite direction. The changes had the desired effect as Sampson scored the last two points of the game to leave the sides level on 1-4 each.

The omens favoured St. Peter's for the replay as all four of their previous Croke Cup wins had been achieved at the second time of asking. However, showing a marked improvement on their performance in the drawn game, St. Flannan's ran out 2-9 to 0-10 winners at Semple Stadium to be crowned All-Ireland champions after a three-year lapse. The Wexford side made the early running and had opened up a 0-5 to 0-1 lead before Gearóid Mannion's goal left just the minimum between the teams at the half-way stage. That timely score gave St. Flannan's a big lift and they were further boosted by the second half introduction of midfielder, Louis Mulqueen, who had been injured in the drawn match. Within a minute of the restart, the Harty champions had restored parity and then a second goal from Dick Quirke put them firmly in the driving seat.

St. Flannan's had opened up a six-point gap before St. Peter's came back at them. The game was on a knife edge when the winners' centre back John Murphy stepped up to slot over a free from 90 yards. The same player followed up with another free from distance to seal victory for the Clare men. The victory was "the icing on the centenary celebration cake", according to the 'Irish Independent.'

"Going to Thurles the first day, I didn't feel entirely confident, as the big fear was that we had climaxed for the Harty final. I had felt a little unwell with nerves on the bus before the game and sure enough, we played very poorly and were lucky to come out with a draw. I gave one of my worst ever performances on a hurling pitch that day. The feeling in the camp was better for the replay. We learned from the mistakes we made the first day and turned in a very workmanlike display. In the end, we beat a fantastic and elegant Wexford team and it was a very satisfying victory for us, especially as it was achieved in our centenary year. The return to Ennis after big match success was always very enjoyable," Peter says, while adding modestly that, "maybe musical, academic and other successes should have received similar treatment".

Peter has nothing but good things to say about Fr Willie Walsh and Fr Hugh O'Dowd, the clerical duo who masterminded the All-Ireland victory. "They were two great men. Fr Willie used to say, 'get to the ball first and then let it go' and we executed this plan to great effect. Fr Willie and Fr Hugh showed us at a young age how to play to our strengths which is a blueprint for whatever you do in life. They prepared us for life and showed us what can be achieved through hard work, preparation and dedication. They showed us the importance of laying out your stall and seeing your positives." Peter also acknowledges the support other teachers in St. Flannan's gave the hurlers in their run-up to big games.

Peter represented his beloved Clarecastle at every level, commencing his senior hurling club career, aged just 17. "I cherish the memories, even those when we played in fields with cow-dung and branches used for goals," he laughs. He also represented Clare at minor and Under-21 level, being on the losing side in a Munster Under-21 final against Tipperary in 1985. "Playing for Clare was a tremendous boost as I felt I was punching above my weight," he says modestly. While studying medicine in UCG, Peter won an All-Ireland Freshers hurling medal and also played in the Fitzgibbon Cup. Due to his medical commit-

ments, however, his hurling career petered out somewhat, although he did line out for less well-known clubs such as Castlebar Mitchels, Cuchullains in Armagh and St. Paul's, Belfast. "I couldn't afford to pick up finger or hand injuries because of my work as a surgeon, and I was also restricted in my ability to travel to training," he explains. Through his job as an ENT (Ear, Nose, Throat) surgeon, Peter has attended to many players who have sustained facial and head injuries from playing hurling and says, "I very strongly believe that full facial helmets should be made compulsory by the GAA at all levels, including senior. Technology will improve the helmets and hurling is the safest of all contact sports if the helmet is worn."

Peter now lives in Belfast with his wife, Marian (neé Keohane), from Cratloe, and their four young children. He confesses that the standard of hurling in his domicile is "not of the standard" he was used to as a young boy. He looks forward to the day when a reunion is organised for the St. Flannan's team of 1982. "I've met Ray Sampson and Michael Kelly at hurling championship matches in Munster, but the meetings have been far too seldom, and when I meet Conor Fanning, who is a GP, we seldom turn the conversation round to hurling," he concludes. Naturally, he was "buoyed" by Clare's senior successes in the mid-1990s, and was particularly delighted for his fellow-Clarecastle men, Anthony Daly, 'Sparrow' O'Loughlin, Alan Neville, Fergus Tuohy and Kenny Morrissey.

Peter Leyden is in no doubt but that "St. Flannan's is one of the best hurling nurseries in Ireland." He concedes that "nowadays there is a more inclusive emphasis there on all sports and traditions," but is somewhat concerned about the "computer game culture among young people". However, he will always treasure the Harty and Croke Cup wins of 1982 in hurling, "the most exciting game in the world".

1983 – ALL-IRELAND SEMI-FINAL
24 April 1983, Cloughjordan

St. Flannan's, Ennis 4-7
(T. Murnane 1-5, A. Hanly 2-0, D. McInerney 1-1, R. Sampson 0-1)

St. Joseph's, Garbally 0-11
(M. Sheil 0-5, P. J. Lynch 0-2, T. Monaghan 0-2, G. Curley 0-1, C. Noone 0-1)

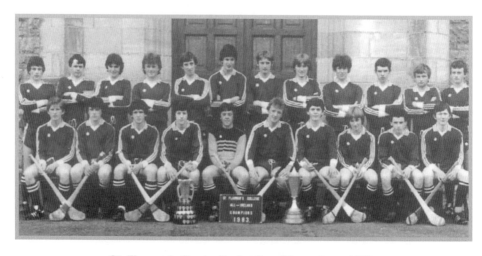

St. Flannan's, Ennis, Croke Cup Champions, 1983.
Back row, left to right: Sean McCarthy, Andrew Hanly, Kieran O'Neill, John Herbert,
Niall Romer, Niall Fanning, Eddie Casey, Tom Quinlivan, Enda O'Flaherty, Enda Colleran,
Niall Conroy, Brian Kelleher.
Front row, left to right: Gearóid Purcell, Rory Brislane, Dick Quirke, John Russell,
Brendan Flynn, Ray Sampson (capt), Timmy Murnane, Declan McInerney,
Gerard O'Loughlin, Michael Hogan.
Missing from photo: Denis Houlahan.
(Photograph courtesy of Ollie Byrnes, author of Blue is the Colour, Hurling at St. Flannan's)

1983 – ALL-IRELAND FINAL
8 May 1983, Thurles
Referee: John Moloney (Tipperary)

St. Flannan's, Ennis 0-16

Brendan Flynn
(Clare)

Denis Houlahan
(Limerick)

Rory Brislane
(Tipperary)

Eddie Casey
(Clare)

John Russell
(Clare)

Ray Sampson (*capt*)
(Limerick)

Sean McCarthy
(Clare)

Enda Colleran
(Clare)

Niall Romer
(Clare) (0-2)

Tom Quinlivan
(Clare) (0-1)

Dick Quirke
(Tipperary) (0-8)

Timmy Murnane
(Limerick) (0-2)

Andrew Hanly
(Clare) (0-1)

Enda O'Flaherty
(Clare) (0-1)

John Herbert
(Limerick)

Sub: Declan McInerney (Clare) (0-1) (for Casey).

Kilkenny CBS 2-4

Alan McCormack
(Kilkenny)

Derek Shelly
(Kilkenny)

Michael Maher (*capt*)
(Kilkenny)

Paul O'Dwyer
(Kilkenny)

Joe Kennedy
(Kilkenny)

Paddy Fennelly
(Kilkenny)

Frankie Morgan
(Kilkenny)

Billy Ayres
(Kilkenny)

Seamus Nicholson
(Kilkenny)

Richard Moran
(Kilkenny) (0-1)

Jackie Lee
(Kilkenny)

Billy Walsh
(Kilkenny) (0-1)

Pat Cass
(Kilkenny) (1-0)

Eddie O'Leary
(Kilkenny) (1-2)

Simon Walton
(Kilkenny)

Sub: Eamonn Lawless (Kilkenny) (for Nicholson).

Ray Sampson

Despite their early dominance of the competition with an astonishing four-in-a-row in the mid-1940s, it wasn't until the early 1980s that St. Flannan's again managed to retain the Croke Cup. A member of both the triumphant 1982 and 1983 sides was Ray Sampson, with the Limerick man having the honour of captaining the Ennis school to victory in the latter year.

The eldest of seven children, Ray was born and reared in Knocklong, County Limerick. His father Edmund (Ned) played hurling and football as did all of his uncles, while there was also a tradition of hurling on his mother's side. Ray attended Hospital Primary School where he was introduced to hurling by his teacher, Sean Smith. "I fell in love with the game straightaway," he remembers.

In September 1978, Ray packed his bags for the famous St. Flannan's in Ennis. One of his earliest secondary school memories is of St. Flannan's winning the 1979 All-Ireland title with 15 Clare men in the starting line-up. Ray was full of admiration for players such as Gerry McInerney and Seanie McMahon and his "immediate ambition was to make the Harty team." Ray's first success with the Ennis college was a Munster under 15-and-a-half championship. He only ever lost one competitive game in the colours of the famed Ennis hurling academy, and that was a Dean Ryan Cup final to a Teddy McCarthy-inspired North Monastery side in 1981. Ray graduated to the Harty Cup team in 1981/82 and played in an unaccustomed role of corner back through-

out most of the campaign. Despite winning the Munster and All-Ireland crowns, Ray says he "hated playing corner back, as all my hurling up until then had been played at either midfield or centre forward. But it was only afterwards that I realised why Fr Walsh, Fr Gardiner and Fr O'Dowd had played me there.

According to Ray, being named captain for the 1983/83 campaign was "one of the best honours I have ever had", as he expected either Dick Quirke or John Russell to have been given the honour. The year didn't get off to a great start, however, with St. Flannan's losing to St. Kieran's, Kilkenny, in the annual game for the old All-Ireland trophy. He vividly recalls, "I was brutal in that game and I went to Fr Walsh a few days later and promised him that I wouldn't be as poor again." Ray kept his word and, after accounting for De La Salle of Waterford "in a good tough game" in their championship opener, St. Flannan's went on to retain the Harty Cup with a replay victory over North Monastery. St. Flannan's were somewhat fortunate to draw the first game 0-9 each in Emly, but were full value for their 1-6 to 0-7 win in the replay. "We played very well in the replay," Ray recalls. "I started the game at midfield before moving to centre back where I had a great battle with Teddy McCarthy, who was some man to jump for a ball."

St. Flannan's weren't at their best in the All-Ireland semi-final against St. Joseph's, Garbally, at Cloughjordan, but still emerged as 4-7 to 0-

11 winners. Ray scans his old scrapbook from his schooldays and sums up that particular game by saying, "we won it and that's all that counted". That set the scene for the All-Ireland final against Kilkenny CBS at Semple Stadium. "Everyone expected St. Kieran's to come out of Leinster, but Kilkenny CBS won through instead. There was a great buzz in the school coming up to the Croke Cup final, with students practising chants. Even the food got better," Ray jokes.

In the final in Thurles, Kilkenny CBS played the better hurling in the first half to lead by 2-3 to 0-5 at the break. Indeed, the 'Irish Independent' describes St. Flannan's as being "particularly ragged" in the opening half. However, the Harty champions were a different team after the break, shooting 0-11 while restricting their opponents to a solitary point from a '65'. It was no coincidence that St. Flannan's dramatic improvement followed a series of astute changes made by the team management. "The result was a performance with fire and determination," the 'Irish Independent' reported. "We made hard work of beating them, and it was only in the last 20 minutes that we pulled away. I did reasonably well, but I'd never be happy with my own game". For Ray, the most difficult part of the day was still to come - making the victory speech - as evidenced by his caption in the aforementioned scrapbook, 'Those blasted speeches'! "Irish wasn't my best subject in school so making the speech wasn't something I was looking forward to. Fr Walsh wrote out the speech for me and I got through it somehow and I didn't mind once I got to the English bit," he laughs. To this day he fondly recalls "the great hype when we got back in the school as All-Ireland champions".

The 1983 All-Ireland success was masterminded by Fr Willie Walsh and Fr Hugh O'Dowd, and Ray is full of praise for both men. "The two priests worked very well together. Fr Hugh loved first-time hurling, like the old Munster championship. Everything was done meticulously and, from a tactical point of view, they were both ahead of their time. Every possible scenario was covered beforehand. If the opposition had a danger man, our

best back was designated to mark him. Whenever we played Farranferris, we had a specific game plan for them. They played the running game which the Cork team now favours and we always had a plan to counteract that. Then, we had a different plan when we played North Mon." Ray feels St. Flannan's owes a huge debt of gratitude to its boarders for providing the backbone to so many successful hurling teams. "When fellas live together for five years, a special bond inevitably develops. Hurling was the big thing in Flannan's - all that you have to do is to walk down the school corridor and see the pictures on the wall for proof of this." Ray was also a noted footballer with St. Flannan's and was part of the team which suffered a narrow defeat to eventual Hogan Cup champions Coláiste Chríost Rí in 1983. "We had some very good footballers. Enda O'Flaherty, who was full forward on the hurling team in '83, was one of the finest underage footballers I've ever seen," he says.

After losing two Munster minor hurling finals with Limerick in 1982 and 1983 (both to Tipperary), Ray graduated to the county senior side in the latter part of 1984. He won a National League medal the following spring, comfortably defeating a Clare side, ironically littered with St. Flannan's past pupils, in the final. However, disappointment followed in the Munster championship when Limerick lost to Cork. Ray starred for the Shannonsiders in their Munster Under-21 championship win of 1986 (defeating Clare in a replayed final), but they were subsequently beaten in the All-Ireland semi-final by a Joe Cooney-inspired Galway. In 1988, Ray emigrated to the US where he won two New York championships with the Limerick club. "It was either hurling or work those days", Ray says nostalgically. A very capable New York side, with Ray in its ranks lost the National Hurling League final to Kilkenny in 1990 in Gaelic Park. "D.J. beat us that day," Ray recalls.

However, he returned home on a number of occasions to assist Garryspillane and Limerick in crunch matches. He won a county intermediate championship medal with 'The Bouncers' in 1991 and the following year he came off the bench to score the winning point as Limerick had a memorable National League final triumph over the then All-Ireland champions, Tipperary at the Gaelic Grounds. Ray returned to Ireland for good in 1996 and played a county final with Garryspillane (losing to Patrickswell) before hanging up his hurl in 2003. He watched with delight last year when Garryspillane finally won their first county senior championship after overcoming Kilmallock in the decider.

One of Ray's biggest regrets in hurling is not winning a Munster championship medal. "When I started playing with Limerick, we had a strong team which contained the likes of Mossie Carroll, Joe McKenna, Pat McCarthy, Liam O'Donoghue and Shane Fitzgibbon. We won the league in '85, but never fulfilled our potential in the championship. Cork and Tipperary were both very strong and it was a pity that there was no 'back door' in those days."

Since retiring from hurling, Ray has taken a big interest in clay pigeon shooting and has ambitions to represent his country in the sport in the near future. Ray is so immersed in shooting that for over five years he has run his own gun and outdoor recreational store, Lazy Dog Ltd, just outside Knocklong. He is happy to report that "it's a growing business". He had previously worked in the construction and bar trades. Ray is married to Donegal woman, Mary (neé Carlin) and they have three young children, Cody (5), Shania (3) and Mackenzie (6 months). He still follows the fortunes of his alma mater and insists that the great bond which existed in his day will never be lost to St. Flannan's. He remains in touch with a few of his school team-mates, particularly John Herbert and Niall Conroy.

Ray Sampson has nothing but fond memories of his five years as a boarder in Ennis' most famous secondary school. "I loved Flannan's with a passion and will till the day I die. Fellows who mightn't be your best friends were like brothers once you put on that blue jersey", Ray concludes. His meticulously-assembled scrapbook will ensure that those great memories are never forgotten.

1984 – ALL-IRELAND SEMI-FINAL
15 April 1984, Birr

St. Kieran's, Kilkenny 3-8
(L. Egan 1-4, E. Keher 1-1, E. Morrisey 1-0, T. Holohan 0-2, T. McCluskey 0-1)

Our Lady's, Gort 1-5
(J. O'Sullivan 1-0, J. Lee 0-3, T. O'Driscoll 0-1, S. O'Donoghue 0-1)

St. Finbarr's, Farranferris, Croke Cup Champions, 1984.
Back row, left to right: Conor Noonan, Jim Deane, Martin Casey, John McSweeney, Damien Wallace, Dan O'Connell, Arthur Tobin, Tom Kearney, Finbarr Daly.
Middle row, left to right: Jim O'Connell, Pat Whelton, Allen Murphy, Brian O'Neill, Mr John 'Kid' Cronin, Pat Tobin, Tom Kingston, Pat O'Callaghan, Mr Sean O'Riordan, Pat Bozynski, Declan Kenneally, John James Murphy.
Front row, left to right: Fr Johnny Collins, Aidan Crowley, Pat O'Brien, Bishop John Buckley, Barry Harte (capt), Bishop Michael Murphy, Mark Foley, D.J. Kiely, Fr Michael Ó Dálaigh.
(Photograph courtesy of Tim Horgan, author of Farna's Hurling Story)

1984 – ALL-IRELAND FINAL
6 May 1984, Croke Park
Referee: Michael Kelleher (Kildare)

St. Finbarr's, Farranferris 1-15

Tom Kingston
(Cork)

Allen Murphy　　　　**Pat Whelton**　　　　**Brian O'Neill**
(Cork)　　　　　　　　(Cork)　　　　　　　　(Cork)

Conor Noonan　　　　**Pat O'Brien**　　　　**Pat Tobin**
(Cork) (0-1)　　　　　　(Cork)　　　　　　　　(Cork)

Declan Kenneally　　　　**D. J. Kiely**
(Cork) (0-1)　　　　　　　(Cork) (0-6)

John McSweeney　　**Barry Harte (*capt*)**　　**Martin Casey**
(Cork) (0-1)　　　　　(Cork) (0-3)　　　　　　(Cork)

Aidan Crowley　　　　**Mark Foley**　　　　**Finbarr Daly**
(Cork) (0-3)　　　　　　(Cork) (1-0)　　　　　(Cork)

Subs: Tom Kearney (Cork) (for Casey), Pat O'Callaghan (Cork) (for Daly),
Arthur Tobin (Cork) (for McSweeney).

St. Kieran's, Kilkenny 0-8

Pat Foley
(Kilkenny)

Tony Byrne　　　　**Pat Carroll**　　　　**Tommy Ryan**
(Kilkenny)　　　　　(Kilkenny)　　　　　(Kilkenny)

Tomás McCluskey (*capt*)　　**Willie Dwyer**　　**Tim Phelan**
(Kilkenny)　　　　　　　　　(Kilkenny)　　　　(Kilkenny)

Lorcan O'Neill　　　　**John Holohan**
(Kilkenny)　　　　　　　(Kilkenny)

Liam Egan　　　　**John Feehan**　　　　**Walter Purcell**
(Kilkenny) (0-6)　　　(Kilkenny)　　　　　(Kilkenny)

Eamon Keher　　　　**Tom O'Sullivan**　　　　**Eamonn Morrisey**
(Kilkenny) (0-1)　　　　(Tipperary)　　　　　　(Kilkenny) (0-1)

Barry Harte

In the GAA's Centenary Year of 1984, the renowned Cork hurling nursery, St. Finbarr's, Farranferris, put a decade of failure and disappointment behind them to regain the Croke Cup. The Farna team was captained by Timoleague's Barry Harte, who was one of several West Cork men to feature on that all-conquering side.

Barry was the first of four sons of butcher, Dan Harte and his wife, Mary to come to Farna. At one stage all four lads were in St. Finbarr's, but unlike Barry, his brothers Ken, Cecil and Ciaran did not make the Harty teams. Barry's name has been indelibly linked with that of former Cork star, Mark Foley, ever since they were young boys growing up in the village of Timoleague. When Barry and Mark finished in primary school, they agreed to continue their education as boarders in St. Finbarr's, with Mark's father, Michael, driving the two nervous youngsters to their new 'home' back in September 1979. When Barry arrived in the famous Cork city nursery some 27 years ago, the senior hurling team had endured a miserable run in the Harty Cup which saw them fail to win a match in quite a few years. The glory days of the late 1960s and early 1970s seemed but a distant memory. However, during Barry's six years at Farna, a major hurling revival took place which culminated in the All-Ireland final victory over St. Kieran's College in 1984 and he became part of the college's hurling folklore.

According to Barry, Farranferris had a long tradition of attracting pupils from the football strongholds of West Cork. "They attracted a huge number of boarders from West Cork", adding that, "if you had aspirations of joining the priesthood or playing hurling, that's where you were directed! Most of us coming in from West Cork wouldn't have played hurling before. It wasn't like going into St. Kieran's where you would have had played hurling from an early age. We had to pick up the skills of the game quickly and when you'd come up against the likes of North Mon at under 14 level, it would usually be a rude awakening for you, when hurling was played at a different pace." As it happened, the Croke Cup winning team was backboned by West Cork men. "You had the likes of Allen Murphy, Pat Whelton, Pat Tobin, Con Noonan, Pat O'Brien, as well as Mark Foley and myself," Barry reflects. "The vast majority of us played for junior 'B' hurling clubs. You actually could say that Pat Whelton and Pat Tobin were privileged because they played for a junior 'I' team," he jokes.

Barry acknowledges that the return of legendary coach, Fr (Canon) Michael O'Brien to Farna in 1982 was a big factor in their return to prominence. But it was his successor and school vice-principal, Sean O'Riordan who actually delivered the silverware. "Fr O'Brien came back as an external trainer in '82, I feel at the instigation of Fr John Buckley, who was a very ambitious man and he brought a level of professionalism to the set-up," Barry recalls. "The expectation and mindset rose to a different level. He was at the cutting edge of training teams and went on to train the Cork seniors to win the All-Ireland in 1984. Even though I was only in third year at the time, he included me on the '82 team which lost the Harty Cup semi-final to St. Flannan's. I missed a couple of goal chances to win the game and that is still a big regret of mine, even though I was only 14. Flannan's went on to win the All-Ireland and they beat us again in '83, around the same time as Fr O'Brien took the Cork job. During his two years, he put the structures in place for what was to follow." Despite being a rival of Fr O'Brien's from their time with Glen Rovers and Blackrock respectively, Sean O'Riordan was viewed as a natural successor to the 'Archdeacon'. Prior to his appointment as manager in 1984, O'Riordan had trained some of the future Harty players at Under-15 level for the White Cup which provided the springboard for the Croke Cup success. Many of those players, including Barry went on to win Dean Ryan Cup medals in 1982 and collected All-Ireland 'B' football medals in 1983.

Yet, by far the best wine was left till last when a great Farranferris team reclaimed the Harty Cup and won the televised All-Ireland decider against St. Kieran's. Few people knew Seanie O'Riordan better than Barry, who clearly regards him as an outstanding hurling coach. "He was meticulous in everything that he did. He brought the whole thing to a new level. It was the first time we had ever heard about gyms, physios and diets. We felt that the rugby internationals would have been the only guys on such programmes! He was ten years ahead of his time and the emphasis was very much on fitness. He had trained us all the way up through the ranks and he saw 1984 as his big opportunity to prove his worth as a top-class manager.

Seanie made me captain and was totally professional in everything that he did. He even took the training to Dunmanway because of the big West Cork contingent. He trained us hard there - I would say it was as tough as any training I did with any team." Barry also praises Fr Johnny Collins as "a very nice man and a great hurling man". Indeed, he states that "the teachers in general showed great goodwill

towards the hurlers and had a paternal interest in the lads".

Barry remembers that there was less pressure on Farna in 1984 than in the previous two years when Fr O'Brien was at the helm. "Because Fr O'Brien was such a high-profile name, big things were expected of us in '82 and '83, whereas the same level of expectation wasn't there when Seanie took over. This undoubtedly worked to our advantage and we received a further boost when D.J. Kiely and Declan Kenneally came back as repeats. They added a bit of steel to the team," Barry says. 1983/84 was the first year the Harty Cup was run in its entirety after the Christmas break and the Farna lads actually trained during the school holidays over the festivities. However, despite being supremely fit, the Farranferris boys almost came a cropper against an unheralded Cashel CBS team in the first round. "It was a nightmare," Barry recalls. "It was a tough, dogged affair and we were greatly relieved to salvage a draw, despite the fact that we had an extra man for about 40 minutes. Cashel had a monster of a guy at centre back called Pat O'Donoghue who, luckily for us, was sent off." Farna looked comfortable when they led by 0-6 to 0-3 at half-time, but Cashel grimly fought their way back and edged in front before D.J. Kiely forced a replay with a last-gasp sideline cut. The replay was equally as competitive, though not nearly as ill-tempered as the drawn encounter. St. Finbarr's prevailed by the minimum margin, with a first half goal from Barry Harte and "a phenomenal save" by goalkeeper, Tom Kingston from Walter O'Carroll in the dying moments proving decisive. Cashel were also left to rue a missed '65' which would have sent the game into extra-time.

That victory set up an all-Cork clash with North Mon in the semi-final on St. Patrick's Day. Barry remembers, "instead of going home for St. Patrick's Day, we stayed back in the college and it proved to be a great team-bonding exercise. North Mon were the traditional giants and had a huge pick and whereas we were nearly all from the country, their team was made up entirely of city guys. It was the first time we were at the same table as them in ten years and there was between 10,000 and 15,000 people in Páirc Uí Chaoimh for what was an eagerly-awaited game."

In a contest which lived up to all expectations and more, Farranferris got off to an explosive start which yielded three goals in the opening five minutes. North Mon were always playing catch-up after that, but Farna still needed to call on all their battling qualities and fitness to hold on for a 4-8 to 3-8 victory. Barry himself scored a hat-trick of goals as Farna qualified for their first Harty Cup final in ten years.

Farna's opponents in the final were Limerick CBS and once again, a replay was needed to separate the teams. Despite dominating the drawn clash, the Cork lads couldn't put Limerick away and were reeled in by a late rally which culminated in Pat Davoren scoring the equalising goal from a 30-yard free. Sean O'Riordan rejigged his team for the replay and these changes had the desired effect as Farna coasted to an 11-point victory. The Shannonsiders played with the aid of a strong wind in the first half, but only led by two points at the break. In the second half, Farranferris took complete control with two goals from debutant, Pat O'Callaghan propelling them to a 4-9 to 1-7 victory and a seventh Harty Cup success. "We beat them in a replay in Kilmallock after drawing the first game in Charleville. They were trained by the former Offaly captain, Pat Fleury and were a tough team. There was a lot of acrimony in the replay but it was one-sided and proved to be an anti-climax. It was a great achievement to beat Limerick CBS when you consider they had eight players who went on to win All-Ireland minor medals with Limerick that same year. By contrast, we had only three players - D.J. Kiely, Tom Kingston and myself - on the Cork team which lost to Limerick in the first round of the Munster championship."

So, it was on to the All-Ireland final at Croke Park against old rivals St. Kieran's. The arduous campaign in Munster had seasoned the Farna boys for another hectic game but, to their surprise, the Kilkenny side were easily disposed of. "It was another anti-climax, but I think the tough Munster campaign stood to

us. We were battle-hardened, and St. Kieran's seemed to freeze on the day," Barry feels. "We travelled up to Dublin on the Saturday and attended the colleges football final. This helped us savour the big match atmosphere. Ironically, losing All-Ireland semi-finalists Coláiste Chríost Rí had only beaten us narrowly earlier in the Munster campaign in what was our first year back in the 'A' football championship." Indeed, Barry recalls that he missed what would have been a winning goal in that particular Corn Uí Mhuirí match, prompting Farna football captain Finnbarr Daly to joke that Barry "missed it deliberately to concentrate on the hurling"!

"We stayed the night in the Ashling Hotel and returned to Croke Park the following day for our own final. Sean O'Riordan sang, 'I did it my way', in the bus en route to GAA headquarters to rouse the troops. It was great to win, especially in Centenary Year when such a big deal was made of all competitions." The 'Irish Independent' felt the final "fell well below expectations" with the Cork lads "always that shade faster, stronger and more skilful" than St. Kieran's. The Croke Cup was effectively destined for Leeside by the interval, at which stage Farna led by 1-10 to 0-4, the goal coming from Mark Foley, who played with his jaw wired following the Harty final replay and, according to Barry, "was a stone lighter than usual". Tom O'Riordan's newspaper report concluded that, "there was simply no denying the merit of St. Finbarr's victory." Barry got through his speech with no great discomfort and he recalls "great razzmatazz back in Cork" that evening. 1984 was even more special for Barry, as he skippered Munster to the special colleges inter-provincial competition held in Centenary Year. Barry repeated his Leaving Cert at Farna in 1985 when "a tough dogged St. Flannan's team caught us on the hop", thereby relieving St. Finbarr's of their provincial and All-Ireland crowns. In fact, in his four years playing Harty Cup for Farna, Barry suffered defeats at the hands of the Ennis college on three occasions.

On leaving Farna, Barry won an All-Ireland minor hurling medal in 1985 and an Under-21 medal (although unfortunately injured for the final) in 1988 with Cork. He also played with the county juniors but only managed to play National League games with the Rebels' senior team. He also represented UCC in the Fitzgibbon Cup (with Mark Foley inevitably as a colleague and Fr O'Brien as coach), before furthering his studies in Trinity College in Dublin. Barry went on to qualify as a dentist, but in recent years changed his career path and he is now involved in property development. He is married to Barbara (a pharmacist) and they live in Timoleague with their three children - Brad, Clara and Elsa. Barry was actively involved in the now-defunct Farranferris Past Pupils Union and actually played football for Argideen Rangers until last year.

In 1993, Barry led Argideen Rangers to their first South West junior hurling success and 12 months later, he became the first Carbery man to raise the Cork senior hurling county championship trophy. As Carbery selector Eddie McSweeney remarked after the historic 1994 county final win over Midleton, "Barry Harte is a lucky captain for any team to have leading them." No doubt, these sentiments were echoed at the team of 1984's ten-year reunion. "A lot of lads scattered over the years but, in recent times, fellows are coming back. Nowadays, a core of us would be drinking buddies," Barry concludes. With St. Finbarr's no longer operational as a secondary school, undoubtedly their fifth and last Croke Cup winning team is the subject of many a regular toast in pubs and clubs by the banks of the Lee.

1985 – ALL-IRELAND SEMI-FINAL
21 April 1985, Limerick

North Monastery, Cork 2-11
(R. Feeney 1-1, K. Cotter 0-4, F. Horgan 1-0, K. McGuckian 0-3,
G. Riordan 0-2, T. O'Keeffe 0-1)

St. Joseph's, Garbally 0-7
(M. Duignan 0-3, A. Ryan 0-2, E. Lynch 0-2)

North Monastery, Cork, Croke Cup Champions, 1985.
Back row, left to right: Br Nevin, Ger O'Riordan, Kieran Keane, Sean Hennessy,
Tony O'Neill, Martin Lynch, Donncha O'Brien, Paul Hurley, Rory O'Connor, Paul O'Neill,
Derry Murphy, Mr Murt Murphy.
Middle row, left to right: Ken Cotter, Ray Murphy, Tony Wall, Mark O'Connor,
James Kenneally, James Dean, John O'Riordan, Matt Twomey, Jim Kelleher.
Front row, left to right: Derek Jeffers, Rodney Feeney, Christy Connery, Tony O'Keeffe,
Frank Horgan (capt), Kieran McGuckian, Barry Coutts, Maurice Honohan, John Healy.
(Photograph courtesy of Gerry Kelly and Liam O'Brien, c/o North Monastery, Cork)

1985 – ALL-IRELAND FINAL
12 May 1985, Portlaoise
Referee: Seamus Brennan (Galway)

North Monastery, Cork 2-7

James Kenneally
(Cork)

Christy Connery Mark O'Connor Kieran Keane
(Cork) (Cork) (Cork)

John Healy Kieran McGuckian Derry Murphy
(Cork) (Cork) (Cork)

Barry Coutts Ken Cotter
(Cork) (Cork) (0-2)

Ger O'Riordan Frank Horgan (*capt*) Tony O'Keeffe
(Cork) (0-2) (Cork) (0-1) (Cork)

Paul O'Neill Donncha O'Brien Rodney Feeney
(Cork) (0-1) (Cork) (2-0) (Cork) (0-1)

Sub: John O'Riordan (Cork) (for O'Keeffe).

Birr Community School 3-4

Cathal Ryan
(Offaly)

Brendan O'Dwyer David Harding Ger Connors
(Offaly) (Tipperary) (Offaly)

Raymond Kelly (*capt*) Michael Hogan Damien Geoghegan
(Offaly) (Offaly) (Offaly)

Niall Gath Padraig McGuinness
(Offaly) (1-0) (Offaly)

Declan Cleare Daithi Regan Declan Pilkington
(Offaly) (1-0) (Offaly) (Offaly) (0-1)

Gary Cahill Patrick Hogan Brian Guinan
(Offaly) (1-2) (Offaly) (Offaly) (0-1)

Sub: Tony Middleton (Tipperary) (for P. Hogan).

1985 – ALL-IRELAND FINAL (REPLAY)
19 May 1985, Limerick
Referee: Seamus Brennan (Galway)

North Monastery, Cork 4-11

James Kenneally
(Cork)

Christy Connery   Mark O'Connor   Kieran Keane
(Cork)   (Cork)   (Cork)

John Healy   Kieran McGuckian   Ken Cotter
(Cork)   (Cork)   (Cork) (0-4)

Barry Coutts   Derry Murphy
(Cork)   (Cork) (0-1)

Tony O'Keeffe   Martin Lynch   Paul O'Neill
(Cork)(0-2)   (Cork)   (Cork)

Rodney Feeney   Donncha O'Brien   Frank Horgan (*capt*)
(Cork) (0-1)   (Cork) (1-2)   (Cork) (3-0)

Subs: John O'Riordan (Cork)(0-1) (for O'Neill), Paul Hurley (for O'Keeffe).

Birr Community School 1-5

Cathal Ryan
(Offaly)

Brendan O'Dwyer   David Harding   Ger Connors
(Offaly)   (Tipperary)   (Offaly)

Raymond Kelly (*capt*)   Michael Hogan   Damien Geoghegan
(Offaly)   (Offaly)   (Offaly)

Niall Gath   Padraig McGuinness
(Offaly) (1-0)   (Offaly)

Declan Cleare   Daithi Regan   Declan Pilkington
(Offaly) (0-1)   (Offaly) (0-1)   (Offaly)

Gary Cahill   Patrick Hogan   Brian Guinan
(Offaly) (0-1)   (Offaly)   (Offaly) (0-2)

Subs: Tony Middleton (Tipperary) (for Harding), Paul Hoare (Offaly) (for McGuinness),
Tony Bennett (Offaly) (for Guinan).

Frank Horgan

Few players have left such an indelible mark on a Croke Cup final as Frank Horgan did in 1985, when as the North Monastery captain, he scored three goals in the replay of that year's final. Ironically, the hat trick came from an unaccustomed corner forward role, as the Cork school won their fourth All-Ireland senior hurling colleges title.

Frank is not aware of a hurling background in either his mother or late father's background. He attended Little Island National School in East Cork and occasionally games were played between schools in the parish. Frank's four older brothers had gone to North Mon before him and one of them, John, won Harty Cup and Croke Cup medals in 1980. Another brother, Kieran, was a regular on an unsuccessful North Mon team that featured future Cork hurling and football maestro, Teddy McCarthy. Having spent the early years of his secondary school education in Coláiste Mhuire, Cobh, where he hurled without success, Frank actually didn't go to the Mon until fifth year. "At that time they were getting stricter on taking people from outside. Obviously Little Island is a good distance from North Mon. I wanted to get at the hurling and the Harty so I followed my older brothers to the Mon eventually," Frank recalls. For Frank, travelling to school in the Mon involved an arduous journey. He had to be up before 7.30 am to catch a train into the city. Then he faced a 35-minute walk to school. "You can imagine lugging three hurleys, a gear bag and your schoolbooks up to the Mon and then going training at 4 o'clock, and running from there back to the train station at 5.30 or 6 o'clock to get home," says Frank.

In his first year in the Mon, Frank was a sub on the Harty side, but he made the starting team for the following two years. In 1983/84, the Mon were beaten in the semi-final of the Harty Cup by St. Finbarr's, Farranferris, who went on to win the All-Ireland. Frank was chosen as captain for the 1984/85 campaign by his fellow players and he remembers the day well. "Murt Murphy put us all in a room and basically said 'lads, pick your captain' and the lads picked me. I was a bit surprised but glad to have got it." There was no real expectation that the Mon were capable of going all the way to Harty Cup and All-Ireland glory. "The one thing about the team was that we had no outstanding player," says Frank, who reckons it was probably a plus in that the team was not overly-dependent on any one individual.

North Mon played Cistercian College, Roscrea in the first round of the Harty Cup. "If I remember rightly, we were under right pressure to win that game right to the very end. They missed a goal in the last minute which was vital," says Frank. "Kieran McGuckian, our centre back, had a stormer of a game that day. We just hung in there and we were lucky to come out of there, being honest." Nenagh CBS provided the opposition in the next round. "I think we walloped them and we went through it fairly comfortably," recalls Frank. That easy victory saw North Mon qualify for a semi-final clash with De La Salle of Waterford. "They give us a right good game. I think we pulled away in the second half. We might have been a bit cocky going out against them."

The Harty Cup final pitted the Mon against St. Flannan's, Ennis, and the match took place in Charleville. The Mon were under "fierce pressure" because of a less than impressive record against the Clare school in previous Harty finals. "One thing that struck me was that our goalkeeper, James Kenneally, had an outstanding game," Frank remembers. Ironically, Gerard O'Riordan had started the year as the Mon goalie but he was later moved outfield. Midfielder Barry Coutts, despite being small in stature, had a reputation as a "teak tough" player and Frank recalls that Coutts had a "fabulous game" in the Harty final. The Mon were against the wind in a low-scoring first half. "Ger O'Riordan broke through and scored a vital goal just before half-time. It was a brilliant goal and it really set us up for the second half and we won comfortably enough in the end." The Mon were victorious on a final scoreline of 5-6 to 1-7. St. Joseph's, Garbally were the Mon's opponents in the All-Ireland semi-final in Limerick. The Munster champions won the game in convincing fashion by 2-11 to 0-7. According to Frank, the Ballinasloe side "had quite a few decent hurlers", including Michael Duignan, who went on to win two All-Ireland senior medals with Offaly.

Naturally, the Mon was gripped by huge excitement in the build-up to the All-Ireland final against an almost entire Offaly-born team, Birr Community School. The final, which took place on May 12th in Portlaoise, ended in a draw, North Mon 2-7 Birr CS 3-4, despite the Harty champions looking well in control when leading by 1-6 to 1-1 at the interval. "I think we went a couple of points ahead and they came back into the game and drew it at the end. They probably deserved a draw over the 60 minutes," Frank sportingly concedes. Indeed, Tom O'Riordan in the 'Irish Independent' credits Birr with "a magnificent fightback". Frank's contribution to the game was curtailed by an injury he sustained during

the first half. "After about 20 minutes I was running through and I got a fierce dead leg. I can remember being in the shower at half-time trying to sort it out." Although he managed to complete the game, the injury left Frank a very doubtful starter for the replay, which took place in Limerick a week later.

"If you had asked me on the Tuesday, I would have said there was no way I was going to be able to play. Even though I was telling them 'yeah, I'm playing', I was still iffy about it myself." The injury meant Frank didn't have the required level of mobility to play in his normal centre half forward position. Hence the switch for a heavily-strapped Frank to left corner forward. Frank feels his hat trick was helped by "mistakes from the Birr defence". All three of his goals came during the first half, when the Mon were playing with the wind. Birr failed to score during the opening half, with the half-time score reading 3-7 to 0-0. "We scored a fourth goal in the second half but I think the game was really over at half-time. They were trying to get back into it and it was a case of us battening down the hatches." There was very little thought given to who would captain the team if injury prevented Frank from playing. As far as Frank remembers, Barry Coutts was the vice-captain. Recalling his acceptance speech, Frank says, "The main man to thank on the day was our trainer, Murt Murphy". Frank describes Murphy as "an excellent coach". "Stopping the opposition from playing was an important part of his philosophy and he placed great emphasis on skills like blocking and hooking. Preventing opponents from striking the ball cleanly and working as a team were cornerstones of his approach. There were some teams we played who could have been better than us but we never allowed them to play. Defensively from 1 to 15 we were an excellent team," Frank concludes. Donal O'Grady, who later became Cork senior hurling manager, also coached teams during Frank's time in the Mon. With the All-Ireland final replay taking place on May 19th, the Leaving Cert quickly appeared on the horizon. "It was a bit of a shock to get back into the books alright," says Frank, who also played football for the

Mon but confesses to something of "a lack of interest" in the big ball game.

In 1984, Frank won the Cork intermediate hurling championship with his club, Erin's Own, their first-ever county title. The following year, Frank faced a school versus club conflict when Erin's Own had a senior championship match a week before the drawn All-Ireland colleges final. As North Mon captain, Frank felt duty bound to ensure he was fit for the Croke Cup decider. "I told the club, 'look, I'll only get one chance to play in an All-Ireland final with my school, so I won't be togging out'. I wasn't very popular but it was my decision. In the end, the school said, 'go ahead and play with them if you want', but I said, 'I can play with Erin's Own for the next 20 years but I'm only get one lash at this'." Unfortunately, Erin's Own were beaten in the first round of that year's senior championship, which was then played on a knockout format. The club was demoted back to the intermediate grade but they quickly earned a return to the senior ranks, where they have remained ever since. During his club career, Frank crossed paths with many of his 1985 Mon team-mates in the Cork hurling championship, such as Kieran McGuckian (Glen Rovers) and Christy Connery (Na Piarsaigh).

Although he didn't play minor for Cork, Frank was a member of the Cork Under-21 team which won the All-Ireland in 1988, hammering Kilkenny by 4-11 to 1-5 in the final. After 1988, a virus knocked him out of his stride, both for work and for hurling. However, he did make a number of appearances for the Cork seniors in the National Hurling League, but he never made the team for the championship. At club level, Frank enjoyed notable success with Erin's Own, captaining them to their inaugural senior county title in 1992. "It was a huge thrill. The previous year we were beaten quite easily and a lot of

people were talking about maybe regrading and, all of a sudden, we had the county cup in our back pocket." Tony O'Keeffe (the only North Mon team-mate from 1985 whom he continues to meet regularly nowadays), also helped Erin's Own to make history in 1992, while Cork hurling legend, Brian Corcoran was "the mainstay" of that team. In the Munster club championship which followed, the Cork side were defeated after a replay by Kilmallock of Limerick. Frank was still hurling at senior level for Erin's Own up to a few years ago. He played in the 2000 Cork county final when Erin's Own were defeated by Newtownshandrum, who have enjoyed huge success in recent years. When Frank stepped down from playing senior, he lined out for the Erin's Own juniors, reaching a couple of East Cork finals in the process. He also won a Cork junior football medal with Erin's Own in 1994.

Since hanging up his hurl, Frank has had more time to play golf, a sport he enjoys immensely. Now living in Glownthaune in East Cork, in recent years Frank has worked for Cork-based pharmaceutical company, Pfizer, where he is employed as a production coordinator. He is married to Maura (née McCarthy), whom he jokes is "more into shopping than hurling", and the couple have three young children, Stephen (9), Eoin (6) and Aoife (2). The two boys "love sport" and are "hurling mad". However, geographical considerations mean it is unlikely they will follow their father's footsteps into the Mon.

Frank Horgan has nothing but fond memories of his time in North Monastery. "I loved it, I'd do it all again," he says. However, these words are hardly surprising when one considers the contribution Frank made to the school's success on the hurling fields in 1985, in conjunction with colleagues he fondly recalls as "a great bunch of lads".

1986 – ALL-IRELAND SEMI-FINAL
13 April 1986, Tynagh

Birr Community School 2-10
(B. O'Dwyer 1-1, G. Cahill 0-3, J. Errity 0-3, P. Guinan 1-0, V. Dunne 0-1,
M. Hogan 0-1, D. Regan 0-1)

St. Joseph's, Garbally 1-5
(D. Curley 1-3, M. Duignan 0-1, J. Shiel 0-1)

Birr Community School, Croke Cup Champions, 1986.
Back row, left to right: Declan Sherlock, David Harding, Brendan O'Dwyer, Daithí Regan,
Barry Gleeson, Padraig McGuinness, Victor Dunne, Billy Dooley.
Front row, left to right: Declan Pilkington, Joe Errity, Gary Cahill, Michael Hogan (capt),
Brian Hennessy, Damien Geoghegan, Johnny Pilkington.
(Photograph courtesy of Billy Dooley)

1986 – ALL-IRELAND FINAL
27 April 1986, Portlaoise
Referee: Pat Delaney (Laois)

Birr Community School 5-8

Barry Gleeson
(Tipperary)

| **Brian Hennessy** | **Damien Geoghegan** | **Declan Sherlock** |
| (Offaly) | (Offaly) | (Offaly) |

| **Victor Dunne** | **Michael Hogan** (*capt*) | **Declan Pilkington** |
| (Offaly) | (Offaly) (0-1) | (Offaly) |

| **Padraig McGuinness** | **Brendan O'Dwyer** |
| (Offaly) | (Offaly) |

| **Joe Errity** | **Daithí Regan** | **David Harding** |
| (Offaly) (2-0) | (Offaly) (1-1) | (Tipperary) |

| **Gary Cahill** | **Billy Dooley** | **Johnny Pilkington** |
| (Offaly) (0-4) | (Offaly) (1-1) | (Offaly) (1-0) |

Subs: Justin Ryan (Offaly) (for D. Pilkington), Declan O'Meara (Tipperary) (0-1) (for Harding).

North Monastery, Cork 1-8

James Kenneally
(Cork)

| **Mark Hooley** | **Kieran Keane** | **Paul Jeffers** |
| (Cork) | (Cork) | (Cork) |

| **Finbarr Wall** | **John Healy** (*capt*) | **Rory O'Connor** |
| (Cork) | (Cork) | (Cork) |

| **Mark McElhinney** | **Paul Cummins** |
| (Cork) (0-1) | (Cork) (0-1) |

| **Georgie Healy** | **Martin Lynch** | **Tony O'Keeffe** |
| (Cork) (0-1) | (Cork) (0-1) | (Cork) (0-3) |

| **Finbarr Healy** | **Donncha Hurley** | **Rodney Feeney** |
| (Cork) | (Cork) (1-1) | (Cork) |

Sub: Timmy Harte (Cork) (for F. Healy).

Billy Dooley

A new name was inscribed on the Croke Cup in 1986 when a star-studded St. Brendan's Community School team from Birr recorded a thoroughly deserved All-Ireland final victory over their hitherto bogey team, North Monastery of Cork. The team was captained by centre half back, Michael Hogan and featured a youthful Billy Dooley from the famed Seir Kieran clan at full forward.

Billy Dooley hails from one of the best known hurling families in the country. The Dooley brothers, Joe, Billy and Johnny, were synonymous with Offaly's All-Ireland triumphs of 1994 and '98, and Joe was also a member of the 1985 All-Ireland winning side. Two other brothers, Seamus and Kieran, also played hurling with the Faithful County.

"I come from a family of five boys and four girls. All of the boys played for Offaly at some level or another and, with the exception of Seamus, we all went to Birr Community School," he explains.

Growing up in the hurling-mad village of Clareen in South Offaly, it was inevitable that Billy and his brothers would take up hurling. It also helped that their family background was steeped in the game. "Our uncle Joe hurled with Offaly and our grandfather on my mother's side, Jim Carroll, won an All-Ireland junior medal with the county in 1923. He played with Coolderry and people in Coolderry like to think that's where the hurling in our family came from," Billy jokes.

Billy attended Seir Kieran National School in Clareen and won a Cumann na mBunscol

title with them before entering Birr Community School, where he spent six years between 1981 and 1987. Unlike most of the traditional hurling schools, Birr didn't take boarders and Billy and his brothers travelled in and out by bus. "On the evenings when you'd stay back for training, you'd have to thumb home," he recalls, "as you made a lot more sacrifices to play in those times". The school's Leinster winning team of 1980 included the likes of the late Aidan Rosney, Paddy Corrigan, Ken Hogan and his own brother Joe, and these were players whom Billy looked up to. Billy lost Leinster finals at Under-14 and Under-16 level, but those disappointments were forgotten about when Birr landed the biggest prize in colleges hurling in 1986. "Looking back, we were unfortunate enough all along until we came to senior," Billy reflects.

In their first game of the 1985/86 campaign, the Leinster semi-final, the Offaly school got the better of St. Peter's, Wexford, by 3-6 to 3-3, with Billy chipping in with a crucial late goal. That set the scene for a provincial final showdown with traditional giants St. Kieran's, Kilkenny, in Rathdowney and, after a keenly-contested first half, Birr clicked into top gear after the restart to run out easy winners by 5-6 to 0-6. "It was close enough at half-time, but we pulled away for an easy enough victory in the second half. Offaly hurling was on a high at the time and I suppose that anytime you beat a Kilkenny team, it was a feather in your cap. That win gave us extra confidence." After retaining their Leinster title in impressive style, Birr Community School set their sights on All-Ireland glory. Billy sat out the All-Ireland semi-final, which was played "on a wet, sluggish old day" in Tynagh, when Birr defeated St. Joseph's, Garbally, by 2-10 to 1-5, after trailing by two points at half-time. Interestingly, Billy's future Offaly senior hurling team-mate, Michael Duignan, was among the scorers for the Galway outfit.

Billy can vividly remember the build-up to the All-Ireland final which was played on April 27th. "Everything in the school nearly came to a complete standstill. The principal, Br Denis, had been the driving force behind hurling in the school for many years and, even though he wasn't directly involved with the '86 team, he gave us great support and did all that he could to ensure that we were successful. You could say it was a case of third time lucky. We owed North Mon one after they beat us in the 1980 final and again in 1985 after a replay. I didn't play in '85, but we had eight or nine survivors on the following year's team and they were a little more in earnest about it. Lucky enough, it worked out for us."

The final was a typically tense affair and both teams struggled to find any rhythm in the early stages. North Mon had wind advantage in the first half, but had to wait until the 24th minute for their first break when Donnacha Hurley picked up a loose ball from Rodney Feeney's blocked attempt to finish to the net. Birr hit back three minutes later when Johnny Pilkington fired home after Gary Cahill's centre was poorly dealt with by North Mon goalkeeper Jim Kenneally. That goal left the sides level on 1-4 apiece at the interval.

The Birr fans had reason to be optimistic as the second half got underway and they were in full voice when Daithí Regan sent a long ball to Billy Dooley, who shot a crucial goal. The Mon responded with a point from Martin Lynch, but by now Birr had the scent of victory in their nostrils and went further ahead when Regan scored their third goal. Again, the holders responded - this time with a brace of points - but two more goals from Joe Errity put the result beyond all doubt.

"The All-Ireland final was very similar to

the Leinster final in that we only got on top in the second half," Billy recalls. "We played against the wind in the first half and got to half-time on level terms. Shortly after half-time, I scored a goal and we tagged on a few quick scores after that to put ourselves in a winning position. We cruised to the final whistle."

Michael Hogan had the tremendous honour of captaining Birr Community School to their first All-Ireland victory and, later in the year, he skippered Offaly minors to All-Ireland success. Billy rated Michael as "a right good centre back". A celebratory meal and disco ensued that night in Birr but Billy feels that "times were a lot simpler then".

Birr Community School's rise to prominence coincided with Offaly's emergence as a hurling power. When the amalgamated Birr school won their first Leinster senior colleges title in 1980, Offaly also won their first provincial senior championship. Birr had to wait five years longer than their county counterparts to achieve a breakthrough at All-Ireland level, but, when it came, nobody was surprised, not least the 'Irish Independent' reporter who covered their Croke Cup winning performance. He wrote, "the ultimate prize came to those who never lost faith in their own ability when Birr Community School proudly lifted the Croke Cup high in the sky at O'Moore Park, Portlaoise. They finally took the All-Ireland Colleges hurling crown at the expense of North Monastery, Cork, who denied them last year. This is the reward for many years of hard work and endeavour with total commitment all the way."

"It was the first All-Ireland that group of players won and it helped to kick off our hurling careers. Five or six of us went on to have a lot of success with Offaly," says Billy. He went on to play for Birr Community School in 1987 when they relinquished their Leinster and All-Ireland titles at the provincial final stage to St. Kieran's, with almost a completely new team being edged out in a Portlaoise thriller by 4-8 to 3-9. Other games which Billy enjoyed in secondary school were basketball and soccer, but "hurling was very much number one".

Billy is lavish in his praise of Padraig Horan who, after skippering Offaly to their first Liam McCarthy Cup success in 1981, masterminded Birr's historic All-Ireland victory. "We couldn't have had a better man over us than Padraig Horan. He was a big Offaly star at the time and we all looked up to him. He was a very determined player who never stood back as a hurler. He'd go through a brick wall if he had to and I think that was something that rubbed off on all of us. He received good assistance from Jimmy Dunne, who was our PE teacher, while Br Denis, Joe Kane and Frank Bergin were also very supportive of hurling. Br Denis would always give us his points of view but he left Padraig very much in charge on match days."

Like many of his Birr Community School team-mates, Billy won All-Ireland minor medals with Offaly in 1986 (as a playing sub) and 1987, defeating Cork and Tipperary respectively. In 1989, he played on the team which lost narrowly to Tipperary in front of a huge crowd in Portlaoise, in the All-Ireland Under-21 final. Despite that reversal, which remains one of Billy's "biggest regrets", he graduated to the Offaly senior team in 1990 and won a National League medal the following year. "A couple of injuries" ruled Billy out of the 1992 and 1993 championship campaigns, but he returned to play a starring role in Offaly's dramatic All-Ireland final victory over Limerick in 1994. He won a second All-Ireland senior medal in 1998, after a never-to-be-forgotten 'back door' campaign. He also collected Leinster medals in 1994 and 1995, winning All-Star awards in both these years for good measure. He retired from inter-county hurling in 2000.

With his beloved Seir Kieran, he won four county senior championships in 1988, 1995, 1996 and 1998. "However, we struggled a bit in the Leinster club championship once we got of Offaly," he laments. In his younger days, Billy also captured county Under-16 and minor 'B' titles and he continues to line out for the club's senior and junior teams to this day. "It's good exercise nowadays," he jokes.

Billy is married to Kinnity native, Fiona (née Maher), and they have three young sons, Sean (6), Conor (4) and Gearóid (2). "They already have hurleys in their hands", he says with pride. He is employed by Offaly County Council and is also a part-time farmer, a dual role which, when combined with family life, gives him very few opportunities to play golf. "I only played it a couple of times," he notes. Billy still lives in Clareen, "50 yards from my original home place" and, while he has kept in touch with many of his former Birr Community School colleagues, there are some he has "only met once or twice in ten years". Sadly, one team-mate from 1986, Brendan O'Dwyer, is since deceased. Billy still goes to the occasional Birr CS game but confesses that "Wednesday games just don't suit me".

"Some young lads give out about school but they were happy days for me in Birr," Billy Dooley concludes. "I hold that Croke Cup medal in very high regard." Over 20 years on, the 1986 success remains the school's only All-Ireland triumph, but it certainly acted as a springboard for Offaly's glorious period at senior inter-county level in the 1990s.

Author's Note:
   The Birr Community School captain from 1986, Michael Hogan, was not available for interview.

1987 – ALL-IRELAND SEMI-FINAL
12 April 1987, Athenry

St. Flannan's, Ennis 2-15
(T. Canny 0-7, P. Healy 1-1, G. Rodgers 1-0, R. McMahon 0-3,
M. McNamara 0-2, J. Quinlan 0-1, A. Neville 0-1)

St. Joseph's, Garbally 1-5
(D. Tiernan 1-0, D. Curley 0-3, C. Colohan 0-1, J. Campbell 0-1)

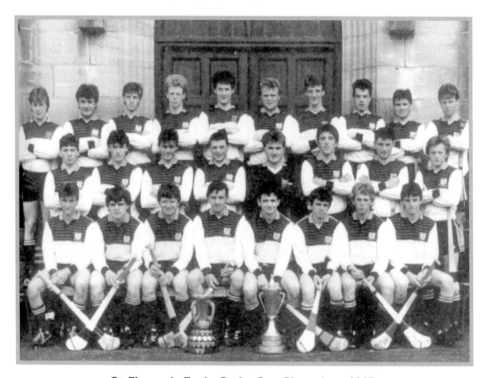

St. Flannan's, Ennis, Croke Cup Champions, 1987.
Back row, left to right: Eoin Maher, Pat Healy, Alan Neville, James McInerney, Sean Lyne,
Eibhear Slattery, Kevin McInerney, Noel McMahon, Robert Linnane, Oliver Mescall.
Middle row, left to right: Michael O'Doherty, Pat Conlon, Anthony Daly, Pat Heffernan,
Tom Hennessy, Darragh O'Neill, Michael McNamara, Turlough Herbert.
Front row, left to right: Richard McMahon, Joe O'Gorman, Tim Canny, Ger Rodgers,
Justin Quinlan (capt), David Fitzgerald, Michael O'Callaghan, Fergus Tuohy.
(Photograph courtesy of Ollie Byrnes, author of Blue is the Colour, Hurling at St. Flannan's)

1987 – ALL-IRELAND FINAL
10 May 1987, Birr
Referee: Noel O'Donoghue (Dublin)

St. Flannan's, Ennis 4-11

Tom Hennessy
(Limerick)

Anthony Daly   **Turlough Herbert**   **Oliver Mescall**
(Clare)   (Limerick)   (Clare)

Darragh O'Neill   **Pat Heffernan**   **Kevin McInerney**
(Limerick) (0-1)   (Limerick) (0-1)   (Clare)

Eibhear Slattery   **Justin Quinlan** (*capt*)
(Clare)   (Tipperary)

Michael McNamara   **Tim Canny**   **Pat Conlon**
(Clare) (1-1)   (Clare) (0-5)   (Limerick) (0-1)

Richard McMahon   **Pat Healy**   **Michael O'Doherty**
(Clare) (1-0)   (Clare) (1-0)   (Galway) (1-2)

St. Kieran's, Kilkenny 1-7

Jimmy Conroy
(Kilkenny)

Padraig McCluskey   **Fran Whelan**   **Padraig Larkin**
(Kilkenny)   (Kilkenny)   (Kilkenny)

John Crosbie   **Pat O'Neill**   **Paul Fahy**
(Kilkenny)   (Kilkenny) (1-3)   (Kilkenny)

Adrian Ronan   **Dominic Bradley**
(Kilkenny) (0-3)   (Kilkenny)

Kevin Conroy   **Richie O'Neill**   **Paul Brennan**
(Kilkenny)   (Kilkenny)   (Kilkenny)

D. J. Carey   **Declan Forristal**   **Briain Ryan** (*capt*)
(Kilkenny) (0-1)   (Kilkenny)   (Kilkenny)

Sub: Dick Dooley (Kilkenny) (for Crosbie).

211

Justin Quinlan

St. Flannan's College has produced many outstanding teams down the years. Some would argue, however, that the 1987 side, captained by Tipperary man, Justin Quinlan was the pick of the lot. Justin was born in Birmingham, but returned with his family to Tipperary at the age of four. He attributes his love of hurling to his father, John, a native of Cappawhite, whom he describes as being "a great hurling man and a big influence to this day." Justin received his primary education at Monastery CBS in

Tipperary town where he played both hurling and football. He subsequently spent two years in Abbey CBS secondary school before leaving to attend St. Flannan's as a boarder. "I went to Flannan's in 1985, the year I sat my Inter Cert. My older brother, Damien had been in Flannan's before me and, while he didn't win anything with them, he went on to win Fitzgibbon Cup medals with UCC," he explains. Justin recalls hurling as a young boy with Damien, who was constantly hitting sliotars, often alone against the wall. Later, Justin did the same in the handball alleys in St. Flannan's. "It was a great way to get your reflexes going. There was a side alley where we used to play backs and forwards. It was really tough, physical stuff and you soon learned that attack was the best form of defence. There was a lot of sledging and flaking and I learned the hard way," he recalls with a smile.

Justin made the Dean Ryan Cup team in his first year at St. Flannan's and was disappointed

when they lost to Midleton CBS in the final. However, it was nothing compared to the disappointment his team-mates felt, having also succumbed to the same opposition 12 months previously in the White Cup. Justin played Harty Cup for two years, but in his first year on the team in 1985/86, St. Flannan's were knocked out in the first round by De La Salle, Waterford. "Gary Loughnane was captain that year and we were disappointed to go out in the first round. I was very surprised to be picked at midfield for that game. Fr Willie Walsh told me that De La Salle had a guy he wanted me to mark and that's how I ended up in midfield." He remembers being even more surprised when he was chosen to captain the Harty team in 1986/87. "I'll never forget it," he says. "The Harty panel was named in the Science Lab and I was announced as captain for the year. I questioned the decision at first because there were some fantastic players on that team and players who were more skilful than I was. I thought Pat Heffernan or Darragh O'Neill would get the nod, but Fr Walsh and Fr Gardiner chose me because I had been voted in as a prefect and the priests must have felt the players would get behind me."

As it transpired, St. Flannan's steamrolled their opponents en route to winning the Harty Cup. They beat St. Colman's 2-12 to 1-5 in the first round, Thurles CBS 0-12 to 1-4 in the quarter-final and North Monastery 2-14 to 1-5 in the semi-final. In the final at Kilmallock, the Clare-based boys produced a magnificent performance to overcome the favourites, Midleton CBS by 3-12 to 2-6. "That was the final we wanted. It was won in the dressingroom really. The rallying cry was, 'they took the Dean Ryan off us, they took the Under-15 off us, but they aren't going to take the Harty off us.' We scored three goals in the first half and I can still remember the third. Pat Heffernan sent in a free, the ball bounced in the square and ended up in the net. We added another four or five points against a strong wind in the second half and ended up as very convincing winners," Justin recalls with delight.

With Kevin McInerney and Michael O'Doherty on board for the All-Ireland series, after being over-age for the Harty campaign, St. Flannan's easily accounted for Garbally College, Ballinasloe by 2-15 to 1-5 in the All-Ireland semi-final to set up a showdown with St. Kieran's in the final in Birr. Traditionally, games between the two college superpowers have been keenly contested but on this occasion, St. Flannan's were far superior as they powered to an easy win. In stark contrast to their Kilkenny counterparts, the St. Flannan's forwards flourished with all six getting on the scoresheet and the full forward line of Richard McMahon, Pat Healy and Michael O'Doherty notched up 3-2 between them. St. Flannan's were slow to get out of the starting blocks and after only three minutes, they were a goal down when Pat O'Neill drove a penalty to the roof of the net. However, the Harty champions gradually took over and led by 3-7 to 1-5 at the interval. In the first minute of the second half, St. Kieran's missed a glorious chance to haul themselves back into contention when O'Neill drove his second penalty wide. Following that let-off, St. Flannan's tightened their grip on proceedings and they cruised to a tenth All-Ireland victory.

"After winning the Harty, the pressure was off us to a certain extent and we were able to express ourselves that bit better in the All-Ireland series. There wasn't the same hype for the All-Ireland final as there was for the Harty final and I think that suited us," Justin says. "The All-Ireland final turned out to be a one-sided game. From 1 to 15, we fought tooth and nail to win possession. That's always a good sign and we broke down more teams by doing that. We always got great support, especially from the boarders who rarely got out and so they looked forward to the Harty campaign with great anticipation. There was always a huge sense of unity among the boarders." When being presented with the Croke Cup, Justin jokes that, as he had done when receiving the Harty Cup, he confined his content as Gaeilge to, "a chairde"!

Justin recalls how professional St. Flannan's were in their approach to each Harty campaign. "I can remember us taking glucose drinks on the bus up to the All-Ireland final in Birr. We even had 'flu jabs at the start of the year. Very few teams were taking those sort of precautions back then. Nothing was left to chance and we had Dr Colm Flynn to thank for that."

Justin is fulsome in his praise of Fr Willie Walsh and Fr Seamus Gardiner, who masterminded the 1987 success. "Fr Walsh was very shrewd on the sideline and had his homework done on every team before we played them. He was a grandmaster. He was able to see things happening straight away and knew what moves to make. Fr Hugh O'Dowd had been with Fr Walsh up until the start of that campaign when he went to Zimbabwe. Fr Gardiner replaced him and was another very knowledgeable hurling man. In training, he took the forwards and Fr Walsh looked after the backs." Justin also represented St. Flannan's in football and remembers Fr Oliver O'Doherty as being the driving force behind the big ball game in the hurling-dominated college.

"A few of the older priests in St. Flannan's said we were the best team ever to come out of the school," Justin proudly states. "We were a very well-balanced team and were superbly prepared. We beat all the top teams convincingly and there was never any let-up in any of our performances." Writing in the 'Irish Independent' following St. Flannan's 4-11 to 1-7 trouncing of old rivals St. Kieran's in the 1987 All-Ireland final, GAA correspondent, Tom O'Riordan concurred with the view that it was the Ennis stronghold's greatest ever team. "Such has been the quality of their performances since the campaign began in early February that it could well be argued this is the finest hurling side ever to come out of St. Flannan's. They had far too much power and strength for St. Kieran's, whose inability to score was a real Achilles heel and a burden they were unable to carry."

Justin played minor hurling and football for Tipperary and was a member of the side which lost the 1987 All-Ireland minor hurling final to Offaly, a game he feels that "Tipp threw away". On that occasion, he marked Johnny Pilkington. A few years later, he won an All-Ireland junior hurling medal with Tipperary in a team which also featured his brother, Damien. An all-round sportsman, he played rugby as a scrum-half with Clanwilliam for 16 years, where his team-mates included unrelated Irish international, Alan Quinlan. He is delighted to have won Munster Challenge Cup medals, but his hurling career petered out as a result. Nowadays, Justin lives in Tipperary town and works as a barber in Limerick. He has a 15-year-old son, Craig, who plays both tennis and golf. Justin still occasionally meets some of his colleagues from 1987, describing them as "all really nice guys".

Justin Quinlan has nothing but fond memories of his time in St. Flannan's and recalls how the school's successes gave Clare hurling supporters great belief during the many lean years for the county. "Every time St. Flannan's won something it gave Clare hurling a boost. The county team was down for a long time, and Flannan's achievements gave supporters something to cling onto. I got on great with the Clare people and there wasn't the same intense rivalry between Tipp and Clare then as there is now". Ironically, much of this was caused by the arrival on the scene in the mid-1990s of a great Banner senior team captained by Anthony Daly, who had been a team-mate of Justin's in 1987, on perhaps St. Flannan's finest ever team.

1988 – ALL-IRELAND SEMI-FINAL
24 April 1988, Portumna

St. Kieran's, Kilkenny 3-8
(A. Ronan 1-5, D. J. Carey 1-1, S. Lawlor 1-0, T. Shefflin 0-2)

St. Mary's, Galway 0-4
(L. Turley 0-2, P. Coyne 0-1, B. Cloherty 0-1)

St. Kieran's, Kilkenny, Croke Cup Champions, 1988.
Back row, left to right: Adrian Ronan, Padraig McCluskey, Declan Forristal, Dominic Bradley,
Noel Maher, Johnny Holohan, Robert Cody, Pat O'Neill.
Front row, left to right: Briain Ryan, Tommy Shefflin, Paul Brennan, Jimmy Conroy (capt),
Padraig Larkin, D.J. Carey, Dick Dooley.
(Photograph courtesy of Tom Brett, Kilkenny)

1988 – ALL-IRELAND FINAL
8 May 1988, Waterford
Referee: John Moore (Waterford)

St. Kieran's, Kilkenny 3-10

Jimmy Conroy (*capt*)
(Kilkenny)

Padraig Larkin
(Kilkenny)

Declan Forristal
(Kilkenny)

Robert Cody
(Kilkenny)

Padraig McCluskey
(Kilkenny)

Johnny Holohan
(Kilkenny)

Dick Dooley
(Kilkenny)

Noel Maher
(Kilkenny)

Dominic Bradley
(Kilkenny) (0-1)

Adrian Ronan
(Kilkenny) (1-3)

Briain Ryan
(Kilkenny) (1-1)

Paul Brennan
(Kilkenny) (0-1)

D.J.Carey
(Kilkenny) (0-2)

Pat O'Neill
(Kilkenny) (0-1)

Tommy Shefflin
(Kilkenny) (0-1)

Sub: Eddie Teehan (Kilkenny) (1-0) (for Maher).

Midleton CBS 2-7

Robert Ronayne
(Cork)

Eamonn Coughlan
(Cork)

Eamonn Murphy
(Cork)

Brian Corcoran
(Cork)

John Kelleher
(Cork)

David Quirke
(Cork) (1-2)

Timmy Dineen
(Cork)

Peter Smith
(Cork)

Liam Cashman
(Cork)

Kevin McCarthy
(Cork)

Timmy Kelleher
(Cork)

John Dillon (*capt*)
(Cork) (0-3)

Fergal Abernethy
(Cork)

Paudie O'Brien
(Cork) (1-1)

Connie Regan
(Cork) (0-1)

Subs: Tom Scanlon (Cork) (for Abernethy), Brian Cotter (Cork) (for Cashman).

Jimmy Conroy

St. Kieran's long wait for an eighth All-Ireland title finally ended in 1988 when they defeated Midleton CBS in the final. It had been 13 years since their last All-Ireland victory and goalkeeper Jimmy Conroy had the great honour of holding aloft the Croke Cup after the famine was ended.

Of Laois parentage, Jimmy played hurling from an early age. "We were hurling since we could stand," he jokes. He was part of a very successful James Stephens underage team that won every honour available to them, including an All-Ireland Féile na nGael title when they beat Na Piarsaigh of Cork on a remarkable scoreline of 1-0 to 0-0 in the final. "Hurling was the game every youngster in Kilkenny played when I was growing up. My late father, Peter, played hurling and football for Laois, and he was my primary source of encouragement," says Jimmy, whose three brothers also attended St. Kieran's. Jimmy explains how he became a goalkeeper. "There used to an Under-14 street league in Kilkenny and I was mad to play. I was very young and small at the time and they put me in goal as a way of keeping me quiet! I must have shown some aptitude for it because they kept me there after that," he says modestly.

Jimmy spent six years in St. Kieran's as a day pupil. When he entered the school in September 1982, there were no obvious star players for him to look up to. "Maybe it was something to do with the fact that St. Kieran's weren't winning All-Irelands at the time, but there weren't many big names. The likes of Pat Dwyer and Eamon Morrissey were there, but it was only in later years when they played for Kilkenny that they blossomed." Jimmy played juvenile and junior hurling with St. Kieran's before graduating to the senior team in 1987, with his older brother, Kevin as a teammate. St. Kieran's went all the way to the All-Ireland final where they suffered a crushing 1-7 to 4-11 defeat by what many felt was the finest team ever to come out of St. Flannan's. As it happened, that game was to prove to be the only one he ever lost in a St. Kieran's jersey!

"The magnitude of that defeat to Flannan's really hurt us. It played on our minds and there was a fierce determination in the team to make amends. St. Kieran's has a great heritage and history in colleges hurling, and I think this worked to our advantage. The black and white-hooped jersey was always worth a couple of points to us. Teams feared us, even when we were ten points down in a game, they were looking over their shoulder, expecting us to come back. We seemed to have that extra edge over everyone else," he remembers.

Jimmy admits that he was surprised to be handed the captaincy at the start of the 1987/88 campaign. "I didn't expect it for the simple reason that the captaincy was normally given to a boarder rather than a day pupil.

Maybe I was chosen because I had played for the Kilkenny minors against Offaly in Croke Park the previous year. James Stephens were also county minor champions at the time and that could also have been a factor. It was a great thrill to captain St. Kieran's to an All-Ireland title. It was great to end up in the same company as people like Eddie Keher and Ted Carroll in the photos on the walls of the college."

With players of the calibre of D.J. Carey, Adrian Ronan and Pat O'Neill eligible once again, St. Kieran's were determined to go a step further in 1988. They cruised through Leinster, inflicting heavy defeats on St. Brendan's Community School, Birr by 3-12 to 1-4 in Rathdowney and Cistercian College, Roscrea by 1-14 to 0-3 in Athy, en route to the final. The subsequent rout of Enniscorthy CBS by 8-17 to 1-6 was only a point short of the record margin in a Leinster final. The hapless County Wexford team were never in the hunt in the showdown, again in Athy, with Adrian Ronan shooting an amazing 4-9 and D.J. Carey a further 2-5. In the All-Ireland semi-final against St. Mary's, Galway, in Portumna, St. Kieran's ran out comprehensive 3-8 to 0-4 winners.

"We had a comfortable enough run to the All-Ireland final. In saying that, we were more hopeful than confident going into the game against Midleton. They were appearing in their first All-Ireland final and had some great players like Brian Corcoran, who was only 15 or 16, but even then was a horse of a player. We had a lot of respect for them because Cork teams are always competitive," he says. An estimated 4,500 supporters made their way to a sun-splashed Walsh Park in Waterford for what would prove to be a thrilling contest. Midleton settled quickest and after John Dillon hit the opening point, Paudie O'Brien swooped for a goal in the fifth minute. St. Kieran's got back into the game when Adrian Ronan took a pass from D.J. Carey in the seventh minute and raced through the defence before shooting to the net.

Carey levelled before David Quirke restored Midleton's lead with an excellent point after 14 minutes. That was the Cork side's final score of the half, however, as Kieran's enjoyed a period of dominance. Unanswered scores from Ronan (two),

Tommy Shefflin and Briain Ryan helped them to a 1-5 to 1-2 lead at the break.

Within 90 seconds of the restart, Midleton had restored parity when Quirke hammered home a penalty. It was tit-for-tat after that and, with less than five minutes remaining, a Paudie O'Brien point was all that separated the teams, 2-7 to 1-9. It was then that St. Kieran's suddenly cut loose. After an incisive burst forward by Ronan, the ball broke kindly to Briain Ryan who blasted to the net. Before Midleton could recover, Padraig McCluskey won the puck-out and booted it up to Ronan whose neatly placed centre was flashed home by substitute Eddie Teehan. Paul Brennan added a point to put the seal on a dramatic, if somewhat flattering, 3-10 to 2-7 victory for the Leinster side. As the 'Irish Independent' reported, "It is a matter of record that Kilkenny hurling teams are at their most lethal when faced with imminent defeat."

"We hit a good few wides, but I still think we deserved to win. It was a tough game and Midleton could have pulled it off. The school had been down in the dumps for a long time. The atmosphere in the school was probably not as good as it is now. I don't think the win was as appreciated as much as it should have been, but that didn't bother us. It was a great team to be a part of and we obviously had some outstanding players. D.J. Carey was small as a young fellow, but unbelievably skilful. I remember him scoring five or six goals against me as an Under-12. He grew a bit after that and those extra few inches probably helped him to become one of the greatest hurlers of all-time."

Jimmy is lavish in his praise of Nicky Cashin, the Waterford man who masterminded the '88 All-Ireland triumph. "Nicky was a great trainer and an inspiration to every player. He studied the opposition very closely and knew their strengths and weaknesses. He never went through the motions and it was a great credit to him to give up his free time for three evenings a week. A lot of St. Kieran's success over the years is down to him." Other staff whom Jimmy recalls for their "fanaticism about hurling" include Fr Paddy Bollard and Fr Pat Comerford.

Jimmy had double reason to celebrate in 1988 as he was also part of the Kilkenny minor team that recorded an impressive victory over Cork in the All-Ireland final. He won an All-Ireland Under-21 medal in 1990 when the Cats accounted for Tipperary in the final. He played a number of challenge matches for the Kilkenny senior team, but never figured in league or championship. After a spell in Waterford RTC, Jimmy studied Chemistry in UCD, and won a Fitzgibbon Cup with the Belfield outfit in 1992/93. He spent the summer of 1993 in the USA and that signalled the beginning of the end for his hurling career. "There was no shortage of players in James Stephens and they probably felt that I wasn't committed enough. I lost interest a bit and I stopped playing hurling completely around 1995 or '96," Jimmy relects.

Jimmy works as an industrial chemist with pharmaceutical giants, Schering Plough in Wicklow. He lives in Kilkenny with his wife, Áine and their two young children, Peter (2) and Róisín (1). While he enjoys a game of golf, his work commitments restrict his time on the golf course.

Not only was the 1988 success a major breakthrough, it also heralded the start of a golden period for the famed Kilkenny nursery. St. Kieran's went on to complete a three in-a-row of All-Ireland wins in 1990 and put two more titles back-to-back in 1992 and '93. "We like to think that we started the winning run and showed the way for the teams that followed us. We were all good friends and that stood to us," Jimmy Conroy says. "Kieran's was a daunting place when you started but it was a great school with great teachers, both academically and on the hurling fields," he concludes.

1989 – ALL-IRELAND SEMI-FINAL
23 April 1989, Ballinasloe

St. Flannan's, Ennis 1-16
(J. O'Connor 0-6, L. Meaney 1-0, C. Clancy 0-3, A. Whelan 0-3, P. Markham 0-2,
D. Maher 0-1, S. Sheedy 0-1)

St. Mary's, Galway 0-5
(P. Howley 0-2, J. Flannery 0-1, P. Coyne 0-1, A. Fury 0-1)

St. Kieran's, Kilkenny, Croke Cup Champions, 1989.
Back row, left to right: Barry Power, Bobby Dillon, Timmy Finlay, Robert Cody, William Carrigan,
Joe Dermody, Tom Lawler, Michael Holohan, Philip Carroll, Jack Carey, P.J. Delaney.
Middle row, left to right: Noel Maher, Sean Ryan, D.J. Carey, Dick Dooley, Pat O'Neill (capt),
Conor Manogue, Canice Brennan, Andy Comerford.
Front row, left to right: Ciaran Phelan, Tadhg Donoghue, Philip Larkin, Pat Leahy, Mr Nicky Cashin.
(Photograph courtesy of Tom Brett, Kilkenny)

1989 – ALL-IRELAND FINAL
7 May 1989, Nenagh
Referee: Willie Horgan (Cork)

St. Kieran's, Kilkenny 3-5

Conor Manogue
(Kilkenny)

Barry Power   **Michael Holohan**   **Robert Cody**
(Kilkenny)   (Kilkenny)   (Kilkenny)

Jack Carey   **Pat O'Neill** (*capt*)   **Bobby Dillon**
(Kilkenny)   (Kilkenny) (0-1)   (Kilkenny)

Noel Maher   **Philip Carroll**
(Kilkenny)   (Kilkenny)

Andy Comerford   **Dick Dooley**   **Timmy Finlay**
(Kilkenny)   (Kilkenny)   (Laois)

Canice Brennan   **D. J. Carey**   **Ciaran Phelan**
(Kilkenny) (0-1)   (Kilkenny) (3-3)   (Kilkenny)

St. Flannan's, Ennis 1-9

David Fitzgerald
(Clare)

Ray O'Halloran   **Francis Corey** (*capt*)   **Kevin Sammon**
(Clare)   (Clare)   (Clare)

Pat Markham   **Ger Moroney**   **Michael McCarthy**
(Clare) (0-4)   (Clare)   (Clare)

Liam Meaney   **Stephen Sheedy**
(Limerick/Cork)   (Clare)

Tony McEnery   **Michael Holland**   **Andrew Whelan**
(Clare)   (Limerick) (1-0)   (Clare)

Daragh Maher   **Conor Clancy**   **Jamesie O'Connor**
(Tipperary)   (Clare) (0-3)   (Clare) (0-2)

Sub: Fergus Callinan (Clare) (for Maher).

Pat O'Neill

After ending a 13-year wait for All-Ireland honours in 1988, St. Kieran's put Croke Cup title wins back-to-back for the first time in 1989. It was entirely fitting that the team should be captained by Pat O'Neill, a survivor from the successful side of the previous year and one of the greatest centre half backs ever to grace the colleges scene.

The youngest of five children, Pat's earliest hurling recollections are of playing the game with his brothers, Michael, Matt and Shane, and sister, Mary, in the field behind the family home in Gowran. Their father, John, had played hurling with St. Kieran's back in the 1940s as well as the local club, Young Irelands, so it was easy to see where their interest in the game came from. Pat received his primary education at Gowran National School where the school principal, John Knox and another teacher, Dick O'Neill were major influences on him. "They were a super help", he recalls.

In September 1983, Pat entered St. Kieran's as a boarder, following the same path his brothers had taken a few years earlier. "Matt and Shane were subs on the team that lost to Farranferris in the 1984 All-Ireland colleges final," he explains, "and I started in St. Kieran's the night Kilkenny won the 1983 All-Ireland. I can remember the excitement in Kilkenny when the team arrived back with the Liam McCarthy Cup that night. I got in trouble", he jokes, "as I just had to go down town to see the cup."

Pat's early memories of secondary school concern Tommy Shefflin, (Henry's brother), who became a good friend of his, together with the since deceased Richie Kearns, who "were always pucking a ball around in the school, even in the morning and at lunch time." Despite it being a lean time for St. Kieran's in terms of hurling success, the school still had its star hurlers. "In the early days, I used to look up to Eamon Morrissey and Tony Byrne, who was also from Gowran. Pat Heffernan was an outstanding colleges hurler too. At that time, though, Birr and St. Peter's were the top teams in Leinster and Kieran's were struggling a bit," Pat reflects.

Pat didn't have to wait long for his first taste of success. "We beat Kilkenny CBS to win the Leinster juvenile title in 1984 and I was marking my own clubman, Cathal Fitzgerald, in that final. Adrian Ronan was our star player at the time. He was head and shoulders above everyone else," Pat says, as he pictures the young prodigy "wearing Weetabix stickers on his helmet". He smiles when he recalls getting "a little hook" on a crucial late chance for Cathal Fitzgerald. Further success followed at junior level and Pat graduated to the senior team, but a five-goal hammering by All-Ireland champions-elect, Birr Community School, was a bitter pill to swallow in the 1986 provincial final in Rathdowney. Revenge was sweet a year later against the same opposition in Portlaoise, on a scoreline of 4-8 to 3-9, but "an outstanding" St. Flannan's team defeated St. Kieran's in the

All-Ireland decider "on a hot day in Birr". This, despite Pat giving the Kilkenny college a dream start when he drove a penalty to the roof of the net. He later drove another penalty wide, but it was academic as the Ennis lads romped to an emphatic 4-11 to 1-7 victory.

Not surprisingly, St. Kieran's were determined to go a step further in 1988 and Pat had a pivotal role in "a very special team" who cruised through Leinster and the All-Ireland semi-final, before defeating Midleton CBS to bridge an astonishing 13-year gap and regain the Croke Cup. Pat lined out in the final in an unaccustomed full forward role, having torn ligaments in his ankle four weeks before the final. He got the plaster off for the final and he remembers "great celebrations" at the final whistle, adding that, "the year before stood to us".

After capturing their first All-Ireland title since 1975, St. Kieran's weren't about to give up their silverware easily. "Everyone said the team wasn't as good as the previous year. They were probably right in a way, but the team of '89 had great spirit." Preparations for the All-Ireland defence began in earnest with the announcement that Pat would captain the team, an appointment which didn't surprise anyone. "When our manager, Nicky Cashin told me that Jimmy Conroy was going to be captain in '88, I didn't mind because I knew I had another year. I had captained various underage teams in Gowran, so I had a fair idea that it was coming to me the next year. There was a great buzz knowing that." After easily accounting for St. Peter's in their first outing of the 1988/89 campaign (4-17 to 1-7), St. Kieran's needed two attempts to see off the challenge of Birr in the Leinster final. The teams drew 1-7 each in Portlaoise, before St. Kieran's prevailed by 2-11 to 1-9 in the replay at the same venue.

The Kilkenny side went straight through to the All-Ireland final where they faced St. Flannan's in Nenagh. "We were delighted to get a rattle at Flannan's", Pat recalls. The Clare side led by 1-6 to 1-2 at the interval but St. Kieran's stormed back, with future legend, D. J. Carey in sensational scoring form to claim their ninth title. In the 'Irish Independent', Tom

O'Riordan wrote, "history will show that it was a team effort which earned St. Kieran's the All-Ireland Colleges title at the expense of St. Flannan's under a warm sun at McDonagh Park, Nenagh, but it's doubtful if they would have succeeded without the efforts of three splendid individual performances." Firstly, he refers to DJ Carey, who "gave a superb display of marksmanship, scoring 3-3 of his side's tally". Secondly, he highlights "the skill, control and tenacity of centre forward, Dick Dooley". Thirdly, "there was Pat O'Neill, the Kieran's captain who was an absolute colossus at centre back".

It was a hugely satisfying result bearing in mind what had happened two years previously. "St. Flannan's had hammered us in the '87 final, and it was very sweet in '89," Pat says. He felt "no extra pressure as captain" before adding jokingly that, "the worst bit was making the speech". Recalling the post-match celebrations, Pat remembers, "there was a great buzz in the school for a few days afterwards but it didn't really hit us until our picture with the Leinster and All-Ireland cups was taken in front of St. Kieran's. It's a big thing to have your picture up on the walls of the school alongside all the great St. Kieran's teams of the past."

Pat is full of praise for Waterford native, Nicky Cashin, the man who transformed St. Kieran's fortunes in the late 1980s. "Nicky changed everything when he took over the management of the team. He was absolutely exceptional. He was a great motivator and he had a way about him. He knew how to get the best out of everyone. Pat also fondly recalls Fr Paddy Bollard, Fr Fergus Farrell and Seamus Knox, who trained teams at juvenile and junior level, as "outstanding coaches". He also praises "two very good men over the school football teams" in Tommy Lanigan and Neil Connolly, while accepting that a few Laois boarders helped to strengthen the team in the big ball game.

Pat won All-Ireland minor and Under-21 medals with Kilkenny in 1988 and 1990 respectively, before graduating to the county senior team in 1991 when the Cats were beaten by Tipperary in the All-Ireland final.

However, they more than made amends in 1992 and 1993 with victories over Cork and Galway respectively. Pat won an All-Star award at centre half back in the latter year. He rotated between centre back and full back in the years that followed, but was disappointed to lose two more All-Ireland finals to Offaly and Cork in 1998 and 1999. He retired from the inter-county game in 2000.

At club level, Pat has also enjoyed plenty of success with Young Irelands. He won a minor championship in 1989, an intermediate three years later and senior championships in 1996 and 2002, before hanging up his hurl for good. He simplifies their club successes as follows, "It was a matter of getting the ball down to Charlie (Carter) and D.J. (Carey)". Pat managed Rower-Inistioge for seven years, a period which included an Under-21 championship win in Kilkenny, and coached Blacks and Whites to Kilkenny and Leinster junior title successes. In 2006, he coached his beloved Young Irelands.

Pat is married to Carlow woman, Siobhan (née Kealy), whose uncle Mick Morrissey won two All-Ireland medals with Wexford in 1955 and 1956. They live just outside Gowran and have three young children, Padraic, Méabh and Eoin. Since leaving school, Pat has worked with Suir Engineering in Mooncoin, a company which is always a force to be reckoned with in the All-Ireland inter-firms competition. He still keeps a close eye on how his alma mater fare on the hurling fields and can envisage his two sons challenging for places in the famous black and white hoops when they grow up. Pat remains in touch with a number of his former team-mates from secondary school, while Charlie Carter is a very close friend. Indeed, Pat recalls that Charlie left St. Kieran's at a young age to work on the family farm having, remarkably, struggled to make the college teams in his early years. He is also very friendly with Philip Larkin (a sub in 1989) and Tommy Shefflin from his schooldays.

Nowadays, Pat can point across the fields from his house to where the legendary Fr Tommy Maher lives, referring to the man whose words on hurling brought silence to the O'Neill's kitchen any time he visited, as "the biggest influence on us all". In the same way that the ageing clergyman will forever be considered a legend in St. Kieran's as a coach, Pat O'Neill, the young man who held aloft the Croke Cup in 1989, will always be revered as a superb defender for school, club and county.

1990 – ALL-IRELAND SEMI-FINAL
15 April 1990, Birr

St. Kieran's, Kilkenny 4-7
(A. Comerford 1-5, C. Brennan 1-0, P. J. Delaney 1-0,
M. Casey 1-0, P. Larkin 0-1, S. Ryan 0-1)

St. Mary's, Galway 2-3
(D. Moore 1-0, K. Greally 1-0, P. Howley 0-2, J. O'Brien 0-1)

St. Kieran's, Kilkenny, Croke Cup Champions, 1990.
Back row, left to right: Eddie Dwyer, Philip Larkin, J.J. Drennan, Clive Kenny, Ger Power,
Pat Purcell, Philip Carroll, Sean Ryan, Joe Dermody.
Middle row, left to right: Mr Tommy Lanigan, Niall Skehan, Bryan Hanrahan, P.J. Delaney,
Noel Maher (capt), Barry Power, Andy Comerford, Ted Carroll, Eugene Somers.
Front row, left to right: Michael Owens, Larry Mahony, Tobias White, Canice Brennan,
David Walsh, Conor Manogue.
Missing from photograph: John McNena, Martin Carey.
(Photograph courtesy of Tom Brett, Kilkenny)

1990 – ALL-IRELAND FINAL
6 May 1990, Mitchelstown
Referee: J. J. Corcoran (Galway)

St. Kieran's, Kilkenny 2-10

Conor Manogue
(Kilkenny)

Barry Power
(Kilkenny)

Larry Mahony
(Kilkenny)

Bryan Hanrahan
(Kilkenny)

Philip Larkin
(Kilkenny)

Pat Purcell
(Kilkenny) (0-1)

Eddie Dwyer
(Kilkenny)

Noel Maher (*capt*)
(Kilkenny) (0-2)

Philip Carroll
(Kilkenny)

Andy Comerford
(Kilkenny) (0-3)

Canice Brennan
(Kilkenny) (0-1)

Sean Ryan
(Kilkenny) (0-1)

P.J.Delaney
(Kilkenny) (2-0)

Ger Power
(Kilkenny)

Joe Dermody
(Kilkenny) (0-2)

Sub: Tobias White (Kilkenny) (for Dwyer).

St. Flannan's, Ennis 0-7

Bernard Scanlon
(Clare)

Karl Quinn
(Clare)

Fergus Callinan
(Clare)

Billy Piggott
(Clare)

Tomás Corbett
(Clare)

Alan Murphy
(Clare)

David McCarthy
(Clare) (0-2)

Liam Meaney
(Limerick/Cork) (0-1)

Stephen Sheedy
(Clare)

Declan Tobin
(Clare)

Jamesie O'Connor (*capt*)
(Clare) (0-3)

Tony McEnery
(Clare) (0-1)

James Healy
(Clare)

Enda Cotter
(Clare)

Andrew Whelan
(Clare)

Subs: Seamus McKeogh (Tipperary) (for Cotter), Kenneth Arthur (Clare) (for McEnery).

Noel Maher

"When you were going to school in St. Kieran's, sometimes you forgot your school books or your homework, but you never forgot to bring your hurl with you." So says Noel Maher with a smile, as he reflects on captaining St. Kieran's, Kilkenny, to victory over arch-rivals St. Flannan's, Ennis, in the Croke Cup final in 1990 on a scoreline of 2-10 to 0-7, thereby completing a hat trick of All-Ireland victories.

Noel, who hails from a typical rural background, is the youngest of five children and has two brothers and two sisters. Both of his brothers, Jim and Philip, who went on to become good club hurlers with Graigue-Ballycallan, also attended St. Kieran's. Noel always remembers Jim coming home from school saying, "St. Kieran's is the place to be, it's a great hurling academy." Sadly, Noel's father, Jimmy, who had a great love of hurling, died just a year after Noel guided St. Kieran's to All-Ireland victory in 1990.

One of Noel's big influences in his early years of hurling was his national school teacher of the time Jim Neary. Jim, who later became school principal, "was a great hurling teacher," Noel recalls. "We were in a little rural school with small classes of 20 which were split between boys and girls. Yet, Jim guided our school to over a dozen Roinn 'A' county finals. That was a great achievement for a small school because we always came up against the bigger schools like Kilkenny CBS in the finals and we won a fair share. They were like David against Goliath clashes, but Jim taught us heart and determination and in the long run that stood to us. In those days, it was hurling and handball only and nothing else, but we had a great time," Noel reflects.

It was in these games that Noel first came across the likes of D. J. Carey, Adrian Ronan and Pat O'Neill who were later to become his team-mates in secondary school, in the famous black and white hoops. Noel originally was a day pupil in St. Kieran's, boarding only in his final year. Hurling instantly took over his life from the day he entered the hallowed grounds of Kilkenny's best-known secondary school. "On our school breaks we would rush down to the handball alley to play hurling and then, at dinner time, out onto the field to play. We ate, slept and talked hurling. It was hurling all the time as there were leagues and various competitions always being organised or even 'three-goals-in' by ourselves. Lads always had their hurls. It was part of their school kit. It wasn't uncommon to see guys carrying hurls on their backs coming or going to school," Noel says.

Séamie Knox, Tommy Lanigan and Nicky Cashin are just three of the names that spring to mind when Noel looks back on the trainers and coaches who improved his hurling skills in St. Kieran's. "Séamie Knox taught us Maths and Science. He was very passionate about the game of hurling. He guided us to the Leinster juvenile final where we played Castlecomer CS. We drew the first game and lost the replay by a point. I don't think Séamie ever forgave us for that. He was devastated and I think we got lots of extra homework for a few weeks after that defeat!" Noel jokes. "Tommy Lanigan was a great trainer and then Nicky Cashin was an exceptional guy. He was our History teacher but, to be honest, it was all hurling. He was great at the psychology of hurling. He would explain to us why a guy passed a ball; what should happen when a quick free is taken; where a corner back should be at each moment of the game and what a player should be trying to achieve in each position. It was great and a lot better than learning History," Noel quips.

Noel played on the St. Kieran's senior team of 1987/88 while still in third year and also on the 1988/89 team, when St. Kieran's won both All-Irelands. This double was all the more noteworthy in that the school had failed to win the Croke Cup since 1975, a totally unacceptable period of 13 years by St. Kieran's standards and had never won back-to-back All-Irelands over the years. "Those first two years were hugely enjoyable. We had very talented players, so much so that your place on the team was always up for grabs. It was so enjoyable playing with players of the calibre and quality of D.J. Carey and Adrian Ronan. You could pass the ball over your head and just watch them beat two or three players and then pop the ball over the crossbar. I remember looking at our opponents and looking at the expressions on their faces wondering, 'just how do we mark these guys?' We knew what it was like as we were up against them all the time in training," Noel remembers.

"It never sank in until 1990, that I had a chance of winning three Croke Cup medals in-a-row," Noel reflects. When he recalls his appointment as captain of the St. Kieran's senior team in 1989/90, he says he was shocked even though it was his third year on the team. "We had just played our first game of the season and it was a challenge game. It was a wet miserable day and I had just played a truly awful game. Our trainer Tommy Lanigan called me over and, just when I thought he was going to have strong words with me over my performance, he told me he had chosen me as

captain. Naturally, I was delighted but a little shocked at the timing of the announcement," Noel says modestly.

A victory over Castlecomer CS by 1-16 to 1-6 in Ballyragget eased St. Kieran's into their Leinster campaign. Noel then takes up the story. "Our second game against Good Counsel in Athy I should remember well, but in fact I can't remember most of it because I ended up concussed. On a miserable day, I came off the pitch looking like 'Elephant Man'. I had received two awful wallops, one while I was going on a solo run and, as a result, I needed seven stitches. I played on and we won 1-10 to 1-5, but after the game I was dropped off at the hospital where I was kept for four or five days to monitor my concussion. Ironically, years later, I ended up very pally with Roddy McDermott from that New Ross team. We feared Kilkenny CBS in the Leinster final, as they were the team to beat and had very good players in the likes of Dan O'Neill and Davy Byrne. But we had great camaraderie and character and, on the day, we were fired up because people had written us off. It was a fine day in Nowlan Park and everything we did came off. Every ball hopped in our favour and we played well to win by 2-9 to 1-7. In every game you could say a particular guy played extremely well for us. The Leinster final was the game in which I felt I played well." The All-Ireland semi-final saw St. Kieran's defeat St. Mary's, Galway 4-7 to 2-3 in Birr. We won handier than the scoreline would suggest. I remember P. J. Delaney had a magnificent game that day.

"The target now was three in-a-row and while people outside didn't believe we would win, because St. Flannan's had beaten us well in a challenge game earlier in the year, Tommy Lanigan kept believing in us and drilled this belief into us," Noel recalls. The final against St. Flannan's was played in Mitchelstown where Noel had to mark Liam Meaney at midfield, whom he refers to as "a perfect gentleman but a very strong hurler and the engine of their team". Noel's role was "to curtail Liam Meaney, so it was easy to focus on the job even though it was a tough one". The game was still in the balance midway through the second half, when St. Flannan's created a goal chance when the Kilkenny boys were ahead by only 1-6 to 0-6. However, Noel recalls that "their player got hooked and the ball was launched to the other end of the pitch where we got a point and I think that was the turning point. After that we got a goal and with the assistance of the wind we held on to win 2-10 to 0-7. Liam and I had a great clean, sporting battle and I clearly remember with about three minutes to go Liam turning around to me and saying 'I think ye have it now' which was very nice of him." P. J. Delaney was described as "devastating" by 'Irish Independent' reporter, Tom O'Riordan who declared St. Kieran's to be "deserving winners" of a contest where, "on many occasions we saw the style, the skill, the speed and the panache of Kilkenny hurling".

Noel was pleased that he was a little more prepared for the speech after winning the All-Ireland, as he had got caught out at the Leinster final. After the provincial success, just as he was being presented with the cup, someone said to him, 'now you have to say a few words' and Noel froze and didn't even know his own name! "This time I was aware of what to say, although I hadn't written any notes as I felt it would have been bad luck. It was normal for some of the players to repeat the Leaving Cert if they thought the team coming up the following year had a reasonable chance of winning another All-Ireland. However, nobody thought we had a chance, so some lads who could have repeated the school year were raging they didn't repeat when they heard we had won another Croke Cup!"

Mention of the upcoming state exams came as a shock to Noel at the celebration dinner later that night. We went back to Hotel Kilkenny and Fr Flavin stood up and praised us all saying, "I didn't think ye would do it but don't forget ye have the Leaving Cert in three weeks time so settle down." With these words, Noel found it difficult to finish his soup! "All the talk up until now was about hurling but suddenly the Leaving Cert was just around the corner. Thankfully, most of the panel were conscientious about their studies

and it showed as they went on to work in a variety of good careers."

Over a decade and a half later, Noel speaks fondly of the St. Kieran's mentors from 1990. "Our trainer, Tommy Lanigan was a Laois man and he loved hurling and it showed. He put his heart and soul into it. He had a huge ability to talk." Tommy was assisted by Art Anglin ("an absolute gentleman"). Noel recalls the duo as being "very organised and we looked up to them as teachers and respected them greatly. On the pitch, we would have died for each other. There would be two of us chasing one of our opponents everytime," he says.

Having completed his Leaving Cert, Noel attended the University of Limerick for a year, where he studied Applied Maths and played hurling on the Freshers team with such noted hurlers as Brian Lohan and Fergal Hartley. His father's death in 1991 resulted in Noel keeping a more watchful eye on the farm back home. He then chose a different career path. "I don't know why I wanted to join the Defence Forces as there was no army tradition in my family," Noel says, "but I have no regrets." However, from a hurling point of view, his army commitments, particularly when based in Cork, greatly restricted his ability to tog out for both his club, Graigue-Ballycallan and his county, for whom he was unable to add to his All-Ireland minor medal won as a panellist in 1988. Also, a hamstring injury prevented Noel from taking up an offer to join the Kilkenny senior panel and he confesses, "I really missed the game back then." He feels that because of the geographical constraints he "lost heart", while he also reckons that his time out of the game meant that he lost his speed over those first vital 15/20 metres.

Despite playing midfield for Galway IT and winning a Division 2 Fitzgibbon Cup medal, Noel eventually faded away from hurling to become a "family man and social hurler". After marrying well-known camogie player, Gillian Dillon, whose father is the legendary ex-Kilkenny hurler Pa, the newly-weds settled in the parish of Freshford. They are the proud parents of what Noel jokes is "a full back line" of James (10), Patrick (8) and Darragh (4).

"Already they are mad into hurling", he says, before modestly adding that "they may have picked up most of their skills from their mother". While he tries to find time to play the odd round of golf, Noel continues to hurl away and his ambition is "to help Freshford back up to the senior ranks as we have been there or thereabouts the past few years". Since joining the army in 1991, Noel has studied Electronics and in recent years has been based in The Curragh. Now an army captain, he has travelled to the Lebanon and Bosnia ("both very interesting experiences") where he has utilised his skills as an artillery weapons instructor.

Reflecting on the changes in education and his own alma mater in particular, Noel reckons, "it's a shame that all the boarders in the colleges are finished. The schools are gone very professional with endurance training and early morning sessions; it's gone very serious. There needs to be a balance restored between discipline, education and sport." He confesses to have lost touch with most of his former St. Kieran's team-mates from 1990.

"Lots of the lads were good friends but basically we have all lost touch," Noel laments. "I've run into past players from St. Flannan's and Good Counsel through my work, but I also keep an eye out for the St. Kieran's results. Hopefully they will continue to win All-Ireland titles and beat St. Flannan's in the finals, as we had great battles down the years," he concludes wryly.

Innocent memories flood back to Noel Maher from his time in St. Kieran's, like "sneaking out for tea and a bun to High St, while the teachers searched the pubs and the snooker halls for us". However, when asked about the likely destination for his sons when their time comes to attend secondary school, his true colours come out. "They will have a choice, Kieran's or Kieran's!" He would love the so-called "full back line" to have "an appreciation of winning and losing and being part of a team". However, they will find it difficult to emulate their father's achievements, as one of only a handful of players to have won three Croke Cup medals, the last as captain in 1990.

1991 – ALL-IRELAND SEMI-FINAL
13 April 1991, Whitegate

St. Flannan's, Ennis 1-7
(B. Scanlon 0-4, M. Daly 1-0, F. O'Connor 0-1,
C. O'Doherty 0-1, G. Quinlan 0-1))

St. Raphael's, Loughrea 0-9
(M. Headd 0-5, T. Kavanagh 0-1, J. Flanagan 0-1, D. Keane 0-1, J. Murray 0-1)

St. Flannan's, Ennis, Croke Cup Champions, 1991.
Back row, left to right: Tom Riordan, Frank McGrath, Barry Quinn, Ronan O'Hara,
Tadhg Lyne, Martin Daly, Karl Quinn.
Middle row, left to right: Mr Mike McInerney, Gary Quinlan, Ollie Baker, David Pyne,
Christy O'Connor, Kieran Kennedy, Bernard Cosgrove, Colm O'Doherty, Mr John Minogue.
Front row, left to right: Fergal Hegarty, Francis O'Connor, Bernard Scanlon,
Tomás Corbett (capt), James Healy, Johnny Collins, Stephen McNamara, Seamus McKeogh.
(Photograph courtesy of Ollie Byrnes, author of Blue is the Colour, Hurling at St. Flannan's)

1991 – ALL-IRELAND FINAL
27 April 1991, Thurles
Referee: Pat Delaney (Laois)

St. Flannan's, Ennis 1-15

Christy O'Connor
(Clare)

Johnny Collins   **Tom Riordan**   **Bernard Cosgrove**
(Clare)   (Cork)   (Clare)

Seamus McKeogh   **Tomás Corbett (*capt*)**   **Karl Quinn**
(Tipperary)   (Clare) (0-1)   (Clare)

Kieran Kennedy   **Ronan O'Hara**
(Kerry)   (Clare) (0-1)

Francis O'Connor   **Gary Quinlan**   **Martin Daly**
(Galway) (0-2)   (Tipperary)   (Clare) (1-3)

Colm O'Doherty   **James Healy**   **Bernard Scanlon**
(Galway) (0-1)   (Clare) (0-1)   (Clare) (0-6)

Sub: Tadhg Lyne (Clare) (for Collins).

St. Kieran's, Kilkenny 1-9

Sean Foley
(Kilkenny)

Shane Doyle   **Barry Power**   **Michael Owens**
(Kilkenny)   (Kilkenny)   (Kilkenny)

Ciaran Connery   **Pat Farrell**   **Barry Smith**
(Kilkenny)   (Kilkenny)   (Kilkenny)

Andy Comerford (*capt*)   **Peter Barry**
(Kilkenny) (0-1)   (Kilkenny)

Martin Carey   **Liam Smith**   **Damien Hurley**
(Kilkenny)   (Kilkenny)   (Kilkenny) (1-0)

Declan Morrissey   **Brian Kenny**   **P.J. Delaney**
(Kilkenny)   (Kilkenny) (0-1)   (Kilkenny) (0-7)

Subs: Nicky Lacey (Laois) (for B. Smith), Richie Kelly (Kilkenny) (for Barry).

Tomás Corbett

After losing the Croke Cup deciders of 1989 and 1990 to St. Kieran's, arch-rivals St. Flannan's bounced back in emphatic fashion in 1991 to deny their Kilkenny counterparts a four in-a-row of All-Ireland successes, a unique record proudly held by the Ennis college since the mid-1940s. For winning captain, Tomás Corbett, the victory was the fulfilment of an ambition he had harboured since 1982 when his older brother, Johnny won an All-Ireland medal in the famous blue and white colours.

The Corbett family lived a mere five-minute walk from the gates of St. Flannan's. Tomás is not aware of any great sporting tradition in the background of either of his parents (both Clare natives) and he has only vague memories of Clare's great National League successes in the mid 1970s. For his primary education, Tomás attended Ennis Boys' National School, where one of the teachers, Peter Maher taught him the skills of the game. "Peter used to coach us every evening," he recalls. "I also benefited from the expert coaching of Paddy Duggan, who did great work with the underage in Éire Óg. The club was very successful at underage level and I won every medal all the way up to Under-21."

Tomás has three brothers, all older, who had attended St. Flannan's before him. Only one, Johnny, hurled but with great success. "I can still remember the excitement in our house the day Johnny set off to play for St. Flannan's in the Harty final against North Mon

in 1982. I was only nine at the time but I was old enough to realise just how big an occasion it was for our family and for St. Flannan's," Tomás says. "Bus loads left from the college that morning for the final and I looked on with envy as they passed by our front door on their way to Emly. I had to be content with a seat in my father's car and Flannan's ran out convincing winners before going on to beat St. Peter's in the All-Ireland final after a replay." After witnessing these triumphs, Tomás looked forward to the day he too would wear the St. Flannan's colours. "I thought John Russell was phenomenal and that's who I wanted to be", he reflects.

Nine months after he first walked through the thick teak doors of St. Flannan's, Tomás travelled with the rest of the school to Birr to see one of the really great St. Flannan's teams win the All-Ireland title. "That was the team containing Anthony Daly, Pat Healy, Turlough Herbert, Fergie Tuohy and Pat Heffernan. No team got near them, not even a St. Kieran's team that had D. J. Carey and Pat O'Neill playing for them. It was a phenomenal team, one of the greatest of all time," he feels. Tomás represented St. Flannan's at juvenile and junior level before graduating to the senior panel in 1989/90. The team was captained by future Clare legend, Jamesie O'Connor and after failing to make the starting line-up for the opening game of the Harty Cup, Tomás established himself at wing back thereafter. The Ennis boys beat Nenagh CBS by 0-10 to 0-3 in the Harty decider, but had to settle for second best against St. Kieran's in the All-Ireland final.

Fortunately for Tomás, he had another year of Harty hurling to look forward to and the opportunity to make amends for the defeat to St. Kieran's. The year got off to a great start for him when he was named captain, something he never expected. "I was very surprised to be given the captaincy. It was a huge privilege to be leading the team out, especially being from the town, and fortunately the team was successful." Such was the strength and ability of the 1990/91 St. Flannan's team, that three of Clare's 1995 All-Ireland winning side - Ollie Baker, Stephen McNamara and Fergal Hegarty - had to be content with places on the bench as the Ennis boys blazed a path to Harty and All-Ireland glory.

A first round victory over Ballincollig CBS was followed by one of St. Flannan's toughest games against St. Colman's, Fermoy, when they struggled to come away with a win. Limerick CBS also provided stiff opposition in the semi-final. "They were a tough nut to crack and we were lucky to scrape through. Dave Clarke, who was phenomenal for such a small man and who later went on to play for Limerick in the 1994 and 1996 All-Ireland finals, had an unbelievable game at centre half back. He almost beat us on his own," Tomás remembers. In the final at Charleville, St. Flannan's cantered to a 4-16 to 1-7 victory over a very disappointing North Monastery outfit. Left corner forward Bernard Scanlan top-scored for Flannan's who collected their third Harty Cup on the trot and their 16th in all. "Everything went our way against North Mon. We were well tuned in for it and the game was over with 20 minutes to go. While people were saying it was a poor final, we took great satisfaction from winning it. The Harty Cup was what you always aspired to winning and it didn't matter how you did it. Sadly, I think the introduction of the 'back door' system in recent years has devalued it somewhat," Tomás opines.

St. Flannan's facile win over North Mon was hardly ideal preparation for the All-Ireland semi-final against St. Raphael's in Mountshannon and they very nearly came a cropper against the Cyril Farrell-coached Loughrea side. Tomás recalls, "a last-minute goal from Martin Daly got us out of jail." Daly, later better known as a Clare senior footballer, had been dropped but came on as a sub and scored a goal from some 40 yards out which gave St. Flannan's victory by 1-7 to 0-9. "Even though we didn't play well, we showed a lot of character and belief in ourselves, and never gave up. It was one of those occasions when the great tradition of Flannan's stood to us. We knew they would be well coached but St. Raphael's didn't have the same belief and you got the feeling they were always looking over their shoulder."

After their great escape in the All-Ireland semi-final, the feeling among the St. Flannan's players and management was that their name was on the Croke Cup and so it proved when they recorded a 1-15 to 1-9 victory over St. Kieran's in the final at Semple Stadium. It was sweet revenge for 1989 and 1990, while there was the added satisfaction of putting a halt to St. Kieran's bid for a fourth successive All-Ireland title (and, as it transpired, what would have been an incredible six-in-a-row by 1993). "When we played St. Kieran's earlier in the year for the old All-Ireland cup, there was very little between us, even though there was a lot of shadow boxing, but we clearly had the edge when it mattered most. We won the game by six points and were never really in any danger of losing. I'll never forget an incident involving P. J. Delaney, who was the one to watch as far as the Flannan's backs were concerned. Delaney started the game well, but our full back, Tom Riordan from Cork, came out and sickened him with a shoulder. That put a premature end to his gallop and we put down a marker from the start," Tomás recalls. "Throughout the game, lads put their bodies on the line for the cause. We put 110 per cent effort in and, in the last few minutes, it was in the bag."

The 'Irish Independent' picked out Tomás Corbett as "having an outstanding game at centre half back", further stating that "revenge was indeed sweet" after the reversals of 1989 and 1990, but "on this occasion, there was no doubting the superiority of the Clare lads".

Needless to say, Tomás was bursting with pride when he finally got his hands on the Croke Cup. After his speech ("containing the usual two lines in Irish"), the newly-crowned champions headed back to a rousing welcome in Ennis. "It was a wonderful feeling, something I had always dreamed of doing. There was a great hullabaloo when we went back to Flannan's with the cup and there were a few bonfires lit as well."

Tomás is loud in his praise of the All-Ireland winning management duo of John Minogue and Mike McInerney. "You couldn't speak highly enough of the two lads. They did a huge job. They had a very good relationship with the players, were very shrewd on the line and were good motivators. We used to train four days a week, from Monday to Thursday, for an hour-and-a-half. The emphasis was very much on ball work and not on the physical aspect of the game. That made the training all the more enjoyable. It was as close to professional as you could get." With "study having taken a back seat in 1991", Tomás returned to St. Flannan's to repeat the Leaving Cert but was overage for the 1991/92 Harty team.

Tomás had further reason to celebrate in 1991 when he skippered the Éire Óg minors to league and championship honours. He was Clare minor captain in 1991 and played in the Under-21 grade for the county in 1992, 1993 and 1994. In the latter year, Tomás captained the Banner side which lost the Munster final to Waterford by 0-12 to 1-12. "We had the likes of Ollie Baker, Eamon Taaffe and Christy O'Connor on that team, and Mike McNamara was training us. We should have had Waterford beaten at half-time, but failed to put them away and we eventually lost to a late goal from Paul Flynn," he ruefully reflects.

Tomás played Fitzgibbon Cup hurling with UCG for three years but has no silverware to show for his efforts. From there, he graduated with a B.Comm and eventually qualified as an accountant in 1999. Nowadays, he is a partner in Carey & Corbett Financial Solutions in Ennis and he lives in the town with his wife

Dearbhla (neé Hassett), who is teaching in Scariff, and they have a young daughter, Ava. Tomás played for Clare during the 1994/95 National League, but had departed for London by the time Ger Loughnane's charges set out on the road to a first Liam McCarthy Cup win in 81 years. He was on the extended panel when the Banner County regained the All-Ireland crown two years later but didn't actually pick up a winner's medal. "While I was thrilled to see Clare win in '95, there was also a sense of frustration at not being involved. Looking on to the pitch and seeing three lads that had been subs on the Harty team only four years earlier made it all the harder to take," he admits.

Ironically, while registered with the Brian Boru club, Tomás won an All-Ireland 'B' hurling championship medal with London in 1995, with opposing St. Kieran's captain from four years earlier, Andy Comerford, also in the ex-patriates' ranks. London subsequently lost to Down in the All-Ireland quarter-final by 0-9 to 0-16 at Ruislip, a game Tomás feels the outsiders "could have won". He played with Éire Óg seniors until 2004 and still plays at junior level. Tomás plays "a small bit of golf" and he also dabbled at rugby, soccer and Gaelic football. Indeed, he played on various St. Flannan's football teams and won a Clare senior football championship medal with Faughs (an amalgamation of Éire Óg and St. Joseph's, Doora-Barefield) in 1994.

Tomás Corbett keeps in regular contact with many of his old St. Flannan's team-mates and attended the 10-year reunion of the all-conquering 1991 team five years ago. He also attended the function in 2000 which honoured all of St. Flannan's Harty Cup winning captains. He recalls his alma mater as "an excellent school" where pupils got "an all-round education". Naturally, he has particularly fond memories of proudly representing the famous nursery on the GAA fields of Munster and Ireland in colleges hurling. "That was pure hurling", Tomás concludes.

1992 – ALL-IRELAND SEMI-FINAL
5 April 1992, Trim

St. Colman's, Fermoy 1-12
(W. Hegarty 1-2, A. Kenny 0-4, K. Begley 0-2, K. Morrison 0-1, S. Cotter 0-1,
P. O'Connor 0-1, I. Lynch 0-1)

St. Patrick's, Maghera 0-3
(M. Collins 0-1, P. McCormick 0-1, M. McCormick 0-1)

1992 – ALL-IRELAND SEMI-FINAL
12 April 1992, Tullamore

St. Kieran's, Kilkenny 4-13
(B. Dalton 1-2, J. Hanrahan 1-1, C. Muldowney 0-4, C. Connery 1-0, M. Owens 1-0,
L. Smith 0-2, P. Barry 0-2, C. Kenny 0-1, R. Kelly 0-1)

St. Raphael's, Loughrea 3-3
(T. Kavanagh 2-1, J. Flanagan 1-2)

St. Kieran's, Kilkenny, Croke Cup Champions, 1992
Back row, left to right: Ciaran Muldowney, Alan Forde, Sean Foley, Kyran Vaughan,
Michael Fitzgerald, Chris Foley, Mr Tom Hogan, Lorcan Carroll, Liam Smith, Justin Hanrahan,
Damien Hurley, Mr Art Anglin.
Middle row, left to right: Nicky Lacey, Brian Cahill, Joe Philpott, Richie Kelly,
Ciaran Connery (capt), Martin Carey, Clive Kenny, Peter Barry, Shane Doyle, Mr Tommy Lanigan.
Front row, left to right: Ken Hughes, Eugene Somers, Brendan Dalton, Vincent O'Brien,
James Young, Michael Owens.
Missing from photograph: Ollie Blanchfield.
(Photograph courtesy of Tom Brett, Kilkenny)

1992 – ALL-IRELAND FINAL
26 April 1992, Thurles
Referee: Terence Murray (Limerick)

St. Kieran's, Kilkenny 1-7

Martin Carey
(Kilkenny)

Chris Foley
(Tipperary)

Shane Doyle
(Kilkenny)

Nicky Lacey
(Laois)

Michael Fitzgerald
(Kilkenny)

Ciaran Connery (*capt*)
(Kilkenny)

Joe Philpott
(Kilkenny) (0-1)

Michael Owens
(Kilkenny)

Justin Hanrahan
(Kilkenny) (0-1)

Clive Kenny
(Kilkenny) (0-2)

Liam Smith
(Kilkenny) (0-2)

Richie Kelly
(Kilkenny)

Brendan Dalton
(Kilkenny)

Ciaran Muldowney
(Kilkenny) (1-0)

Peter Barry
(Kilkenny)

Subs: Ken Hughes (Kilkenny) (0-1) (for Kelly), Damien Hurley (Kilkenny) (for Muldowney).

St. Colman's, Fermoy 0-8

Barry O'Grady
(Cork)

Brian McCarthy
(Cork)

John O'Brien
(Cork)

Patrick Sheehan
(Cork)

Johnny Sheehan
(Cork)

Fergal McCormack
(Cork)

Ian Lynch
(Cork)

Aidan O'Brien
(Cork) (0-1)

Sean Cotter
(Cork)

Kieran Begley (*capt*)
(Limerick)

Trevor Slattery
(Cork) (0-1)

Pat O'Connor
(Cork) (0-2)

Willie Hegarty
(Cork) (0-1)

Kieran Morrison
(Cork) (0-1)

Aidan Kenny
(Cork) (0-2)

237

Ciaran Connery

"St. Kieran's was a Catholic school, but to be honest, hurling was the real religion there." So says Ciaran Connery, who captained St. Kieran's to their 1992 Croke Cup hurling triumph over St. Colman's, Fermoy, in a closely-fought final in which St. Kieran's ran out winners on a scoreline of 1-7 to 0-8.

A native of Conahy, a small parish in North Kilkenny, Ciaran says that Conahy Shamrocks provided plenty of opportunities for Ciaran and his friends to acquire the skills of hurling. Although only a small club, they reached many underage county finals during Ciaran's teenage years, reaching Under-12, Under-16 and minor finals. "Hurling was very enjoyable back then. We had no nerves or negative thoughts," Ciaran says." I admired great clubmen like Nicky Brennan, now the president of the GAA, his brother, Kieran, Tommy Downey and, in later years, Dermot Healy. Tommy Downey stayed with the underage teams all the way through and these were the type of people we wanted to emulate growing up in Conahy, where there was a great bond among the players and the community.

It is no surprise that Ciaran turned out to be successful on the hurling field as he grew up in what he describes as "a sports-mad family." Ciaran's mother, Catherine Ryan (from Watergrasshill) won a junior All-Ireland camogie medal with Cork in 1973 and played senior camogie with Kilkenny. Her brother, Eamon played football with Cork in the 1960s before going on to coach the Rebels in senior football. More recently he has also achieved a double coaching the Ladies senior footballers to two All-Ireland titles in 2005 and 2006. Another uncle, Michael, played minor hurling for Cork before joining the priesthood. On the other side of Ciaran's family, his father Donal played hurling for Freshford, while his aunt, Mary Connery, was a highly renowned camogie player winning a Gaelic Press All-Star Award in 1967. Ciaran is the eldest of six children, with his only brother, Daire, going on to emulate him by winning a Croke Cup medal in 2000. His four sisters, Fiona, Eimear, Sinéad and Áine - are all accomplished sportspersons in their own right, all four being adept at both camogie and hockey. Fiona has 50 senior international hockey caps for Ireland.

Ironically, if it wasn't for the fact that Ciaran was two months underage to attend Kilkenny CBS, his illustrious hurling career in their great local rivals, St. Kieran's would probably have never taken place. It was only in the interview for the CBS that Ciaran discovered he didn't fulfil the age requirement for the Christian Brothers school and so, at the eleventh hour, he enrolled in St. Kieran's. "In St. Kieran's you were there for a good education but the school revolved around hurling. Lads walked into class with their hurl and during every break we played hurling, even if it was up against the wall. The hurl would be glued to you. I remember one day in particular when I was in first year and D. J. Carey, Adrian Ronan and Pat O'Neill all walked by me and I just stared at them in awe." Ciaran recalls.

Surprisingly, Ciaran was not on any of the juvenile or junior teams in St. Kieran's. "Maybe I was too small but I only got involved in the senior teams in fourth and fifth year. I'll never forget having to mark P.J. Delaney every day in training for a whole year and never being able to hold him scoreless. The best I could do was to hold him to a single point. I also remember Andy Comerford as a fantastic player and captain, but we lost a possible four-in-a-row as St. Flannan's proved stronger on the day in 1991. I have to say I was surprised to be appointed captain in 1992 by Tommy Lanigan. In first year, I remember looking up to the senior hurlers in admiration, but now suddenly I was the school captain. It was a fantastic feeling."

St. Kieran's found their path through the Leinster championship a relatively straightforward one. They defeated old rivals, St. Peter's, Wexford, in the first round by 2-11 to 0-6, before overcoming Castlecomer CS on a scoreline of 4-7 to 0-5 in their next encounter. Kilkenny CBS were their opponents in the semi-final. St. Kieran's saw off their great rivals by a six point margin, 1-11 to 1-5, with Clive Kenny grabbing the St. Kieran's goal (in a game where, if circumstances had been different almost six years earlier, Ciaran could have been wearing the CBS colours). Indeed, Ciaran jokingly recalls that "a good friend of mine tried to knee-cap me in that game"! It was a hat-trick of fellow County Kilkenny opponents for St. Kieran's as they wrapped up their provincial campaign with a comfortable win over Callan CBS by 2-13 to 2-2 to record their 40th Leinster title.

Remembering those games fondly, Ciaran says, "the common trait in those games was that we didn't start them very well. The first ten or 15 minutes were very tough. Our big rivals were Kilkenny CBS and they were a dogged team to play against. We were surprised to be up against Callan in the Leinster final but we respected them as a hurling team. Callan got an early goal but I remember telling our lads, "that is too early to matter." We got three points back but they replied with another goal. Despite that, I was happy enough with the way we were playing. We had an excellent set of forwards in Brendan Dalton, Ciaran Muldowney and Richie Kelly, all fantastic men to get scores. I was more nervous with the Leinster Cup in my hands than I was before any game. The hurling was easy but making a speech was significantly more difficult," Ciaran jokes.

St. Raphael's, Loughrea, trained by Galway's Cyril Farrell, were St. Kieran's opponents in the All-Ireland semi-final which was played in Tullamore. There was a very strong blustery breeze which was in St. Kieran's favour in the first half and Ciaran modestly remembers "scoring an unintentional goal from a '65 that afternoon." He further recalls that, "In the second half they had the wind which made it very difficult for us. We had to move the ball a lot on the ground but, thankfully, our forwards were excellent once they got the right ball," and the Kilkenny lads coasted to a 13-points victory.

"There was a fabulous build-up to the final around the college. My mind wasn't on our lessons at all, to be honest. Tommy Lanigan had the training sessions going exceptionally well. There was a great buzz around. I remember we held a team meeting in the run-up to the final and as we left the classroom about 200 students from all the other classrooms stood up and gave us an unbelievable reception. It left the hairs standing on the back of my neck. In fairness, we had been gearing up to play St. Flannan's in the final but it was St. Colman's who upset the form book to reach the Croke Cup final."

The day of the final couldn't have been worse weather-wise. There was a gale force wind and it was lashing rain, leaving conditions heavy underfoot. "At half time after playing with the wind we were only two points up (1-4 to 0-5) and the atmosphere in the dressing room was fairly grim. We hadn't played well but everybody decided to get stuck in and to do their best. In the second half they missed a few chances and that affected them while we grew in determination. As captain, I was conscious that we needed to battle for every ball and everyone responded to that demand. I wasn't really aware of the extra

239

responsibility, but I was going to lead by example. If I faded, that wasn't going to send a great message out. Martin Carey made some spectacular saves in goal that day and set up some rallying counterattacks. He hadn't played in goals for us until the final as Ollie Blanchfield had been our 'keeper up until then. In the end we had that bit of luck although it was very tight on the day." Cliona Foley reported in the 'Irish Independent' that it was "a most disappointing match, marred by the atrocious weather conditions." Indeed, she reckoned that, "the ground reduced to a sponge on which the ball was miserably deadened".

Once again, although overjoyed at winning, Ciaran didn't enjoy the speech-making in front of a big crowd but nonetheless, "I was very proud lifting the Croke Cup and I thanked everyone before entering the dressing rooms to start off the wild celebrations. There was a great buzz inside and it followed through to the college where we were all able to hold our heads high, having represented our school and winning the All-Ireland title." Indeed, the only cloud on the horizon was the Leaving Cert and it was Ciaran's mother who refocused his mind on these exams after the celebrations were over. "The thoughts of having lost the Croke Cup final the year before made me even more determined to win the final and especially when I was captain. But I still remember after the cup was won, my mother sending me up to my room to study with a glass of milk and a packet of digestive biscuits to keep me quiet," he recalls with a smile.

When Ciaran reflects back on the mentors who had a major influence on his hurling career in St. Kieran's, he praises Tommy Lanigan as "an excellent coach and a good communicator, who was very well organised with a specific game plan. Tommy was good at analysing other teams' strengths and weaknesses and informing us before the games. Invariably he was right. For example, he would have his homework done and it worked to our benefit on a few occasions". Tommy was also successful in training the James Stephens club and Ciaran had "great time for his scientific approach and his skills work back then".

Selector Art Anglin was "a quiet man who

was involved for many years and whose opinion was always respected", while Denis Philpott, whose son, Joe was a team-mate of Ciaran, was "another teacher in the college who had a great passion for hurling". At inter-county level, Ciaran gained an All Ireland minor hurling medal with Kilkenny in 1991, but missed out on playing as he had snapped ligaments in his shoulder. The following year, he was on the Cats' side which lost to Galway in the All-Ireland semi-final, on a day he remembers that Francis Forde excelled for the Tribesmen, while Ciaran's colleague, Eddie O'Dwyer sustained "a horrific knee injury". At Under-21 level, Ciaran won a Leinster medal in 1995 but lost out to Tipperary by seven points in the All-Ireland final.

By now, Ciaran had joined the army and he acknowledges that, "the army training was fantastic and helped to forge friendships which will last a lifetime. However, there wasn't much spare time for hurling and for those couple of years, hurling had to take a back-seat."

While in college in Galway, Ciaran played in the Trench Cup for Galway RTC, in addition to playing junior and intermediate hurling for Kilkenny for a number of years, narrowly losing a junior All-Ireland final to Galway in 1996 and an intermediate decider to Limerick in 1998. Ciaran never made the black and ambers' senior team. "Kilkenny have a conveyor belt of hurlers and, if you're not on it at the right time, you won't make it," Ciaran says philosophically. At club level, he recalls playing his first senior game for Conahy Shamrocks at the tender age of 16, "because the club was so small". In his first full year with the club in 1991/92, they slipped back down to the intermediate grade and, after six or seven years there, they were relegated to junior. In his time, he captained the club at various intervals.

Overall, trying to work in Dublin, live in Cork and play hurling in Kilkenny became too difficult to accommodate everything - on top of which there was a stint overseas in the Lebanon. "It all became too difficult to manage and, when I was posted to Cork, I joined another fantastic club, Blackrock," he says. "I was very fortunate to win the county final with Blackrock in my first year in 2002. I only joined them in May, but there were a few injuries and I ended up playing wing back against Newtownshandrum in the final, where we won by four points. They gained revenge against us in 2003, but I have enjoyed hurling with the senior team in Blackrock where there is a great buzz on championship days." This enjoyment continued, despite what he calls the recurrence of "niggly groin injuries" over the past few years.

Ciaran is married to a Kilkenny woman, Ann (neé Holohan), "whose sporting passions are scrabble and supporting Kilkenny", and they live in Cork, with Ciaran now based in Collins Barracks as an army captain. He rhymes off lads he hopes will be life-long friends from his days in St. Kieran's. He still sees Ciaran Muldowney, Michael Fitzgerald and Shane Doyle "on the odd occasion" and, as there has been no team reunion from 1992 as of yet, Ciaran confesses to only meeting other former hurling colleagues, "every now and then".

He has greatly enjoyed his involvement with the Defence Forces hurling team and playing in very competitive tournaments involving Bank of Ireland, AIB Bank. Ciaran's involvement with the Defence Forces team has also seen him travel as far afield as Australia, for a trip he considers to have been "a fantastic success". Indeed, Ann's appointment in the summer of 2006 to Indianapolis, in her chosen career in the pharmaceutical industry, has brought a further overseas dimension to Ciaran's hurling exploits. A three-year commitment in the American home of the Indy 500 motor races has got him involved in promoting hurling in the locality, with games against Purdue University (an hour's drive away) helping to improve his new side's hurling skills. Ciaran also coaches hurling to 14 to 16-year-old lads in a nearby High School. The Americans whom he coaches are "mad for the game", according to Ciaran.

It wasn't until quite recently that Ciaran Connery discovered from his mother how close he came to enrolling in Kilkenny CBS, rather than St. Kieran's. Quite how such a move would have effected the destination of the Croke Cup in 1992, we'll never know. However, Ciaran still looks out for the St. Kieran's results, but concludes (tongue-in-cheek, in Ann's company) that, "if we ever move back to Kilkenny and have kids, we'll obviously send them to the CBS"!

1993 – ALL-IRELAND SEMI-FINAL
4 April 1993, Athboy

St. Kieran's, Kilkenny 1-15
(O. O'Connor 0-7, R. Moore 1-1, K. Hughes 0-2, D. Hurley 0-2, B. Dalton 0-2, J. Young 0-1)

St. Patrick's, Maghera 0-3
(M. McCormick 0-3)

1993 – ALL-IRELAND SEMI-FINAL
4 April 1993, Ennis

Our Lady's, Gort 1-9
(E. Taaffe 0-5, A. Quinn 1-0, M. Lynskey 0-3, E. Costelloe 0-1)

St. Michael's CBS, Limerick 2-5
(T. Houlihan 1-2, P. Neenan 1-0, D. Hennessy 0-1, J. O'Donnell 0-1, A. Shanahan 0-1)

St. Kieran's, Kilkenny, Croke Cup Champions, 1993.
Back row, left to right: Mr Denis Philpott, Oliver Carter, Martin Phelan, Damien Hurley,
William Quinn, Derek Delaney, Rory Moore, Pat Comerford, Denis Drennan,
Eamonn Delahunty, Robert Kearney, Stephen Drennan, Mr Art Anglin.
Middle row, left to right: Barry Ryan, Eoghan Farrell, Shane Doyle, Chris Foley,
Joe Philpott (capt), James Young, Brendan Dalton, Ollie O'Connor, Kryan Vaughan, Ken Hughes.
Front row, left to right: Mr Seamus Knox, Brian Kelly, Brian Cahill, Ollie Blanchfield,
Eoin Carey, Vinny O'Brien.
(Photograph courtesy of Tom Brett, Kilkenny)

1993 – ALL-IRELAND FINAL
25 April 1993, Nenagh
Referee: Timmy Lyons (Limerick)

St. Kieran's, Kilkenny 3-15

Ollie Blanchfield
(Kilkenny)

Brian Cahill
(Kilkenny)

Shane Doyle
(Kilkenny)

Brian Kelly
(Kilkenny)

Vinny O'Brien
(Kilkenny)

Chris Foley
(Tipperary)

Joe Philpott (*capt*)
(Kilkenny)

Eoghan Farrell
(Kilkenny) (0-1)

Damien Hurley
(Kilkenny) (1-1)

James Young
(Kilkenny) (0-1)

Martin Phelan
(Kilkenny) (0-1)

Ken Hughes
(Kilkenny) (1-1)

Brendan Dalton
(Kilkenny) (0-2)

Stephen Drennan
(Kilkenny) (1-0)

Ollie O'Connor
(Kilkenny) (0-8)

Sub: Kyran Vaughan (Tipperary) (for O'Brien).

Our Lady's, Gort 1-10

Ronald Ryan
(Galway)

Peter Huban
(Galway)

Colman Cooney
(Galway)

Oliver Taaffe
(Clare)

Derek O'Connor
(Galway)

Oliver Clancy (*capt*)
(Clare) (0-1)

Ivan Linnane
(Galway)

Kieran Fahy
(Galway)

Julian Conneely
(Galway)

Michael Lynskey
(Galway) (0-1)

Eamonn Taaffe
(Clare) (0-5)

Brian Murray
(Galway) (0-2)

Shane Linnane
(Galway) (1-1)

Ollie Fahy
(Galway)

Enda Costello
(Galway)

Joe Philpott

Seldom in the history of the Croke Cup has a team cruised through their matches with such ease as St. Kieran's in 1993 and, in their seventh consecutive All-Ireland final appearance, Joe Philpott led them to their fifth All-Ireland title in six years.

Joe has a very strong hurling background with his mother hailing from Gorey and his father being a Cork man. His parents met when his father, Denis, a former inter-county footballer with the Rebel County, taught in County Wexford, but his switch to the staff of St. Kieran's was to bring a wealth of coaching experience to the famous Kilkenny nursery. From a very young age, Joe was brought along to matches and training sessions as Denis was heavily involved in the local Dicksboro club and St. Kieran's sides. Joe has three sisters and one brother, Kieran, who went on to win a Croke Cup medal in 1996.

The underage street leagues were Joe's first real taste of competitive hurling, as he confesses that "there were hurling teams, but they weren't very good" in primary school, as the co-educational amalgamation of St. Canice's and Loreto had about a two-to-one ratio of girls over boys.

It was inevitable that Joe would attend St. Kieran's with his father on the teaching staff there. "I got a little bit of slagging at the start from the other lads because Dad was teaching there, but it wasn't a big issue," he reflects. "To be honest I played more soccer than hurling in my first few years in St. Kieran's, but there were some talented players coming together in a range of sports. Our Under-16 side won Leinster championships in soccer, hurling and Gaelic football." He recalls that Adrian Ronan was "the superstar" in the school in the late 1980s, after a 13-year Croke Cup famine was ended. "I also remember Dad bringing me along one day to watch this new guy from first year playing. His name was D.J. Carey and his skill level was absolutely phenomenal. Adrian was the better known player and physically bigger, but D.J. always had the potential to be the star."

Joe made the senior hurling team as a third year, but had the misfortune to miss the 1991 All-Ireland final due to a broken collar bone picked up at a Dicksboro training session, a week before the defeat by St. Flannan's. He was replaced for the Croke Cup showdown by future Kilkenny star, Peter Barry. "Our junior side that year was exceptional. There were seven of us on the senior team and the future was very bright," he recalls. Sure enough, St. Kieran's went on to win their 11th All-Ireland title in 1992, with Joe lining out at left half back. However, he concedes that "St. Colman's, Fermoy, should have beaten us in the final."

Due to his longevity on the team, Joe felt that "the captaincy was down to two of us for 1992/93 - myself and Shane Doyle". Joe was delighted to get the nod and, as it transpired, St. Kieran's "weren't really tested all year". They opened their campaign with a comfortable 2-18 to 1-6 victory over Callan CBS in Thomastown and they followed this up with an emphatic demolition of St. Peter's Wexford, at Dr Cullen Park in Carlow, in the Leinster final, winning by 8-10 to 2-8. Brendan Dalton notched 3-1 and Ollie O'Connor 2-4, as St. Kieran's pulled away in the second half after a tight opening half an hour. "We had two great corner forwards in Brendan Dalton and Ollie O'Connor. They were two totally different players though. Brendan was tough, but Ollie was pure hurling. He was an unbelievably skilful hurler. We were surprised Ollie didn't make a breakthrough on to the Kilkenny senior side, but he was so good he was probably brought along when he was too young." St. Kieran's then dismissed the challenge of St. Patrick's, Maghera in the All-Ireland semi-final in Athboy in County Meath. The game had been switched from nearby Trim due to adverse weather conditions. "In ways, even though they were an Ulster team, it proved our stiffest contest. St. Patrick's just played 11 or 12 defenders that day and sat on the fence," Joe recalls. However, in the end, the Leinster champions won on a scoreline of 1-15 to 0-3.

Waiting for St. Kieran's in the All-Ireland final were Connacht champions, Our Lady's, Gort, who had a one-point win over St. Michael's CBS, Limerick, in their semi-final. "I wasn't too surprised that we were playing Gort in the final," Joe says, "as I had been on the Kilkenny minor team in 1992 against Galway and had played against some of the players from Gort and they had some very good hurlers." For once the big occasion got to Joe and nerves got the better of him before the Croke Cup final. "For the first time I had a sleepless night before a game. I used never get nervous but I was that night, possibly because I was captain. Even at half-time, I was absolutely shattered," he confesses.

However, as John Martin reported in the 'Irish Independent' the following day, "St. Kieran's were masters in every department." He went on, "midway through the first half St. Kieran's were clear by seven points and wasting precious few chances. It looked as if we were in for a very one-sided game but, to

their credit, Our Lady's, Gort, put a respectable complexion on the final scoreline." At half-time the score was 2-7 to 0-7 in favour of St. Kieran's. Early in the second half, inspired by future Clare star, Eamonn Taaffe, Gort managed to cut the deficit to three points. However, a goal from St. Kieran's halted Gort in their tracks when Ken Hughes whipped across a wonderful ball to Ollie O'Connor who applied his usual expert finish. Indeed, apart from a Shane Linnane goal, the Galway lads failed to score in the last 21 minutes. In reality, St. Kieran's won without having to get into full stride. Although he recalls being presented with the Croke Cup "in the middle of the pitch in Nenagh", remarkably, Joe's recollections of the previous finals are "more vivid". Perhaps, winning was becoming all too easy for St. Kieran's at this juncture.

Joe points out that Seamus Knox, who trained the winning team, deserves great credit for St. Kieran's success. "Seamus was a great motivator and put one hundred per cent into training, while never letting us neglect our school work. He was a great Maths and Science teacher and, if we had any problems he would bring us in for extra lessons. He was a very genuine guy." Of course, Joe's father, Denis, coached the side and this brought double joy to the Philpott household throughout the campaign. Joe also lauds the work of Tommy Lanigan, the Under-14 coach, and Art Anglin, who was "a good man to look at games and analyse them". Overall, scoring a total of 14 goals and 58 points and conceding just 4 goals and 27 points in four games, proves just how convincingly St. Kieran's won the title in 1992/93. The same year, the hurling-mad college also won the Leinster Schools soccer competition. Joe scored an equaliser (which he modestly calls "a fluke") in that year's first round, the only match he played. Indeed, he jokes that "I only played that day because I hadn't my homework done!"

Joe's hurling career came to an abrupt end, by his own choice, just a couple of years after leaving St. Kieran's. "I played minor with Kilkenny in 1992 and we won the Leinster Final, but we lost the All-Ireland semi-final to Galway after a replay. We should have won the drawn game but they were far superior in the replay. I was then a sub on the Kilkenny Under-21 side, but by then I had lost interest. Possibly, I had too much success with St. Kieran's but the drive wasn't there and I had developed different interests." Joe reckons he played his last competitive game of hurling when just 20 years of age. In recent years, he has played some "casual five-a-side soccer and a bit of squash".

After leaving St. Kieran's, Joe attended Cork RTC, and studied Applied Physics and Instrumentation. He went on receive a Bachelor of Science degree. He has travelled extensively, to Australia, the US and Asia but is now employed as an engineer by Schering Plough Avondale, based in Rathdrum, County Wicklow. Joe has met many of his St. Kieran's colleagues since they captured their 12th Croke Cup but, nowadays, he only meets Shane Doyle and Vinny O'Brien on a regular basis. His father only retired from teaching in St. Kieran's in recent times so, inevitably, talk at the dinner table kept Joe up to speed on the hurling fortunes of his alma mater over the years.

"It seemed like some lads played hurling in St. Kieran's, all day, every day," Joe concludes. "We even played a form of handball in the alleys with our hurls." This obsession with the ancient game helped a rampant college side sweep all before them in 1993, evoking "very fond memories" for Joe Philpott and his father-cum-coach, Denis.

1994 – ALL-IRELAND SEMI-FINAL
17 April 1994, Belfield

North Monastery, Cork 1-16
(M. Daly 1-2, D. O'Sullivan 0-5, K. Egan 0-4, P. Ryan 0-4, A. Coughlan 0-1)

Cross and Passion, Ballycastle 0-7
(A. McCloskey 0-2, C. McGaughan 0-2, J. McKay 0-2, D. Connolly 0-1)

1994 – ALL-IRELAND SEMI-FINAL
17 April 1994, Nenagh

St. Mary's, Galway 3-13
(D. Burke 1-5, A. Kerins 0-6, P. Ryan 1-0, D. Fahy 1-0, B. O'Donnell 0-1, L. Keane 0-1)

St. Kieran's, Kilkenny 1-16
(P. J. Cody 0-8, M. Connolly 1-0, B. Dalton 0-3, B. Kelly 0-2,
M. Phelan 0-1, D. Duggan 0-1, E. Behan 0-1)

North Monastery, Cork, Croke Cup Champions, 1994.
Back row, left to right: Br Martin O'Flaherty, Adrian Coughlan, John Fennelly, Christy Hartnett,
Graham O'Connor, Seán Óg Ó hAilpín, John Anderson, Colin O'Sullivan, Mr Séamus Ó Ruiséal.
Middle row, left to right: Barry Henneberry, Padraig Harrington, Kevin Egan, Mark Daly,
Jim Mehmet, Brian Kidney, Paul Morrissey, Pat Ryan, Damien O'Sullivan, Derek French.
Front row, left to right: Mr Gerry Kelly, Kieran O'Shea, Liam O'Keeffe, Brian Hurley (capt),
Gerard Shaw, Mick Aherne, Mr Nicky Barry.
(Photograph courtesy of Gerry Kelly and Liam O'Brien, c/o North Monastery, Cork)

1994 – ALL-IRELAND FINAL
24 April 1994, Nenagh
Referee: Pat Delaney (Laois)

North Monastery, Cork 1-10

Brian Hurley (capt)
(Cork)

Mick Ahern　　　　　**Brian Kidney**　　　　　**Jim Mehmet**
(Cork)　　　　　　　　　(Cork)　　　　　　　　　(Cork)

Gerard Shaw　　　　　**Kevin Egan**　　　　**Seán Óg Ó hAilpín**
(Cork) (0-1)　　　　　　(Cork) (1-3)　　　　　　(Cork) (0-1)

Liam O'Keeffe　　　　　**Paul Morrissey**
(Cork)　　　　　　　　　　(Cork)

Pat Ryan　　　　　　**Kieran O'Shea**　　　　**Adrian Coughlan**
(Cork) (0-1)　　　　　　(Cork)　　　　　　　　(Cork) (0-1)

Mark Daly　　　　**Damien O'Sullivan**　　　**Colin O'Sullivan**
(Cork)　　　　　　　(Cork) (0-3)　　　　　　　(Cork)

Sub: Graham O'Connor (Cork) (for O'Keeffe).

St. Mary's, Galway 1-6

Mark Kerins
(Galway)

Stephen Hynes　　　　**John O'Connor**　　　　**Brian Heavey**
(Galway)　　　　　　　(Galway)　　　　　　　(Galway)

Paul Clancy　　　　　**Jeffrey Lynskey**　　　**Ronan Dempsey**
(Galway)　　　　　　　(Galway)　　　　　　　(Galway)

Brian Carr (capt)　　　　**Dara Faherty**
(Galway)　　　　　　　　　(Galway)

Brian O'Donnell　　　　**Dara Burke**　　　　**Damien Fahy**
(Galway) (1-0)　　　　　(Galway) (0-2)　　　　(Galway) (0-2)

Liam Keane　　　　　**Padraic Ryan**　　　　**Alan Kerins**
(Galway)　　　　　　　(Galway) (0-1)　　　　(Galway) (0-1)

Brian Hurley

The last of North Monastery's 20 Harty Cup final wins came in 1994 and the renowned Cork hurling nursery went on to capture their fifth All-Ireland title that same year. The captain of the team for those triumphs was their outstanding goalkeeper Brian Hurley.

Brian hails from a background with very strong GAA ties and he admits to having grown up with a hurley in his hand. His father, Donal, has always been "steeped in the GAA" and he won a Corn Uí Mhuirí medal with Coláiste Íosagáin, Ballyvourney in 1954. Having started his early education in Glasheen National School, Brian moved on to the North Mon Primary School, ironically being taught there by his father, where another teacher, Denis Burns was "a great influence". Brian's mother, Kitty (née Barry Murphy), is a first cousin of one of Cork's most revered sporting figures, Jimmy Barry Murphy. Kitty's father, Dinny, captained Cork to Liam McCarthy Cup glory back in 1929 and Kitty herself represented the county in camogie. Brian is the youngest of a family of four and both of his brothers, Diarmuid and Donncha wore the Mon's famous blue and white jersey. Donncha was part of the Mon team which retained the Harty Cup in 1986, before losing their All-Ireland title to Birr Community School.

Winning the Harty Cup was a dream for Brian and his contemporaries virtually from the moment they entered the Mon. He looked up to players such as Barry Egan, in the hope that advancement in his teenage years would enable him to replicate his hero's skills. Brian did not enjoy much success at juvenile or junior level. Having previously played a lot of hurling as an outfield player, it was around this time that Brian was switched on a long-term basis to goalkeeping duties. Gerry Kelly and Nicky Barry were coaching in the Mon at the time, while future Cork manager, Donal O'Grady was also involved with the school's underage teams. Messrs Kelly and Barry were joint-trainers of the Mon's senior team in 1994 and Brian describes both of them as "characters" and "great hurling men". "Gerry and Nicky had the foresight to see I could play in goal. They were a great influence on my career and I have to thank them for everything they did for me. Gerry was my Maths teacher at the time, but we didn't always do a whole lot of Maths when the conversation switched to hurling," Brian jokes. However, for Brian's first actual experience of playing between the posts, we have to go back a bit further. He remembers volunteering to play in goal on the first occasion he walked in to the dressing room at the famed St. Finbarr's club. He was only six or seven years of age at the time.

After playing in the White Cup and Dean Ryan Cup, with no tangible reward, Brian went on to play for the Mon's Harty team for three years, all as an imposing netminder. He describes the Munster senior semi-final defeat to a Fergal McCormick-inspired St. Colman's, Fermoy in 1992 as "harrowing", but adds that the experience stood him in "good stead". Frustration was also the experience the following year, when the Mon lost to Limerick CBS, again Harty champions-elect, also in Buttevant and by now something of "a hoodoo pitch". However, preparations for the 1993/94 campaign began early, indeed before the academic year even got under way. Brian saw the captaincy as "a great honour", reckoning it was based on "longevity on the team".

The first round of the Harty Cup was against Scariff Community School, with the Mon winning 2-9 to 0-3. "Our backs were to the wall early in the game. We made very hard work of it, but eventually we pulled away in the second half," Brian recalls. The Mon faced Charleville CBS in Fermoy in the next round and Brian admits his side were fortunate to come away with a 1-11 to 1-9 win. "They were an unknown quantity at the time and we didn't play well at all." A very young Neil Ronan played for Charleville in that game, while his older brother, Darren was another key player. Seán Óg Ó hAilpín, destined to become one of the GAA's most recognisable stars in recent years, was on the 1994 Mon team and he marked Darren Ronan in that game. But it was the younger of the two Ronan brothers who caused the most problems. "We didn't defend at all properly that day and Neil Ronan punished us. As far as I can remember, he got five points in the first half," Brian says. However, the Mon, despite being down to 14 men, managed to turn things around in the second half. "We fought hard and eventually won it by default at the end." To this day, when Brian meets players from that Charleville team, they say it should have been their Harty Cup that year.

Due to fixture turmoil in the province over an issue of player eligibility when transferring between schools, there was a long delay before the Mon eventually took on Thurles CBS in the semi-final, which was played "in very heavy conditions" in Mitchelstown. "Our defence came to the top again that day," Brian recalls. The Mon played with "a very strong wind" in the first half but failed to build a decent lead. However, they "defended like lions" in the second half and

this was enough to see them through on a 2-6 to 1-5 scoreline. The only cloud on the Mon's horizon was the injury sustained by corner-back, Mick Ahern.

However, he was given the all-clear to play in the Harty final, which took place just a week later. Fermoy was the venue for the final and it was an all-Cork affair on a wet day against Midleton CBS. "They had Joe Deane, Donal Óg Cusack in goals, as well as Mickey O'Connell. They had a lot of very strong minors, but they were young. We had a little bit of experience and a bit of unity," Brian says. "We were 0-5 to 0-3 up at half-time after playing with a very strong wind. We got the greatest roasting of all time at half time," Brian continues. He reckons the Mon delivered "the best defensive display" he ever witnessed in the second half of that final. "We had good players; great winners in my opinion. They proved it afterwards in their careers." The Mon's defensive excellence in the second half was reflected by the fact that Midleton managed to score just one point when backed by "a gale-force wind". The final score was 1-9 to 0-4. Kevin Egan pointing a '65' into the teeth of the wind is one of Brian's enduring memories from that final.

The All-Ireland semi-final against Cross and Passion, Ballycastle, took place in UCD's grounds in Belfield. While Brian and his teammates were in awe of the "fantastic complex", the game itself was never really a contest and, with Kevin Egan delivering "a marvellous display", the Mon ran out comfortable winners by 1-16 to 0-7. "We had a little too much class for them," Brian recalls. Victory came at a price, however, with centre half forward, John Anderson breaking his hand during the game. The injury meant Anderson was unable to play in the Croke Cup decider. "He was gutted. He's still, to this day, a fantastic, passionate hurler," Brian states, while conceding that it was an accidental collision with a team-mate that caused John's injury.

Leinster kingpins, St. Kieran's, Kilkenny were surprisingly defeated by St. Mary's, Galway in the other All-Ireland semi-final. Brian admits it was a "boost" to hear that St. Kieran's had been knocked out. "It gave us a little bit of a spur that we had the ability to go on and win it." Although Brian said there was "pressure" on the team going into the final, he felt it was lessened because the main goal, the Harty Cup, had already been achieved. "Anything after that was a bonus." The build-up to the final included singing practice among the school's supporters to ensure the team had sufficient vocal encouragement on the big day. "Everyone rallied in behind us. Brother O'Flaherty and Mr Ó Ruiséal, the principals in both sections of the Mon at the time, were fantastic influences. Their help and support for that team was only unbelievable."

The final was played in Nenagh and, upon winning the toss, Brian opted to play with the wind. "We were so strong defensively that we would try and hold on in the second half," he explains. However, he admits he was worried during the first half as his side "were making no inroads at all" against "a good Galway defence." Seán Óg Ó hAilpín was moved to full-forward during the first half, a switch that Brian describes as "the funniest move of all time". It was indicative of the Mon's struggles up front. Seán Óg scored one point while in his unaccustomed position. "That was the one score I ever saw him get until I saw him scoring against Clare in the 2005 All-Ireland semi-final," Brian quips. The Mon led 0-6 to 0-2 at half time. "The scoreline at half time didn't do us justice as we dominated the first half." Normality was restored for the beginning of the second half, as Seán Óg returned to more familiar territory in the half-back line. After receiving a "rallying call" at the interval, the Mon players turned around to face the elements in the second half. "We frustrated them and we had a bit of class up in the forward line. Unfortunately we lost Liam O'Keeffe with a broken finger in the final but Graham O'Connor came in to the forward line and was a huge influence." In the end, the Mon emerged victorious on a 1-10 to 1-6 score-line. Cliona Foley in the 'Irish Independent' felt that, "fans of St. Mary's, Galway, may have trailed from the ground declaring that they had thrown away an historic chance to become the first-ever Connacht winners of the Croke Cup".

In Brian's view, the contribution of Kevin Egan was once again immense. Egan scored a goal from a penalty and ended with a tally of 1-3 from centre half back. The 'Irish Independent' also called Brian Kidney "both brave and brilliant", and further lauds Brian Hurley's goalkeeping at crucial junctures. Indeed, such was the post-match excitement that the captain recalls how he thanked St. Jarlath's (regular Connacht football kingpins), rather than St. Mary's in his victory speech! In terms of the homecoming, Brian vividly recalls the "hysteria" of the welcome when the team returned to the northside of Cork city. They received a very special "ovation" when they arrived at Na Piarsaigh, who had seven players on the panel. "We got plenty of support and everyone knew what winning an All-Ireland meant to the school." Brian and his team-mates were granted "a little bit of scope" with their Leaving Cert preparations. It was just as well, too, with French and Irish oral exams taking place very close to the All-Ireland final!

In his second year as a Rebel County minor, Brian also captained the Cork Under-18s in 1994, winning the Munster title before losing to Galway in the All-Ireland final. Alan Kerins, who played corner-forward for St. Mary's in the Croke Cup final, was in goals for the Galway minors in the Irish Press Cup decider. Brian remembers ruefully that Cork didn't give the young Galway goalie, then only 16 years old, enough to do in that final as the young Tribesmen won by 2-10 to 1-11. Brian played for the Cork Under-21s in the 1995 Munster championship, but he lost his place to Donal Óg Cusack in 1996 and 1997. Brian was the sub 'keeper as Cork won the 1996 Munster Under-21 title and the All-Ireland crown in 1997. "I was also a sub to Ger Cunningham with my club so I was getting very few games. Ger was the best goalie I've ever seen. Donal Óg was playing a lot of matches with his club, and with his division at the time, and he went on to be a fantastic 'keeper and still is, as well as being a great friend," Brian sportingly acknowledges.

In terms of success with his club, Brian's earliest recollection is winning an All-Ireland Féile Under-14 football title. Brian won two minor county medals with St. Finbarr's and later went on to win an Under-21 county medal. Alas, major senior hurling honours have eluded him, with St. Finbarr's county championship ambitions thwarted on a number of occasions by a then "star-studded" divisional team, Imokilly. Brian also played a lot of football for the 'Barr's, generally operating in the forward line. Brian reckons Cork hurling stars like Ronan Curran and Seán Óg Ó hAilpín are good enough to play inter-county football. However, inter-county dual players are almost an extinct species nowadays and Brian has sympathy for Cork football manager, Billy Morgan. "A lot of the better club players in the county are only playing one grade at inter-county level." Nowadays, Brian is a selector with the St. Finbarr's senior hurling team, alongside Jimmy Barry Murphy. He enjoys this role and also still plays football for the club at junior level.

A single man and living in Cork city, since his schooldays, Brian has been employed in EMC, an American multinational corporation which deals in the storage of information software. The company has facilities in Ovens and Little Island and Brian's role involves commuting between the two locations in County Cork. He is a work colleague and close friend of the man who wore the Mon number 3 jersey in 1994, Brian Kidney, joking that "a full-back and a goalkeeper are always buddies". While he enjoys the occasional round of golf, the shift work involved in his job often hinders his social life.

With Brian Hurley as the organiser-in-chief, he and his colleagues met up two years ago for a tenth anniversary celebration in Mulligan's pub in Cork. There was a huge turnout for the occasion and the former schoolmates watched the video of the 1994 Harty final and compared each other's school-day scrapbooks (Brian has kept a comprehensive one himself). In 2000, Brian was selected as goalkeeper on the Millennium Harty Cup team. The team was based on players' performances in the famous Munster colleges senior hurling championship from 1965 to 2000 and he was delighted to get the nod for the number one jersey ahead of illustrious names such as Donal Óg Cusack and Clare's Davy Fitzgerald. The selected team was presented to the crowd at half time in the 2000 Harty final. It was yet another accolade for Brian to treasure and a measure of his contribution to an outstanding North Monastery team who conquered Munster and Ireland in 1994.

1995 – ALL-IRELAND SEMI-FINAL
2 April 1995, Navan

St. Raphael's, Loughrea 3-27
(K. Broderick 2-5, C. Earls 0-8, T. Daniels 1-2, K. Keane 0-4, C. Hynes 0-3, E. McMahon 0-2, N. Shiel 0-2, V. Maher 0-1)

Cross and Passion, Ballycastle 0-2
(C. McGaughan 0-1, L. McMullan 0-1)

1995 – ALL-IRELAND SEMI-FINAL
23 April 1995, Dungarvan

Midleton CBS 0-10
(J. Deane 0-4, M. O'Connell 0-3, L. Walsh 0-1, P. Mullaney 0-1, J. Cotter 0-1)

Good Counsel, New Ross 0-5
(M. Redmond 0-3, M. Doyle 0-1, R. Purcell 0-1)

St. Raphael's, Loughrea, Croke Cup Champions, 1995.
Back row, left to right: Kevin Broderick, Niall Sheil, Vincent Maher, John Loughnane, Justin Whyte, Kevin Sweeney, Eddie McMahon, Trevor Daniels.
Front row, left to right: Cathal Hynes, Keith Daniels, Stephen Morgan, Cathal Murray, Clement Earls, Kenneth Keane, Raymond Keane, Cathal O'Reilly (capt).
(Photograph courtesy of Cathal O'Reilly)

1995 – ALL-IRELAND FINAL
30 April 1995, Limerick
Referee: Timmy Lyons (Limerick)

St. Raphael's, Loughrea 5-10

Stephen Morgan
(Galway)

Justin Whyte   **John Loughnane**   **Raymond Keane**
(Galway)   (Galway)   (Galway)

Cathal O'Reilly (*capt*)   **Kevin Sweeney**   **Cathal Murray**
(Galway)   (Galway)   (Galway)

Cathal Hynes   **Kenneth Keane**
(Galway)   (Galway) (2-0)

Clement Earls   **Vincent Maher**   **Eddie McMahon**
(Galway) (0-5)   (Galway)   (Galway) (0-1)

Trevor Daniels   **Kevin Broderick**   **Keith Daniels**
(Galway) (0-2)   (Galway) (3-1)   (Galway) (0-1)

Sub: David Brett (Galway) (for Loughnane).

Midleton CBS 3-5

Donal Óg Cusack (*capt*)
(Cork)

Brian O'Callaghan   **Tom O'Brien**   **Padraig Barry**
(Cork)   (Cork)   (Cork)

Tony Hickey   **Pat Walsh**   **Daire Cott**
(Cork)   (Cork)   (Cork)

Alan Kelliher   **John Cotter**
(Cork)   (Cork)

Diarmuid O'Sullivan   **Michael Dunne**   **Michael O'Connell**
(Cork)   (Cork)   (Cork) (0-3)

Conor Lehane   **Joe Deane**   **Pat Mullaney**
(Cork)   (Cork) (3-1)   (Cork) (0-1)

Subs: Paul Kelliher (Cork) (for Barry), Edward O'Flynn (Cork) (for Lehane),
Liam Walsh (Cork) (for O'Sullivan).

Cathal O'Reilly

The wonderful renaissance in Connacht hurling commenced with the Galway senior team's great progress in the 1970s, culminating in the memorable lifting of the Liam McCarthy Cup by Joe Connolly on September 7th, 1980. Further success ensued at minor, Under-21 and Railway Cup level. However, it wasn't until 1995 that the elusive Croke Cup crossed the Shannon when St. Raphael's, Loughrea, captained by Cathal O'Reilly, achieved the distinction in the 44th staging of the prestigious competition.

Cathal, who has two brothers and a sister, is a native of Loughrea, where his father had moved to work in 1977, a year before Cathal was born. He confesses that he has "loved the game of hurling" from his childhood days. In this regard, he received "great support at all times" from his parents. He speaks very highly of the contribution of Frank Burke, who took over as principal of the national school in Loughrea in 1988. He credits the Galway GAA County Board chairman with "totally revolutionising hurling at primary level" in the town.

This interest was further nurtured from the moment Cathal entered St. Raphael's as a first year in 1990. Success came very soon in the form of Connacht juvenile and junior titles. "The same lads came through together and we formed a great bond", Cathal recalls, adding that "Loughrea is a rich hurling area, surrounded by great hurling clubs, Sarsfields, Kiltomer and Athenry". St. Raphael's is a co-educational day school, with a student population in Cathal's time of around 500, of which roughly half were boys. The school was making great strides at senior level in the early 1990s. All-Ireland semi-final defeats by eventual champions, St. Flannan's, Ennis in 1991 (by one point) and St. Kieran's, Kilkenny in 1992, augured well for the future. Young Cathal looked up to older fellow pupils such as Tomás Kavanagh. "He was an absolutely outstanding centre back", Cathal reflects. At inter-county level he admired his fellow county man, Pete Finnerty, and as the years progressed, Clare's Brian Lohan. At a local level, his own younger brother, Kieran and his team-mate throughout secondary school, Kevin Broderick, were inspirational figures for him.

The man most commonly associated with the rise and rise of St. Raphael's is Cyril Farrell. Cyril's contribution to Galway's cause at all levels is well documented, but his appointment as principal at the school forced him to take something of a back seat in hurling matters. This enabled Athenry man, John Hardiman, to come to the fore and Cathal is loud in his praise of both men for developing and encouraging the game in St. Raphael's. St. Mary's, Galway, and Portumna CBS were the Loughrea side's most difficult opponents at that time. Remarkably, Cathal made his senior debut in 1993 as a 14-year-old full back, a position he retained the following year when St. Mary's won out in a great Connacht final.

Cathal recalls that after the 1994 defeat by

St. Mary's, the team "made a pact" to go all the way to All-Ireland glory the following year, much to the amusement of, among others, Cathal's father. Such was the unity of purpose among the squad in 1994/95 that, entirely of their own volition, the players organised training over and above the official sessions. "It was not unusual to have twice daily get-togethers and occasionally we would meet up on the St. Raphael's pitch all seven days of the week." The captaincy issue was not finalised until after the Christmas break as a number of players had led out the team in various challenges and minor competitions prior to the festive period. However, Cathal was voted in as skipper by his fellow players early in the new year of 1995.

Cathal has fond memories of the all-conquering championship campaign which ensued. Victories over St. Mary's, Galway and Presentation, Athenry were followed by a Connacht final win over arch-rivals, Portumna CBS. The All-Ireland semi-final against "unknown opponents", Cross and Passion, Ballycastle was plain-sailing on April 1st at the UCD grounds, with the Ulster boys on the wrong end of a 34-point hammering. St. Raphael's All-Ireland final opponents were Midleton CBS, whose only previous appearance in the decider had been as runners-up to St. Kieran's, Kilkenny seven years earlier. "We knew very little about the opposition except they had a number of key quality players, such as Joe Deane and Mickey O'Connell", Cathal recalls. "We knew we'd be definitely up against it, as they had a good record in Munster and had beaten the Leinster champions (Good Counsel) in the semi-final".

Cathal estimates that about 2,000 people made the journey to Limerick to support the St. Raphael's side in their quest to bring the Croke Cup west of the Shannon for the first time. Three goals in a 15-minute spell in the first half paved the way for the Galway school's triumph. "Our defence was very big and strong, despite John Loughnane's minor injuries from a car crash the night before, and we had a great forward division as well", Cathal reflects. Three-goal hero, Kevin Broderick, "an absolutely brilliant player",

comes in for special praise from his captain. Indeed, the future Galway senior star netted after only 35 seconds and his side were well in control by the half-time interval when they led by 3-9 to 1-3. Overall, the Connacht representatives turned in what the 'Irish Independent' described as "a stunning display" and, as countless teams found to their cost over the ensuing years, the Midleton goalkeeper and team captain, Donal Óg Cusack, is seldom beaten five times in a game.

"Raphael's rejoice", was the headline in the 'Irish Independent' match report. And rejoice they did! Indeed, the enormity of their win on the last day of April in the Gaelic Grounds didn't fully sink in until the new champions arrived to a heroic welcome back as bonfires blazed in Loughrea. A few weeks later, former Galway star of the 1950s, Fergus Benson, called up for a cup of tea to the O'Reilly household and emphasised the ground-breaking nature of 16-year-old Cathal's achievement, in conjunction with his very talented and wholehearted colleagues.

Cathal continued his interest in the fate of St. Raphael's after he left the school. He attended their games in the few years after he sat the Leaving Certificate but has "lost touch somewhat since". However, he is disappointed that some recent teams have lost heavily in Connacht. He feels that "the same crop of players isn't there" anymore. His brother, Kieran, represented St. Raphael's at all levels and was a sub on the defeated Croke Cup finalists in 1998. His alma mater's last appearance in a Croke Cup final in 2004 ended in a hammering from a powerful St. Kieran's side. Indeed, this result acted as a major prompt for the colleges' powers-that-be to introduce a 'back door', with the Connacht champions now facing an annual All-Ireland quarter-final.

An unfortunate hand injury sustained while pursuing a carpentry apprenticeship in 1996 completely curtailed Cathal's hurling for a year after the accident and, to this day, he has difficulty hurling in the wintertime. In 1997, he commenced studying Industrial Engineering and Information Systems and he graduated in May 2001 with a first class honours degree from NUIG. His return on the hurling field was an emotional one when introduced as a Loughrea sub, to a rousing reception from a 10,000 strong crowd, in the 1998 Galway SHC semi-final, only to be faced with the daunting task of marking Athenry's Joe Rabbitte! He was a member of the Galway minor team which lost the 1996 minor decider to Tipperary and was a sub on the county Under-21 team which lost the All-Ireland final to Kilkenny, three years later.

At club level, he has accumulated an array of county medals, from Under-14 right up to Under-21. However, study commitments meant that he was not a part of the historic Loughrea team who ended a 65-year famine earlier this year when they ousted reigning All-Ireland champions, Portumna, in the Galway SHC final. Clearly, he is held in high regard by hurling folk in the town, having been awarded Senior Club Player of the Year in both 1999 and 2002. One of his main ambitions is to return to the club senior team next year.

Cathal continues to live near home, residing as he does in Clostoken, some five miles from Loughrea. He continued his studies as a post-graduate (to the detriment of hurling) and, having previously worked with Boston Scientific (Ireland) Ltd as a business strategist, Cathal changed employers in April 2006 and is now employed as a Lean Manufacturing consultant with KPI Consulting Ltd, based in Galway. In this specific field of expertise he received a distinction from Cardiff University earlier this year.

After a few informal Christmas get-togethers, the all-conquering St. Raphael's of Loughrea squad had a formal reunion in April 2005. Over 250 people attended for a tenth anniversary celebration in the local Meadow Court hotel. Souvenir jumpers and plaques were presented on the night to panel members, most of whom attended the function.

"It's still great to talk about it. The memory of 1995 will always remain in my life. The bond was something special. I've never been involved in a team with the same commitment", Cathal O'Reilly concludes. After several near-misses by Connacht teams, the team he led out in Limerick on April 30th, 1995, finally broke the mould and completed a grand slam of elite hurling titles for the western province.

1996 – ALL-IRELAND SEMI-FINAL
31 March 1996, Navan

St. Kieran's, Kilkenny 0-18
(J. Coogan 0-7, J. Staunton 0-5, G. Kennedy 0-2, P. Delaney 0-2, M. Fogarty 0-1, B. O'Shea 0-1)

St. Mary's, Belfast 0-4
(J. Flynn 0-2, K. Grego 0-1, C. Magee 0-1)

1996 – ALL-IRELAND SEMI-FINAL
31 March 1996, Nenagh

St. Colman's, Fermoy 1-15
(T. McCarthy 0-11, D. Barry 1-1, W. O'Donoghue 0-2, J. McCarthy 0-1)

St. Raphael's, Loughrea 2-7
(V. Maher 1-1, C. Earls 0-4, N. Kelly 1-0, N. Shiel 0-1, C. Hynes 0-1)

St. Kieran's, Kilkenny, Croke Cup Champions, 1996.
Back row, left to right: Michael McGrath, John McEvoy, Bob Aylward, Gerry Kennedy,
Tomas O'Dowd, Aidan Cummins, Brian O'Shea, Henry Shefflin, Eoin Drea,
Podge Delaney, Patrick Holden.
Middle row, left to right: Mr Pat Murphy, Brian Holohan, Willie Maher, Barry O'Donnell,
Michael Ryan, Sean Dowling, Jimmy Coogan, Alan Geoghegan, John Staunton, Mr Aidan Finnan.
Front row, left to right: Mr Denis Philpott, J.P. O'Neill, Michael Fogarty, David Carroll (capt),
Joe Young, Kieran Philpott, Donncha Fahy, Michael Kavanagh, Fr Jim Cassin.
(Photograph courtesy of Tom Brett, Kilkenny)

1996 – ALL-IRELAND FINAL
28 April 1996, Croke Park
Referee: Aodán MacSuibhne (Dublin).

St. Kieran's, Kilkenny 1-14

Joe Young
(Kilkenny)

Kieran Philpott   **Sean Dowling**   **Michael Kavanagh**
(Kilkenny)   (Kilkenny)   (Kilkenny)

Aidan Cummins   **David Carroll (*capt*)**   **Michael Fogarty**
(Kilkenny)   (Kilkenny) (0-1)   (Kilkenny)

John McEvoy   **Tomas O'Dowd**
(Laois) (0-1)   (Kilkenny) (0-1)

Willie Maher   **Donncha Fahy**   **John Staunton**
(Tipperary) (1-1)   (Tipperary) (0-1)   (Kilkenny) (0-3)

Henry Shefflin   **Jimmy Coogan**   **Podge Delaney**
(Kilkenny) (0-1)   (Kilkenny) (0-3)   (Kilkenny) (0-2)

Sub: Brian O'Shea (Kilkenny) (for McEvoy).

St. Colman's, Fermoy 2-6

Derek Slattery
(Cork)

Wesley Walshe   **Niall Fitzgerald**   **David Relihan**
(Cork)   (Cork)   (Cork)

William Twomey   **Luke Mannix**   **James Murray**
(Cork)   (Cork) (0-1)   (Waterford) (0-1)

Eoin Murphy   **Paul Cotter**
(Waterford)   (Cork)

Elton Pierce   **Timmy McCarthy (*capt*)**   **David Barry**
(Cork) (0-1)   (Cork) (0-2)   (Cork)

David McInerney   **John McCarthy**   **Will O'Donoghue**
(Cork)   (Cork)   (Cork) (2-1)

David Carroll

"This one is for you, Dad," said David Carroll, as he held aloft the Croke Cup, in front of an emotional crowd in Croke Park on Sunday April 28th, 1996. The St. Kieran's captain had just emulated the achievement of his father in 1957, but sadly Ted Carroll had passed away only four months before the Kilkenny college's 13th All-Ireland triumph.

David, whose mother Angela (neé Lenihan) hails from Irishtown, is the youngest of five children. His brothers Pat, Donal and Ted (a winning Croke Cup panellist in 1990) all played in various grades of hurling for St. Kieran's, while his sister, Helen played camogie. After his outstanding playing career with Kilkenny came to an end, Ted Carroll became the secretary of the Kilkenny County Board. Because of the huge workload which this involved, David grew familiar with the ongoing pandemonium in the house, including fixture congestion and ticket requests, especially as Kilkenny were more or less always involved in the latter stages of the chase for the Bob O'Keeffe and Liam McCarthy cups. "The house would be besieged by people in search of final tickets," David recalls.

Naturally, hurling was part and parcel of David's life from when he was a very young boy. He still recalls the Christmas morning ritual of playing a fun game of hurling with his cousins, the O'Neills and the Hendersons, in James' Park. Having attended Kilkenny CBS Primary School, David found it awkward at first when switching to rival college, St. Kieran's for his secondary education.

"Suddenly the lads I played with in primary school were now the arch-enemies, so matches between Kilkenny CBS and St. Kieran's always held that extra bit of bite for me," David says. "While I was aware that my father had won the Croke Cup with St. Kieran's, he never dwelled on that success. However, his influence over me was reflected in the hurling tips he gave me, while pucking a ball around the nearby fields or bringing me to watch St. Kieran's play".

"Having watched St. Kieran's play for a number of years before I entered the college myself as a student, I was fortunate to witness some of the best college sides ever. In the late 1980s, there were players of the calibre of D. J. Carey, Adrian Ronan and Pat O'Neill. Later on, when I was in first and second year, I admired the likes of P. J. Delaney, Philly Larkin, Andy Comerford, Ollie O'Connor, Joe Philpott and Brendan Dalton." David remembers that success on the field was almost taken for granted in St. Kieran's. "We used to expect to have the day after the Croke Cup final free, as it was anticipated that we would earn this annual holiday for the celebrations." His first hurling memory from St. Kieran's was of a juvenile trial game where "it seemed there were thousands waiting on the sideline to get on and show their skills, like a Cecil B. De Mille film. It showed the strength in depth available when players like Martin Comerford, Eddie Brennan and Derek Lyng rarely featured on the St. Kieran's teams yet, but went on to achieve massive success with Kilkenny seniors in later years," David reflects. "Any blank wall without a window was used to practise your hurling skills."

There were mixed fortunes for David in his early years hurling for the college as he won juvenile and junior titles with St. Kieran's, but also lost some particularly heartbreaking finals at these levels. "We lost to Good Counsel in juvenile and also to Kilkenny CBS at junior level and I remember on the way home from the latter game wondering if I should have gone to the CBS instead of St. Kieran's. I got some slagging from my mates over that result," David says, with a smile. "We were blessed with some first-class trainers back in those days," David recalls. "Trainers such as Séamus Knox, Denis Philpott and Adrian Finan left no stone unturned in their effort to improve our game. I remember, in one of my first training sessions, walking across to fetch a lose sliotar and receiving a severe telling off from Séamus Knox for not sprinting out to get the ball and sprinting back, but we learned quickly what was expected of us."

David graduated to the senior team in his Transition Year in 1993/94 and played at left half back on the St. Kieran's side which lost to St. Mary's, Galway, in extra time on a scoreline of 3-13 to 1-16, in the All-Ireland semi-final played in Nenagh. Indeed the college team itself was going through a transition of sorts at the time. "We had a young team in 1995, but we lost the Leinster final to Good Counsel by 1-8 to 1-6 and we weren't allowed forget that result for some time, having won the previous eight provincial senior titles in-a-row."

Having captained both the juvenile and junior sides and gained invaluable senior experience over the previous two years, it was no great surprise when David was named as captain of the senior team in 1995/96. However, his world turned upside down a few days before Christmas in 1995 when his highly-revered father, Ted, died suddenly while out walking in Kilkenny city. "There wasn't really time to dwell on his passing. Between the hurling matches, the training and the Leaving Cert, I was kept busy and these things helped

get me over it," David recalls in a sombre tone.

The Leinster campaign was by no means plain sailing for St. Kieran's, starting with a tough struggle in a closely-contested semi-final against St. Peter's, Wexford. The previous year's conquerors, Good Counsel, awaited in the Leinster final. "We could never understand how Good Counsel managed to have a strong hurling and football side in senior colleges, as we found it difficult concentrating on the hurling alone," David recalls. In the end, St. Kieran's barely overcame the New Ross college by 1-7 to 1-6 in Nowlan Park with Joe Young emerging as a real hero that day, producing many fine saves. "We were delighted to win in front of a big crowd who were there to see a National League tie between Kilkenny and Tipperary which followed our game." Páirc Tailteann, Navan, was the venue as St. Kieran's eventually comfortably defeated St. Mary's, Belfast in the All-Ireland semi-final, after the Kilkenny lads experienced a shaky start. Denis Philpott was the manager of the St. Kieran's team and David recalls that he regularly got the 'Cork Examiner' newspaper and kept an eye on the Harty Cup matches. Paper cuttings of the impressive progress of St. Colman's in Munster were placed prominently on the school noticeboard, so the team members were well aware that the Fermoy college had a very strong team. "One journalist reported that St. Colman's were the best-ever college side, but we weren't lacking in confidence as we had a very good record against Harty Cup winning sides."

St. Kieran's were extremely well prepared for the big day. Training was switched to the wider James Stephens pitch to give the team an added advantage, but David recalls they were under no illusions that they were the underdogs going up to Croke Park. Having turned in some unspectacular performances along the way, there were some major changes made to the team structure. Donncha Fahy was placed at centre forward while Tomas O'Dowd and John McEvoy were the new midfield partnership.

On All-Ireland final day, the favourites led by 2-5 to 0-7 at the interval. However, the message from Denis Philpott during the break was straightforward, "you have the wind. Stay calm and take your points." Cliona Foley started her match report for the 'Irish Independent' the following day by stating, "never underestimate Kilkenny hurling nursery, St. Kieran's." Clearly, David Carroll and his colleagues agreed. "St. Colman's were meant to be unstoppable but we had a strong team. Our performance that day was as close to perfection as I ever remember. There were no real stars on the field as all six forwards plus the two midfielders got on the score sheet." The only other player to register a score for the Kilkenny side was David himself, playing at centre half back. "Yes, I remember being surprised when that shot went over," he says modestly. Indeed, the captain played a vital role in what was effectively the match-winning goal when his '65' in the 50th minute was deliberately lobbed short for Willie Maher to flick the ball overhead to the back of the St. Colman's net. The Harty champions were left to rue their inordinate number of wides but St. Kieran's were far-from-lucky All-Ireland champions for the 13th time.

Dedicating the victory to his late father Ted, David says, "I remember trying to mention everybody in my victory speech. So many people played a part in our win. Adrian Finan, Pat Murphy, Art Anglin, Tom Luby and, of course, Denis Philpott. We were on an absolute high heading back into Kilkenny and our Irish teacher, Mick Dermody attempted to sing his version of 'An Poc'. However, Denis Philpott was quick to remind us that we were still representing the college during our celebrations. There was a great bond among the players. We only had a few boarders back then and, in fairness, they had it tough. Between school lessons, hurling training, matches and study in the evening and only getting one good meal during the day, we suddenly realised why they were so mean on the pitch," David jokes. "Ironically, you'd often come up against some of your college team-mates when playing club minor games and suddenly they'd be trying to break you up, but there was always a little extra buzz in seeing guys you played with making the breakthrough on to the county

team. On reflection we were looked after extremely well in St. Kieran's and it's only after leaving that you realise how privileged we were to have attended the place," David reflects.

Recalling Denis Philpott's role in St. Kieran's historic win David says, "Denis got involved with Dicksboro but was more noted as a football man having arrived from St. Finbarr's and having trained UCC Sigerson Cup teams. He was 100 per cent focused at all times and tolerated nothing less. We always prepared very diligently. The training sessions were hard and intense and they concentrated on continuous ball work and, as a result, we got fit without realising it."

After completing his Leaving Cert, David studied primary teaching in St. Patrick's, Drumcondra, which proved to be something of a culture shock, on a number of fronts. " There were 200 in my year and just 20 of them were guys. This had its strong points, but a good hurling team for the college was not one of them", he jokes. In St. Pat's, David appreciated St. Kieran's even more, as he met lads from other counties who were not quite as enthusiastic as he was about playing hurling. Playing with the Erin's Hope team, David saw the other side of the coin as he was occasionally forced to get lads out of bed to fulfil Dublin Under-21 fixtures. "The game obviously wasn't taken as seriously in some parts of the country as it was in Kilkenny, but nonetheless hurling in St. Pat's was enjoyable," David reflects.

After studying for three years in St. Pat's, David taught in St. Canice's National School in Kilkenny for just over five years. Having studied psychology, David went to work in the National Children's Hospital in Tallaght before going to Exeter University in England where he undertook a Masters in Psychology. Naturally, this complicated his availability to play and train with Dicksboro. "I was flying over and back every weekend to play intermediate with Dicksboro, as we always had a challenge game or training. I often practised my hurling skills up against a wall in Exeter to keep sharp and I have to admit I got a few funny stares from people passing by. However, we reached the All-Ireland intermediate club final and won it in Croke Park, and that was a tremendous day for the club and that made all the travelling worthwhile." Dicksboro had only re-formed in the 1970s and gradually went from strength to strength, under "excellent trainers like Denis Philpott and Pat Henderson". The 'Boro' won the Kilkenny intermediate title in 1991 and, ultimately, the senior crown in 1993. "Dicksboro always had a strong side, so I never really featured in the senior team until I was 22", David concludes.

In what he describes as a "chequered underage inter-county career", David played minor and Under-21 for the black and ambers. It was heartbreak for the Cats as they lost to Galway in the 1994 All-Ireland minor semi-final with the last puck of the ball, while a hiding by Cork ensued in 1995, in the All-Ireland final in the same grade. Defeat in the Leinster Under-21 championship by Wexford in 1997 was followed by another heavy defeat, this time by Galway, in the penultimate stage of the 1998 championship. However, David is quick to point out that many of the players on these sides which suffered bad beatings later

went on to win senior All-Ireland medals with Kilkenny. Unfortunately, David never made the Kilkenny senior team as the competition is "just too fierce". While he concedes that he now "regularly attends weddings of his contemporaries", David remains "whatever the opposite is of being married"! At the time of writing, he laughs that "it is time to go looking for a job", after all the time, energy and money he has devoted to third level study.

In addition to keeping an eye out for St. Kieran's results, David Carroll also takes great pride in seeing young players he coached as kids in St. Canice's break onto Kilkenny teams, at various grades. Indeed, he is quick to point out that, such is the competition for places in St. Kieran's, that quite a few players who failed to make the black and white-hooped jersey have gone on to greatness in the black and amber stripes. "The GAA rely heavily on schools like St. Kieran's to breed champions at adult level," concludes the young man, whose replication of his father's achievement in holding aloft the Croke Cup, in particularly poignant circumstances, remains unique in the illustrious history of colleges hurling.

1997 – ALL-IRELAND SEMI-FINAL
13 April 1997, Tullamore

St. Colman's, Fermoy 4-18
(N. Ronan 1-11, E. Fitzgerald 2-3, I. Gardiner 1-1, S. Kearney 0-1,
D. McInerney 0-1, J. O'Driscoll 0-1)

St. Mary's, Belfast 1-6
(C. Magee 1-0, T. Maguire 0-3, J. Flynn 0-2, K. Grego 0-1)

1997 – ALL-IRELAND SEMI-FINAL
13 April 1997, Nenagh

Good Counsel, New Ross 4-10
(P. Sheahan 2-2, M. Doyle 0-7, R. Codd 1-0, T. Howlin 1-0, M. O'Neill 0-1)

St. Raphael's, Loughrea 1-7
(K. Colleran 1-0, G. Keary 0-3, E. McMahon 0-2, E. Rocks 0-1, K. Daniels 0-1)

St. Colman's, Fermoy, Croke Cup Champions, 1997.
Back row, left to right: Shane Murphy, Pierse Davern, Pat O'Riordan, Conor O'Kane,
Jerome O'Driscoll, Neil Ronan, Paul Sheedy, Stephen Dennehy, Barry O'Connell,
Eoin Fitzgerald, Aidan Hogan.
Middle row, left to right: Mr Denis Ring, Shane Kearney, Peter Murphy, Ian Gardiner,
Finbarr Foley, Niall Fitzgerald, Paddy Mullins, Derek Slattery, Sean Slattery, David McSweeney,
Gerry O'Riordan, Mr Tom Barry, Mr Dermot Coakley.
Front row, left to right: David Relihan, Paudie Burke, Wesley Walshe, Mr John Hickson,
Luke Mannix (capt), Fr Denis Kelleher, Paul Cotter, David McInerney, Damian McNamara.
(Photograph courtesy of Donal O'Connell and Dermot Coakley, c/o St. Colman's, Fermoy)

1997 – ALL-IRELAND FINAL
27 April 1997, Croke Park
Referee: Pat Horan (Offaly)

St. Colman's, Fermoy 4-20

Derek Slattery
(Cork)

Stephen Dennehy   **Niall Fitzgerald**   **Wesley Walshe**
(Cork)   (Cork)   (Cork)

David Relihan   **Luke Mannix (*capt*)**   **Peter Murphy**
(Cork)   (Cork) (0-1)   (Cork)

Conor O'Kane   **Paul Cotter**
(Cork) (0-1)   (Cork) (0-1)

Ian Gardiner   **Shane Kearney**   **David McInerney**
(Cork) (0-1)   (Cork)   (Cork)

Eoin Fitzgerald   **Neil Ronan**   **Jerome O'Driscoll**
(Cork) (2-3)   (Cork) (1-7)   (Cork) (1-6)

Subs: Finbarr Foley (Cork) (for O'Kane), Paddy Mullins (Cork) (for E. Fitzgerald), Paul Sheedy (Cork) (for Ronan).

Good Counsel, New Ross 0-9

Niall Mackey
(Kilkenny)

Tom Digby   **Philip Wallace**   **Martin Bolger**
(Kilkenny)   (Wexford)   (Kilkenny)

Nicky Kenny   **Michael Redmond**   **Paul Doyle (*capt*)**
(Kilkenny)   (Wexford)   (Wexford)

Nigel Higgins   **Tomas Howlin**
(Wexford)   (Wexford) (0-1)

Micheal O'Neill   **Paul Sheehan**   **Michael Doyle**
(Wexford)   (Kilkenny) (0-2)   (Kilkenny) (0-6)

Keith O'Grady   **Robbie Codd**   **John Barron**
(Wexford)   (Wexford)   (Kilkenny)

Subs: Shane Barron (Wexford) (for Howlin), James Tierney (Kilkenny) (for O'Grady), also Padraig Kehoe (Wexford).

Luke Mannix

The 1990s saw a major revival in the hurling fortunes of St. Colman's, Fermoy. The North Cork school won Harty Cups in 1992, 1996 and 1997 and also captured their second All-Ireland title in the latter year, under the captaincy of local lad, Luke Mannix.

Luke, whose only sibling is an older sister Siobhán, grew up in Fermoy and played hurling from the age of six. His father was "always keen on sport, but not hurling in particular".

Luke's next-door neighbours, who were a few years older, were very involved in hurling and they got him interested. In national school, his teacher, Paul Cotter was also "a great hurling man" and he was another big influence on Luke. In September 1991, he entered St. Colman's as a day pupil where he spent the next six years. "Hurling was a massive part of school life," he remembers. "One of the first things I noticed when I started in Colman's were the pictures on the wall of the various Harty teams. There were six or seven pitches across the road from the school and no matter how good or bad a hurler you were, you were brought out to play. Denis Ring, Fr Donal Roberts, Dermot Coakley and Donal O'Connell were the men involved with the various hurling teams at that time."

When Luke started in St. Colman's, there was no shortage of hurling heroes for him to look up to. "The likes of Fergal McCormack, John Sheehan and Ian Lynch were part of an exceptionally strong team that defeated St. Flannan's in the 1992 Harty final. I was in first year at the time and I can remember the thrill of going to Kilmallock on the bus to see them play. They were 12 or 13 points down at half-time, but came back to win in the second half. I wanted to emulate what they achieved and thankfully, I managed to do so a few years later." Luke enjoyed phenomenal success with St. Colman's. He won an Under-15 White Cup medal and, along with Paul Cotter who was midfield on the 1997 All-Ireland winning side, played on three successful Dean Ryan Cup sides. "We won the Dean Ryan three years running and that was the springboard to our Harty and All-Ireland wins," Luke points out.

Luke played Harty Cup hurling for three years, making his debut in 1995 when St. Colman's were eliminated in the first round by Limerick CBS. The Fermoy school made amends for that disappointment the following year when they regained the Harty Cup after a four-year lapse with victory over Nenagh CBS in the final. However, for many, the highlight of the campaign was a second round victory over St. Flannan's of Ennis. St. Colman's went on to contest the 1996 All-Ireland final in Croke Park, but were forced to give second best to a star-studded St. Kieran's, Kilkenny outfit. "They were just too strong for us on the day," Luke recalls. "They had fellas like Henry Shefflin and Donncha Fahy and they also knew what was required to succeed at that level, having been in numerous finals over the years. We were absolutely gutted on the long journey back to Fermoy. But looking back on it now, I would say that winning the Harty Cup satisfied our ambitions for that year. We didn't have the same desire to win the All-Ireland as we had to win the Harty."

With ten of the 1996 panel on board again in 1997, St. Colman's set their sights on the big prize. "When we came back after the summer holidays in September 1996, our sole intention was to win the All-Ireland. One of the players we lost was Timmy McCarthy, who had carried us in a good few of the previous year's games, but that loss was offset by the arrival of Neil Ronan, who came to us from Charleville CBS. He gave us that extra edge up front and he was the icing on the cake really." Luke can still remember the circumstances in which he was made captain of the 1996/97 team. "Denis Ring stopped me in the school corridor one day, brought me into one of the classrooms and gave me the good news. Being honest, it didn't come as a huge surprise to me because I was in my final year and had captained the White Cup team a few years earlier. I was there the longest with Paul Cotter and one or other of us was going to get the captaincy."

St. Colman's eased past De La Salle, Hospital in the first round of the Harty Cup, winning by 2-26 to 1-6. St. Flannan's were seen as the biggest threat to Luke and his colleagues in their quest to retain the Harty Cup, so the Cork side's joy was understandable when, for the second year in-a-row, they knocked out their great rivals, this time by 1-12 to 1-5 in the quarter-final. In the penultimate round, St. Colman's recorded a comprehensive win over Thurles CBS by 2-18 to 0-7 and history once again repeated itself when Nenagh CBS were defeated in the provincial decider. On the eve of St. Patrick's Day 1997 in Clonmel, St. Colman's triumphed by 1-17 to 0-8. Neil Ronan bagged 1-10, with Luke himself contributing 0-3 from long-range placed balls. "Nenagh were strong down the middle and had a big performer in Richie Flannery, but we were better balanced and that's what stood to us as we ran out comfortable winners," Luke says. St. Colman's once again had things very much their own way in the All-Ireland semi-final against St. Mary's, Belfast, in Tullamore on April 13th, with Neil Ronan scoring a whopping 1-11 as the Munster

champions powered to a facile 4-18 to 1-6 success.

"We were more ambitious the second year", Luke remembers, "and we wanted to win the All-Ireland so badly. We travelled up the day before the final and stayed in Maynooth College that night. We were extremely focused, everything was prepared to perfection. It was also a very emotional occasion for us because we knew it would be our last time to play together in Croke Park." Luke concedes that he "would have loved another crack at St. Kieran's, but you can only beat what's in front of you" and, on this occasion, it was first-time finalists, Good Counsel of New Ross.

The County Wexford side matched St. Colman's for much of the first half and trailed by just three points, 0-7 to 0-10, two minutes before the break. However, an Eoin Fitzgerald goal, followed by a point from Ian Gardiner, put St. Colman's 1-11 to 0-7 in front at half-time and left Good Counsel with a mountain to climb. The floodgates opened when Jerome O'Driscoll nipped in for a second goal just four minutes after the restart. At the opposite end, St. Colman's goalkeeper, Derek Slattery killed off Good Counsel's hopes of staging a recovery when he produced two brilliant saves inside a minute from Michael Doyle and Paul Sheehan. Showing no mercy to the opposition, Colman's moved up a gear and a quick 1-1 from Neil Ronan inside 30 seconds had the Cork support in full voice. In the final quarter, Eoin Fitzgerald burst through to boot home a goal. St. Colman's eventual winning margin was a massive 23 points.

"After losing last year's Croke Cup decider with six of yesterday's starters, St. Colman's came to GAA headquarters in determined mood. A superb performance by their defence and full forward line deservedly gave them their second title - 20 years after their only previous victory," the 'Irish Independent' reported. "All eyes were on Fermoy's stunning full forward, Neil Ronan who, despite obviously carrying an injured ankle, still managed to top score on 1-7. But on either side of him, Jerome O'Driscoll (1-6) and Eoin Fitzgerald (2-3) for once, equalled, and at times, outdid

Ronan. Fellow Cork minor, Fitzgerald gave an outstanding display of fearless fielding and tireless running to stand out as man of the match."

Luke's personal memories of the final are vivid. "It was a hot day and the size of the pitch took us by surprise. We started well. Conor O'Kane, who had been a sub up to the final, scored the first point. Neil Ronan and Jerome O'Driscoll were popping over the points and we kept our foot on the pedal until the very end." Indeed, it wasn't till very recently that Luke was told that the match had been so one-sided that Good Counsel sub Padraig Kehoe came on for the final minutes without having actually replaced a starting colleague! "It was a dream come true to win the All-Ireland. It had been my aim for six years. After the final whistle, I was literally dragged off the pitch by a steward and I was up in the stand receiving the cup before I knew it. Fr Denis Kelleher had prepared the speech for me in Irish and I got through it alright. There were huge celebrations afterwards. We got a Garda escort into Fermoy. Everyone was delighted for us - it meant an awful lot to the pupils and staff of the school, and to the people of Fermoy."

Denis Ring's name is indelibly linked with successful St. Colman's teams and Luke is full of praise for his former coach. "Denis took over the training after Fr Kelleher became school president. He brought a new dimension to our game and was the main driving force behind our successes. He knew the strengths and weaknesses of his players and he knew how to improve your game and how to cajole players. He was meticulous in his planning and I'm sure everyone in Colman's is grateful to him for all he has achieved. In general, all the teachers were very accommodating towards the hurlers and lads actually did quite well in the Leaving Cert." Luke also played football for the school and "one big regret" he has is that he never won silverware in the big ball game with St. Colman's. He recalls with gratitude the work done for Gaelic games in the school by Fr Denis Kelleher and Gus Kelleher.

Luke played minor hurling for Cork in 1996, but the Leesiders' Under-18s lost to "an exceptional" Tipperary side, who went on to win the All-Ireland title. Two years later, he won an All-Ireland Under-21 championship medal with the Rebel County. A powerful side, including Donal Óg Cusack, Diarmuid O'Sullivan, Wayne Sherlock, Sean Óg Ó hAilpín, Neil Ronan, Timmy McCarthy and Joe Deane, beat Galway by 2-15 to 2-10 in the final. However, in 1999, Clare dethroned Luke and his colleagues in the first round in Munster. While he played senior hurling for Cork in challenges and the Oireachtas Cup, Luke never held down a regular slot for competitive games.

After leaving St. Colman's, Luke studied for a B Comm in UCC, followed by a Masters in Electronic Commerce, and he was part of the Fitzgibbon Cup winning side in 1998. In the final the Cork university defeated Waterford IT by 2-17 to 0-13 in Limerick, but this result was reversed the following year. He now lives in London with his partner, Julie, whom he has known since his schooldays. He works in the finance section of the Musgrave Group, while continuing with his part-time accountancy studies at night. He plays hurling with Robert Emmets in London and has represented Fermoy in junior hurling and intermediate football over the years. He describes himself as "a social golfer".

St. Colman's, Fermoy, remained a force into the early years of this decade, winning three Harty Cups on the trot between 2001 and 2003, and All-Irelands in 2001 and 2002. However, it was the 1997 All-Ireland triumph which effectively kick-started the winning run. "We were probably an inspiration to the teams that followed us in the same way as the 1992 team was an inspiration to us," says Luke Mannix, who continues to keep an eye out for his alma mater's results, over nine years after he held aloft the Croke Cup. Indeed, he retains "very positive memories" of St. Colman's and regularly meets a number of his 1997 team-mates on his frequent trips home to Fermoy.

1998 – ALL-IRELAND SEMI-FINAL
5 April 1998, Thurles

St. Flannan's, Ennis 1-8
(J, Casey 1-5, C. O'Reilly 0-1, T. Carmody 0-1, S. Mullane 0-1)

Callan CBS 1-6
(J. Gormley 1-0, J. O'Neill 0-2, G. Cleere 0-2, C. Herity 0-1, J. P. Corcoran 0-1)

1998 – ALL-IRELAND SEMI-FINAL
5 April 1998, Drogheda

St. Raphael's, Loughrea 2-16
(K. Daniels 2-4, G. Keary 0-9, A. Morgan 0-1, N. Kelly 0-1, S. Morgan 0-1)

St. Mary's, Belfast 0-5
(M. McCullough 0-2, C. Herron 0-1, H. Kennedy 0-1, P. Kelly 0-1)

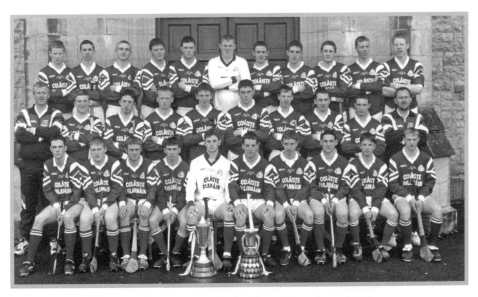

St. Flannan's, Ennis, Croke Cup Champions, 1998.

Back row, left to right: Colman Shouldice, Tony Griffin, Tony Carmody, James McInerney, Brian Geary, Shane O'Neill, Gary Farmer, Gerry Quinn, Michael Greaney, Conor Plunkett, Kenneth Kennedy.

Middle row, left to right: Mr Mike McInerney, Dermot Gleeson, Tomas McNamara, Tadhg McNamara, Diarmuid McMahon, Mark Fitzgerald, Ronan Hickey, John Casey, Robert Conlon, Mr John Minogue.

Front row, left to right: Cathal O'Reilly, Michael Hehir, Patrick McCormack, Michael Shannon, Garrett Howard, Brian Clancy (capt), Shane Mullane, Hugh Flavin, Brian McMahon, Gearóid Considine.

(Photograph courtesy of Fr John Jones, Mountshannon)

1998 – ALL-IRELAND FINAL
2 May 1998, Croke Park
Referee: Aodán Mac Suibhne (Dublin)

St. Flannan's, Ennis 2-16

Garrett Howard
(Tipperary)

Tomas McNamara   **Kenneth Kennedy**   **Conor Plunkett**
(Clare)   (Clare)   (Clare)

Brian McMahon   **Brian Geary**   **Dermot Gleeson**
(Clare)   (Limerick)   (Tipperary)

Gerry Quinn   **Gearóid Considine**
(Clare) (0-2)   (Clare) (0-1)

Brian Clancy (*capt*)   **Tony Carmody**   **Cathal O'Reilly**
(Clare) (0-1)   (Clare) (0-2)   (Limerick) (1-2)

Michael Greaney   **John Casey**   **Shane Mullane**
(Galway) (1-0)   (Clare) (0-7)   (Limerick) (0-1)

St. Raphael's, Loughrea 1-11

Johnny O'Loughlin
(Galway)

Keith Egan   **Damien McClearn**   **John Conroy**
(Galway)   (Galway)   (Galway)

Cyril Murray   **Stephen Morgan**   **Paul Tierney**
(Galway)   (Galway) (0-1)   (Galway)

Donal Ward   **Anthony Keane (*capt*)**
(Galway)   (Galway) (0-1)

Gavin Keary   **John Dooley**   **Padraic Garvey**
(Galway) (0-6)   (Galway)   (Galway)

Niall Kelly   **Keith Daniels**   **Aidan Morgan**
(Galway) (0-2)   (Galway) (1-1)   (Galway)

Brian Clancy

Not since the drought of 1958 to 1976, had St. Flannan's senior hurlers endured a trophyless period lasting as long as seven years. So when Newmarket-on-Fergus' Brian Clancy led them back to Harty and Croke Cup glory in 1998, there was as much relief as anything else after what must have seemed an eternity for the famous Ennis nursery.

Hurling has been in Brian's background for many years and his grandfather, James Clancy, actually played on the first Clare team

to win an All-Ireland senior title in 1914 (at a time when the All-Ireland trophy was called the Croke Cup!) "I played hurling with Newmarket from Under-10 upwards," he explains. "I attended Quin Primary School, where we had a strong team, but didn't win anything. Hurling has always been in my family, and my father, Tommy, always encouraged me to play. My older brothers, Derek and James also attended St. Flannan's, without actually making the Harty team, so I had no choice in the matter," Brian jokes.

As a first year day pupil, Brian greatly admired Richard Woods, James Healy and Brian Tobin, who were some of the marquee names on the St. Flannan's team at that time. "Richard Woods was a fellow I looked up to when I started in Flannan's. He was also from Newmarket and was centre back on the Harty team. He went on to play for Clare afterwards." Brian played on the St. Flannan's Under-15 and Under-17 teams before graduating to the Harty team in his Leaving Cert

year of 1996/97. He had figured on unsuccessful White Cup and Dean Ryan Cup teams before then, and it looked as though his chance of winning silverware with Flannan's had passed when, under the tutelage of Eamon Giblin and Peter Quinn, they were well beaten by St. Colman's, Fermoy, in the 1997 Harty Cup. However, his decision to repeat the Leaving Cert the following year ensured a highly successful climax to his time in St. Flannan's.

Although Brian was just one of a handful of survivors from the 1997 team, St. Flannan's were able to field an exceptionally strong side in 1998. This was due, in no small part, to the arrival into the school of Clare All-Ireland minor winners, Kenneth Kennedy and Brian 'Beano' McMahon, as well as Limerick's Brian Geary, all as repeat Leaving Cert students. "To get those three lads on board was a huge boost. They added strength to the team and people were referring to us as potential All-Ireland champions before the campaign ever started," Brian recalls. "Clare's victories in the All-Ireland senior and minor finals the previous year had brought a winning feeling to the county. However, I can't say for sure if it was a factor in our success. St. Flannan's has a huge tradition in colleges hurling and would always fancy their chances at the start of a Harty campaign."

Brian was handed the captaincy in the dressing room before an early season challenge match against Coláiste Chríost Rí. "It was a fierce proud moment for me as I wasn't expecting it," he says modestly. Despite being understrength for their opening game in the

Harty Cup against Thurles CBS, St. Flannan's emerged as comfortable 3-11 to 1-4 winners. In the semi-final, they exacted sweet revenge on their 1997 conquerors, St. Colman's with an absorbing 0-10 to 0-8 victory, in "a bit of a grudge match in Kilfinnan". The signs looked ominous for St. Flannan's when they went in at the break on level terms after playing with the aid of a strong wind. The Fermoy lads had opened up a 0-8 to 0-6 lead with a few minutes to go, but St. Flannan's scored the last four points to take the spoils and qualify for the final. "That was easily our most satisfying win. Conditions weren't conducive to a high-scoring game and it was like the Harty and All-Ireland victories rolled into one," Brian remembers. In the provincial final, St. Flannan's accounted for Limerick CBS by 0-12 to 0-5 to claim their 17th Harty Cup. The final failed to live up to expectations but, from Brian's viewpoint, "It was just a matter of winning it and we were relieved to get the Harty Cup. In Flannan's, that's what you want to win - you probably don't know the All-Ireland is for the Croke Cup!" Surprise Leinster champions, Callan CBS provided a much stiffer test for the Ennis lads in the All-Ireland semi-final. Played in wet conditions at Semple Stadium, the game was always close with St. Flannan's just about edging the verdict on a 1-8 to 1-6 scoreline. The closeness of the game came as no surprise to Brian, who states, "they had beaten a particularly strong St. Kieran's team in the Leinster final and we knew they were bound to be good. It was a tough game and it was great to get over it."

Similarly, Brian confesses that he "didn't know a lot" about All-Ireland final opponents, St. Raphael's, Loughrea. "We knew they would be tough opposition. Cyril Farrell and John Hardiman were coaching them and they had the likes of Gavin Keary and Keith Daniels who were on the Galway minor team that played Clare in the previous year's All-Ireland final", he recalls. As it transpired, "It was a very exciting game and we were delighted to come out on the right side of the result. It was a huge occasion - the school chartered a special train to Dublin and it was a big thing for us to tog out in the dressing rooms in the new Cusack Stand. It was a dream come true parading behind the band."

A Cathal O'Reilly goal in the dying minutes proved decisive as St. Flannan's lifted the Croke Cup for the 12th time. In a tight opening to the game, Shane Mullane set up Michael Greaney for a third-minute goal. However, St. Raphael's were back on level terms by the end of the first quarter. St. Flannan's led by 1-6 to 0-5 at the break and it remained close until the last 10 minutes when O'Reilly's goal put St. Flannan's 2-10 to 1-9 ahead. That score effectively broke the Galway side's resistance and the Ennis lads emerged victorious by a somewhat flattering eight-points margin, after what the 'Sunday Independent' called "a pulsating final".

Brian remembers the great celebrations on the pitch afterwards and "being dragged away from them by a steward who brought me up to the Hogan Stand to receive the cup", adding that, "I didn't over-complicate the speech for myself!"

St. Flannan's were guided to success in 1998 by John Minogue and Mike McInerney. Brian is well qualified to talk about the triumphant management duo. "John and Mike were two very experienced coaches whom I would rate highly. We trained four evenings a week and all the training was skills-based. It was total hurling and because we were playing so much of it, the fitness looked after itself. The two lads had a great relationship with all the players and were very approachable. Of the two, John was probably the 'bad cop', but just like Mike, who was the 'good cop', he had the best interests of the team at heart. There was no real dominant speaker. We also got great support from Fr Moloney and Fr Jones, the college President, while the addition of Jamesie O'Connor to the teaching staff at that time further increased the profile of hurling in the school. The boarders and day pupils got on well together and were treated equally by everyone. The hurlers were well looked after. The winning feeling had come to Clare at that stage, although Flannan's teams had never felt inferior."

Brian wasn't a member of the All-Ireland winning Clare minor team of 1997 but after skippering St. Flannan's to national glory, he made the 1998 county minor side which lost the All-Ireland quarter-final to Galway. That loss was quickly forgotten about, though, when he captained Newmarket-on-Fergus to a county minor championship a few weeks later. When Newmarket won the Clare Under-21 championship in 2001, Brian was again captain and he played on the county team in that age-group that year. He also represented the Banner County at intermediate level but work and club commitments meant that he never made the senior panel. He has since skippered the club's senior team, but so far championship success has eluded him. "We're desperate to win a senior championship at this stage. Newmarket is the most successful club in Clare hurling, but we haven't won a championship in 25 years. At the moment, we have a young team which will probably take another year or two to fully mature", he reckons, while he is bitterly disap-

pointed at his club's failure to Wolfe Tones in the 2006 county final.

After completing his secondary education, Brian studied Computer Systems at the University of Limerick. He represented UL in the Fitzgibbon Cup and also won a Munster Freshers title with them before dropping off the course after a year and beginning an apprenticeship as a blocklayer. Brian is now self-employed in Newmarket and has three people working for him in his blocklaying business.

Brian Clancy has remained in close contact with many of his St. Flannan's team-mates from 1998, often through club hurling in County Clare, and he attended the function that honoured the colleges' Harty Cup winning captains earlier in the decade. "Those lads will always be my friends and Flannan's will always be a good school," he concludes with pride.

1999 – ALL-IRELAND SEMI-FINAL
27 March 1999, Nenagh

St. Flannan's, Ennis 2-16
(A. Quinn 1-5, B. Gantley 0-4, R. Conlon 1-0, T. Griffin 0-3, T. Carmody 0-2,
D. Kennedy 0-1, B. Dunne 0-1)

Gort Community School 0-10
(D. Greene 0-3, S. Coen 0-2, S. Carey 0-1, D. Fitzsimons 0-1, A. Diviney 0-1,
C. Brennan 0-1, J. Gantley 0-1)

1999 – ALL-IRELAND SEMI-FINAL
28 March 1999, Parnell Park

St. Kieran's, Kilkenny 3-19
(E. Kelly 1-8, B. Carroll 0-6, D. Dowling 1-1, S. Hennessy 1-0, P. Reid 0-3, G. Whelan 0-1)

Ulster Colleges 0-6
(K. O'Connell 0-3, P. Kirk 0-1, C. Herron 0-1, S. McGourty 0-1)

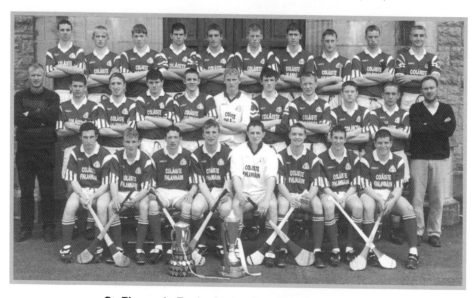

St. Flannan's, Ennis, Croke Cup Champions, 1999.
Back row, left to right: Tony Griffin, Justin McMahon, Kenneth McNamara, Ronan O'Looney,
Gerry Quinn, Brian Culbert, Fergal Lynch, Pat Culhane, Conor Plunkett, Tony Carmody.
Middle row, left to right: Mr Mike McInerney, Gerard O'Grady, Tom McNamara,
Declan Walsh, Gary Farmer, Barry Nugent, Dermot Gannon, Tadhg McNamara,
Damien Kennedy, Andrew Quinn, Mr John Minogue.
Front row, left to right: Robert Conlon, Brendan Gantley, Brendan Dunne,
Dermot Gleeson (capt), Sean Hawes, Sean Arthur, Mark Kelly, Derek Quinn.
(Photograph courtesy of Fr John Jones, Mountshannon)

1999 – ALL-IRELAND FINAL
18 April 1999, Croke Park
Referee: Pat Horan (Offaly)

St. Flannan's, Ennis 2-15

Sean Hawes
(Clare)

Gary Farmer
(Clare)

Ronan O'Looney
(Clare)

Tom McNamara
(Clare)

Justin McMahon
(Clare)

Conor Plunkett
(Clare)

Dermot Gleeson (*capt*)
(Tipperary)

Gerry Quinn
(Clare) (0-2)

Tony Griffin
(Clare)

Damien Kennedy
(Clare) (0-1)

Tony Carmody
(Clare) (1-0)

Robert Conlon
(Clare)

Brendan Gantley
(Galway) (0-2)

Brendan Dunne
(Tipperary) (0-3)

Andrew Quinn
(Clare) (1-7)

Subs: Declan Walsh (Clare) (for McNamara), Brian Culbert (Clare) (for Conlon).

St. Kieran's, Kilkenny 2-10

Jamie Power
(Kilkenny)

Mark Phelan
(Kilkenny)

Martin Óg Kennedy
(Kilkenny)

Brendan Griffith
(Kilkenny)

Tim Murphy
(Kilkenny)

Damian Walsh
(Laois)

Paddy O'Brien
(Kilkenny)

Hugh Gannon (*capt*)
(Kilkenny)

John Coogan
(Kilkenny)

Eoin Kelly
(Tipperary) (1-7)

James Moran
(Tipperary)

Gary Whelan
(Kilkenny)

Brian Carroll
(Offaly) (0-3)

David Dowling
(Kilkenny)

Patrick Reid
(Kilkenny) (1-0)

Subs: James O'Keeffe (Kilkenny) (for Coogan), Shane Hennessy (Kilkenny) (for Moran).

Dermot Gleeson

After ending their seven-year drought in 1998, St. Flannan's were back in the winning groove and they successfully defended their Harty and All-Ireland titles in 1999. Tipperary man, Dermot Gleeson was a key player in both years and had the great honour of captaining the Ennis nursery to their 13th Croke Cup victory in 1999.

Dermot, the eldest of a family of five (four boys and a girl) grew up in the North Tipperary village of Killoscully. This familiar-sounding village is nowadays often used to film scenes for Pat Shortt's popular comedy programme, 'Killinascully'. Dermot played his early hurling with Ballina, on the Clare border, before his "hurling-mad" father, Michael, helped to form a new juvenile club called Ballinahinch, which catered for young players in Ballinahinch and Killoscully. Dermot was one of the fledgling club's first recruits and he was to the fore as they made remarkable progress over a short period of time. Martin O'Brien, who is Dermot's cousin, was the first player from the parish to play minor hurling for Tipperary, a feat which Dermot would later emulate.

Dermot has been obsessed with the game of hurling for as long as he can remember. The idea of attending St. Flannan's first entered his thoughts as a ten-year-old when he was returning home from a National League match between Tipperary and Clare in Cusack Park, Ennis. "On our way back from the game, we passed a big stone building and I asked my Dad what it was. He replied, 'that's St. Flannan's - the home of hurling' and proceeded to tell me that my cousin Fr James Grace was teaching there. When he told me that that's where all the good hurlers go to school, I made it clear to him that I wanted to go there when I finished primary school. Sure enough, two or three years later, that's where I went."

Dermot entered St. Flannan's as a boarder in 1994, where he would spend six years, repeating his Leaving Cert there in 2000, but unfortunately he was overage for the Harty team that year. Known as 'Chops' to his school-mates, Dermot's early heroes in the school included Rory Gantley, John Reddan, David Forde, Ger Looby and Stiofán Fitzpatrick ("legends in the school"), even if the senior team was going through a lean period by acceptable standards in the college. Dermot recalls how there was so much hurling talent when he went into St. Flannan's that their internal 'A to L' and 'M to Z' teams actually met in the Clare county final for first year students. "It reflected the strength of hurling in the school. We were able to put out two teams that no other school in Clare could live with. At the start, there were hundreds of young lads out training", with Dermot wondering would he ever make the breakthrough.

He recalls losing a White Cup Munster Under-15 championship final to Thurles CBS, but he made amends the following year when winning a Dean Ryan Cup medal. His progress was clearly being noted by the senior mentors as he graduated to the Harty team in 1996/97, at which stage he felt "a boy among men", and St. Flannan's lost at the penultimate round to St. Colman's, Fermoy. However, that disappointment was forgotten about in 1998 when Dermot was on board as the Ennis school savoured Harty and All-Ireland glory, winning the All-Ireland final against St. Raphael's of Loughrea at Croke Park, by 2-16 to 1-11

Dermot can vividly recall the moment when he was informed he would be captain for the 1998/99 campaign. "I felt it was probably between myself and Gearóid Considine but, when Gearóid didn't return in September, that made me the frontrunner. However, it was a big downer for me that my best friend and a fabulous hurler was gone. Mike McInerney brought me out to the hurley shed and that's where he gave me the good news."

St. Flannan's easily accounted for newly-promoted Hospital De La Salle in their opening defence of the Harty Cup. They went on to defeat St. Michael's CBS, Limerick in a repeat of the previous year's final, in the quarter-final in Nenagh, this time by a three-goal margin. The champions then headed to Feenagh for the Munster semi-final, where they edged out St. Colman's, Fermoy, by 0-10 to 0-8. In the final on March 7th, they faced old rivals, St. Finbarr's, Farranferris with Feenagh again the venue. The Cork side set the early tempo and opened up a big lead before St. Flannan's finally clicked in to gear and pulled clear for a 1-14 to 1-8 victory. "They were seven points up at half-time, before we eventually woke up", Dermot recalls, "and we blitzed them in the second half. John Gardiner was starting to break through at that time and I can remember Farranferris bringing him on in the second half."

Dermot and his St. Flannan's team-mates overcame Gort Community School by 2-16 to 0-10 in the All-Ireland semi-final at Nenagh. Dermot feels that the involvement of four former Gort players in the St. Flannan's camp added considerable spice to the contest. "There was a right bit of needle in it. Brendan Gantley and Justin McMahon, both of whom made the team, as well as Robert McTighe and John Loughnane, neither of whom did, had left Gort to come to Flannan's the previous

year. In the build-up to the game, there were all sorts of claims that we had poached them because they were good hurlers, but that wasn't the case, as they came to Flannan's of their own accord."

Three weeks later, St. Flannan's were forced to call on all of their renowned battling qualities to hold on to their provincial and All-Ireland crowns. It proved to be a reversal of sorts of the 1957 final between the same two schools. According to Shane Scanlon in the 'Irish Independent', "there were shades of Offaly's 1994 All-Ireland win as St. Flannan's, Ennis, retained their All-Ireland Colleges SHC 'A' title with a storming finish that stunned St. Kieran's, Kilkenny, in a dramatic final at Croke Park." Truly, the Croke Cup final against their longstanding foes, bore witness to one of the great colleges hurling comebacks. Six points in arrears with 12 minutes remaining, the Clare outfit looked dead and buried but, displaying a never-say-die attitude, they roared back to win by six and leave their Kilkenny opponents shell-shocked.

St. Kieran's were quickly in to their stride and had 1-3 on the scoreboard after only five minutes. However, by half time, St. Flannan's were behind by just the bare minimum, 0-7 to 1-5, but midway through the second half, they trailed by 0-10 to 2-10. St. Flannan's then sprung to life with the introduction of Brian Culbert in the 45th minute. In the final quarter, St. Flannan's remarkably scored 2-5 without reply. The 'Irish Independent' described it as "an amazing finish to a final that, for the most part, failed to live up to its pre-match billing". From Dermot's perspective "it was unbelievable how we came back to win that final. We had only 12 minutes to turn it around, and we somehow managed it."

Dermot was marking his fellow Tipp man and future senior inter-county star, Eoin Kelly. The pair knew each other well but friendship was forgotten when the Croke Cup was at stake. One moment from the game still sticks out clearly in Dermot's mind. "Gerry Quinn put in an unbelievable tackle on St. Kieran's midfielder, John Coogan. Quinn was a fierce strong fella and Coogan came off injured not long after that." Dermot remembers "amazing scenes at the final whistle. I was very proud to be captain of that Flannan's team. There was great camaraderie between the lads. They would stand on their heads for you - that's the type of lads they were." Indeed, Dermot was unlucky not to pull off an amazing provincial double in 1999, as he was centre half back with the St. Flannan's footballers who lost by just three points to Tralee CBS in the Corn Uí Mhuirí final.

The 1999 All-Ireland success was master-minded by Mike McInerney and John Minogue. "They were the perfect partnership," Dermot recalls, "even though they were totally oppo-site in a way. Mike was very shrewd, he stood back and took everything in. By contrast, John wouldn't hold back if you made a mistake. They left nothing to chance; there wasn't a stone left unturned. The school principal, Fr Brendan Moloney, was also very good to us. They looked after us very well with gear and so on."

Dermot played inter-county minor hurling for three years and was also on the Premier County Under-21 team for three campaigns, ironically losing out each year to Limerick. He was centre half forward on the Tipp minor team which won the Munster championship in 1999, but lost the All-Ireland final by three points to Galway. He gained a measure of revenge the following year when he won an All-Ireland intermediate medal, defeating the Tribesmen in the decider. He was called up to the senior panel for the National Hurling League by then manager, Nicky English at the beginning of 2001, but wasn't involved when Tipperary won the Liam McCarthy Cup later that year.

At club level, Dermot has won a Tipperary junior championship medal with Ballinahinch. However, after taking up employment with Morrissey Construction in Charleville, he transferred to Newtownshandrum and helped them to win Cork and Munster titles in 2005. He also won a Fitzgibbon Cup medal with University of Limerick, from where he gradu-ated with a Business Studies degree. He now works in Limerick with the accountancy firm of BDO Simpson Xavier and retains his ties with Tipperary by playing rugby with Newport, while he also enjoys an occasional game of golf.

Dermot Gleeson "enjoyed every minute" of his time in St. Flannan's. "I played any sport which got me out of class," he jokes. He remains in touch with quite a number of his team-mates, in addition to joint-manager, Mike McInerney. He is sad to see the end of board-ing in the school but, no doubt, his nine-year-old brother, David, who is "mad keen to go to Flannan's", will make it over to Ennis as a day pupil. Young David's ambition will be to repeat his brother's heroics on the hurling fields in the late 1990s.

2000 – ALL-IRELAND SEMI-FINAL
2 April 2000, Nenagh

St. Kieran's, Kilkenny 2-14
(B. Carroll 1-6, E. Kelly 0-6, L. Heffernan 1-0, P. Reid 0-1, S. O'Neill 0-1)

Gort Community School 0-11
(A. Diviney 0-5, P. Mahony 0-3, B. Coen 0-2, S. Carey 0-1)

St. Kieran's, Kilkenny, Croke Cup Champions, 2000.

Back row, left to right: Ned Sweeney, Ken Coogan, Shane Hennessy, Michael Walsh,
Robert Aylward, Brendan Doyle, Peter O'Neill, John Lennon, Michael Connolly, Dick Fitzpatrick.
Middle row, left to right: Stephen Dunne, Michael Rice, Derek Brennan, Ger Prendergast,
Brian Hogan, James Moran, Jackie Tyrrell, Enda Cleere, Pat Reid, Seaghan O'Neill.
Front row, left to right: Mr Adrian Finan, Eoin Kelly, Brian Carroll, Brian Dowling, Tommy Walsh,
Tim Murphy (capt), Liam Heffernan, Joe Delaney, Michael Drennan,
Daire Connery, Mr Pat Murphy.
(Photograph courtesy of Tom Brett, Kilkenny)

279

2000 – ALL-IRELAND FINAL
16 April 2000, Nenagh
Referee: Johnny McDonnell (Tipperary)

St. Kieran's, Kilkenny 1-10

Derek Brennan
(Kilkenny)

Daire Connery　　　**James Moran**　　　**Tommy Walsh**
(Kilkenny)　　　　　(Tipperary)　　　　(Kilkenny)

Brian Hogan　　　**Ken Coogan**　　　**Jackie Tyrrell**
(Kilkenny)　　　　(Kilkenny)　　　　(Kilkenny)

Tim Murphy (*capt*)　　　**Shane Hennessy**
(Kilkenny) (0-1)　　　　(Kilkenny)

Seaghan O'Neill　　　**Eoin Kelly**　　　**Michael Walsh**
(Kilkenny) (0-1)　　(Tipperary) (0-7)　　(Kilkenny)

Brian Carroll　　　**Peter O'Neill**　　　**Liam Heffernan**
(Offaly)　　　　(Kilkenny)　　　(Kilkenny) (1-1)

Sub: Ned Sweeney (Kilkenny) (for M. Walsh).

St. Flannan's, Ennis 0-9

Derek Quinn
(Clare)

Kenneth McNamara　　**Ronan O'Looney** (*capt*)　　**Alan O'Loughlin**
(Clare)　　　　　(Clare)　　　　　(Clare)

Robert Conlon　　　**John Culkin**　　　**Andrew Fleming**
(Clare)　　　　(Galway) (0-1)　　　(Clare)

Fergal Lynch　　　**Justin McMahon**
(Clare)　　　　(Clare)

Damien Kennedy　　**Jonathan Clohessy**　　**Gerard O'Grady**
(Clare) (0-2)　　　(Clare)　　　　(Clare)

Brendan Gantley　　　**Brian Culbert**　　　**Andrew Quinn**
(Galway) (0-1)　　　(Clare)　　　　(Clare) (0-5)

Sub: Niall Moran (Limerick) (for Clohessy).

Tim Murphy

There was more than just the Croke Cup at stake in Nenagh, on April 16th, 2000. The 'big two' of colleges hurling were locked at 13 titles each and the bragging rights would be very precious over the ensuing 12 months. So when Tim Murphy held aloft the famous trophy that day on behalf of St. Kieran's, after a four-point defeat of St. Flannan's, it was a particularly special moment for the famous Kilkenny college.

Tim is a native of Danesfort and he received his early education in the local national school. There was also a school in Cuffesgrange, which was the other side of the parish and one in Burnchuch at that time also. The Danesfort primary school team was comprised of children from all three schools. "You'd be playing beside lads you wouldn't actually be going to school with, but that made little difference either way, as everybody knew everybody regardless," he recalls. They "toiled away" in Roinn C for years. "I was never more than a good Roinn C hurler in those days," he says modestly, "and never had the opportunity to come across the city boys up in Roinn A, so I never really improved." He remembers wanting to go to St. Kieran's because, initially, he liked the uniform! "My older brothers went there, so naturally at that age I was inclined to want to go anyway, but what sealed it was when Kieran's won the 1993 All-Ireland final and, when I saw all the press that it got, I was hooked."

Tim's father and namesake didn't attend St. Kieran's but, by all accounts, Tim reckons his father was "a very decent hurler" in his day. "I've heard it so many times after matches, lads coming up saying how good he was and that he could have played for Kilkenny, but for Pat Henderson. Himself, Frank Minogue and Dick Mahony are reckoned to be the three best hurlers Danesfort ever had."

"I had six good years in Kieran's and I must say that I enjoyed them. When I made the juvenile panel in first year, that's when I started improving as a hurler. All of a sudden, we were training three times a week after school, and training hard I might add. Seamus Knox and Tom Hogan were over the team and we beat St. Peter's in the final. In the space of one year in secondary school, I was now fit as a fiddle and I could hit the ball comfortably off my left," Tim recalls. He was overage in second year and didn't play junior that year, but did the following year when St. Kieran's lost the final to Kilkenny CBS by two points. Tim remembers his side "starting terribly and conceding two goals". It's a defeat, just over ten years on, that galls him still. "It was one of the biggest disappointments I've had on the field. I had a few friends playing for the CBS, so I suppose I'll give them that one!"

In his early years in St. Kieran's, Tim looked up to the likes of Henry Shefflin, Willie Maher, Michael Kavanagh and Sean Dowling. "I remember one time, I think I was in second year, and we had just got out for mid-term. It was raining and freezing; pure miserable. Everybody had gone home for the holidays and there were just a few of us waiting round for the bus, or whatever, up by the changing rooms. The boys were out trudging through it all on a Friday afternoon, with Denis Philpott barking at them. I don't think it's just the talent that has Kieran's so successful, but that sort of dedication as well."

In all, Tim was on the St. Kieran's senior panel for three years. The second of these, in 1999, brought heartbreak when St. Flannan's late surge brought them a record-equalling 13th Croke Cup. However, "1999/2000 was a great campaign", Tim recalls. "It was my third involved with the seniors, and maybe that's why, but Adrian Finan and Pat Murphy pulled me from class one day and asked me would I like to be captain. I jumped at it! I honestly didn't expect it, but I also knew right there I'd be lifting the All-Ireland, so I wasn't going to say 'no'. I knew we'd win because we had narrowly lost the previous year to Flannan's, who had a great team but lost most of it, and we had an even better team that year. Tommy Walsh, Jackie Tyrrell, Brian Hogan, Ken Coogan, Eoin Kelly, Brian Dowling, Michael Rice, Brian Carroll. All these boys were playing for their counties. So we had the players without a doubt and there was no question we'd be prepared with Adrian Finan and Pat Murphy over us."

As it turned out, St. Kieran's won every game they played that year - challenges, league and championship, even beating St. Flannan's in an All-Ireland final dress rehearsal, in the annual match played for the old Croke Cup. In Leinster, St. Kieran's beat two County Wexford teams en route to reaching the final - St. Peter's, Wexford, and Good Counsel, New Ross. In Carlow, in the provincial decider, Dublin Colleges provided Tim and his colleagues with "by far our toughest game in Leinster", before St. Kieran's pulled away in the closing stages to retain their crown. They then had to shrug off the challenge of Gort Community School in the All-Ireland semi-final, leaving age-old foes, St. Flannan's, lined up on April 16th, 2000, in Nenagh.

"The final was tense," Tim reflects. "I remember not being too happy with the rain, because that didn't suit us one bit. Not that we couldn't roll up the sleeves and dig in, which we had to do, but because I thought on a good spring day we could play some stuff. As it turned out it was a slog and a hard one and we had heroes all over the field. The six backs were outstanding and James Moran had the

game of his life at full back. Jackie Tyrrell and Brian Hogan cleaned up as wing backs. Shane Hennessy and myself, I think we won the midfield battle, though it wasn't pretty as we were mostly just slipping and sliding all over the place, trying to pull on balls. Eoin Kelly was a powerhouse up front and, on a day for battling, the likes of Liam Heffernan and Peter O'Neill worked their socks off. The day didn't suit the likes of Brian Carroll, who had been superb all year, but you couldn't ask any more from him."

In the 'Irish Independent', Paddy Hickey reported, "the heartbreak of last year's All-Ireland defeat was most emphatically exorcised by St. Kieran's." The only goal of the game came in the 28th minute from Liam Heffernan, with many present feeling his shot was for a point, but the goalscorer himself adamant he was lobbing the losers' goalkeeper, Derek Quinn. This left the Kilkenny lads ahead by 1-4 to 0-4 at the interval. There was never much between the sides and it was appropriate that Tim ended match scoring with an 80-metre free. The celebrations matched the achievement and Tim has very fond memories of the rejoicing that took place in Reid's of Ballyhale on the Sunday and Monday nights!

After leaving St. Kieran's, Tim went on to UCD where he studied Economics for four years. He won a Fitzgibbon Cup medal in first year, when UCC were defeated in a replayed final at Nenagh. He represented Kilkenny at underage and "flirted with the county senior panel at one point, but it wasn't to be". In recent years, Tim has undertaken a lot of travelling round the world and, at the time of writing, he is based in Bondi, Sydney in Australia, where he works for UBS Global Asset Management.

Such are Tim Murphy's itchy feet, that he intends to do even more globetrotting before returning to Ireland. No doubt, when he finally resettles he will link up with many of his St. Kieran's team-mates from 2000, when the talk of their outstanding win against St. Flannan's in a real crunch Croke Cup decider will be high on the agenda. All will be in readiness at Reid's in Ballyhale!

2001 – ALL-IRELAND SEMI-FINAL
8 April 2001, Clonmel

St. Colman's, Fermoy 2-7
(A. O'Shaughnessy 1-3, B. Carey 1-1, D. Fitzgerald 0-2, S. Kearney 0-1)

Dublin Colleges 1-5
(J. Twomey 1-0, C. Keaney 0-2, S. Quinn 0-1, S. Hiney 0-1, S. Fee 0-1)

St. Colman's, Fermoy, Croke Cup Champions, 2001.
Back row, left to right: John Mulchinock, Richard Relihan, Brendan Healy, Eamonn Condon, Stephen Molumphy, Paul Dowling, Jonathan O'Shea, Noel O'Riordan, Pa Boyce, Maurice O' Brien, Dessie Fitzgerald, Seamus Stack.
Middle row, left to right: Mr Denis Ring, Anthony Walsh, Maurice McNamara, John G. Kelly, Stephen Coughlan, T. J. Begley, Denis Fitzgerald, Donal Houlihan, Brian Lane, Tom Lyons, Richard Murphy, Shane Kearney, Mr Michael Doolin.
Front row, left to right: Mr John Hickson, Tadhg Healy, Matthew Fitzgerald, Brian Carey (capt), Ms Joan Hunter, Ms Bridie McDonald, Brian Murphy, Paul Kearney, Aidan Kearney, Fr Denis Kelleher.
Missing from photograph: Andrew O'Shaughnessy.
(Photograph courtesy of Donal O'Connell/Dermot Coakley, c/o St. Colman's, Fermoy)

2001 – ALL-IRELAND FINAL
5 May 2001, Croke Park
Referee: Pat Ahern (Carlow)

St. Colman's, Fermoy 2-10

Denis Fitzgerald
(Cork)

Matthew Fitzgerald   **Richard Murphy**   **Brian Murphy**
(Cork)   (Limerick)   (Cork)

Richard Relihan   **Tadhg Healy**   **Aidan Kearney**
(Cork)   (Cork)   (Waterford)

Maurice O'Brien   **Dessie Fitzgerald**
(Limerick)   (Cork) (0-1)

Shane Kearney   **Brian Carey** (*capt*)   **Seamus Stack**
(Waterford)   (Cork)   (Cork)

Andrew O'Shaughnessy   **John Mulchinock**   **Paul Kearney**
(Limerick) (2-8)   (Cork)   (Waterford) (0-1)

Subs: Stephen Molumphy (Waterford) (for P. Kearney).

Gort Community School 2-7

Michael O'Donoghue
(Galway)

Eoin Ruane   **Joseph O'Leary**   **Shane Burke**
(Clare)   (Galway) (1-0)   (Galway)

Steve Moylan   **Shane Kavanagh**   **Matthew Fitzsimons**
(Galway)   (Galway) (0-2)   (Clare)

Cathal Forde   **Conor Crotty** (*capt*)
(Galway) (0-1)   (Galway)

Tommy Lee   **Iarlaith Tannian**   **Colm Burke**
(Clare) (0-1)   (Galway)   (Galway)

Cathal Connolly   **Joseph Gantley**   **David Greene**
(Galway) (0-1)   (Galway) (1-1)   (Galway) (0-1)

Subs: Martin Nestor (Galway) (for Lee), Gary Forde (Galway) (for Ruane),
Ray Glynn (Galway) (for Forde), Niall Curtin (Galway) (for S. Burke).

Brian Carey

When Mallow lad, Brian Carey, led St. Colman's to their third Croke Cup success on May 5th, 2001, the Fermoy school firmly established itself as a major hurling nursery. Ironically, some 28 years earlier, his father, Eugene, had experienced great frustration when he was a member of a St. Colman's side which was unbeaten but was thrown out of the Harty Cup.

Brian has loved the game of hurling from day one, and he jokes that, "I think I was born with a hurley in my hand." Having started the game with a strong Mallow team when just seven years of age, Brian was fortunate to win plenty of underage county titles. He attended Rahan National School and his father's alma mater, St. Colman's, Fermoy, was always going to be the next port of call in his education. Eugene had donned the famous green and white jersey in 1972/73, the year that St. Colman's were ejected from the Harty Cup by the GAA powers-that-be. This followed an objection from North Monastery (whom they had beaten by 3-8 to 3-3) about whether their registration with the Munster Council had met the required deadline. As it transpired, it was to be another four years before the Croke Cup entered the hallowed walls of the famous Fermoy secondary school for the very first time.

Brian's desire to wear the St. Colman's jersey was further increased once he saw them play North Monastery in a Harty Cup game, "with Timmy McCarthy marking Seán Óg". He admired players like McCarthy, as well as Luke Mannix, Will Twomey, Eoin Murphy and Paul Cotter. "Luke Mannix, in particular, was a very good role model, as he was good at school, a good leader and had a good personality." Brian has two siblings (including an older sister) but his younger brother, Myles, was sent to the Presentation Brothers in Cork, where "he enjoys playing rugby", as the boarding section of St. Colman's is now closed down.

Brian's introduction to hurling in St. Colman's was a tough one. "I remember my first training session. I was marking Brian Murphy and that proved a bit of an eye-opener," Brian modestly remembers. He experienced mixed fortunes as St. Colman's won the Cork Colleges juvenile title, but lost out in the Dean Ryan Cup to Midleton CBS and St. Flannan's, Ennis. "However, all these competitions were good experience and it was an education to play against such good young players," Brian reflects. While just 15 years of age, Brian forced his way onto the senior panel in St. Colman's but he feels he was "brought along just for the experience". Despite this, he got a late run against St. Flannan's, who won a Harty hat-trick between 1998 and 2000, with St. Colman's failing even to reach a provincial decider in those three years.

In Brian's Leaving Cert year people were hinting to him that he would be made captain but he didn't fully expect it. "I suppose I was on the panel for four years and Brian Murphy had been there that long also, but he had been captain the previous year." St. Colman's road to the All-Ireland final started out with a "fairly handy victory over Cashel CBS in Clonmel". Brian explains, "That was a great start as we had a very young team, some of whom were playing their first championship game." St. Finbarr's, Farranferris proved a stiffer test in the Munster quarter-final played in Watergrasshill. "A good Farranferris side included John Gardiner, but it was extra special for us to beat them as we gained revenge for the previous year and they were close rivals of ours." Unknown to Brian that day, his father had been taken ill and, sensibly, he wasn't told until after the game. "We didn't really play well in the semi-final against Thurles CBS in Nenagh. To be honest, Thurles were up for it but we squeezed through into the Harty Cup final."

Another of St. Colman's great rivals, St. Flannan's, awaited them in the decider. "Flannan's had previously beaten us in the Dean Ryan Cup. They were the kingpins of Munster hurling but our ambition all along was to win the Harty Cup. We had been aiming at Flannan's and we knew their players. Our trainer, Denis Ring, had unbelievable detail on them as he had studied them in previous matches and he'd know how many times a player would strike off which hand, which way they would play a ball and their strong and weak players. His homework on any opposition really was fantastic," Brian remembers. "That Harty Cup final in Feenagh was one of the best games I ever played in. We won by three points (2-12 to 0-15) and a half an hour after the game we were still on the pitch. The whole place went mad and it was such a great feeling, as so much work had gone into it."

Having won the Harty Cup, Brian and his team-mates were determined to win the Croke Cup. "St. Colman's had won a fair few Harty Cups but only two Croke Cups, so this was a great motivating factor for us." On April 8th in Clonmel, surprise Leinster champions, Dublin Colleges were St. Colman's opponents in the All-Ireland semi-final. "I had played against the Dublin county minor side so I knew all about them. Conal Keaney, in particular, was a big worry for us. I got a goal with about seven or eight minutes to go and it was probably the worst goal I have ever scored. Their 'keeper miscontrolled the ball and I ran

in and pulled on it, but it got stuck in the muck. I remember trying to kick the ball, which was black at this stage, over the line. No one could really see the ball but I think the referee just awarded the goal because I had my hands raised and I jumped up in celebration," Brian jokes. "But it didn't matter as, two minutes later, Andrew O'Shaughnessy got the ball and stuck it in the back of the net and there was no doubt about that one." St. Colman's eventually won by 2-7 to 1-5 and Brian says, "it was good that we got a tough close game as we had a full month before the Croke Cup final. The school and the town of Fermoy really got behind the team at that stage. There were flags everywhere."

Even though St. Colman's faced a Connacht team in the Croke Cup final they didn't underestimate them. "Gort Community School were our opponents but we knew we were up against it as we had played Loughrea and they had been brilliant. Also, Galway were always strong at minor level," Brian reflects. "On the day, Andrew O'Shaughnessy basically won that final for us as he scored 2-8. Andrew was a class act so our aim was to get the ball to him. He was knacky and always in the right place at the right time." John Harrington, reporting for the 'Irish Independent', clearly concurred. His headline "O'Shaughnessy inspires", preceded a glowing tribute to the young Limerick man, the star of a game he describes as, "a slow burning fuse that only caught fire in the second half". He went on, "The first period was a joyless 30 minutes, marred by poor striking and sloppy shooting, the second was an explosive cocktail of powerful hurling and deadly finishing. In the end St. Colman's victory was easily explained. They had Andrew O'Shaughnessy and Gort didn't."

In the first half of the Croke Cup final of 2001, the sides seemed to be suffering from big match nerves. Defences were on top, and the quality of the game was disappointing, with both teams guilty of some very poor wides. Gort led 0-4 to 0-3 at the break but the match finally came to life when O'Shaughnessy hit two quickfire goals in the opening five minutes of the second half. While the first was a scrambled affair, the second was a rasper. According to the 'Irish Independent', "the St. Colman's forwards seemed pedestrian in the first half but were running like prize greyhounds in the second." A tactical decision by the St. Colman's management to play with a two-man full forward line paid off, as it gave O'Shaughnessy the room to wreak havoc." Indeed, three O'Shaughnessy points in less than ten minutes gave St. Colman's a six point lead and Gort looked dead and buried. However, the match was thrown wide open when a Joseph Gantley goal for Gort left just three points between the teams. Three more O'Shaughnessy points left the Connacht champions six points in arrears once more with just six minutes left on the clock. A goal from a penalty from Gort full back, Joseph O'Leary on the stroke of full time gave the underdogs hope, but it ultimately proved to be merely a consolation score.

Moments later, Brian Carey became the 50th young man to receive the Croke Cup. "My speech wasn't spectacular; it was one of few words. Indeed, I recall doing an interview for TG4 the week before where my Irish wasn't the best at describing the messy goal I got against Dublin Colleges," Brian jokes. "I recall the crowd going mad and we went back to school and there was a stand out for us. We paraded the cup and even some of the older players joined the teachers in the pub!" Reflecting on the mentors who inspired St. Colman's to their Croke Cup success, Brian is again loud in his praise of Denis Ring. "Denis was our PE teacher and we went through thorough preparation before each game. He was unique and we never had a trainer like him. Denis lifted the whole hurling scene in St. Colman's. You only have to look at the record before he arrived, and then look at his record there in the school. There was a huge transformation. Michael Doolin was also a great GAA man. An Offaly man, he was a great football trainer and we had a decent football team too, but the teams were often very mixed so the training end of things would overlap. A lot of the team were boarders back then and after two and a half hours' training the lads would settle into their study for the night."

Others who spring to Brian's mind for their promotion of Gaelic games in St. Colman's are Fr Donal Roberts, Tom Barry and Donal O'Connell. On a personal level, Brian was always very grateful to his parents for their unwavering support, and also to his "hurling mad" grandmother!

Despite playing for Cork minors in the 2001 All-Ireland final where the Rebels lost to Galway, Brian didn't make the county Under-21 side. "The competition in Cork is very strong and, to be honest, the dedication to inter-county hurling didn't really appeal to me on top of the pressure of college. I had hurled a lot in Colman's and I felt I needed a break." Brian's initial third level hurling career centred around Fitzgibbon Cup hurling with UCC, but he never managed to garner a winner's medal.

"Playing for your club is everything and I am very happy playing with Mallow," Brian says. "We play at intermediate level in hurling and in the senior grade for football. We generally feature in the latter stages of the championship and the club is developing nicely. Hurling was always my game. I was never great at football as I felt I never had the pace for it, while I also played a little rugby." Brian undertook an Electronic Engineering degree course in UCC and then headed to Edinburgh to study for a Masters. The British GAA championships have been a real highlight of his time in the UK. "Over 20 teams converge on the likes of Birmingham for the championships. It was great craic." In late 2006, Brian was appointed to a senior role in the Exploratory Resources section of Shell UK, based in Dorset, but still plans to commute "for the hurling"! He has a long-term girlfriend, Aisling Birmingham from Fermoy.

It is over five years since St. Colman's won the All-Ireland colleges senior hurling title and, while there has been no formal reunion yet, Brian Carey would love to meet up with his many friends and team-mates again. His main sporting ambition is to play senior club hurling in County Cork with Mallow. He hopes to achieve this in the near future and, in doing so, reproduce the form which saw him captain St. Colman's to their wonderful Croke Cup win in 2001.

2002 – ALL-IRELAND SEMI-FINAL
14 April 2002, Kilmallock

St. Colman's, Fermoy 4-15
(A. O'Shaughnessy 1-6, S. Molumphy 1-1, L. Philpott 1-1, M. Allen 1-1, P. Kearney 0-4,
J. O'Donnell 0-1, E. Condon 0-1)

Mercy College, Woodford 0-5
(A. Garvey 0-2, K. Holohan 0-2, D. Kelly 0-1)

St. Colman's, Fermoy, Croke Cup Champions, 2002.
Back row, left to right: Donal Houlihan, Brian Hogan, Michael Allen, Kieran Curtin, Paul Kearney,
Eamonn Condon, Daniel Carroll, Stephen Molumphy, Gerry O'Connor, Padraig Cotter,
Colm O'Connell, Brian Lane, Maurice McNamara, Padraig Hyland,
Patrick Kirby, Stephen Barrett.
Middle row, left to right: Mr David Rea, Mr Denis Ring, Colm Coakley, Brendan Healy,
Shane Hickey, John O'Donnell, John G. Kelly, Denis Fitzgerald, Eoin O'Donovan, Ger Cahill,
Fergus Browne, Joey O'Herlihy, Conor Griffin, Barry Sheehan, James Dorgan,
Mr Donal O'Connell.
Front row, left to right: Mr John Hickson, Barry Fitzgerald, Andrew O'Shaughnessy,
Luke Philpott, Maurice O'Brien (capt), Aidan Kearney, Seamus Stack,
Richard Relihan, Fr Donal Roberts.
(Photograph courtesy of Donal O'Connell/Dermot Coakley, c/o St. Colman's, Fermoy)

2002 – ALL-IRELAND FINAL
28 April 2002, Thurles
Referee: Aodán Mac Suibhne (Dublin)

St. Colman's, Fermoy 0-11

Denis Fitzgerald
(Cork)

James Dorgan
(Cork)

Brian Lane
(Cork)

Eamonn Condon
(Cork) (0-1)

Richard Relihan
(Cork) (0-1)

Maurice O'Brien (*capt*)
(Limerick)

Kieran Curtin
(Cork)

Seamus Stack
(Cork)

Aidan Kearney
(Waterford) (0-1)

Patrick Kirby
(Limerick) (0-2)

John O'Donnell
(Cork)

Stephen Molumphy
(Waterford) (0-1)

Andrew O'Shaughnessy
(Limerick) (0-3)

Luke Philpott
(Cork)

Paul Kearney
(Waterford) (0-2)

St. Kieran's, Kilkenny 2-4

Richie Power
(Kilkenny)

Dermot Nolan
(Kilkenny)

John Lennon
(Kilkenny)

David Prendergast
(Kilkenny)

Ger Holden
(Kilkenny)

John Tennyson
(Kilkenny)

Padraig Kennedy
(Kilkenny)

Michael Rice (*capt*)
(Kilkenny) (1-1)

Brendan Doyle
(Kilkenny)

Sean O'Connor
(Dublin) (0-1)

Mark Heffernan
(Kilkenny)

Eamon O'Gorman
(Kilkenny)

Eoin Reid
(Kilkenny) (1-1)

Seaghan O'Neill
(Kilkenny)

James Fitzpatrick
(Kilkenny) (0-1)

Sub: Willie McCormack (Tipperary) (for Doyle).

Maurice O'Brien

In the early years of the new Millennium, St. Colman's, Fermoy had arguably the most consistent teams in colleges hurling. The North Cork school won three Harty Cups in-a-row between 2001 and 2003 and two All-Ireland titles, the second of these in 2002 under the captaincy of Limerick lad, Maurice O'Brien.

Hurling success came early for Maurice when he helped Glenbrohane National School to win their first Cumann na mBunscol title. His background is steeped in hurling. "All of my family hurled with Glenrue and my older brother, Michael won an All-Ireland minor medal with Limerick in 1984. I'm also a second cousin of Ned Rea, who played on the last Limerick team to win the Liam McCarthy Cup in 1973," Maurice explains. Along with fellow Limerick man, Andrew O'Shaughnessy (who was destined to become a massive name in Harty and Croke Cup circles), Maurice entered St. Colman's as a boarder in September 1997. The school was still basking in the warm afterglow of its second All-Ireland triumph and he had many heroes to look up to, including Neil Ronan, Paul Murray, Damien McNamara, Mike Fitzgerald and Eoin Fitzgerald.

Over the next five years, Maurice achieved major success in the famous green and white colours. He collected a variety of medals at juvenile and junior levels in Munster before graduating onto the senior team. He played Harty Cup hurling for three years and was a substitute in the previous year. In his first year as a member of the Harty team, St. Colman's

made an early exit to St. Finbarr's, Farranferris, in Buttevant. They regrouped for the 2001 campaign and ended the year as Harty and All-Ireland champions, with Maurice at midfield in their narrow All-Ireland final win over Gort Community School. When St. Colman's began their Harty Cup defence in October 2001, Maurice was surprised to find himself in the role of captain. "Even though I'd been captain all the way up, I didn't expect to be given the captaincy that year. I was very surprised when Denis Ring broke the news to me because there were a lot of good players on that team and any one of them could have been captaincy material," he says modestly.

Boasting many of their 2001 All-Ireland winning side, St. Colman's encountered few problems en route to retaining the Harty Cup in 2002. In the first round at Ballylanders, they walloped Limerick CBS by 5-21 to 0-4, a result which stands as the Sexton Street school's heaviest ever defeat in the competition. Indeed, Maurice jokes that, as the match was played "up the road from home", it gave him the opportunity to avail of "a nice home-cooked dinner"! The North Cork team led by 4-12 to 0-3 at half-time and could even afford to take their foot off the pedal somewhat in the second half. Next up for St. Colman's were Coláiste an Phiarsaigh of Glanmire, who provided them with their toughest game of the Harty campaign. St. Colman's were forced to start without three injured regulars, including Maurice, but still held too many aces for their opponents. The Fermoy side led by 0-7 to 0-4 at the interval, but were hauled back onto level terms and it needed the introduction of their injured trio of Maurice O'Brien, Aidan Kearney and Patrick Kirby for them to prevail by 2-12 to 1-6, with Andrew O'Shaughnessy scoring both of their goals. O'Shaughnessy was again among the goals as Colman's accounted for Cashel CBS by 4-6 to 0-3 in the semi-final at Mitchelstown. The final, which was played in Clonmel, was even more one-sided with St. Colman's destroying Templemore CBS on a 2-18 to 0-6 scoreline. "Glanmire were the only team to really test us in Munster and we got a fair scare," Maurice remembers.

The Fermoy lads enjoyed another comfortable victory (4-15 to 0-5) over Mercy College, Woodford of Galway in the All-Ireland semi-final, to set up a meeting with St. Kieran's in the Croke Cup decider. "St. Colman's had a poor record against St. Kieran's in All-Ireland finals over the years and this was something Denis Ring kept harping on about. That was the motivation for us. The atmosphere in the school was electric leading up to the game and we were anxious not to let anyone down."

The final was played in dreadful conditions at Semple Stadium. The 'Irish Independent' reported, "the match was never going to live up to its lofty billing - the weather took care of that. Driving wind, hail and rain meant resolve and bravery were always going to be more valuable commodities than fancy stick work - and neither team was lacking". Both teams struggled to adapt to the conditions and the match remained scoreless until the 13th minute when Michael Rice's sideline cut from 40 yards was inadvertently helped into his own net by St. Colman's wing back, Kieran Curtin. However, the reigning champions trailed by only the minimum at half-time, with the wind at their backs for the second half. The Cork side resumed with three more points in-a-row from Andrew O'Shaughnessy, wing back Richard Relihan and Paul Kearney. St. Kieran's looked in trouble but just a minute after Kearney's score, they went up the field and regained the lead with a goal from Eoin

Reid. It was nip and tuck from there on and the winners led by two points with time running out. There was one final scare though as goalkeeper, Denis Fitzgerald was forced to tip over Eoin Reid's goalbound shot. Moments later, the final whistle sounded with St. Colman's holding on for a 0-11 to 2-4 victory.

"There was huge relief when the game was over. It was a desperate day for hurling. It was also the most intense match I've played in," Maurice says. "We conceded a soft goal in the first half, but fought hard to get back into contention before half-time. We played well after the break, but were under pressure right up to the end when Denis Fitzgerald produced a vital save." In the 2001 final against Gort, Andrew O'Shaughnessy scored 2-8 of St. Colman's overall total of 2-10. By contrast, his tally in the 2002 decider was 0-3, with just 0-1 coming from play. "No-one would have given us a chance if they had known beforehand that Andrew would only score a point from play. He had given a great scoring display in 2001, but didn't get the same space against St. Kieran's. The 2002 final was much more of a team effort. We had a good spread of scorers with one of our corner backs, Eamonn Condon even getting on the score-sheet. In my speech, I said the same few words I had said after the Harty! But there was great hype back in Fermoy as he were brought in on an open-top trailer. The pouring rain didn't stop people turning up." In the days ahead, the celebrations were great, with Maurice recalling that "it was then time for a belated crack at study"!

The 2002 All-Ireland success was masterminded by Denis Ring and his management team of Donal O'Connell, Dermot Coakley and Fr Donal Roberts. Maurice has nothing but praise for Ring, who subsequently managed the Cork minors. "The attention to detail was something else. Denis studied other teams and had all their strengths mapped out before we played them. Every possible angle was covered. We trained as hard as any team - twice a day, four days a week during lunchtime and after school, day pupils and boarders alike." Maurice also represented St. Colman's in football and was a member of the team which gave Coláiste na Sceilge a major scare in the Munster Colleges SFC 'A' semi-final of 2002. He remembers Michael Doolin and Gussy Kelleher as being the main promoters of the big ball game in the school.

2001 and 2002 were remarkably successful years for Maurice O'Brien and Andrew O'Shaughnessy as they also garnered All-Ireland Under-21 medals with Limerick, having played without tangible reward at minor level for the Shannonsiders. Another St. Colman's team-mate, Patrick Kirby, joined them on the 2002 winning side. Maurice was on the county senior panel in 2003 and 2004 for the National Hurling League, but his only championship appearance was against Offaly in the All-Ireland Qualifiers. He is now back on the Limerick panel, after a year's absence. In 2005, he lined out at wing forward on the Garryspillane team which captured the Limerick SHC for the first time. It was a huge achievement for the club who had been threatening to make a breakthrough for some

time, even if disappointment followed when they were knocked out of the Munster championship in the first round by Waterford's, Ballygunner.

Maurice O'Brien is studying Quantity Surveying at Limerick IT. As part of his course, he is currently on work experience with his uncle's company, PK O'Brien and Associates, in Terenure. He has played Fitzgibbon Cup hurling with Limerick IT, but much to his regret, he wasn't involved when they won the prestigious third level competition in 2004, having taken a year out to go working at the time. He says he will never forget his time in St. Colman's, the success he enjoyed and the great friends he made. "I've very fond memories of St. Colman's. I still keep in contact with some of the lads and keep an eye out for their results. I recently met a member of the 1948 team which reached the All-Ireland final, at a golf classic, and I'm proud to be associated with such a traditional school", he concludes.

2003 – ALL-IRELAND SEMI-FINAL
6 April 2003, Boherlahan

St. Kieran's, Kilkenny 2-20
(J. Fitzpatrick 0-6, E. O'Gorman 1-2, M. Bergin 1-1, M. Nolan 0-3, R. Power 0-3,
J. Murphy 0-2, E. Reid 0-1, J. Quane 0-1, J. O'Neill 0-1)

Gort Community School 0-4
(D. Kennedy 0-3, K. Diviney 0-1)

St. Kieran's, Kilkenny, Croke Cup Champions, 2003.
Back row, left to right: Neal Prendergast, Shane Prendergast, Kevin Lanigan, Richie Power,
David Prendergast, James Connolly, Eamonn O'Gorman, Eoin Reid, Niall McEvoy, John Tennyson,
Aidan Ryan, Mr Tom Hogan.
Middle row, left to right: Mr John Quane, Patrick O'Flynn, James Farrell, Philip Walsh,
John Walsh, Patrick Butler, George Hickey, Patrick Hogan, Padraig Treacy, Michael Bergin,
Mr Art Anglin, Mr Ken Archibold.
Front row, left to right: Mark Aylward, Donncha Cody, Jamie Quane, Damien Bergin,
Darren O'Neill, James Fitzpatrick (capt), John Murphy, Maurice Nolan, Niall Fennelly,
William Norton.
Missing from photograph: Richie Hogan.
(Photograph courtesy of Tom Brett, Kilkenny)

2003 – ALL-IRELAND FINAL
26 April 2003, Clonmel
Referee: Sean McMahon (Clare)

St. Kieran's, Kilkenny 1-15

James Connolly
(Kilkenny)

Donncha Cody
(Kilkenny)

John Tennyson
(Kilkenny)

Neal Prendergast
(Kilkenny)

Patrick Butler
(Kilkenny)

David Prendergast
(Kilkenny)

John Walsh
(Laois)

James Fitzpatrick (*capt*)
(Kilkenny) (0-4)

Darren O'Neill
(Kilkenny) (0-2)

John Murphy
(Kilkenny) (0-1)

Eamonn O'Gorman
(Kilkenny) (0-1)

Richie Power
(Kilkenny) (0-4)

Maurice Nolan
(Kilkenny) (0-1)

Eoin Reid
(Kilkenny) (1-0)

Michael Bergin
(Kilkenny) (0-2)

Subs: Damien Bergin (Laois) (for Murphy), Kevin Lanigan (Tipperary) (for Nolan), James O'Farrell (Kilkenny) (for Butler), Shane Prendergast (Kilkenny) (for Power), Jamie Quane (Kilkenny) (for Bergin).

St. Colman's, Fermoy 1-4

Denis Fitzgerald
(Cork) (1-0)

Colm O'Connell
(Cork)

Brian Lane
(Cork)

Eamonn Condon
(Cork)

Kevin O'Mahony
(Limerick)

Aidan Kearney
(Waterford)

John O'Donnell
(Cork)

Seamus Stack
(Cork)

Padraig Cotter
(Cork)

Colm Coakley
(Cork)

Paul Kearney
(Waterford) (0-1)

Patrick Kirby
(Limerick) (0-1)

Andrew O'Shaughnessy (*capt*)
(Limerick) (0-2)

Michael Allen
(Cork)

Fergus Brown
(Cork)

Subs: Stephen Barrett (Cork) (for Cotter).

James 'Cha' Fitzpatrick

Revenge was sweet for St. Kieran's, Kilkenny, in 2003 when, under the captaincy of James 'Cha' Fitzpatrick, they defeated the holders, St. Colman's, Fermoy, to regain the Croke Cup. After their agonising loss in the previous year's final, St. Kieran's were a driven team and they produced an accomplished performance to not only beat their fierce Cork rivals, but also stop them from achieving a three-in-a-row of All-Ireland successes.

Now recognised as one of the most versatile hurlers in the country, 'Cha' comes from a family of six boys and three girls in the South Kilkenny hurling stronghold of Ballyhale. His background is steeped in hurling. "My father, Edward who was in Kieran's for a few years, captained the Kilkenny minors and my grandfather, John won All-Ireland senior medals in 1932 and '33. My older brother, Dick was a sub on the St. Kieran's All-Ireland winning team in 2000, so hurling was always a part of my life," he explains. Of farming stock, the nickname 'Cha' was given to James because, as a child starting school, his hair was so blond he was likened to a Charolais bull! "Nobody calls me James anymore," he jokes. He received his primary education at Ballyhale National School where the principal, Joe Dunphy, made a big effort to promote hurling. "Joe was a great man. He ran school leagues and that's where it all started for me."

In September 1997, 'Cha' entered St. Kieran's as a day pupil, making the 40-mile round trip to Kilkenny by bus. Having been part of county underage development squads, 'Cha' had no problems settling in. "I knew several of the lads when I started in Kieran's, including John Tennyson and Richie Power. I've hurled with them all the way up," he says.

The player 'Cha' admired most during his early years in St. Kieran's was Tipperary sharpshooter, Eoin Kelly, who was one of the stars of the 2000 All-Ireland success. "Eoin was the big name in the school at that time. Hurling was a big deal in St. Kieran's. From looking at the old photos of players like Eddie Keher and Ted Carroll, you quickly became aware of the school's great hurling tradition and you hoped one day to have your photo up on the wall." 'Cha' won a Leinster juvenile title before graduating to the senior team in 2001. Then managed by Adrian Finan, who later coached James Stephens and the Kilkenny minors, St. Kieran's were beaten in the provincial semi-final by Dublin Colleges, but they bounced back in 2002 to capture the Leinster title and reach the All-Ireland final which they lost to St. Colman's by 2-4 to 0-11 "on a miserable wet day in Thurles".

"We were devastated to lose that final and we were determined to make amends the following year," 'Cha' reflects. "When I came back to do my Leaving Cert after the summer break, the team manager, Tom Hogan called me aside and asked me would I like to be captain and I said, 'no problem at all; I'd love the challenge'. We were very determined in 2003 as we didn't want to be remembered for being the team that lost two All-Ireland finals on the trot. A good few of us had played in the 2002 final, and 2003 was our last chance to win an All-Ireland medal with St. Kieran's. We trained hard that year, often up to six or seven times between Monday and Friday, including out at Kilkenny Castle Park. Thankfully, everything paid off."

A fired-up St. Kieran's encountered few problems in retaining their Leinster crown. They opened their provincial campaign with a comfortable 3-14 to 1-7 victory over Cistercian, Roscrea at Portlaoise. In the semi-final, the champions produced a stunning second half display to overcome city rivals, Kilkenny CBS by 4-14 to 2-7 at Nowlan Park. The CBS put it up to the match favourites, though, and at half-time were full value for their 2-7 to 2-5 lead, despite having played against the wind.

However, St. Kieran's showed a vast improvement after the break with a 31st minute goal from Eoin Reid giving them the impetus they needed to go on and book their place in the final. A 3-10 to 0-11 victory over St. Peter's, Wexford, at Dr Cullen Park saw St. Kieran's retain their provincial crown in impressive fashion. When the teams met in a league encounter earlier in the year, St. Peter's had recorded a surprise win in Power Park on a remarkable scoreline of 5-6 to 0-20, but on this occasion, their Kilkenny opponents held all the aces. The writing was on the wall for the Wexford lads after 13 minutes when Michael Bergin blasted the opening goal. On the stroke of half-time, 'Cha's' free was flicked to the net by Eoin Reid, giving Kieran's a 2-6 to 0-4 lead at the break. Within a minute of the restart, Reid added his second goal to put the Kilkenny side 11 points clear and effectively end the game as a contest. St. Peter's did manage four unanswered points midway through the half, but whatever hopes they had of making up the deficit were ended when midfielder Darren Foran was issued with a straight red card for a wild pull late in the game. "We won, but we knew there was a lot of improvement needed", 'Cha' recalls.

St. Kieran's booked their place in the All-Ireland final following an emphatic 2-20 to 0-4 win over Gort CS at Boherlahan. The bigger and more skilful of the two sides, Kieran's never looked back after centre forward, Eamonn O'Gorman goaled to give them a 1-4 to 0-1 lead. By half-time, Kieran's had increased their advantage to 1-8 to 0-3. The second half turned into a rout for the Leinster champions, whose second goal was scored by corner forward, Michael Bergin in the 43rd minute.

The St. Kieran's players had no difficulty motivating themselves for the All-Ireland final at Clonmel, especially as St. Colman's were their opponents. "St. Colman's were going for the three in-a-row and they were also the favourites. But we knew that if we played to the best of our ability we could win," 'Cha' says. St. Kieran's used their wind advantage to great effect in the opening half and played some majestic hurling to career into a 0-9 to 0-1 interval lead. When St. Colman's blood substitute Mark Cleary was red-carded just before half-time, the way was clear for the winners-elect to coast home to a 1-15 to 1-4 success. The Kilkenny lads were out of sight when full forward, Eoin Reid crashed home their only goal just after the restart. Once Reid's goal went in, the game died as a contest. Indeed, the 'Irish Independent' reported, "it's a pity that the elements and the sending off militated against a level playing field, but it is hard to see how even St. Colman's at their very best could have bettered this perfectly balanced St. Kieran's team." 'Cha' remembers being "on a high" for a few weeks after the All-Ireland final. "Then we had to knuckle down to the Leaving!"

A key factor in St. Kieran's victory was the successful curbing of St. Colman's dangerman, Andrew O'Shaughnessy, who famously scored 2-8 in the All-Ireland final two years earlier. "The management duo of Tom Hogan and John Quane had their homework done on St. Colman's and John Tennyson was magnificent on O'Shaughnessy," 'Cha' notes.

"Tom and John were a great partnership. Tom looked after the hurling side of things as regards positional strategy, and John did all the fitness work and drills with us. Ken Archibold and Art Anglin were two others who were also a big help to us. I remember Brian Cody came into the school a few days before the final to give a great speech."

Many of the 2003 St. Kieran's team also won All-Ireland minor medals with Kilkenny in 2002 and 2003, including 'Cha', who fondly remembers "the golden years for Kilkenny minors". In 2004, he captained the Kilkenny Under-21s to a facile All-Ireland victory over Tipperary at Nowlan Park. "I broke my collarbone in the first half, but I was still able to collect the trophy afterwards," he remembers. He made his championship debut for the Kilkenny senior side against Clare in the 2004 All-Ireland quarter-final replay, and he accepts it was "a big step-up from underage, suddenly playing on the same team as D.J. (Carey)". A broken wrist in 2005 was part of a none-too-memorable year for 'Cha', but 2006 has proven to be an incredibly fruitful year, both for club and county. With Ballyhale Shamrocks, he won Kilkenny and Leinster medals. In the black and amber colours of Kilkenny, he garnered Leinster and All-Ireland medals at both Under-21 and senior level and

a National League memento. Just to round it all off, he was named at midfield on both the GPA Team of the Year and the All-Stars.

'Cha' studied Engineering in UCC for three years, but recently began studying for a potential career in primary school teaching, having enrolled in St. Patrick's, Drumcondra. He played with UCC in the 2004 Fitzgibbon Cup final which the Cork university lost to Waterford IT by 0-9 to 0-11.

When speculating on possible future stars for St. Kieran's, a reference is made in the last chapter of Enda McEvoy's 'Fennessy's Field' to "some fair-haired youth off the Ballyhale Shamrocks team that captured Féile na nGael honours", as that book went to press in 1998. Clearly, that young boy went on to fulfil the author's expectations and, in the process, led a terrific team in black and white hoops to a memorable Croke Cup success in 2003. James 'Cha' Fitzpatrick looks set for more glorious years as one of the many great players to represent the Kilkenny Cats, whose hurling education took place in St. Kieran's.

2004 – ALL-IRELAND SEMI-FINAL
3 April 2004, The Ragg

St. Kieran's, Kilkenny 0-17
(R. Power 0-8, D. O'Neill 0-2, N. McEvoy 0-2, N. Prendergast 0-1, S. Prendergast 0-1,
M. Aylward 0-1, D. Bergin 0-1, R. Hogan 0-1)

St. Flannan's, Ennis 1-8
(C. Ryan 1-0, B. Gaffney 0-3, K. Kennedy 0-3, J. McInerney 0-1, S. O'Brien 0-1)

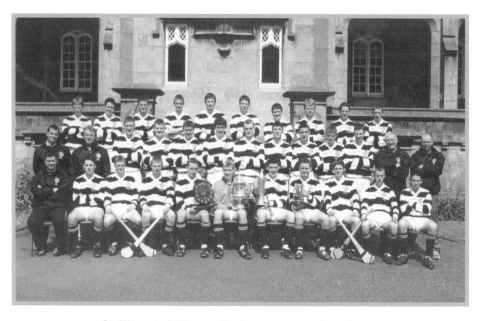

St. Kieran's, Kilkenny, Croke Cup Champions, 2004.
Back row, left to right: Thomas Keogh, Adrian Harkin, Philip Walsh, Niall Fennelly,
Shane Prendergast, Pat Butler, J.J. Farrell, Jamie Quane, Niall Tennyson, Paddy Kennedy.
Middle row, left to right: Mr Tom Hogan, Mr John Quane, Eamonn Walsh, Richie Power,
T.J. Reid, Donncha Cody, Kevin Lanigan, Neal Prendergast, Shane Campion, Padraig Treacy,
Jason Dermody, Mr Art Anglin, Mr Ken Archibold.
Front row, left to right: Mr Pat O'Flynn, Willie Norton, Maurice Nolan, Mark Aylward,
Richie Hogan, Paddy Hogan, John Walsh (capt), Damien Bergin, Michael Bergin,
Donncha Fitzpatrick, Kieran Brennan.
Missing from photograph: Darren O'Neill, Niall McEvoy.
(Photograph courtesy of Tom Brett, Kilkenny)

2004 – ALL-IRELAND FINAL
4 May 2004, Parnell Park
Referee: Johnny McDonnell (Tipperary)

St. Kieran's, Kilkenny 3-20

Paddy Hogan
(Kilkenny)

Willie Norton   **Donncha Cody**   **Eamonn Walsh**
(Kilkenny)   (Kilkenny)   (Kilkenny)

Pat Butler   **John Walsh (*capt*)**   **Neal Prendergast**
(Kilkenny)   (Laois) (0-1)   (Kilkenny)

Darren O'Neill   **Damien Bergin**
(Kilkenny) (0-1)   (Laois)

Richie Power   **Shane Prendergast**   **Jamie Quane**
(Kilkenny) (1-9)   (Kilkenny) (0-1)   (Kilkenny)

Richie Hogan   **Niall McEvoy**   **Mark Aylward**
(Kilkenny) (0-5)   (Kilkenny)   (Kilkenny) (2-1)

Subs: Maurice Nolan (Kilkenny) (0-1) (for McEvoy),
Jason Dermody (Kilkenny) (for S. Prendergast), Pauric Treacy (Kilkenny) (for Butler),
Kevin Lanigan (Tipperary) (0-1) (for O'Neill), Philip Walsh (Kilkenny) (for R. Hogan).

St. Raphael's, Loughrea 1-6

Fergal Hynes
(Galway)

Alan Whyte   **Shane Flaherty**   **Patrick Deeley**
(Galway)   (Galway)   (Galway)

Daragh Earls   **Martin Ryan (*capt*)**   **Thomas Earls**
(Galway)   (Galway)   (Galway)

Francis Kerrigan   **Raymond Regan**
(Galway) (0-2)   (Galway)

Sean Kelly   **Brendan Dooley**   **Kevin Hynes**
(Galway) (0-1)   (Galway)   (Galway)

Ian Burns   **Gary Kilcar**   **Keith Haverty**
(Galway)   (Galway) (0-2)   (Galway) (1-1)

Subs: Daniel McKeigue (Galway) (for Burns), Raymond Dervan (Galway) (for Kilcar),
Fiachra Cooney (Galway) (for Kelly), Kieran Kennedy (Galway) (for Deeley).

John Walsh

When St. Kieran's most recently won the All-Ireland colleges senior hurling championship, the captain was a Laois man, as was the case with the famous Kilkenny college's first success in 1948. John Walsh proudly received the Croke Cup in Parnell Park on May 4th, 2004, almost 56 years to the day since Lar Dunphy held aloft the original trophy in nearby Croke Park.

John is from the parish of Ballinakill, a village which borders County Kilkenny and has a strong hurling tradition. This being the case, it comes as a surprise when John says that he played little or no hurling in primary school. "I went to Knock National School and hurling wasn't really promoted there. Every so often, Noel Delaney would call to the school and teach us football and hurling skills. But while we had a football team, there was no organised hurling played really." Hurling was in John's blood, however, and it was inevitable that he would take up the game. "My mother is from Ballyouskill in North Kilkenny, while my father P.J. played for Ballinakill and was a member of the history-making team that won three Laois Under-21 championships in-a-row. I started hurling with the club at the age of eight under the guidance of Liam O'Shaughnessy and the interest grew from there."

On completing his primary education, John had the choice of attending one of four secondary schools, but his love of hurling meant it was a no-contest. "I could have gone to Heywood Community School, Roscrea or Knockbeg, but I chose St. Kieran's because of its proud hurling tradition," he says. "I can remember Nicholas Lacey from Ballinakill playing for St. Kieran's in 1991 and '92, and in '99 my brother, Damian was centre back on the team which lost the All-Ireland final to St. Flannan's. Damian was on both the Laois minor hurling and football teams at that time and he had switched to St. Kieran's after three years in Roscrea. He was someone I looked up to. Also, as a first year in Kieran's, I greatly admired the likes of Tipperary's Eoin Kelly, who was always a very friendly and modest fellow, and Kilkenny's Tommy Walsh," both of whom went on to become superstars at senior inter-county level.

John's hurling career in St. Kieran's was very successful from start to finish. In his first two years, he featured on Leinster juvenile winning teams and was awarded Juvenile Hurler the Year in 2001. After winning a Leinster junior medal in 2002, he was one of "four or five" players added to the senior panel. St. Kieran's won the Leinster title that year, but disappointment followed when they lost to St. Colman's, Fermoy in the All-Ireland final. The following year, John established himself at wing back on the senior team and revenge was sweet for St. Kieran's when they defeated St. Colman's in the All-Ireland final. "It was a sweet win, not just because we got revenge for the previous year, but because we stopped Colman's from winning the three-in-a-row," John recalls, particularly having gone through the pain barrier by playing the final with a broken thumb.

John skippered St. Kieran's to win the Leinster senior hurling league in December 2003, but it still came as a surprise to him when he was appointed captain for the championship campaign. "I was told I would be captain at a players' meeting just before Christmas. I had captained the team during the league, but I had no inclination that I was going to keep the captaincy for the championship, as it could easily have been Donncha Cody or Richie Power, to name just two. It was a great honour to be made captain and to follow in the footsteps of all the great players who have captained Kieran's in the past."

"Under the management of Tom Hogan and John Quane, we trained awful hard, up to five times a week, in all sorts of conditions. We had been successful all the way up through the ranks, and we really wanted that All-Ireland title," John says. St. Kieran's had a big win over St. Mary's of Enniscorthy in the first round in Carlow Town's pitch, before facing a much sterner challenge from Dublin Colleges in the Leinster semi-final at Portlaoise. Despite being reduced to 14 players early in the second half, the Kilkenny school dug deep to run out winners by 2-13 to 1-8. The sides were level at 0-4 apiece at the interval and, for John, the highlight was Richie Hogan's 40-metre handpass to set up Darren O'Neill for a crucial first goal midway through the second half. "I would say that was our toughest game of the championship. It was a real dogfight until Darren's goal." In the Leinster final at Dr Cullen Park in Carlow, St. Kieran's locked horns with old rivals, St. Peter's. A disappointingly small crowd turned up to witness the All-Ireland champions strut their stuff but St. Kieran's were in control of proceedings from an early stage and won by 0-13 to 1-4, despite conceding a late goal. "St. Peter's are always a tough team to play against. Any time we went down to Wexford to play them it was like going to Galatasaray," John jokes. "We were up for a battle and not just our team, but our panel was so strong that there was never a doubt in my mind that we would come away with anything less than a win."

Fielding nine of their 2003 All-Ireland winning side, St. Kieran's powered past another of their keenest rivals, St. Flannan's, Ennis, in the All-Ireland semi-final at The Ragg in County Tipperary. They laid the foundations for a 0-17 to 1-8 win by forging into a 0-10 to 0-2 lead at the break and Colin Ryan's 58th minute goal for the Harty champions came too late to effect the issue. For many neutrals, the draw which pitted the Leinster and Munster champions together for a semi-final, meant that a lop-sided final was a distinct possibility. "In hindsight, the Flannan's game was possibly seen as the All-Ireland final. Connacht champions, St. Raphael's of Loughrea, did not appear to be as strong a side as the team which made history nine years earlier by bringing the Croke Cup across the Shannon for the only time in the competition's history," John recalls.

"Unlike St. Flannan's or some of the other teams we played, St. Raphael's were a bit of an unknown quantity. We hardly knew anything about them but, in saying that, we gave them the same respect as anyone else and didn't take anything for granted. We met in St. Kieran's on the morning of the game. The mood was very relaxed on the bus. We all knew what we had to do. We did a warm-up in St. Vincent's pitch nearby and we were really focused on the game when arriving at Parnell Park".

However, as it transpired, the game proved to be very one-sided and the issue was never in doubt with John Walsh's men coasting to a facile win. Inspired by Kilkenny minor star, Richie Power who, according to John, "had an unbelievable game, was a step above the rest and contributed 1-9 of our tally", St. Kieran's were on top from start to finish. "We were always in control and I even got on the scoresheet myself," John says, with a smile. The 'Irish Independent' also honed in on St. Kieran's "Power play". While crediting the Galway lads for staying in touch early on, the report states that two late goals in the first half by Mark Aylward opened a huge gap and that "early in the second half, the famous Kilkenny nursery raised their game to a whole different plane". John has fond recollections of receiving the

Croke Cup from fellow Laois man, Bernard Dunne, Chairman of the All-Ireland Colleges Council. "I never felt so good and so proud. It was a relief as much as anything else. I was under pressure beforehand because my brother Damian had missed out on winning an All-Ireland and my father was at every game. Because I was from Laois, I probably felt I had something extra to prove, but things couldn't have worked out better. One of the highlights for me was travelling across the Kilkenny/Laois border with the Croke Cup the following night. A few of the loyal Ballinakill hurling supporters organised a reception for a packed minibus of lads and we had a great night celebrating."

John is wholehearted in his praise of the St. Kieran's management duo of Tom Hogan and John Quane, who had been involved with the winning team from their early days in the school. "Tom Hogan was the main man. He had won an All-Ireland club medal with James Stephens as a player and was also involved with Graigue-Ballycallan when they got to the All-Ireland final a few years ago. So he knew what was required. John Quane was more of a tactics man. Also, Ken Archibold did the physical work with us and Art Anglin was a great man with the stats. Vice-principal, Dick McEvoy, was another great supporter of all grades of hurling in the school."

John is now in his third year of a hurling scholarship in Dublin Institute of Technology, where he is studying Buildings Services Engineering. He is an integral member of DIT's hurling team, having helped them to win the Higher Education Division 2 title last year, and two Kehoe Cup finals appearances in the last two years. Carlow beat them narrowly on both occasions. Earlier this year, John played in the Fitzgibbon Cup, when DIT defeated the Garda Training College, before losing to NUIG in the quarter-final.

John is also a talented footballer and represented Laois at Under-14 and Under-15 level in the big ball game. He also won Under-14 'B' and Under-16 'B' South Leinster football medals with St. Kieran's. Nowadays, the general consensus is that being an inter-county dual player is almost an impossibility, but John is proud to have represented his county in hurling at all levels. He hopes to play senior hurling with Laois for many years to come, and would dearly love to be a part of a successful Ballinakill team. "I got my first taste of senior inter-county hurling last year and it's much different to the colleges scene. Hopefully, I'll have a good innings with Laois and that we can do something in Leinster over the next few years. I won three Under-21 championships with Ballinakill in 2002, '03 and '04, and a fourth in 2006 with the Harps Gaels. Ballinakill is going through a transitional phase at the moment but we should be competitive in the senior championship nevertheless. There's not a lot between all the clubs in Laois," John concludes. In his spare time he has a massive interest in music.

John Walsh and fellow Laois man, Damien Bergin, who was also part of the successful 2004 team, hold the distinction of being the last two boarders to complete their entire secondary education at St. Kieran's.

Naturally, he is regularly in touch with many of his colleagues who brought the Croke Cup to the famous Kilkenny nursery for the 16th time. He retains very fond memories of all involved with that triumph. While John had the honour of being presented with the Leinster and All-Ireland trophies, he claims that "everybody played their part" on that all-conquering side.

2005 – ALL-IRELAND SEMI-FINAL
9 April 2005, Nenagh

St. Flannan's, Ennis 2-13
(C. Ryan 0-7, I. Colleran 1-2, A. Arthur 1-1, C. Coughlan 0-1, B. Gaffney 0-1, J. Neylon 0-1)

Birr Community School 1-14
(P. Cleary 1-0, J. Bergin 0-3, D. Horan 0-2, B. Nolan 0-2, D. Masterson 0-2, M. Mulrooney 0-2,
C. Coughlan 0-2, R. Carroll 0-1)

2005 – ALL-IRELAND SEMI-FINAL
9 April 2005, Nenagh

St. Kieran's, Kilkenny 5-14
(P. Hogan 2-2, R. Hogan 1-4, T. J. Reid 1-3, Martin Walsh 1-0, M. Nolan 0-3, Mark Walsh 0-1,
J. J. Farrell 0-1)

Thurles CBS 2-9
(C. Clohessy 2-0, B. Moran 0-3, P. Burke 0-2, T. Hammersley 0-2, T. Hassett 0-1, M. Cahill 0-1)

St. Flannan's, Ennis, Croke Cup Champions, 2005.
Back row, left to right: Gary Casey, Martin Tierney, Kevin Raftery, Niall Killeen, Paddy Moloney,
George Hannigan, Daniel McMahon, Bernard Gaffney, Jack Neylon, John Moloney,
Marc O'Donnell.
Middle row, left to right: Mr Con Woods, Sean Talty, Conor Neylon, Ciaran O'Doherty,
Damien O'Halloran, Marc O'Halloran, Greg Lyons, Derek Ryan, Gerard Arthur, Conor Tierney,
Mr Jamesie O'Connor.
Front row, left to right: Barry Coffey, Ian Colleran, Colin Ryan, Colm Madden,
James McInerney (capt), Patrick Kelly, Seamus Hickey, Colm O'Connell, John Conlan.
(Photograph courtesy of Fr John Jones, Mountshannon)

2005 – ALL-IRELAND FINAL
2 May 2005, Thurles
Referee: Noel Cosgrove (Tipperary)

St. Flannan's, Ennis 2-15

Patrick Kelly
(Clare)

Ciaran O'Doherty   **John Moloney**   **Marc O'Donnell**
(Clare)   (Clare)   (Clare)

Conor Neylon   **Seamus Hickey**   **George Hannigan**
(Clare)   (Limerick)   (Tipperary)

Damien O'Halloran   **James McInerney** (*capt*)
(Clare) (0-1)   (Clare) (0-2)

Colin Ryan   **Jack Neylon**   **Colm Madden**
(Clare) (0-7)   (Clare)   (Clare)

Bernard Gaffney   **Niall Killeen**   **Gerard Arthur**
(Clare) (1-3)   (Clare) (1-0)   (Clare) (0-2)

Subs: Ian Colleran (Clare) (for Neylon), Greg Lyons (Clare) (for O'Halloran).

St. Kieran's, Kilkenny 2-12

Nicky Cleere
(Kilkenny)

James Dowling   **Shane Campion**   **Eoin O'Shea**
(Kilkenny)   (Kilkenny)   (Kilkenny)

Jason Dermody   **Neal Prendergast**   **John Lawlor**
(Kilkenny)   (Kilkenny)   (Kilkenny)

Patrick Hogan   **Maurice Nolan** (*capt*)
(Kilkenny) (1-1)   (Kilkenny) (0-5)

Mark Walsh   **Jonjo Farrell**   **T.J. Reid**
(Kilkenny)   (Kilkenny) (0-1)   (Kilkenny) (0-2)

Martin Walsh   **Richie Hogan**   **Shane Brennan**
(Kilkenny)   (Kilkenny) (1-3)   (Kilkenny)

Subs: Niall Tennyson (Kilkenny) (for Dermody),
Donncha Fitzpatrick (Kilkenny) (for Martin Walsh).

James McInerney

On the same day that Clare suffered a comprehensive defeat by Kilkenny in the 2005 National Hurling League final in Thurles, St. Flannan's helped to lift the doom and gloom in the Banner County by delivering another All-Ireland colleges senior hurling 'A' title at the same venue, with James McInerney having the honour of receiving the Croke Cup for the 14th time in the school's illustrious history.

One of four children (three boys and a girl), James' hurling talent was obvious from an early age. He was part of successful Newmarket-on-Fergus juvenile teams and also enjoyed a degree of hurling success during his days in Ballycar National School. James acknowledges that St. Flannan's rich hurling heritage was a major factor in his decision to attend the school. "When I was younger, I used to be brought to Flannan's matches and attended a few Harty finals," he explains. "It was the place to play hurling and that was something that obviously appealed to me." His father, Sean, had played hurling for O'Callaghan's Mills and James' older brother, John, had been in St. Flannan's before him. John won a White Cup medal in the famous blue and white colours, while the youngest of the McInerney boys, Alan, is now attending the school.

In 2000, James entered St. Flannan's as a day pupil. His first impressions made a big impact on him, when he saw "all these great teams on the wall". Growing up, as he did, in the glorious 'Ger Loughnane era' in Clare, James craved for success on the hurling fields.

"In 1998, Brian Clancy from Newmarket captained Flannan's to win the All-Ireland and that was something I always wanted to emulate," he reflects. Initially, James won Munster Under-15 and Dean Ryan Cup medals before eventually playing Harty Cup for three years. In 2003, St. Flannan's won all of their games en route to the final, only to lose to St. Colman's, Fermoy, following a replay. The following year, they made amends when they defeated Waterford Colleges in the Harty final at Cashel by 3-15 to 1-8. However, disappointment followed when they succumbed to St. Kieran's in the All-Ireland semi-final. The Kilkenny outfit went on to hammer St. Raphael's, Loughrea, in the final. "Losing the All-Ireland semi-final was awful disappointing. A few days earlier, the Clare minors suffered a heavy defeat to Tipperary in the Munster championship and I think that had an affect on our performance."

At the start of the 2004/05 academic year, James was informed that he had been appointed St. Flannan's senior hurling captain. He recalls, "Con Woods called me into his office and gave me the good news. It didn't come as a major surprise to me because I had captained the Under-15 and Dean Ryan Cup teams. Having said that, I was delighted to be given the captaincy, but the news was tempered by a hamstring injury I picked up two weeks later."

The injury, which was sustained in a club game, forced him to sit out St. Flannan's three pre-Christmas matches against Doon CBS, De la Salle, Waterford and St. Joseph's, Kilmallock. In his absence, corner forward Gerard Arthur assumed the captaincy. James returned for the Harty Cup quarter-final in early February 2005 against Midleton CBS which was played in "atrocious conditions" at Cashel. Late Midleton goals from Padraic O'Sullivan (younger brother of Cork full back, Diarmuid) and Alan Morrissey set up a tense finish, but St. Flannan's held on to win by 1-14 to 2-8. They went on to book their place in the final with a 1-9 to 1-4 win over St. Joseph's, Kilmallock (having led by 1-8 to 0-0 at the interval), but the victory came at a cost for the Clare school who lost their captain to injury in the early stages. "I thought I was right and it was a big blow to suffer the hamstring injury again. It kept me out of the Harty final and the All-Ireland semi-final, and I very nearly missed the All-Ireland final as well," James recalls.

St. Flannan's entered the final against Thurles CBS at Nenagh knowing that victory would give them a record 21st Harty Cup. Leading by 1-5 to 0-2 at the break, the reigning Munster champions survived a spirited Thurles comeback, with three late points from Colm Madden, Gerard Arthur and Niall Killeen sealing a 1-12 to 1-6 success. Afterwards, a track-suited James McInerney joined stand-in captain Gerard Arthur on the winners' podium to receive the Harty Cup.

The Ennis-based lads were given another tough game by beaten Leinster finalists, St. Brendan's Community School, Birr, in the All-Ireland semi-final. The powers-that-be in the GAA brought in a 'back door' route in 2005 (a system which does not endear itself to James) and the Offaly school had availed of their second chance by defeating Connacht champions, Gort Community School in the first-ever Croke Cup quarter-final. St. Flannan's side eventually came through the penultimate tie, but were put to the pin of their collar before they emerged from Nenagh winning by 2-13 to 1-14. On the same programme in the County Tipperary venue, St. Flannan's got a sneak preview of their All-Ireland final opponents. Their 2004 conquerors, St. Kieran's, Kilkenny, easily defeated Harty Cup runners-up Thurles CBS, to set up yet another showdown between the two top hurling nurseries in the country over many years.

Recalling the 'will he?/won't he play?' speculation in the media about his availability for the Croke Cup final, James is clear on his own prognosis. "I'm not sure whether my name was even on the match programme, but I knew the week before that I would be playing. I had been receiving intensive treatment for a number of weeks and I'll always be grateful to Dr Patrick Leahy and Ger Hartman for getting me back to health in time for the final, even though there were concerns about my match fitness."

The 54th Croke Cup final was the middle offering in a three-game programme in Thurles on the May Bank Holiday Monday, sandwiched between the Hogan Cup decider and the National Hurling League showdown. For long periods, the Clare lads held the upper hand, but little separated the teams all through. St. Flannan's had posted two early points before top scorer Colin Ryan (described as a "metronomic freetaker" by the 'Irish Independent') launched a cut goalward and Bernard Gaffney found the net. However, St. Kieran's responded immediately with a similar score from Richie Hogan. Gerard Arthur kept St. Flannan's two clear until just before half-time when Patrick Hogan grabbed a second Kieran's goal to edge them into a 2-5 to 1-7 interval lead. Within four minutes of the resumption, St. Flannan's were back in the driving seat when Niall Killeen soloed through for a great goal. The 'Irish Independent' reported that, "a game that was surprisingly quiet burst into life with five minutes remaining". James McInerney, now at full forward, earned a free that Colin Ryan converted and the Newmarket player then pointed to bring the sides level. After Patrick Kelly had denied Donncha Fitzpatrick with a brilliant save, Gaffney nudged the Banner boys in front and further scores from Ian Colleran and Gaffney put the result beyond doubt.

"We were very hungry for it and I think that showed in the closing stages when we managed to pull away," James says. "I got myself into the game near the end, but struggled to finish after getting a belt in the stomach.

However, Jamesie came over and let me know in no uncertain terms that I was ok! I was delighted to receive the Croke Cup but I was so sick that I wasn't able to complete the lap of honour with the rest of the lads." The winning squad returned that evening from Thurles to "a great civic reception in Ennis".

James is full of praise for the St. Flannan's management duo of Jamesie O'Connor (a boyhood hero of his) and Con Woods. "They were the perfect pairing. Con has lots of experience, he's been teaching in the school a long time and has played for Clare. What can you say about Jamesie? He's a legend in Clare and the tactics and training, which took place three times a week, were top class." Messrs O'Connor and Woods took a big gamble on playing their injured captain, James McInerney, who had played little or no hurling over the previous few months. But the decision to start him, and especially to switch him to full forward for the final quarter, paid rich dividends as he played a key role in the dramatic closing stages. James also lauds the contributions of Alan Dunne and Eamon Giblin for promoting hurling in his alma mater.

James has since been drafted onto the Clare senior panel, describing his promotion as "a massive step-up". He admits that he sometimes has to pinch himself when sharing the same dressing room with some of his heroes, albeit now coming to the end of long inter-county careers with the Banner County. He was on the Clare minor team for three seasons and was a member of the county Under-21 side in 2006. James is studying Civil Engineering at Limerick IT and, naturally enough, he keeps in touch with many of his former St. Flannan's colleagues. Indeed, Colin Ryan and Bernard Gaffney are among his team-mates in Newmarket-on-Fergus. After losing to Wolfe Tones in the Clare senior final in the summer of 2006, the long wait (dating back to 1981) continues for a county title.

James McInerney is hoping for long and successful careers with club and county. Success is now more or less demanded by the hordes of Banner County fans, reared on a diet of Munster and All-Ireland triumphs in the mid to late 1990s. He accepts that these are "changing times for the GAA" but, irrespective of what honours lie ahead for him, James' first medal of real note will always be a proud possession. On May 2nd, 2005, he defied the pain barrier to lead St. Flannan's to a memorable Croke Cup success, aided and abetted by what he describes as "a savage performance" from all his team-mates.

2006 – ALL-IRELAND SEMI-FINAL
1 April 2006, Kilkenny

Dublin Colleges 1-13

(R. O'Carroll 0-4, P. Ryan 1-0, J. Maher 0-3, S. Murphy 0-2, S. O'Rourke 0-1, C. McBride 0-1,
D. Kelly 0-1, J. Cooper 0-1)

Midleton CBS 0-10

(R. White 0-8, B. Lawton 0-1, E. O'Keeffe 0-1)

2006 – ALL-IRELAND SEMI-FINAL
2 April 2006, Nenagh

St. Flannan's, Ennis 1-11

(C. Madden 1-0, C. Nealon 0-3, J. Conlon 0-3, C. Tierney 0-2, B. Coffey 0-1,
D. Ryan 0-1, R. Horan 0-1)

Kilkenny CBS 0-13

(M. Bergin 0-6, M. Kelly 0-2, J. Fitzpatrick 0-2, D. Webster 0-1, J. Comerford 0-1, A. Stapleton 0-1)

Dublin Colleges, Croke Cup Champions, 2006.
Back row, left to right: Paddy Brennan, Dermot Manley, Shane Murphy, Barry Finn, John Sheanon,
Ross O'Carroll, Wayne Brogan, Paul Ryan, Peter O'Callaghan, Simon Lambert, Finn McGarry,
Gary Coleman, David Quinn, Brendan Treacy, Shane O'Rourke, Conor Connolly (capt),
Sean Ryan, Darragh O'Gorman, James Doody, Oisín Gough, Dermot Connolly.
Front row, left to right: Scott O'Brien, David Treacy, Andrew Hopkins, Ben Traynor, Mick May,
Martin O'Sullivan, Dan Keating, Dean Kelly, Darren Whelan, Cian McBride, Joey Maher,
Peter Buckeridge, Mark Brannigan, Jack Gilligan, Jonny Cooper.
(Photograph courtesy of Tony Stack)

2006 – ALL-IRELAND FINAL
1 May 2006, Carlow
Referee: Dickie Murphy (Wexford)

Dublin Colleges 1-11

Simon Lambert
(Dublin)

Shane Murphy　　**Peter O'Callaghan**　　**Mark Brannigan**
(Dublin)　　　　　　(Dublin)　　　　　　　　(Dublin)

John Sheanon　　**Conor Connolly** (*capt*)　　**Brendan Treacy**
(Dublin)　　　　　　(Dublin)　　　　　　　　　(Dublin)

Shane O'Rourke　　**Dermot Connolly**
(Dublin)　　　　　　　(Dublin) (0-1)

Cian McBride　　**Ross O'Carroll**　　**Joey Maher**
(Dublin) (1-0)　　　(Dublin) (0-1)　　　(Dublin) (0-2)

Paul Ryan　　**Jonny Cooper**　　**Dean Kelly**
(Dublin) (0-6)　　(Dublin) (0-1)　　(Dublin)

Subs: Ben Traynor (Wexford) (for Kelly), Peter Buckeridge (Dublin) (for O'Callaghan).

St. Flannan's, Ennis 0-11

Donal Tuohy
(Clare)

Ciaran O'Doherty　　**Conor Cooney**　　**Stephen O'Reagan**
(Clare) (0-2)　　　　(Clare)　　　　　　(Clare)

Eamonn Glynn　　**Seamus Hickey**　　**Derek Ryan**
(Clare)　　　　　　(Limerick)　　　　　(Clare)

Enda Barrett　　**Donnagh Stack**
(Clare)　　　　　　(Cork) (0-1)

Barry Coffey　　**Colm Madden** (*capt*)　　**Ross Horan**
(Clare)　　　　　(Clare) (0-1)　　　　　(Clare)

John Conlon　　**Conor Tierney**　　**Conor Nealon**
(Clare) (0-1)　　(Clare) (0-4)　　　(Clare) (0-2)

Subs: Mark Earley (Clare) (for Coffey), Colm O'Connell (Limerick) (for Horan).

Conor Connolly

Dublin hurling received a major shot in the arm in 2006 when the combined Dublin Colleges became the first team from the capital to claim the All-Ireland colleges SHC 'A' title at the expense of holders and 14-time champions, St. Flannan's, Ennis. Ballyfermot lad Conor Connolly captained the history-making side, who were also the first 'back door' winners of the title. Conor was a fifth year pupil at Coláiste Chillian in Clondalkin when he held the Croke Cup aloft in Dr Cullen Park, Carlow, on May 1st 2006.

beside Round Towers' pitch, making training very convenient. However, with players from 13 schools involved in the Dublin Colleges set-up, you would think that bringing them together would cause problems. This was not the case, as Conor explains. "Because about 15 of us were also on the Dublin minor hurling panel, we combined the training. We trained twice a week at DCU and at Clann na nGael in Ringsend, which has floodlit facilities."

Conor was only a squad member when Dublin Colleges were knocked out of the 2004/05 Leinster championship by St. Kieran's, Kilkenny, in the first round. However, for 2005/06 he was centre back and also captain. On being named captain, he says, "I was handed the captaincy for the league which took place before Christmas, but I thought it would only be a temporary thing. So you could say I was surprised when I was asked to continue in the role for the championship." Under the management of former Offaly player, Vincent Teehan, as well as Declan Feeney and John McEvoy (the latter doubling up as physical trainer), Dublin Colleges opened their Leinster campaign with a 2-10 to 0-7 victory over St. Peter's, Wexford, in Arklow. First half goals from John Sheanon and Darren Whelan put the Metropolitans on their way to a comfortable win. In the semi-final at the St. Loman's club grounds in Mullingar, Dublin Colleges accounted for Birr Community School.

Conor inherited a love of sport from his father, David, who played Leinster schools rugby with Blackrock College and senior rugby with Blackrock as a prop (with future Ireland and Lions flanker Fergus Slattery as a team-mate) and represented the province at Under-19 level. "I have no hurling background, but I was always encouraged to play sport," says Conor, who received his primary education at Gaelscoil Inse Chóir before enrolling at Coláiste Chilliain in Clondalkin. His primary teachers, Cathal Paircéir and Con Ó Tuama introduced him to hurling. Other strong influences on him were his older brother, Liam and Leinster coach, Paul McManus, who trained the teams at Liffey Gaels. According to Conor, "he really showed us what hurling was all about".

Conor participated as Coláiste Chilliain competed in their own right in the Dublin 'C' championship, but they were knocked out in the group stages. His school is located right

This win set up a meeting with Kilkenny CBS in the provincial decider at Dr Cullen Park. Late points from Anthony Stapleton and the outstanding Mark Bergin saw the Kilkenny side claim their first Leinster title since 1983 on a 1-14 to 2-9 scoreline. "We had good wins over St. Peter's and Birr, but for some reason, we didn't perform in the final. The winning feeling wasn't as good at training coming up to that match," Conor concedes. "I don't know what went wrong. It was the first big match most of us had played in and maybe nerves were a factor. Our heads were down in the dressing room afterwards and there were lots of tears, but Declan Feeney came in and told us we weren't going to feel like that again this year. We were still in the running for an All-Ireland and we were determined to make the most of the second chance."

With the provincial runners-up still in contention in what was the second year of the 'back door' experiment, Dublin Colleges were pitted against Harty Cup winners Midleton CBS in the All-Ireland semi-final on April 1st in Nowlan Park. It didn't look good for the Leinster side when they trailed by 0-3 to 0-8 at half-time, but they had been playing against the elements. After the break, the Dublin lads proved they were not in humour for being April 'fools' and they roared back into contention. They were level by the 48th minute thanks to a point from Joe Maher and, in the end, Paul Ryan made amends for an earlier penalty miss with a late goal which put the seal on a 1-13 to 0-10 victory. "We knew that we hadn't done ourselves justice in the Leinster final and that was a big motivating factor when we played Midleton. We were confident of winning, especially as Shane O'Rourke was back from injury and Peter O'Callaghan was back from suspension," he recalls. "Midleton put us under a lot of pressure in the first half, but we were a different team in the second half and totally shocked them."

With defeated Harty Cup finalists St. Flannan's overcoming Kilkenny CBS in the other semi-final the following day, the stage was set for the first Croke Cup final involving two beaten provincial finalists. The Ennis-based boys were bidding to capture their 15th Croke Cup and had the weight of tradition behind them. However, Conor says that Dublin Colleges were "very relaxed before the game, having played in the Leinster final and got used to having nerves".

On the May Bank Holiday Monday, Dublin Colleges returned to Dr Cullen Park, the scene of their Leinster final loss, eager to make amends. Managed by former Clare star, Jamesie O'Connor, St. Flannan's had wind advantage in the first half. However, there was little to choose between the teams until the closing stages of the half when a brace of points from Ciaran O'Doherty and Conor Nealon gave the Ennis boys a 0-8 to 0-4 cushion at the break. The game changed completely in the second half with Dublin Colleges storming back to take control. The only goal arrived in the 42nd minute when Joe Maher set up Cian McBride who finished expertly to the net. That score brought the men from the capital onto level terms, 1-6 to 0-9, and they hit the front two minutes later when Paul Ryan slotted over a free. St. Flannan's piled on the pressure in the closing stages and would have forced extra-time but for a brilliant Simon Lambert save from Nealon in injury-time. "Like the game against Midleton, we didn't start hurling until the second half," Conor reflects. We got a run on Flannan's and we survived a late scare to take the title.

"I had a speech written out and there were very emotional scenes afterwards. We had a meal after the game and later we celebrated back at my house. Everybody was absolutely flying."

While the 'Irish Independent' reported that the new champions produced "a fantastic performance", Conor admits that he was disappointed at the level of support for his team in the All-Ireland final. He would like to see pupils from the schools involved in the amalgamation being given time off to support the team. "Our support was predominantly made up of parents and people involved with the clubs. We didn't get the same support as the other schools. The 'single' schools we played had fans banging drums and singing chants."

Conor is full of praise for the Dublin

Colleges management triumvirate of Vincent Teehan, Declan Feeney and John McEvoy. "The three lads put in a great effort and instilled a tremendous spirit in the team. John McEvoy was a brilliant trainer and made the training very enjoyable. All three were great motivators, but we still had the craic with them before the games."

An equally talented footballer, Conor played for the Dubs in both the Leinster minor hurling and football championships in 2005 and 2006. He treasures his Leinster minor hurling medal from 2005. Conor is still young enough to line out for the Dublin Colleges again for the 2006/07 campaign in his Leaving Cert year and is quietly confident of their chances of further glory.

"Physically, it is becoming too tough to be a dual player nowadays," Conor Connolly concedes. His ambition is to play senior hurling for Dublin in the coming years. "Things are finally starting to happen for Dublin hurling and I would love to be a part of the county's hurling future." If glory days eventually do return for the Metropolitan hurlers, there is very little doubt but that the combined colleges' Croke Cup success, under Conor's captaincy in 2006, will be deemed to have been a key factor in the Dubs' progress in the small ball game.

Appendix A

Croke Cup – Roll of Honour

St. Kieran's, Kilkenny (16)
1948, 1957, 1959, 1961, 1965, 1971, 1975,
1988, 1989, 1990, 1992, 1993, 1996, 2000,
2003, 2004

St. Flannan's, Ennis (14)
1944, 1945, 1946, 1947, 1958, 1976, 1979,
1982, 1983, 1987, 1991, 1998, 1999, 2005

North Monastery, Cork (5)
1960, 1970, 1980, 1985, 1994

St. Finbarr's, Farranferris (5)
1963, 1969, 1972, 1974, 1984

St. Peter's, Wexford (4)
1962, 1967, 1968, 1973

St. Colman's, Fermoy (4)
1977, 1997, 2001, 2002

Limerick CBS (2)
1964, 1966

Templemore CBS (1)
1978

Kilkenny CBS (1)
1981

Birr Community School (1)
1986

St. Raphael's, Loughrea (1)
1995

Dublin Colleges (1)
2006

Appendix B

All-Ireland Senior Hurling 'B' Finals

27/4/68, Croke Park
St. Mary's (Mullingar) **5-8**
St. Mary's (Belfast) 4-7

4/5/69, Portumna
Presentation (Birr) **2-12**
De La Salle (Loughrea) 5-1

26/4/70, Limerick
St. Joseph's (Galway) **6-11**
New Ross CBS 0-3

2/5/71, Croke Park
St. Mary's (Belfast) **4-17**
Presentation (Birr) 4-5

23/4/72, Athlone
St. Jarlath's (Tuam) **6-5**
Presentation (Birr) 4-8

8/4/73, Borrisokane
Presentation (Birr) **5-9**
Nenagh CBS 5-4

28/4/74, Raheny
St. Mary's (Belfast) **3-6**
Charleville CBS 1-9

20/4/75, Croke Park
Good Counsel (New Ross) **4-10**
Roscommon CBS 0-10

16/5/76, Dungarvan
Good Counsel (New Ross) **2-7**
Midleton CBS 2-3

1/5/77, Thurles
Causeway Comp. (Kerry) **2-9**
St. Joseph's (Fairview) 2-5

7/5/78, Roslevan
Charleville CBS **2-10**
St. Raphael's (Loughrea) 3-5

6/5/79, Thurles
Good Counsel (New Ross) **2-4**
Roscommon . . . . CBS 0-5

4/5/80, Roscrea
Cashel CBS **2-16**
Roscommon CBS 2-1

10/5/81, Birr
St. Joseph's (Tulla) **4-11**
St. Vincent's (Glasnevin) 3-2

16/5/82, Thurles
Cashel CBS **2-12**
Callan CBS 2-2

8/5/83, Thurles
Nenagh CBS **1-11**
Callan CBS 1-9

13/5/84, Croke Park
Presentation (Castlecomer) **3-10**
St. Patrick's (Maghera) 0-8

5/5/85, Birr
Presentation (Athenry) **4-7**
Oatlands CBS 3-7

11/5/86, Cloughjordan
Nenagh CBS **2-4**
Cistercian (Roscrea) 1-6

10/5/87, Birr
Shannon Compehensive **3-8**
Cistercian (Roscrea) 2-4

8/5/88, Waterford
Castlecomer CS **4-8**
Scoil Mhuire (Kanturk) 3-4

7/5/89, Marino
De La Salle (Hospital) **3-13**
St. Louis (Ballymena) 3-6

6/5/90, Ballinasloe
Scariff CS 1-15
Presentation (Athenry) 1-11

27/4/91, Thurles
Callan CBS 1-14
Coláiste an Spioraid Naomh (Cork) . . . 1-10

27/4/92, Tullamore
Abbey CBS (Tipperary) 4-8
Roscommon CBS 1-7

25/4/93, Clonmel
Hamilton HS (Bandon) 5-9
Patrician (Ballyfin) 3-7

8/5/94, Kilkenny
Our Lady's (Templemore) 3-8
Callan CBS 0-8

7/5/95, Navan
Doon CBS 5-11
St. Patrick's (Maghera) 0-4

28/4/96, Carrick-on-Suir ·
De La Salle (Hospital) 1-13
Enniscorthy CBS 0-4

27/4/97, Nenagh
St. Clement's (Limerick) 1-8
Cistercian (Roscrea) 0-7

2/5/98, Croke Park
Portlaoise CBS 4-13
St. Cuan's (Castleblakeney) 1-7

18/4/99, Croke Park
Enniscorthy CBS 4-11
St. Caimin's (Shannon) 0-17

16/4/00, Clonmel
Cistercian (Roscrea) 3-14
St. Declan's (Kilmacthomas) 4-6

7/5/01, Swords
Mercy College (Woodford) 4-13
Callan CBS 2-10

28/4/02, Thurles
Abbey CBS (Tipperary) 3-11
Castlecomer CS 1-13

26/4/03, Clonmel
Castlecomer CS 1-12
St. Joseph's (Borrisoleigh) 1-8

1/5/04, Navan
Cistercian (Roscrea) 2-13
St. Patrick's (Maghera) 2-10

30/4/05, Templemore
Enniscorthy CBS 3-8
Charleville CBS 0-13

1/5/06, Navan
St Patrick's Maghera 3-12
Bagenalstown CS 1-12

Appendix C

**All-Ireland Senior Hurling 'B'
Winning Captains**

1968 - Gerry Whelan
1969 - Michael Kennedy
1970 - Gerry Glynn
1971 - Kieran Donnelly
1972 - John Power
1973 - Michael Brophy
1974 - Paddy Mallon
1975 - Davy Kehoe
1976 - Ray Harte
1977 - Sean Flaherty
1978 - Ger Howard
1979 - Philip Cahill
1980 - Gerry Morrissey
1981 - Andrew Walsh
1982 - Niall Ryan
1983 - Martin Hynes
1984 - Martin O'Neill
1985 - Niall Cannon
1986 - Michael Gaynor
1987 - David McGettrick
1988 - James Brennan
1989 - Michael Ryan
1990 - Kevin McNamara
1991 - Adrian O'Sullivan
1992 - Brian Lacey
1993 - Dan McCarthy
1994 - David Kennedy
1995 - Paul Keane
1996 - Eamonn Cronin
1997 - Paul Carey
1998 - Brian Fitzpatrick
1999 - Michael Jacob
2000 - Peter Garvey
2001 - Trevor Cavanagh
2002 - Andrew Morrissey
2003 - Peter O'Donovan
2004 - Eamonn Lee
2005 - Garrett Sinnott
2006 - Sam Dodds